Life after Foster Care

Life after Foster Care

Improving Outcomes for Former Foster Youth

Loring Paul Jones

PRAEGER™

An Imprint of ABC-CLIO, LLC

Santa Barbara, California • Denver, Colorado

Library of Congress Cataloging-in-Publication Data

Names: Jones, Loring Paul, author.
Title: Life after foster care : improving outcomes for former foster youth / Loring Paul Jones.
Description: Santa Barbara : Praeger, [2018] | Includes bibliographical references and index.
Identifiers: LCCN 2018013292 (print) | LCCN 2018026772 (ebook) | ISBN 9781440857416 (ebook) | ISBN 9781440857409 (alk. paper)
Subjects: LCSH: Foster children—United States. | Foster children—United States—Care.
Classification: LCC HV875.55 (ebook) | LCC HV875.55 .J656 2018 (print) | DDC 362.73/3—dc23
LC record available at https://lccn.loc.gov/2018013292

ISBN: 978-1-4408-5740-9 (print)
        978-1-4408-5741-6 (ebook)

22 21 20 19 18   1 2 3 4 5

This book is also available as an eBook.

Praeger
An Imprint of ABC-CLIO, LLC

ABC-CLIO, LLC
130 Cremona Drive, P.O. Box 1911
Santa Barbara, California 93116-1911
www.abc-clio.com

This book is printed on acid-free paper ∞

Manufactured in the United States of America

Contents

CHAPTER ONE

Foster Care and the Transition to Young Adulthood

Americans consider the biological and nuclear family to be the optimal environment in which to raise children. However, sometimes parents are unable to provide the expected care for and socialization of their children, or they may intentionally harm their offspring. In order to protect these children, we remove them from their homes and place them in foster care. Foster care is meant to be a safe, substitute, and temporary family. The public policy goal is to provide these children with *permanency*, defined as an exit from the child welfare system into a safe and long-term family (or family-like) living arrangement. The preferred permanency outcome is to reunify foster children with their biological family, but permanency can also take the form of adoption, a legal guardianship, or care provided by a relative (Adler, 2001; Wulczyn, 2004). Despite the public policy mandate to reunify children with their family of origin, some youth remain in the system until they reach the age of majority. These youth do not achieve permanency: they leave care to go to independent living or some other living arrangement. As legal adults they are essentially discharged to "self" (U.S.D.H.H.S., 2012).

What youth aging out of foster care share with all emerging adults are the common needs to become employed, to be financially independent, to acquire the skills to enable them to live autonomously, to develop satisfying relationships with others, and to be integrated into the community as productive and valued members. Mastering these tasks is a challenge for most young people. However, youth in foster care face unique and additional challenges because of their life circumstances both before and after they entered care. Former foster youth have never known the love and security that comes from a stable family life. Not only are they victims of maltreatment, but they also have most probably grown up in poverty. They likely have grown up in homes where there has been parental dysfunction (mental health problems, substance abuse disorders, domestic violence, incarceration, etc.) (Crosson-Towers, 2007). They have experienced the emotional trauma and mental health difficulties caused by abuse and loss, and the potential disruption of family and community ties inherent in removal from the home.

Foster care should be beneficial for children for a number of reasons. First, in removing a child from their home they receive protection from further maltreatment, which was detrimental to their emotional and physical development. Second, these children have foster parents, who will not only provide protection from further abuse but also attend to their basic needs. Third, foster children have social workers, who provide them with services including health care and mental health treatment to address the problems that have developed because of the abuse and neglect they experienced. These children may not have access to these services in their parental homes. Despite these benefits, going into foster care does pose a number of risks to a child's development that need to be addressed. Fifteen percent of former foster youth in a small nonrandom sample said going into care made their situation worse (Jones, 2015). There are a variety reasons for this negative response. Some foster children do not receive protection from abuse while in care. Maltreatment by substitute caregivers while in foster care does occur, and the needs of many children go unmet due to the lack of the provision of needed services (Kortenkamp & Ehrle, 2002; Mech, 2002). One of the problems foster children face in care is frequent placement changes, which has been associated with many of the problems examined in this book (Ryan & Testa, 2005). Frequent moves while in care can result in additional psychological trauma as children reexperience the trauma from earlier removals.

Youth also enter care with socioeconomic disadvantages that foster care does not erase, and these disadvantages exert an adverse effect on emerging adults, even after long stays in care. Some of the research reported in this book indicates that many former foster youth might not do any better than, and in some cases they do not do as well as, nonfoster youth who grew up in poverty in meeting the tasks of emerging adulthood (Berzin, 2008; Buehler, Orme, Post, & Patterson, 2000; Kerman, Wildfire, & Barth, 2002). Youth leaving foster care also face the challenge that comes with the sudden loss of services and support.

The Transition to Adulthood and Foster Youth

Most of us remember the time of transition from adolescence to adulthood as one of excitement tinged with anxiety. We may have even watched our own children struggle through the period in life called *emerging adulthood* by Arnett (2000, 2004) and assisted them with significant support during this period of change. During this transition phase, a youth is moving from familiar situations into new opportunities and challenges. Anxiety may emerge from the loss of customary environments and concern about one's capacity to meet new challenges. The ease of this transition is dependent not only on a person's own internal resources but also on the support, both tangible and intangible, provided by others. Most of us had the emotional and financial support of parents and family, and we knew we had a fallback position in the family home when we needed refuge. Many of us have also had mentors to help guide us in making career decisions.

The theory of emerging adulthood connotes a changing notion of adulthood, which recognizes that it is taking longer than it once did to become an adult in U.S. society. It is not only the elongated time period it takes to reach full adulthood that is different; youth need more support during the transition period than has been the case in the past. Youth are depending on their parents and family for support until a much later age than had formerly been the custom in U.S. society.

In this difficult and changing context, foster youth are making two transitions. The first transition is the one they share with all youth: the movement into emerging adulthood. The other transition is leaving the child welfare system and its support, protection, and supervision and going to independent living. These youth may not receive the benefit of the elongated period of preparation for adulthood that is inherent in the concept of emerging adulthood. Youth are not expected to become adults overnight just because they meet a chronological age marker, but that is what could, and often does, happen to a youth being discharged from care. Foster youth not only lose the child welfare system's support on leaving care but often do not have the supports from parents or family that most youth can expect as they encounter the challenges of early adulthood. Family ties may be weak or broken because of prior abuse and/or years in care away from family. Even when ties with the family of birth are intact, families may find it difficult to help. Foster youth often come from families with multiple problems and limited resources, and their parents may be unable or unwilling to provide them with assistance. Social policy expects youth to be self-sufficient without parental support or a publicly provided safety net. In short, these youth risk leaving care without the same help that most young people need, depend upon, and receive. The poor outcomes reported in this book are partly a result of this lack of support.

Public policies have as their foundation the belief that youth leaving care can or will shortly attain financial self-sufficiency and emotional independence. Until the passage of the Fostering Connections to Success Act in 2008, the expectation was that foster youth would leave care to live on their own with little or no support. Even today youth often leave care with just a garbage bag containing their belongings, a referral to a homeless shelter, bus fare to their parental home, and possibly, if they are fortunate, some cash. Just 40 percent of youth have at least $250 when they exit foster care. Only a third of these youth have a driver's license, and most do not have either the resources or skills to establish an independent residence. Many youth reach emancipation without completing high school, employment, and a connection to a supportive, caring adult (American Bar Association Commission on Youth at Risk, 2011; Delgado, 2013). Overcoming these challenges is made more difficult by the socioeconomic disadvantages that preceded foster care and that continue after foster care.

The movement from foster care into independence is a crucial opportunity to address disadvantages caused by youth's experiences before foster care. In many cases, society is not making good use of that opportunity. This book is an argument for an extension of foster care with accompanying support to help these youth emerge into adulthood successfully. The moral argument for this approach is that the state has assumed responsibility for these youth by removing them from their families and placing them in out-of-home care. The state, therefore, is obligated to give them the tools to succeed in life after foster care. In early adulthood, these youth need and deserve the support that most youth in this society expect and receive from those who were responsible for them in childhood and adolescence. This book also presents a utilitarian argument in that the research indicates that better prepared and supported former foster youth will have a greater likelihood of success at independent living. This preparation and support is likely to be cost effective in the long term as former foster youth use this assistance to avoid the difficulties noted in the literature that demand a costly public response. These perspectives all point to the need for child welfare agencies and decision makers to give conscious attention to the use of evidence-based practices to deal with the systemic failure to prepare foster youth for adulthood and support them after discharge.

A Description of Youth Leaving Care

From 2010 to 2014 more than a quarter of a million youth entered foster care each year, mostly for reasons of abuse and/or neglect in the family of origin. Neglect is the most common reason for removing a child from their home. About 0.5 percent of children in the United States are in foster care at any time. Almost 6 percent of America's children will spend at least some time in out-of-home care by the time they reach age 18. These children are placed in a variety of settings ranging from homes of relatives to foster families and institutions. These disparate placements are generically referred to as *foster care* in this book (Adoption and Foster Care Analysis and Reporting System, AFCARS, 2015).

Foster children come mostly from families that have incomes that place them below the poverty line, and they disproportionately are racial and ethnic minorities. Two groups especially overrepresented in child welfare caseloads are African American and Native American children (U.S. Department of Health and Human Services, 2014a; Wildeman & Emanuel, 2014). Fifty-eight percent of these foster children were children of color. Twenty-four percent of foster children were African American. At the same time, 48 percent of America's children were minorities, and African American children constituted about 13 percent of the general population (U.S. Census Bureau, 2016). *Disproportionality* is the name given in the policy literature to the overrepresentation of minority children. African American children are particularly vulnerable. Not only are they and Native American children more likely to enter care than are children of other races and ethnicities, but African Americans are also less likely to reunify with their families or leave care through adoption into another family than are other children. Once in the system, minority children receive differential treatment in services that results in unfavorable outcomes that continue at emancipation (Boyd, 2014). Furthermore, they exit care through emancipation in disproportionate numbers (Harris, Jackson, O'Brien, & Pecora, 2009).

The mean age at entrance to foster care is about nine, with a median age of eight, but most of the youth who exit the child welfare system through emancipation went into care during adolescence. Over 91,000 foster children are between the ages of 11 and 15. An additional 66,000 youth in care are between the ages 16 and 20 (U.S. Department of Health and Human Services, 2015a). The entry into foster care in middle childhood raises questions about missed developmental opportunities before a youth enters into care. For most children the experience in foster care is temporary. About 46 percent of the children who left the system in 2014 had been in care one year or less. In 2014, 238,230 youth exited care at a median age of 6 or 7. About 58 percent of these youth returned home to their parents or went to live with other relatives. Another 21 percent found adoptive families, and 9 percent went to live with guardians (AFCARS, 2015). For many foster youth, finding permanency through adoption, guardianship, or reunification is elusive. Unfortunately, federal policy has been less successful in influencing permanency outcomes for adolescents than it has been for younger children. As the median age of exit suggests, reaching permanency goals is easier for younger children. Leaving the system through adoption or reunification is a less likely outcome for adolescent foster children than it is for younger children (Barth, Wulczyn, & Crea, 2005).

Emancipated youth usually have had longer stays in care (U.S. Department of Health and Human Services, 2015b) and thus have a greater opportunity to be exposed to foster care's effects, be they negative or positive. For many of these youth foster care became a permanent situation that continued through their entire childhood. Adolescents in foster care encounter the same challenges as younger children in care, only over a longer time period because of the potential for more extensive disruptions of their family life, living situations, schooling, and support systems (Pecora, 2007).

In 2014, 22,392 youth emancipated, or "aged-out," of foster care when they turned age 18. These youth represent about 11 percent of all exits from the system. Recent trends have suggested emancipation for all youth is becoming a more common means of exit than it had been in the past. After increasing steadily since the late 1990s, the number of young people emancipating from foster care reached its zenith in 2009 (29,500) before beginning to decline. However, the number of youth aging out of care is still historically high. The 2014 number of youth who aged out of care was 20 percent higher than it was in 2004 (Children's Bureau, 2015). Youth who run away from placement are not part of the count of the number of youth exiting foster care. Official figures place the number of runaways at 1,138 in 2014 (AFCARS, 2015), but other sources place the number much higher. Courtney, Terao, and Bost (2004) found that 46 percent of the 17-year-olds they interviewed in three Midwestern States said they had run away from placement at least once. However, many of these youth return to placement and exit care in a more appropriate manner.

Defining Emancipation

This book refers to youth who exit care through reaching the legal age of adulthood as *emancipated foster youth* (EFY). The term *aging out* refers to these youth as well, and refers, the process of preparing youth to leave care as well as the actual exit (Ryan, Perron, & Huang, 2016). The standard usage of *emancipation* means that youth have reached the age where their parents are no longer legally responsible for them and youth are under no obligation to follow their parent's directives. The same is true for EFY and the child welfare system. They are no longer required to answer to the child welfare system, and the system can disengage its support from the youth. Parents do not have a legal obligation to support their emancipated offspring, but most parents do provide considerable support to their transitioning children. EFY cannot count on the child welfare system for the type of support that most youth in the general population receive from their families.

The experiences and needs of another group of foster youth called *former foster youth* (FFY) are also a subject of this book. FFY are those who have been in foster care but who did not exit through emancipation. The number of older foster youth who exit care before emancipation is substantially greater than just youth who age out. Much of the research reported in this book does not make this distinction and uses the terms EFY and FFY interchangeably. As much as possible, I will try to use the terms as defined here.

A subset of these youth who exit care in late adolescence are assumed by public policy to not need independent living preparation or continued support after discharge because of their permanency option. Their adoptive or biological parents or guardians are considered responsible for these youth's independent living preparation. Research findings that describe the outcomes for these youth post–foster care call this assumption into question. Policy and practice recommendations that flow from the research as a means of improving outcomes will be suggested throughout this book.

Concern about the readiness to leave care has spurred the development of legislation aimed at preparing youth to leave care. The majority of the states have taken advantage of federal legislation to extend care up to ages of 19 or 20 or even later (AFCARS, 2015). However, data suggest these efforts are not enough. We know that many of these youth leave care without a plan to achieve independence or the resources needed for independent living. Consequently, their effort to make their way in the world of emerging adulthood often ends badly.

The cumulative research indicates that youth in foster care often do not get the assistance they need to complete high school, go on to college or other educational opportunities, obtain and keep a job, or find and retain stable and safe housing. This book systematically reviews studies of former FFY, which show these youth to be more likely than their nonfoster peers in the general population to be living in poverty, be unemployed, and be dependent on public assistance. After leaving care, many of these youth find themselves in prison, homeless, or parents before they are ready. These findings reveal serious deficiencies in the child welfare system, and specifically in the preparation and support of youth for transition into adulthood.

The Goals of the Book

This book has two overall goals. The first is the examination of three decades of policy, research, and practice on youth leaving foster care in order to:

1. Provide child welfare practitioners, policy makers, and students with state-of-the-art knowledge regarding the current conditions and experiences of former and emancipated foster youth.
2. Provide child welfare practitioners, policy makers, and students with the best and evidence-based practices to improve the outcomes for former and emancipated foster youth.
3. Enhance readers' skills and knowledge for application to improve the services for former and emancipated foster youth.
4. Suggest practical recommendations for practice and policy for assuring better outcomes for former and emancipated foster youth.

The second goal is to inform the practitioners, policy analysts, decision makers, program developers, advocates, educators, and others who work with these youth in other service sectors about the youth's post–foster care functioning. This book examines empirical evidence regarding the effectiveness of efforts to prepare youth for life after foster care and identifies strategies implemented to improve their transition into adulthood.

CHAPTER TWO

The Transition to Adulthood in the United States

Moving out of the family home and establishing a separate residence, and being able to financially support oneself has historically indicated, through much of the twentieth century, that one was becoming an adult. One of the most striking changes in American society in recent decades has been the extension of the time it takes to become an adult in the United States. Arnett (2000) has given the name of *emerging adulthood* to this developmental stage of life that begins at age 18 but extends into a young person's midtwenties, and can sometimes take as long as the early thirties. This period has become a time of semiautonomy for many youth rather than a period of independence. This restricted autonomy is constrained by an extended dependence on parents for financial support, housing, and child care when needed (Osgood, Foster, & Courtney, 2010).

At least part of this development began with changes that occurred in the post–World War II economy, and government policies to support postsecondary education. Generous government support given returning war veterans in the form of the GI Bill meant that more Americans than ever could attend colleges and universities. Unprecedented numbers of Americans flocked to postsecondary education rather than jumping directly from high school into the job market in the pursuit of a place in the middle class. However, the route to financial independence in the postwar era was not solely through college. The United States had a prosperous manufacturing economy in which high school graduates, and in many cases men with less than a high school diploma, could find well-paid manufacturing jobs that provided sufficient income and benefits to ease them into adulthood. These economic opportunities meant that they would be able to support a family and maintain a middle-class lifestyle. Beginning in the 1970s those jobs began to disappear. The result was that for working-class youth, paths to a stable family life began to become more difficult (Bluestone & Harrison, 1982). The demands of the economy required students to seek postsecondary education as the best bet for assuring entry into the middle class. A college degree was no longer perceived as a luxury but rather as a necessity. The resulting need for a longer period of educational preparation meant that many young adults were also delaying marriage and parenting, and they were leaving home at later ages than they had done in the past (Furstenberg, 2010).

In addition to the educational demands, the changing economy has complicated the transition to adulthood. Even before the Great Recession of 2008–2013, economic change had made it more difficult for young people to achieve self-sufficiency and independence. Restricted economic opportunities, stagnant wages, and high housing costs made it difficult for parents to launch their offspring. Census data indicate that youth in the general population are leaving their family homes to establish an independent household at around age 23, and often return home after an initial failed attempt at living independently (Williams, 2005). The average age at which children in America finally depart the home is 28 (Clark & Davis, 2005; Mouw, 2004). This trend of youth remaining in the family home increased during the Great Recession. The percentage of men age 18 to 24 who resided in their parents' home was 53 percent in 2005. In 2011, the percentage of males of this age who lived in their parent's home was 59 percent. The corresponding percentages for females for living with their parents were 46 percent in 2005 and 53 percent in 2011. In 2012, 36 percent of all 18- to 31-year-olds lived in a parents' home (Fry, 2013). Similar increases were noted for youth ages 25 to 34 remaining in the family household (Vespa, Lewis, & Kreider, 2013). However, these trends may not be observed among foster youth. Nationally, 73 percent of 19-year-olds live with the parents. Among discharged foster youth at age 19, only 43 percent of them were living with parents (Pergamit & Johnson, 2009).

These changes have resulted in the transition to adulthood becoming a more gradual process for most youth. Youth become less dependent on their families over time as they develop the ability to meet their own needs (Goldscheider & Goldscheider, 1999). The rise of economic inequality beginning in the 1970s caused many anxious parents to reach the conclusion that in order for their children to remain in the middle class, they must invest more resources in their children over a much longer period, even after they left the family home. Schoeni and Ross (2005) analyzed data collected for the Panel Studies of Income Dynamics and found that even about 20 years ago, parents' financial contributions to their adult children after they left home were substantial. At the time of that research, these parents provided, on average, $2,200 a year to their adult offspring up to age 34 ($3,354 in 2017 dollars).

Youth who maintain positive connections to their parents have a source of help, advice, and tangible resources (e.g., finances and housing) when they face adversity in the transition (Steinberg, 1990).

The research of Cohen, Kasen, Chen, Hartmark, and Gordon (2003) underscores the gradual nature of the transition to adulthood. They found a steady increase in the time that it took a youth to meet the traditional markers of independence. The markers culled from a variety of domains (housing, work, romantic relationships, and parenting) were being reached at later time points than they had been in the past. Today it is not uncommon for youth to delay identifying as an adult until their early thirties when they feel they are financially independent and emotionally mature (Arnett, 2004; Courtney, 2009).

Some researchers use the life course perspective to examine predictable life events such as the transition to adulthood (Elder, 1998; Goldscheider & Goldscheider, 1999). This perspective has hypothesized a predictable sequence of role transitions, beginning with the completion of education, entry into full-time work, the establishment of an independent household, marriage or cohabitation, and parenthood (Elder, 1980). In the past, someone became an adult at the completion, or near completion, of this sequence. For the most part, middle-class youth still adhere to this schedule, albeit at a slower pace than in the past. For less advantaged youth it is difficult to accomplish these milestones in a predictable fashion. Reliance on the family of origin continues for both groups into their thirties or longer for some, but for different reasons. Young middle-class people were willing to remain in the family home to maintain their middle-class status, and as a way of gaining family support to complete the transition sequence (Fussell & Furstenberg, 2004; Rumbaut, Komai, & Morgan, 2007). Disadvantaged youth live at home as an economic survival strategy. In either instance, the financial and emotional burden on families has greatly increased in the past 15 years (Furstenberg, 2010).

Some data is available to support an assertion that less advantaged youth would prefer to leave home earlier than do youth with more resources (Furstenberg, 2010), even though they might not have the financial means to do so (DeMarco & Cosner-Berzin, 2008). Middle-class youth are more likely to be college or university students. These youth may be enjoying a period of semiautonomy from their parents that may be accompanied by part-time work and cohabitation. If these students are living at home, their relationships with their parents are generally better than the relationships that nonstudents have with their parents, particularly when those nonstudents are not working. Parents feel that students are moving toward independence, and are much more willing to contribute support (Aquilino, 1999). Youth from low-income families are less likely to be attending college, or be working, than middle-class youth (Furstenburg, 2010). Rather than receiving financial support from their parents, youth from low-income households are often expected to contribute money to the family household to pay rent, board, and bills. This expectation may place these youth in conflict with their families, as it may pose a barrier to their own investment in their education or restrict their ability to establish an independent household (Kendig, Mattingly, & Bianchi, 2014). However, having to make these contributions does not mean that a youth is unhappy about it. Some evidence suggests that poor and low-income adolescents, who feel obligated to contribute to the household and are able to do so, have elevated feelings of emotional well-being derived from the role fulfillment that assisting one's family provides (Telzer & Fuligni, 2009).

This pattern of leaving home also occurs in other industrial nations, but with some differences. In northern Europe, youth are more likely than their U.S. counterparts to leave home in their teens, largely because of the state supports available to them. Southern European youth may stay in the home longer, but as much for cultural as for economic reasons. The lack of comparable public social supports for transitioning youth in the United States relative to their European peers means that youth in the United States must rely in part on their parents' willingness and ability to support them (Billari, Philipov, & Baizan, 2002). In the United States, if you are not working, jobless benefits are meager compared to what is provided in the rest of the developed world, and those that are available are only given to people with the prerequisite employment histories.

In addition, something that directly affects transitioning youth is that public support for postsecondary education has been declining in the United States, and college costs have been rising. As a result, many youth leave college with massive amounts of debt. This author accompanies a group of American students to a German university during the summer. The U.S. students are always amazed to find that German students receive their postsecondary education at no cost and leave school without debt. The debt taken on by American graduates makes it difficult for U.S. youth to establish an independent household. These deficiencies in public support make family support even more essential (Goldberg, 2012). It should also be noted that the relative lack of public support that the United States provides for children when compared to other industrialized countries means that supports provided to children may come at the expense of parents planning for their own retirement, although parents may be at least partially reimbursed for this contribution when their offspring provide caregiving for their aging parents.

A complicating factor for low-income women in leaving home is that they are more likely than middle-class women to become pregnant during the transition. Pregnancy and the transition to adulthood are discussed in detail in Chapter 11. Forty percent of first births in America occur to unmarried women. Most of these women have not attended or completed college. Almost 50 percent of youth with a high school education or less become parents in their teen or twenties (Vespa et al., 2013). These pregnancies are generally unplanned, interrupt a sequence that could lead to self-sufficiency, and occur to individuals and families with limited resources that complicate the process of completing the life course sequence (Cherlin, 2010). Additionally, these young mothers often have romantic relationships that are fragile and are likely to break up. The fathers tend to have employment problems, mental health and/or substance abuse problems, and possible criminal justice involvement (Huang & Lee, 2008). These women are forced to rely on their families for financial and emotional support. This reliance places more stress on already overburdened families. The corresponding problem for low-income men of color that complicates the transition is criminal justice involvement (Jonson-Reid & Barth, 2000).

Emerging Adulthood

Arnett (2000) has attached the label *emerging adulthood* to this relatively new period of extended preparation for adulthood. Arnett defines this period as a new developmental stage that occurs from ages 18 to the mid- to late twenties where the youth is "in-between the restrictions of adolescence and the responsibilities of adulthood" (2000, p. 14). He asserts that the earlier reference to this stage by Kenniston (1971) as "youth" had limitations because the term has been used to refer to children, adolescents, and young adults in their twenties (Arnett, 1998). Emerging adulthood is seen as a more precise term that refers to a particular time in a person's life. The stage is different from adolescence and the adulthood that follows, and is a bridge between the two. While there is disagreement about whether this bridge is really a new stage of life, most researchers agree that it is taking longer to achieve adulthood in America than it did in the past (Goodkind, Schelbe, & Shook, 2011).

According to Arnett and Taber (1994), reaching adulthood requires change in two developmental domains: the cognitive and the emotional. The cognitive domain includes the capacity to make adult decisions and developing a sense of responsibility to others including a larger society. The emotional realm entails the development of autonomy from parents, not in the psychological sense of separation discussed in previous psychological literature, but as developing an autonomous relationship based on mutuality and reciprocity. The emotional sphere also encompasses the ability to establish intimacy in adult relationships and the development of impulse control with the ability to behave in a socially responsible manner.

This theorizing about a new stage of life occurred in the context of the development of knowledge about how the brain operates. This new knowledge has delineated the differences in brain functioning, development, and behavior between adolescents and adults. Research suggests that parts of the brain are continuing to develop well into a youth's twenties. One of the last parts of the brain to mature, the prefrontal cortex, is that area associated with impulse control (Steinberg, 2005). Youth are still developing competence in executive functioning (Blakemore & Choudhury, 2006). Youth do not have the same ability as adults to make decisions, as they are more likely to be affected by emotions and the need to be accepted by a peer group than are adults. They are more prone to risk taking, less likely to have a future orientation, and they have much more trouble than adults in regulating their strong emotions (Arnett & Tanner, 2006). All of the above could be made worse if they had been subjected to the traumatic brain injury that many abused children experience.

Risk taking is built into the changes taking place in the adolescent brain, and provides opportunities for youth to learn from experiences including those experiments that might end in failure. It is important during the period that youth have adult support to enable them to develop coping and self-regulation competencies and resiliency when there are mistakes (Jim Casey Opportunities Initiatives, 2011).

Defining Adulthood

Emerging adulthood is fraught with ambiguity. Legally, youth know they are adults, but most are unable to do what they have been told makes one an adult, such as being financially independent. Just when someone becomes an adult is open to question. One theory that has examined this question is the life course perspective. Researchers using this theoretical framework typically use large data sets, such as census data, to identify trends in life events within the population (Collins, 2001). This theory emphasizes two domains: the sociological/historical, and the biological and its accompanying maturation. The sociological/historical domain shapes the societal expectations as to what a young person is supposed to be accomplishing at a given chronological age. Biological age, turning age 18 (maturation), is an indicator that the process of transition is accelerating.

Three different levels of analysis are of concern in the life course perspective: individual time, as measured by age and developmental stage; social time, as indicated by the acquisition of socially determined roles; and historical time, by looking at events and conditions that might shape an individual's transition into these roles (Giele & Elder, 1998). An example of historical time impacting transitioning youth and decisions they might make is coming of age during the Great Recession. Transitioning youth found it difficult to secure work at that time, which led to an upsurge in people deciding to become students (Fain, 2014).

Life course theorists have looked at traditional role transitions as the markers of reaching adulthood. The acquisition of new roles means that one has acquired new responsibilities and rights. These transitions include school completion, beginning full-time work, establishing a household independent from the family of origin, perhaps commitment to another person in the form of marriage or cohabitation, and parenthood (Shanahan, 2000). Similarly, Furstenberg, Kennedy, McLoyd, Rumbault, and Setterstein (2004) placed economic self-sufficiency and financial independence, alongside the completion of schooling and ahead of marriage and parenting, as markers of becoming an adult. A central concern is whether transition events occur "on time" or "off course." The timing is largely socially determined by societal expectations about when events ought to occur and by such things as reference group theory. Young adults may be assessing how well they are doing by viewing how others in their peer networks and reference groups are making the transition. Timing is used as a factor by youth and others in the evaluation of their progress toward adulthood (Elder, 1995).

The emerging adulthood perspective is greatly influenced by Arnett (1998, 2003, 2004). His theory is useful in understanding the variability in outcomes that youth have in the transition. Youth have different life experiences and starting points that must be taken into account in judging the progress of the transition (Horrocks, 2002). Arnett's work is based on surveys completed with adolescents and youth of various ethnicities, and has led him to suggest alternate indicators to the life course perspective for identifying when one reaches adulthood. These markers deemphasize the role transitions of the life course perspective. The indicators of adulthood that Arnett maintains have wide agreement in our culture. These are: (1) making one's own decisions, (2) accepting personal responsibility for one's actions, and (3) achieving financial independence from one's family of origin. Arnett describes these markers as individualistic and qualities of character.

Underscoring these markers is the core American value of individualism. Attaining financial independence, and not being dependent on others, is of prime importance in America's conception of adulthood. *Responsibility* is defined as responsibility to oneself, and not as obligations to others. Arnett says that this individualism is tempered by the development of character qualities that emphasize social and communal considerations. An example of this consideration provided by Arnett's research is that youth believe adults were expected to show greater consideration for others and to avoid reckless behavior such as drunk driving that might harm other people. Arnett found that Latinos and African Americans were more adamant about the social and communal aspects of the theory than white respondents were. Minority youth were also more likely than white youth to say that developing the ability to support a family is an indicator of adulthood. Arnett explains this difference through the greater commitment to collective values that is found in minority communities when compared to the majority culture. Arnett's research suggests that white youth do not believe that meeting the traditional transition markers (such as school completion, full-time employment, and marriage) is necessary to determine whether one is an adult. However, minority youth, although they endorse Arnett's alternate markers, are more likely than majority youth to say that the traditional indicators have to be met in order for one to be identified as an adult (Arnett, 2003). This belief is important for child welfare practitioners, as a disproportionate number of children in that system are minorities.

Foster Youth and Their Challenges during the Transition

Foster youth risk leaving care without the same help that most young people need and depend upon. One concept taken from the life course perspective suggested by Singer and Berzin (2015) for use in understanding the unique problems for foster youth in transition is cumulative advantage/disadvantaged theory. Youth enter care with significant socioeconomic disadvantages. This theory suggests that the developmental impact of any transition is determined by the timing of events in a person's life (Elder, 1998). Youth leave care with significant disadvantages, such as not finishing high school. An early transition without support, before one is ready, can lead to a disadvantaged outcome. This outcome hinders youth as they encounter additional life events or transitions. Over time, this leads to an accumulation of other disadvantages (Merton, 1968). These cumulative disadvantages make it difficult to cope with the more complex demands that come with adulthood. The transition to adulthood is difficult even for those who have resources and previous successes at various life stages, but even more so for those with cumulative disadvantages. As an example of this disadvantage, noted in Chapter 6, is that attending underperforming schools prior to entering the child welfare system leads to educational deficits that are compounded by placement changes that hinder school progress. The resulting failure to complete high school means that youth are handicapped in finding well-paying jobs.

The core mission of the child welfare system is to protect children. Because of this mission many foster youth do not get the opportunities to engage in this type of rite-of-passage activities that are part of most emerging youth's transition (Bruskas, 2008; Scannapieco, Smith, & Blakeney-Strong, 2016). Rules meant to keep them safe may have restricted their opportunities to become more independent. Youth leaving care may have not held an after-school part-time job, obtained a driver's license, learned to drive a car, spent a night at a friend's house, or hung out with friends on a weekend night (Scannapieco, 2011).

The transition is a crucial opportunity to intervene to address disadvantages that a youth has experienced; it ought not to be missed. Sawhill, Winship, and

Grannis (2012) assert from their research that failure to have a successful transition to adulthood makes the chances of having a middle-class income at age 40 only 50 percent. These labor economists also note that making a successful transition to adulthood despite previous adverse events carries a 60 percent chance of being middle class at age 40. This finding seems highly relevant for foster youth, as enabling a successful transition may alleviate some of the disadvantages that these youth have accumulated from past experiences.

In a qualitative study that examined why youth leave care early, Goodkind et al. (2011) found that youth often emancipate at age 18, even when they are not ready, out of a desire for independence and autonomy. The youth interviewed concurred with previous views stated by other researchers cited in this chapter that being an adult meant "being able to take care of yourself." They note that this view not only is culturally rooted in American individualism but for foster youth may arise from life history where they learned they need to take care of themselves when the adults in their lives were deficient in providing care. In another qualitative study, transitioning youth reported that the extra scrutiny and supervision they received as foster adolescents made them feel like a child. Rather than experiencing support from the child welfare system during the transition as helpful, as other youth might view assistance from a parent, foster youth may interpret the extension of help as a barrier to adulthood (Cosner-Berzin, Singer, & Hokanson, 2014). This attitude on the part of adolescents—asserting they can do things on their own—may be developmentally appropriate, based on their need for independence (Erickson, 1968).

Independence versus Interdependence

A number of researchers have argued against equating independence with adulthood (Avery & Freundlich, 2009; Goodkind et al., 2011; Propp, Ortega, & NewHeart, 2003). First, these researchers assert that no adult is truly independent, but instead is embedded in a web of social relationships where there is mutual dependency throughout the life cycle. Second, emerging adulthood has as a core underpinning the notion of an extended period of parental dependency noted earlier in this chapter. This dependency period involves a postponement of adult responsibilities. Time spent in attending college is the most obvious example of this delay. An extended dependency may not be possible for low-income youth. Emerging adulthood as conceived by Arnett may be available only to those youth who have the resources to sustain an elongated period of preparation before adulthood (Kendig et al., 2014). Hence, low-income youth are pushed into an ideal of independence that is not expected of other youth. The logic of independent living programs emphasizes the expectation of early independence.

The striving for independence as a marker of adulthood places burdens on foster youth and other vulnerable groups who seek to survive independently.

America's public policy about foster care emancipation has traditionally revolved around independent living and self-sufficiency, which means we expect a much earlier adulthood for foster children than for youth in the general population. According to Propp et al. (2003), the emphasis on independence in independent living programs may be transmitting to youth the cultural notion that it is a sign of weakness to ask for help, which may make them reluctant to try to access services after foster care ends.

These authors also argue for conceptualizing the transition to adulthood as including "interdependence," which is a mixture of dependency and self-sufficiency. A person relies on the assistance of others when he or she lacks skill, confidence, energy, and/or time to cope with the tasks on hand. This assistance is a bridge to developing the ability to handle tasks more autonomously in the future. The notion of interdependent living says that self-sufficiency is necessary but not sufficient. A successful adulthood means having the ability to connect with others in the community and live with them in a way that is mutually beneficial (Pine, Kreiger, & Maluccio, 1990). Interdependence requires transition programs to help youth make those connections. As indicated previously, no one is truly independent. Youth need to be taught to develop the ability to relate to others, assisted to build support systems based on mutuality and reciprocity, and helped to become contributing members to a larger society. All of these should be considered markers of adulthood. This may mean redefining measures of success used in public policy for determining the success of a transition. Most current measures used some variant of self-sufficiency as a measure for determining successful outcomes.

The Transition in the Context of Foster Care

Courtney, Hook, and Lee (2010) used latent class analysis with data from the Midwest Evaluation of Adult Functioning to test Arnett's theory with discharged foster youth (the methodology of this important study is discussed in Chapter 5). This analytic technique gives researchers the ability to break apart research samples into distinct subgroups based on similarities across multiple variables. These researchers found four different profiles of emancipated foster youth (EFY). The first group, *Emerging Adults*, contained 21 percent of youth who fit Arnett's model of emerging adulthood as a gradual approach to meeting adult markers and the avoidance of major difficulties. The largest group of adolescents (36 percent), called *Accelerated Adults*, experienced a quickened rather than a gradual movement into adulthood. This label did not mean unsuccessful, but many of these youth did have problems such as homelessness at some point. Almost all had finished high school, about one-half had at least some college, and one-half had children. Despite experiencing troubles at certain points, they were making the transition (completing high school, establishing an independent household, and raising children). A separate class, called *Struggling Parents* (25 percent), was also growing up faster than their peers. Movement of this group into adulthood was precipitated by a single event, such as reaching the statutory age for discharge from care or experiencing an early pregnancy. This group was disproportionately composed of African American females raising a child. They were less likely than the previous two groups to have a high school diploma or general equivalence diploma, to have any labor force attachment, or to have established an independent household. This group also had a high reliance on public assistance, suggesting that they were not meeting the marker of self-sufficiency. The remaining youth (18 percent) were called *Troubled and Troubling*, a group made up mostly of males who were institutionalized, homeless, incarcerated, or otherwise not self-sufficient or independent (Courtney, Hook, & Lee, 2010).

Munson, Lee, Miller, Cole, and Nedelcu (2013) and Kendig et al. (2014) provide empirical evidence to support the assertion that youth with previous disadvantages are likely to have an accelerated transition to adulthood. This disadvantaged beginning, along with the subsequent involvement in the child welfare system, often causes youth to establish a too-early adulthood. This early coming of age often occurs without the prerequisites for self-sufficiency, such as a completed education. Galambos, Kolaric, Sears, and Maggs (1999) note that the early adulthood of many youth, who grew up in hardship, can create a "pseudomaturity" in which youth mimic adult behaviors without the prerequisite psychosocial maturity. Many of these young adults also have mental health problems because of past traumas. It is unrealistic and unfair to expect independence and self-sufficiency from this group (Singer & Berzin, 2015).

A policy change that would address the barriers to successful transition to adulthood is to extend the time a youth is under care with accompanying support. Although there is support for such initiatives, much debate focuses on how long that extension should be. Should emancipation be assumed to coincide exactly with a youth's eighteenth birthday? Could there be another definition of when someone is ready for adulthood? Although many states have the legal authority to retain jurisdiction beyond age 18, they do so reluctantly, in limited circumstances, and for the briefest time needed to deal with those circumstances (Packard, Delgado, Fellmeth, & McReady, 2008). Although public child welfare agencies cannot provide support for former foster youth (FFY) indefinitely, nor do youth want it, policy makers must recognize and respond to current social and economic trends, such as the increase in age at which youth are leaving home and the pattern of successive returns to the parental home by youth after leaving (Baum, Ma, & Payea, 2013). An extended period of transitional services for all foster youth might help these youth cope with the challenges of emerging adulthood. This extension might provide the same sort of supports afforded to youth in the general population, and would be congruent with the normative transition to adulthood in contemporary America (Osgood et al., 2010). The provision of services to FFY might be thought of as a social investment because of the potential payoffs in future economic stability.

A concept from the United Kingdom called *corporate parenting* has been used by Courtney (2009) to describe the role the state should assume that would enable FFY to emerge successfully into adulthood. In acting as a corporate parent the child welfare system would resemble a family. The corporate family is synonymous with the extended family, which has a broader array of supports than the nuclear family. During the extension period, the state acts as a good parent, that is, as a guide and resource toward a successful transition. The state would do for the youth what is expected of any parent launching a child from the home. The state does not do the actual parenting, but it can make sure that the youth has what they need to be successful. This means they help find helping systems, and other adults, who can carry out parent-like roles until the youth can stand on their own. The child welfare system can bring together the resources of the various service systems that a youth needs to emerge as a successful adult. Child welfare should not take sole responsibility for the transition, but should include other relevant service systems (education, health, income maintenance, vocational training, mental health, housing, etc.) (Schwartz, 2009). We take this up this issue in Chapter 3.

CHAPTER THREE

Toward a National Policy on Transitioning Foster Youth

The policy mandate is to find *permanency* for youth by reunifying foster children with their biological parents, and if that is not possible, to find these children a new home through adoption or guardianship. However, some children do not find permanency and remain in foster care until they reach the age where they are considered to be legally an adult. These youth are referred to as *aging out* or *emancipated*. Research findings have developed an alarming picture of these youth when they leave foster care. The cumulative research has documented the problems and struggles that many former foster youth have in their adaptation to emancipation. This research is reviewed in much detail later in this book, but for now it should be noted that these dismal outcomes have stimulated a strong desire to address the needs of former foster youth at the policy level.

Legislative History on Transitioning Foster Youth

Precursors

The passage of the landmark legislation called the Adoption Assistance and Child Welfare Act of 1980 moved the federal government firmly into the child welfare policy domain by defining permanency options and priorities for system-involved youth. However, the law did nothing to address what happens to youth after they leave foster care. Historically, youth would reach an age when they were no longer considered to be minors, and at that time they were no longer eligible for child welfare services. Nevertheless, when youth left from care, they were often unprepared for life after foster care.

When they had problems and sought help in adult service systems, they often encountered professional helpers who did not understand both their developmental needs and the unique circumstances of former foster youth (FFY). Beginning in the 1980s, concern began to build among advocates about these former foster children as research became available that documented their difficulties. The conclusion among advocates was that better preparation for youth leaving care might alleviate some of the problems noted in the research.

The advocates for foster youth brought the data to the attention of the U.S. Department of Health and Human Services (DHHS), which issued a Request for Proposals (RFP) entitled *Study of the Adaptation of Adolescents in Foster Care to Independence and Community Life* in 1983. This RFP resulted in the funding of several independent living services (ILS) demonstration projects (Propp, Ortega, & NewHeart, 2003). Thus, Congress was prepared to act, which it soon did.

Congress passed a series of legislative acts spanning a couple of decades to provide funding to the states to better prepare youth for the transition from foster care to emerging adulthood. These actions were a recognition that while foster care is meant to be temporary, for many youth the reality is remaining in the system until they age out. It was recognized that the state and federal governments had responsibilities for these youth that did not end with emancipation.

Independent Living Initiative of 1986

The first policy effort came in 1986 with the passage by Congress of the Independent Living Initiative, which amended the Title IV-E of the Social Security Act to provide the states with $45 million to develop independent living programs for foster youth ages 16 to 18 who were Title IV-E eligible (Collins, 2004; Stott, 2013). Funding was allocated to the states according to a formula based on the percentage of youth in the state who received foster care funds in 1984. The aim was to help emancipated foster youth (EFY) develop independent living skills through a teaching program. The significance of the act was that the federal government recognized the importance of preparing youth to leave foster care by dedicating funding for the first time for this purpose (Courtney, 2009).

States were given a great amount of flexibility in the design and implementation of their ILS programs. The basic services required by law included outreach to attract eligible youth to ILS, education and employment assistance, ILS skills training, individual and group counseling, case management, and a written independent-living plan for each participant. The states were encouraged to provide supplemental services, which could include mentoring, ILS training for foster parents, financial stipends, and the development of youth advisory committees to gather youth input on service delivery and needs. However, a U.S. Government Accountability Office report (1999) bemoaned the lack of evaluation to determine the effectiveness of these efforts, and also the great variation in programs found between states. States were reporting wide differences in participation rates by their eligible youth, and nationally, at the time of the report, only about 60 percent of eligible youth were participating. About one-third of states said that less than one-half of eligible youth were enrolled in an ILS program. Another third of the states reported that at least 75 percent of youth needing services were participating. Differences in participation rates was not the only variation noted. Only 23 states provided stipends and other incentives for participation. Just 21 states provided assistance with school tuition and expenses. Another 20 helped with transportation for school or work, and 26 states provided funds to help set up an independent household. Only 5 states provided all of these services.

The act was reauthorized under Public Law No. 100–647 in 1993, which strengthened previous legislation in three ways. First, eligibility was extended to all age-eligible youth regardless of their Title IV-E status. States could also provide follow-up ILS services to EFY until age 21. Funding was also incrementally increased to $70 million, which was intended to be a base for future funding (Mech, 2003). Prior to 1993 the states depended on a yearly authorization by Congress. Therefore, states limited the amount of money and resources they committed to these programs because of uncertainty about future funding (DeWoody, Ceja, & Sylvester, 1993). Once states had some degree of assurance about the level of funding from year to year, they could feel free to engage in planning on behalf of youth. Despite the guaranteed level of funding, most observers thought that not enough money was provided to meet the need for services of all youth who needed assistance (Ryan, Perron, & Huang, 2016).

Foster Care Independence Act of 1999

The next landmark piece of legislation on behalf of FFY occurred when President Clinton signed the Foster Care Independence Act (FCIA) (P.L. 109–169) into law in December 1999. This act doubled the amount of money available for ILS to $140 million ($700 million over five years). In order to access funds, states were required to provide a 20 percent match. The act is also called the Chafee Foster Care Independence Program in honor of Senator John Chafee, a major advocate for foster youth. The legislation is commonly called Chafee. This legislation was a watershed event in its recognition of the need to better serve youth during this critical transition period. The program had five goals:

1. Identify children likely to remain in foster care and provide them with the skills necessary to make the transition to independent living.

2. Assist these adolescents to obtain the education, training, and social services necessary for self-sufficiency.

3. Aid youth in becoming ready for postsecondary education or training.

4. Give these youth the support necessary to cope with the emotional stress inherent in the transition.

5. Provide the social services necessary for EFY to achieve self-sufficiency, and recognize and accept their personal responsibility for adulthood (Collins, 2004).

Medicaid could be extended at the state's discretion for youth until age 21. States were allowed to use 30 percent of the funds available under the FCIA to provide room and board for EFY until age 21. This provision signaled a policy shift from teaching skills to a recognition that certain concrete needs must also be met if services were to be effective. A number of states excluded some youth from participating in programs. For example, Florida limited Medicaid participation to only those students who had a GPA that would have allowed them to be eligible for the state's own independent living program for college students (U.S. Government Accountability Office, 2004).

Youth between 18 and 21 years old had the option to be housed in supervised settings where they could live independently, in kin or non-kin foster care or in a group facility. The states could claim Title IV-E reimbursement for these services. The federal DHHS was required to help the states create more developmentally appropriate living arrangements for this age group (Courtney, 2009).

Chafee required a state's governor to certify in the application for funds that the state would ensure that foster youth would participate directly in designing independent living program activities, and that youth would take responsibility for living up to their part of the program. At the micro level, this has meant the use of a transitioning service plan that included input from youth on goals. At the macro level, it has meant the development of youth advisory boards that gather youth perspectives on policy and planning issues (Collins, 2004; National Foster Care Awareness Project, 2000a).

The FCIA reaffirmed the system's commitment to permanence despite the interest to better prepare youth for emancipation. ILS programs were not supposed to replace the foster care goal of finding adoptive homes for youth who were not able to return to their own families. The FCIA removed family income as one of the barriers to adoption for older youth. The states would be eligible for a doubling of the incentive payments for older children adoption, from $4,000 to $8,000. This provision began for youth age 16 and older in 2010, and eligibility was extended to age 14 and older the following year (American Bar Association Commission on Youth at Risk, 2011). Despite these provisions, Avery and Freundlich (2009) assert that the child welfare workers stop seeking permanency for youth in their teens because they think it is unlikely a permanent home can be found for older youth who have spent years in the system. Such attitudes, they say, undermine a core principle of child welfare practice, finding permanency for youth. Therefore, many youth leave care without a crucial resource, parents (or at least a parent-like adult) and a family, needed to successfully negotiate the transition.

Chafee also addressed the criticism of the previous legislation that there were only minimal efforts to evaluate the effects of ILS programs. The FCIA mandated that the states reserve 1.5 percent of their funding for rigorous evaluations, and the law also funded the Multi-Site Evaluation. This evaluation addressed deficiencies in the ILS literature by subjecting four existing programs to rigorous experimental evaluation (random assignment, two groups, and a longitudinal design). This evaluation was funded as a field test of existing practices, not as a demonstration of potential model programs (Courtney et al., 2011a, 2011b). The funding of demonstrations to identify model programs with empirical support is still a need that has not been addressed. The FCIA also required the Administration for Children and Families to develop a reporting system for the states to provide data to the federal government that could be used to assess the states' performance in providing ILS by tracking youth to age 21 (National Youth in Transition Data Base, 2012). However, the states were not required to begin reporting data until 2011 (Shpiegel & Cascardi, 2015). Initial results from these data collection efforts are discussed in detail in the next chapter.

The FCIA made Title IV-E funds available to Native American tribes for the purpose of ensuring that Indian children had access to extended foster care and the increased guardianships and adoption assistance in the Act (American Bar Association Commission on Youth at Risk, 2011).

Although the program provided tangible benefits such as housing and health care, this support was much less than a parent might provide to a child during the transition, and it would end at age 21. The ending of state care was still abrupt, so youth may still be pushed into an adulthood for which they are not prepared.

A major drawback to the FCIA is that it did not extend Title IV-E reimbursement to eligible youth as an entitlement except for housing. Therefore, most states decided not to take part in the extension, and states were slow to extend Medicaid. The Midwest Study had one state that extended care until age 21 (Illinois), and two that did not (Wisconsin and Iowa), which provided a natural experiment of the effects of the extension. Not surprisingly, Illinois EFY were more likely to have received ILS than youth in the other two states. In fact, Illinois youth were on average two years older when they exited care than youth who left care in the other two states. These additional two years had a positive effect on educational attainments, which are reviewed in Chapter 6 (Courtney, Dworsky, & Pollack, 2007).

In 2004, the GAO reported an increase in participation by eligible youth from their initial 1999 report, but in some states up to 90 percent of foster youth were still not receiving ILS. Two-thirds to one-half of the 17- and 18-year-olds interviewed by Courtney, Terao, and Bost (2004) said they had not received training or services in the domains needed for independent living (vocational, budget, and financial management). Subsequent follow-ups with this sample indicated that it was unlikely they would receive any ILS after age 18 if they left care (Courtney et al., 2007).

The FCIA required that ILS programs be coordinated with special education programs for foster youth with disabilities. However, guidelines for how this was to be done were not provided, leading to the charge that the needs of disabled foster youth are ignored (Geenen & Powers, 2007). A number of states excluded some youth from participating in programs. For example, Florida limited Medicaid participation to only those students who had a GPA that would have allowed them to be eligible for the state's own independent living program for college students (U.S. Government Accountability Office, 2004).

Promoting Safe and Stable Families Amendment (2002)

The next major policy initiative on behalf of EFY was the Promoting Safe and Stable Families Amendment (PSSFA) in 2002 (Public Law No. 107–133). The focus of the legislation was not to teach independent living skills, but to provide educational and economic assistance. Title II of this legislation provided for educational training vouchers (ETVs) to make available financial assistance to youth seeking postsecondary education. This provision provided an additional $60 million for postsecondary education and vocational training assistance for EFY who were age 18 and older, and for FFY who were adopted at age 16 or later. This component of the legislation indicated an interest in the needs of foster children other than just EFY. Youth could receive up to $5,000 a year to pursue college or training until age 23 if they had been participating in the program when they were age 21. However, youth are required to seek all other sources of help such as Pell Grants prior to receiving an ETV (Fernandes, 2006; Stott, 2013). One problem with the PSSFA is that the amount of funding is woefully inadequate. Even if the states applied the entire $140 million a year to educational assistance, that would only translate into about $2,000 a year per youth (Osgood, Foster, & Courtney, 2010).

Fostering Connections to Success Act (2008)

The last piece of federal policy supporting emancipated foster youth came with the Fostering Connections to Success Act (FCSA) (Public Law No. 110–35), which was signed into law by President Bush in 2008. The law is also known as Fostering Connections. The FCSA amended Title IV-E of the Social Security Act to allow the states to extend care for foster youth until age 21. States might also end the provision of care short of age 21 by setting limits for assistance at age 19 or 20. The states can receive entitlement funding to provide these emerging adults with basic needs and case management services. The legislation represents an acknowledgement of the need for the state to act in loco parentis for a vulnerable group of youth into early adulthood. The law recognizes what we know about most youth: they are not ready to be independent and self-sufficient at age 18. The title of the law seems to indicate that the state must help youth make the connections to becoming successful adults (Osgood et al., 2010). States that receive funds are legally responsible for ensuring that basic needs of those who remain in care are met as defined by law. Fostering Connections goes beyond the FCIA, which only gave the option to the states of spending funds on housing and Medicaid. They were now under mandate to do so (Okpych, 2012).

Eligibility for ILS was also widened for younger youth. Youth who moved from foster care to an adoptive family or guardianship after age 16 could receive ILS. States were required to include these services in case plans if appropriate (Child Welfare Information Gateway, 2014).

This law strengthened supports for EFY in three ways. First, the increased age eligibility meant that more youth could receive ETVs. Second, states can choose to provide matching funds to secure federal funding for housing for youth up to age 21. Housing was to be provided in the form of licensed placements with supervision. Housing assistance was given prior to the passage of this act, but only for youth attending high school or a vocational program with an expected graduation date before they turned age 20. Eligibility for services was contingent on the youth meeting at least one of four conditions, attend school, work at least 80 hours a month, participate in an employment readiness program, or have a documented medical diagnosis that precludes taking part in any of the other specified activities. Finally, the FCSA requires social workers to develop the already mandated transition plan for youth within 90 days of the youth's eighteenth birthday. The plan is required to address the youth's options in a number of specific domains: housing, health insurance, education, opportunities for mentorship, and services that would continue after discharge to support these domains (Stott, 2013).

The legal provision regarding housing addresses the need for stable living arrangements. Housing difficulties have undermined efforts to engage these emerging adults with services, and might be necessary to keep them in education programs or employed (Hernandez & Naccarato, 2010). The provision of case management services means that child welfare agencies can play a coordinating role in connecting youth with the various and often fragmented public service systems (postsecondary education, workforce development, health, mental health, and housing) that offer the services necessary for a successful transition (Osgood et al., 2010).

The act mandated the states to develop, with the collaboration of the state's Medicaid agency along with input from pediatricians, a plan for coordinating and monitoring the provision of health care services using the medical home model, and oversight of medication for each child (American Academy of Pediatrics, 2016).

Other Policies That Have Relevance for EFY

Other laws, not specifically written for a child welfare population, have the potential to affect transitioning youth. One of these laws is the Individuals with Disabilities Education Act (Public Law No. 101–476). This law mandates transition services for special education students (who are over-represented in child welfare caseloads) from birth until age 21 (Hill, 2009). Secondary schools are required to begin developing individualized transition plans as part of an individual education plan (IEP) when such students reach age 16. The plan lists long-term goals for education, vocational training, and general life skills, and it must identify the services needed to reach these goals (Gardner, 2008). Schools generally treat foster parents as decision makers even though social workers are the child's legal guardian because of Family Educational Rights and Privacy Act privacy restrictions. Social workers have greater knowledge of and access to resources than foster parents, and their greater participation in the process would aid in transition planning. Some tweaking of the law is needed so that the two systems can increase the efficiency and effectiveness of collaborative transition planning (Powers et al., 2012).

Other policy options that might assist EFY include the Transitional Living Programs (TLP) authorized by the Runaway and Homeless Youth Act (Public Law No. 106–171) should an FFY find themselves homeless. TLP are part of the Runaway and Homeless Youth Program run by the DHHS Family and Youth Services Bureau and provide long-term residential care for homeless youth ages 16–21 for up to 18 months. Many youth exit foster care by running away from placement, and they could benefit from this program as well. This program provides grants to community-based organizations for residential care, life skills training, decision making, relationship building, aid in accessing health care including mental health, assistance with education, and employment (U.S. Department of Health and Human Services, 2015a).

The Higher Education Opportunities Act (Public Law No. 110–315) was amended in 2008 in order to enable foster children to participate in federal TRIO programs. TRIO programs are educational opportunity outreach programs designed to motivate and support students from disadvantaged backgrounds in their educational aspirations. Examples of these programs are Talent Search and Upward Bound. Postsecondary institutions are also required to recruit and serve former foster youth and to develop an institutional climate that is supportive of FFY (Okpych, 2012).

The Family Unification Program is a relatively small program funded by the U.S. Department of Housing and Urban Development (HUD) that provides transitional and personal housing assistance for youth who age out of care. As of the fall of 2013, only 20,500 vouchers for rental subsidies were available. The program assists families involved with the child welfare system whose primary problem is housing, and for whom, if the housing issues are not addressed, the children will need to go into out-of-home care. HUD requires public housing agencies to collaborate with child welfare agencies in order to help child welfare families compete for housing choice vouchers. Youth ages 18 to 21 who have aged out of foster care are also eligible. The vouchers are available only in some communities, and when used for this youth population are good for 18 months. Families have no such limits. Youth receiving vouchers are also eligible for ILS (Dion, Dworsky, Huff, & Kleinman, 2014). HUD also provides housing assistance to "high risk" youth between the ages of 18 and 24 to learn housing construction skills and earn a high school diploma or GED. HUD awards competitive grants to state and local governments to provide education and employment training under federal employment training programs (Gardner, 2008).

Youth would also be eligible for employment and training services funded under the Workforce Investment Act of 1998. These funds can be used to develop subsidized training slots and provide stipends while youth are in training (U.S. Department of Labor, 2000).

The Patient Protection and Affordable Care Act of 2010 (Public Law No. 111–148) provided that as of 2014 all EFY will be eligible for Medicaid coverage until age 26, regardless of their income. However, not all states have taken part in the Medicaid expansion to cover these youth (Houshyar, 2014). At this time, this law is facing repeal by the Trump administration.

Values Underpinning the Legislation

According to Collins (2004) and Osgood et al. (2010) the legislation have as their underpinning the following values: youth development, permanency, self-sufficiency, and social inclusion.

The U.S. Department of Health and Human Services (2003) describes youth development as "a policy perspective that emphasizes providing services opportunities to support all young people in developing a sense of competence, usefulness, belonging, and empowerment." Collins (2004) notes that this stance is not within the historic practice sphere of child welfare, which has tended to view its clients, particularly children, in terms of deficits rather than strengths. The child's viewpoints were often not included in social work decision making. The youth-centered approach affirmed a youth's right to self-determination. Current policy requires youth input, both as an empowering strategy and as an enticement for youth to use services. It may be that youth avoid these services because while in care they feel disempowered by the system. In order to feel independent, youth often need to place some distance between themselves and the system. In addition, the youth development perspective is reflected in the aim to provide services within a normative, nonclinical framework to support youth in the task of coping with the transition (Schelbe, 2011).

The 1986 and 1999 legislation had within their titles and service provisions the underlying value system guiding U.S. youth policy. Youth were to be independent with the desire to reduce dependency on public programs by FFY. The language in all the legislation supports predominant U.S. values of achieving self-sufficiency and accepting personal responsibility. In short, to participate in programs youth must be taking actions on their own behalf such as going to school or working. These expectations are in line with the values of rugged individualism and the Protestant work ethic. Americans expect people to "make it on their own," regardless of their circumstances. These values assume that a person needs to be economically self-supporting in order to be considered a responsible adult (Propp et al., 2003). Such a view minimizes the limitations of the economy in providing for all citizens, and often ends up blaming the victim. Chapter 2 discussed for American youth how extended dependency is the norm. It may be that the focus on self-sufficiency and independence for foster youth is obsolete. These goals are inappropriate for youth who leave care with educational deficits and mental health difficulties. It is assumed that a large majority have experienced some form of trauma from the maltreatment they experienced that can limit their adult functioning.

The states limit the support to only those youth who are attending an educational program and/or who are employed. This philosophy limits ILS support primarily to youth who will most likely make a successful transition out of care. Because of this premise, youth who are not in school or working will find it difficult to take advantage of this support.

A fourth value identified by Osgood et al. (2010) is social inclusion, which is apparent in the 2008 legislation. According to this principle, all citizens in a democratic society have a right to participate in the full range of activities. It seeks to empower individuals to act on their own behalf, emphasizes reciprocity between persons and the government in the provision of services, and underscores the obligations of all parties in both the delivery and receipt of services. ILS programs are supposed to give EFY the skills to participate in a larger society. The legislation also calls for identifying policies that exclude certain groups from participation in the larger society.

Conclusions

This chapter shows the significant policy efforts made over the last 30 years to ease the transition to adulthood for EFY. Funds were made available to set up programs across the country. While we know much about what happens to youth when they leave care, we know very little about how well the programs for transitioning youth work because of the lack of rigorous evaluations. Chapter 4 discusses these programs in detail. Despite the legislative history, current programs for EFY are fragmented and underfunded, do not provide comprehensive services, and do not reach all the youth who need these services in a manner that would help youth transition successfully into adulthood (Packard, Delgado, Fellmeth, & McReady, 2008). Research that will be discussed later in the book supports these assertions. The consensus in the literature is that the money available for ILS programs is not adequate to meet the needs of youth leaving care. These policies have also been deficient in that they do not adequately address the changes discussed in Chapter 2 on how contemporary youth are emerging into adulthood. The current dependence of young adults on their families makes it clear that further extensions of the age limit for the receipt of services are warranted. In most states, youth still only receive services until age 21, despite the considerable evidence that there is still a need for continued assistance after age 21. The emerging-adult research, as well as other research available on transitioning youth, suggests that an individual is not an adult by either biological or social standards until at least age 25 (Jim Casey Youth Opportunities Initiative, 2011). This research indicates continued need for support beyond age 21, and we must not forget those adolescents who leave care before emancipation. These youth may also need independent living assistance. The trend with all of this legislation is to allow the states to use ILS funds for youth at various ages as they approach the transition (National Foster Care Awareness Project, 2000a, 2000b). However, Courtney (2009) asserts that Congress has been ambivalent about extending the age at which EFY would continue to receive services because of a fear of making these youth dependent. This concern is seldom extended to children in the general population, whose families provide them with needed financial and emotional support well after these youth reach age 21.

Making the case for extension may be facilitated by the continuing development of the empirical evidence about the benefits of such an extension. Some evidence is available to suggest that these expenditures would have long-term payoffs. Certainly, discharging youth before they are ready and prepared has fiscal policy implications. Significant costs are generated in the areas of public assistance, services for the homeless, criminal justice involvement, health care for the uncovered, and loss of tax revenue. Packard and colleagues (2008) provide an example on how such an empirical effort would look. They developed a cost-benefit-analysis proposal for extending transitional services to age 23, in which they examined cost and savings over 40 years for a cohort of EFY in the domains of lifetime earnings, taxes paid, incarcerations, and public assistance avoidance. These researchers estimate that such an extension would provide a benefit to cost ratio of $1.50 to $1.00. They estimate that even if only 75 percent successful, the extension would return savings at a rate of $1.20 to $1.00 spent. Kerman, Barth, and Wildfire (2004) completed another cost-benefit analysis with Casey foster youth alumni. These researchers assert on the basis of their findings that a yearly per youth expenditure of between $4,000 to $6,000 over a two-year period after these youth left care would result in fewer education, health, and housing problems, and higher levels of well-being by FFY. In Chapter 6, a cost-benefit analysis completed by Peters, Dworsky, Courtney, & Pollack (2009) provide an example of what improvements in outcomes can be had by just extending care by one year in the area of education.

Some concern has been expressed that extended foster care with a package of services and support may discourage some youth from pursuing legal permanency through reunification, adoption, or legal guardianship. Legal permanency has been the goal of child welfare services since passage of the Adoption Assistance and Child Welfare Act of 1980. However, evidence from extensions of foster care in California and Illinois suggest youth are more likely to remain in care past age 18, not at the expense of legal permanence, but rather as an alternative to undesirable options such as running away from placement prior to discharge or emancipating at age 18 before they are ready (Courtney, 2009; Courtney & Okpych, 2015).

By 2017 24 states and the District of Columbia had taken advantage of the extension and services to youth past age 18 or 19 (Fowler, Marcal, Zhang, Day, & Landsverk, 2017). One reason some states are reluctant to extend care comes from concern about funding in relation to the federal "lookback" provision. This provision is a federal requirement that a child is only eligible for foster care support if the child was eligible for Aid to Families with Dependent Children (AFDC) at the time of removal from the home. If a youth reenters care to take advantage of the benefits, under the law their eligibility for foster care payments is based on their income and assets, not the family's from which they were removed. As the number of youth in care who are eligible under federal lookbacks declines, the state may be faced with spending burdens in extending payments beyond age 18. The lookback provision requires youth to meet an eligibility test that is outdated and almost two decades old. If not repealed it could hinder the states in developing programs that would provide necessary support to transitioning youth (Delgado, 2013).

Another drawback to implementation is that many state statutes require that youth have judicial oversight to receive Title IV-E services, and the laws in those states do not allow judicial oversight after a youth has reached the age of majority. Therefore, in order to take advantage of these provisions for IV-E reimbursement some states will have to change their laws (Fernandes, 2008).

Many adolescents who leave foster care prior to their emancipation date may not be able to access the full range of resources. The bulk of adolescents exiting care go to their families prior to aging out (Wulczyn & Brunner His-lop, 2001). It is assumed that the families then become responsible for the transition. However, many of these families are resource deficient, and the relationships between parent and child may be strained. Their families might not be in a position to assist them with the transition. These youth may be in need of ILS, but are overlooked by current legislation (Courtney, 2009).

Another group left out of the federal legislation are those EFY who are not working or attending school. In order to access services, youth must be engaged in at least one of these two activities or have a medical problem that keeps them from doing so. Youth who are not working or attending school are those who are most in need of services. In short, policies may not address the full range of challenges that these youth face.

CHAPTER FOUR

Independent Living Services

Getting Youth Ready to Leave Care

Readiness for independent living is contingent on an adolescent having tangible life skills (sometimes called *hard skills*) such as being able to find and maintain an apartment or a job, and intangible (soft) skills such as problem solving, stress reduction, and anger management (Leathers & Testa, 2006; Nollan et al., 2000; Ryan, McFadden, Rice, & Warren, 1988). Independent living services (ILS) programs are meant to teach those skills, and are an outgrowth of the U.S. Department of Health and Human Services (DHHS) 1983 request for proposals entitled *Study of the Adaptation of Adolescents in Foster Care to Independence and Community Life*. ILS programs were institutionalized by the Independent Living Initiative of 1986, which was discussed in the last chapter. The actions by the federal government were a response to the problems noted in the research on youth leaving foster care that were also briefly reviewed in Chapter 3 and that we will examine in detail later in this chapter. The intent of these programs was to provide emancipated foster youth (EFY) with the skills needed to live independently (Collins, 2001). ILS programs were initially intended for youth in long-term foster care who did not have a permanency plan, and were offered as youth moved toward emancipation. Efforts and the expenditure of funds were concentrated on preparing youth before they left foster care and given only to those foster youth who were aging out of care. Policies have changed over the years to encourage states to begin the process of independent living preparation earlier in adolescence, and to provide services after a youth leaves care.

ILS were originally intended to teach tangible skills to youth exiting foster care, in four domains: finances, education, employment and health. The Foster Care Independence Act of 1999 (FCIA), widened the eligibility for ILS programs to include youth as young as 14 and allowed the states to provide independent living and transition services until age 21 (Naccarato, Brophy, & Courtney, 2010). In addition, the states began providing concrete benefits to youth leaving care such as Medicaid, housing, and educational vouchers to help offset college costs.

The 1986 ILS legislation and the later FCIA gave the states considerable leeway in designing programs and defining eligibility for services. The United States does have a policy that provides for a broad framework for the design of ILS programs, but the specifics of programs were left up to the states. Funding also varied widely among states. For example, in 2006 West Virginia allocated $476 per youth for ILS, while Montana provided $2,300 per youth (U.S. Government Accountability Office, 2007). Therefore, considerable differences in program implementation are found among the states. Eligibility criteria, length of time services are given, and the adequacy of those services are largely a question of the state in which a youth happens to reside.

The U.S. Government Accountability Office (GAO) (1999) summarized findings from the annual reports from the states for 1987–1996 in order to provide a description of ILS programs. The GAO found wide variations in ILS programs among the states. The GAO noted the number of youth receiving services doubled during the period under review, but that only a portion of eligible youth participated in an ILS program (U.S. Government Accountability Office, 1999). The GAO report identified several other weaknesses with programs. Few evaluations of programs exist, and those that are available lack methodological rigor. Appendix A summarizes the research discussed in this chapter. The GAO asserted that training for employment was inadequate in most programs. Programs did not link youth with potential employers or provide apprenticeships, and available vocational training programs were expensive. The GAO also noted that transitional housing programs and services postdischarge were inadequate to meet existing need. The GAO also recommended more "hands-on activity" for learning skills rather than the didactic, classroom-based training in order to more fully engage youth.

Participation in ILS Programs

In 2004 a GAO follow-up on the early implementation of the FCIA showed wide variations in ILS participation by youth. Of the 40 states reporting, 13 said that at least 75 percent of youth were participating. Five states reported less than 25 percent of youth received ILS (U.S. Government Accountability Office, 2004). Data collected in 2014 show that not all of the youth eligible for ILS actually received those services (U.S. Department of Health and Human Services, 2015a). The Midwest Study reported that although 76 percent of the eligible 17- and 18-year-olds received ILS, only one-third of youth felt prepared for independent living. This finding suggests that independent living preparation for youth leaving care is inadequate. One drawback to participation in ILS programs is the lack of financial support for youth. Many youth thought they would need financial assistance to cover the expense of participating. In the Midwest Study only 12 percent of youth had received a subsidy as an incentive to take part in independent living training (Courtney, Terao, & Bost, 2004). When youth do participate, the adequacy of services is often questioned. Reilly (2003) reported most of the youth in his nonrandom sample of convenience in Nevada had been in an independent living program, but almost none of them had received services or assistance after they left care. Pecora, Kessler, Williams, et al. (2005) said that 70 percent of FFY had received ILS, but only half of those who received services said they were well prepared for life after foster care.

Courtney, Piliavin, Grogan-Kaylor, and Nesmith (2001) interviewed a random sample of Wisconsin older adolescents (n=141) preparing to leave care. On average, youth received training in 13 of 16 independent living skill areas identified as important in that study. Youth generally did not receive training in housing, legal needs, or parenting skills. Eighty-three percent of youth said health education was the most frequently rendered service. Academic support was the most common type of service provided according to findings from the National Youth in Transition Database (NYTD) (2013). The Midwest Study also reported education to be the service most frequently given, with African Americans being the group most likely to receive that service. About 53 percent of youth in the Midwest study received that service (Katz & Courtney, 2015). The least provided service was financial assistance for housing. Only 8 percent of youth received this assistance (Courtney & Dworsky, 2005; Okpych, 2015). Most of the training focused on daily living skills (see Appendix A for a description of these skills). Youth interviewed two years later said their preparation was deficient in that they were not trained on how to secure employment or housing. A qualitative study by Geenen and Powers (2007) found that youth who took part in ILS training felt the preparation for independent living was inadequate and did not prepare them for the real world. Courtney et al. (2004) concluded that although youth receive some ILS training, it might not be comprehensive enough to meet their needs. They measured six domains for independent living skills: education, employment/vocational, financial management, housing, health, and youth development. Depending on the domain measured, they found that one-third to one-half of students had not received any training in that area. A study that used a representative sample of California's foster youth reported that youth felt the least prepared in areas needed for basic survival such as housing, employment, and financial management (Courtney, Charles, Okpych, Napolitano, & Halsted, 2014).

A drop-off in the provision of ILS occurs at age 19. Although Illinois had lagged in the provision of services before youth left care, it did a much better job than the other states in the Midwest Study at reaching youth after their eighteenth birthday. Illinois was the only state in that study to extend foster care beyond age 18. At age 21, 35 percent of Illinois EFY continued to receive services versus 21 percent of youth in the other two states. The lesson according to Courtney (2009) is that youth will use services after emancipation if the state extends foster care. He and a colleague found similar results in a qualitative study they conducted in California. In that study, foster youth were enthusiastic about extended care with services as a way to prevent homelessness and allow youth to focus on their educational or vocational goals (Napolitano & Courtney, 2014).

The FCIA also funded the development of the NYTD, which required the states to report outcome data to the Administration for Children and Families (ACF) so that the federal government could assess their performance on the provision of ILS. (The methodology of this study is discussed in Chapter 5.) The NYTD data from 2012 provided a somewhat more positive picture of the state of ILS programs. Okpych (2015) merged this database with another ACF database called the Adoption and Foster Care Analysis and Reporting System (AFCARS). This merger provided the researcher with a sample of 131,204 foster children to examine the characteristics of ILS. Okpych found that in fiscal year 2011–2012 about 50 percent of youth received at least one ILS with a mean of 2.31 services per youth. Hispanic youth were the most likely, and African Americans were the least likely, group to receive services. Disabled foster youth were more likely than nondisabled youth to have taken part in ILS programs (55 percent vs. 48 percent), suggesting that extra attention was given to special needs youth. Females were more likely to receive services than males. Two reasons were given for the gender differences in service utilization: Women were more likely to pursue education after foster care, which gave them a reason to remain connected to their independent living program. They also had lower incarceration rates than males. Youth in jail or prison are not available for services (Courtney, Dworsky, Cusick, et al., 2009). Okpych (2015) and Courtney et al. (2009) also found that youth in urban areas were less likely to have received ILS than youth who live in suburban or rural areas, which has a disproportionate effect on the ability of minority youth to access services.

Program Components

As stated earlier the GAO (1999) found that ILS programs varied from state to state and even within states. As noted earlier in the chapter, the focus of training was on skills needed for self-sufficiency. Programs used social skill training techniques such as classroom instruction, modeling, role-plays, group work, and in some cases individualized mentoring.

A distinction is made between *hard* and *soft* skills. Hard skills are those that are easily measurable and include employment, educational, and housing maintenance skills. Soft skills include the ability to connect to others, anger management, social development, parenting, health, and mental health maintenance, among others (McMillen, Rideout, Fisher, & Tucker, 1997). According to Iglehart and Becerra (2002), these soft skills receive less attention than hard skills. Hard skills are generally easier to teach and measure, and therefore are favored by ILS programs (Georgiades, 2005).

A debate exists about what to teach or emphasize in ILS curricula (hard or soft skills). McMillen et al. (1997) and Iglehart and Becerra (2002) say the emphasis on the teaching of hard skills with its stress on self-sufficiency is misplaced, particularly in adolescence before youth are able to understand or accept that responsibility. This emphasis may also contribute to the expectations of an accelerated adulthood for EFY. As discussed in Chapter 2, the emphasis on self-sufficiency may be unrealistic and unfair for youth, who are not prepared for it and who already have numerous problems that need to be overcome before self-sufficiency can be considered. However, at least one report from New York State, which drew on the voices of FFY, revealed that the emphasis on soft skills was not what was wanted or needed. The adolescents in that study reported that too much training time was spent on topics such as substance abuse and pregnancy prevention when what they wanted was more time spent on learning about educational options, career planning, and relationship building (Youth Advocacy Center, 2001).

A number of needs assessments have been published that attempted to measure youth reaction to ILS programs and their perspective on what content should be taught. McMillen et al. (1997) gathered data from 25 foster youth for a needs assessment and found that for the most part they were satisfied with their ILS program. This sentiment was also reported in other studies (Cook, 1994; Cook, Fleishman, & Grimes, 1991; Mares, 2010). McMillen et al. (1997) found that curriculum on money management (budgeting, consumer skills, and credit information) was seen as most helpful by participants. Stipends and subsidies received high marks and were a necessity for many youth to participate.

One theme noted in the literature was the importance of staff relationships with the participants. Waldinger and Furman (1994) and Iglehart and Becerra (2002) found that in addition to acquiring independent living skills, what youth most appreciated in their training was the relationship with their ILS workers. These workers were viewed as sources of emotional support, knowledge, and encouragement. Independent living skills specialists were also highly appreciated by youth, and were held in higher regard than the youths' regular social workers as a resource for independent living preparation. Geenen and Powers (2007) report that youth were most satisfied with their ILS program when they had a case manager delegated to them who could individualize their programs. In a number of studies, foster parents were viewed by foster youth as the main source of teaching independent living skills (Courtney et al., 2001; Lemon, Hines, & Merdinger, 2005; Geenen & Powers, 2007). Undoubtedly, this learning from foster parents comes from "hands-on" experience in the home rather than classroom training.

Similar to McMillen et al.'s (1997) findings, many researchers report that social workers received poor marks from EFY regarding how helpful they were in assisting youth to acquire independent living skills. Freundlich and Avery (2006) assert that EFY fault social workers for not involving them in case planning, which causes some youth to disengage from planning for independent living. Caseload size may be the most significant barrier to social workers taking a larger role in ILS (McMillen et al., 1997; Rice & McFadden, 1988). Youth may also favor consultation with independent living workers rather than social workers because they have less authority over them, which youth think may give them more latitude in decision making. McMillen et al. (1997) also speculate that social workers might not have developed the relationship skills needed to interact with adolescents as most of their child welfare clients were younger. Brown and Wilderson (2010) postulate that one group that is particularly hard to reach in ILS programs consist of youth who had frequent placement changes and/or worker changes, which impeded the ability to develop ties to caring adults.

The initial intent of ILS programs was to prepare youth for emancipation, but such programs have evolved toward also providing services for youth after discharge as well. Some programs also provide educational assistance (college tuition and textbook assistance), vocational support, a saving plan that youth can use to build up a cash reserve for emergencies, transitional housing, and mentoring. Although these types of services were not initially widespread, they are becoming more common (McMillen et al., 1997; Montgomery, Donkoh, & Underhill, 2006).

The Research Evidence on Effectiveness of ILS

The GAO (1999) report released almost two decades ago indicated that little research evidence was available to gauge the effectiveness of ILS programs. Since then only five randomized trials, the most rigorous type of research design needed to establish a cause and effect relationship between program participation and outcomes, have been published. Four of these trials were part of the Multi-Site Evaluation of Foster Youth Programs (MEFYP), funded by the federal DHHS as a component of the FCIA. MEFYP examined four specific program models at different sites throughout the country. At

Table 4.1   **Independent Living Skills and Categories**

Category	Skill
Personal Development	Communication, decision making, problem solving, planning, anger management, provision of personal and emotional support, family support, time management, recreational activities
Social Development	Building supportive relationships, learning about community resources, mentoring, marriage, parenting preparation
Daily Living	Housekeeping, nutrition, food purchasing and preparation, laundry, finding housing, financial management
Employment	Career exploration, interviewing for jobs, résumé construction, job finding, job maintenance
Health	Preventative care, accessing health care, substance abuse prevention including avoiding smoking, pregnancy prevention, sexual health and decision making
Education	Completing high school, college application procedures, preparing for college
Other	Legal assistance, help with obtaining documents such as driver's licenses, social security numbers, birth certificates, etc.

Sources: Burt, 2002; Cook, 1994; Maluccio, Kreiger, & Pine, 1990; Mech, 2002; U.S. Government Accountability Office, 1999.

best, the results from this examination are mixed as to whether ILS programs are effective (U.S. Department of Health and Human Services, 2008a, 2008b). The other study that used random assignment tested a self-determination intervention that was part of an ILS program (Powers et al., 2012). Most of the remaining studies listed in Table 4.1 are methodically weak and generally paint a much more positive picture of independent living preparation than the MEFYP. However, observers have noted that because of these methodological weaknesses we really do not know much about the efficacy and workings of these programs.

The weaknesses identified in the research design of these studies include small nonprobability samples, retrospective data collection, lack of comparison groups, and the use of nonstandardized measures, and in some studies significance statistics for findings are not reported. Five of the studies listed in Table 4.1 are the previously mentioned evaluations that used random assignment. One additional study is not an outcome effort, but rather is a description of the recipients of ILS. Two systematic research reviews and one needs assessment are also included in the table. Of the 16 remaining evaluations/studies, 8 utilized small samples (less than 100 participants), 2 evaluations used large samples (n=1,000 at baselines or larger), and 1 study is a secondary analysis of the large Midwestern longitudinal study (n=732) (Katz & Courtney, 2015). Five studies had medium-sized samples (somewhere in between 101 and 445 participants). The use of small samples of convenience gathered from a single site limits statistical power, which can result in positive aspects about ILS programs being overlooked, and the nonprobability sampling methods limit the ability to generalize to larger populations. One exception to sampling concerns is the study completed by Cook et al. (1991) (n=1,644 at baseline). This evaluation is an important early effort funded by the federal government to assess the effectiveness of ILS programs. Another strength of this study is its representativeness. Its weakness is that it was only able to locate about 50 percent of the youth selected for the study for a follow-up interview. It is possible that the nonenrolled youth fared worse than the study participants. Six of the studies utilized comparisons of ILS participants with foster youth who did not participate in ILS activities. One problem noted with some of these comparison studies was that in some instances baseline differences between comparison and treatment groups undermined external validity, or there were no attempts to determine whether comparison group youth might have received independent living training somewhere else. Other questions are raised about the reliance on self-report measures because those responses might not always reflect reality. The time period after discharge covered in most studies was relatively brief. Therefore, we do not know whether the reported outcomes will change over the long term.

Differences between programs in areas such as treatment fidelity efforts, staff adherence to protocols, program length and intensity, curriculum and components, program quality, and efforts to enroll students (how aggressive) were additional weaknesses noted in critiques of the ILS evaluation methodologies (Dane & Schneider, 1998). Therefore, claims about program effectiveness should be viewed with caution.

Outcomes of ILS

Education

One of the studies using experimental design provided the strongest evidence for ILS programs making a positive contribution to emancipation outcomes (Courtney et al., 2011b). This study found that treatment-group youth who had received aggressive outreach and intensive case management were more likely than the controls to remain in foster care past age 18, attend college, and persist in college enrollment. The treatment group was also more likely than the controls to receive educational and employment assistance, money management training, and financial support to find and maintain housing. However, differences between study groups were not found on outcomes relating to employment, economic well-being, housing, delinquency, pregnancy, or readiness for independent living. Researchers cautioned that this sample was made up of youth receiving intensive services from treatment foster care, so the results may not be generalizable to all foster children.

Most of the other studies reported that taking part in an ILS program improved educational outcomes. The studies that showed no relationship between ILS participation and EFY educational efforts were two of the studies that utilized classical experimental design (U.S. Department of Health and Human Services, 2008a, 2008b). Lindsey and Ahmed (1999) found that ILS program participants were more likely to finish high school, attend college, or complete a vocational program. Scannapieco, Schagrin, and Scannapieco (1995) observed statistically significant higher high school graduation rates among ILS program participants when compared with nonparticipants. A later study conducted by Scannapieco, Smith, and Blakeney-Strong (2016) found that youth in Texas who had independent living skills training were more likely to be attending high school, college, or a GED program than were youth without that training. Crucial to success in preparing students to continue their schooling was spending time on planning and goal-setting activities. Harding and Luft (1995) ILS participants were more likely than nonparticipants to have finished a Job Corps training program. None of the studies reported negative outcomes with ILS participation and educational outcomes. However, in the absence of random assignment, we cannot attribute educational success to ILS. It may be that more motivated foster youth and EFY self-select themselves into these programs, and would have succeeded without participating in ILS.

Employment and Finances

Studies by Scannapieco et al. (1995) and Georgiades (2005) reported that significantly more treatment-group youth (ILS participants) were employed at the closure of their case than comparison group youth (youth who did not participate in ILS). Scannapieco et al. (2016) found that working with youth to develop money management skills, helping them navigate transportation problems, and providing mentoring were all associated with finding and maintaining employment. The other studies reported no effects, or insignificant differences when noted. The MEFYP, which used classical experimental design, also showed no effect between program participation and employment (Courtney et al., 2011b). The researchers in that study suggest that the lack of outreach to EFY was the reason that no effect was shown in any domain measured including employment. Barnow et al. (2015) examined

1,058 youth participating in the Casey Family Transition program for two years. The overall findings on employment and housing were described as not "overwhelmingly positive" (p. 166). However, they did report that the longer a youth received services, the more positive the employment and education outcomes. The effect of program duration was strongest when combined with the receipt of job preparation and income support services.

The most frequent request for more training by EFY was in the area of budgeting and financial management (McMillen et al., 1997; Mares, 2010). Youth in the Midwest sample reported that financial aid information was the need most often not met (Katz & Courtney, 2015). Foster youth in two studies were said to be better able to manage their finances after ILS participation (McMillen et al., 1997; Lindsey & Ahmed, 1999). Kerman et al. (2004), while not specifically referring to ILS, found that youth who remained in extended foster care and received services for two years were more likely to be self-sufficient than youth who left care at age 18. The early evaluation conducted by the GAO (Cook, 1994; Cook et al., 1991) found that those youth who received money management skills training were more likely to maintain a job for at least a year and not collect public benefits.

Housing

Most studies that examined housing reported positive outcomes with ILP participation. Several studies have observed that independent living program participants were more likely to be living independently after services (Austin & Johnson, 1995; Lindsey & Ahmed, 1999; Scannapieco et al., 1995). Harding and Luft (1995) reported that ILS participants had more housing stability than the comparison group who moved more often than the ILS treatment group. However, none of these studies claim that ILS prevented homelessness. Courtney et al. (2011b) found that the treatment group in their study was more successful than the controls in obtaining financial support for housing. In contrast, Lemon et al. (2005) did not find a difference between ILS and non-ILS participants on any housing outcomes in their study. Dworsky and Courtney (2009a) in a correlational study found that ILS participation was not associated with housing security. The Midwest Study sample also reported that after financial management, housing was the need most overlooked by independent living programs (Katz & Courtney, 2015).

Other Outcomes

The Midwest study supplies evidence that the provision of ILS services at ages 17 or 18 reduces the expression of unmet needs after discharge (Katz & Courtney, 2015). However, we cannot attribute this finding to ILS preparation. Perhaps, youth with fewer needs self-select into ILS programs, or after discharge their needs were being met by means other than ILS.

Many programs have focused on the teaching of specific skills. For example, one of the skills of money management is the ability to balance a checkbook. Three studies that used comparison groups reported that youth who participated in an ILS program demonstrated more knowledge of independent living skills than youth who did not have independent living skills training (Lemon et al., 2005; Mallon, 1998; McMillen et al., 1997). In addition, Lemon et al. (2005) reported that ILS participants felt better prepared for independent living and were more hopeful about the future than their nonparticipant comparisons. The GAO (1999) and McMillen et al. (1997) reported that when asked, youth generally express satisfaction with their ILS program. Freundlich, Avery, and Padgett (2007) provided data from a New York study of youth who took part in an ILS program. These youth were far more skeptical about their preparation than the previously mentioned studies. The more rigorous MEFYP study in Los Angeles found no differences between treatment and control groups on the acquisition of life skills or any other outcomes (educational attainment, employment, earnings, and avoidance of economic hardship) needed for independent living. The researchers thought the small sample size hampered the statistical significance of their findings. The MEFYP researchers thought their results called into question the effectiveness of classroom training and suggested that alternatives to didactic instruction are needed (U.S. Department of Health and Human Services, 2008a). One of the randomized studies that utilized a self-determination intervention found treatment-group youth reported having a higher quality of life, used more transition services, and took part in more independent living activities than the control group (Powers et al., 2012). These researchers also claim education and employment gains by the treatment group, but they do not report supporting statistics for that claim. Statistical significance was probably omitted because their sample size was too small to find significant difference. This deficit suggests the need for more robust sample sizes in future studies.

Secondary gains beyond the program outcomes have been claimed for ILS program participation. McMillen et al. (1997) reported that youth in their sample said that participation in an ILS program seemed to reduce the feelings of isolation and stigmatization that FFY often experience. A number of studies indicate that ILS participants were more likely to leave care with critical documents such as driver's licenses and birth certificates that all youth should have in their possession when they leave care (Cook, 1991; Courtney et al., 2005; Courtney, Dworsky, Cusick, et al., 2009; Georgiades, 2005; Havalchak, White, & O'Brien, 2008). These items will be necessary as they move further into adulthood.

Factors Predicting Success or Problems in ILS

Mares and Kroner (2011), in a study aimed at identifying factors that predicted risk or success in an ILS program, found that older youth and youth with longer stays in the program had much better outcomes than younger youth and those with short periods of ILS participation. Youth with mental health problems were half as likely as those without such problems to attain favorable outcomes on high school completion, employment, and housing. As in most programs, youth spent much time in the classroom learning independent living skills. The amount of time spent in classroom instruction was not associated with any of the previously mentioned three outcomes. Like the MEFYP evaluations, they suggest that the classroom teaching of life skills was ineffective with this group. Maybe these youth would better respond to home-based skill teaching, and on-the-job learning.

A study of 534 adolescents who were approaching emancipation found placement type to be a good indicator of how well a youth did on a survey of life skills knowledge. Youth in scattered site apartment placements did best on this test followed by youth in foster placements. Group home residents did the poorest in terms of knowledge of life skills. Youth in the first two types of placements may have more opportunity for hands-on experience to learn life skills (Mech, Ludy-Dobson, & Hulsemans, 1994). Because of institutional rules and state regulations, group homes may restrict youths' opportunities to learn skills. For example, state labor laws may not permit residents to cook meals in congregate settings, and thus students lose an opportunity for learning kitchen skills. However, in the Midwest sample, group home youth were more likely to receive ILS than youth in other types of placement. This difference showed up mostly in employment training, perhaps because of contractual agreements to provide those services to youth in congregate care (Katz & Courtney, 2015). The deficiencies noted in the acquisition of ILS knowledge may be related to both the placement context and the means of teaching skills. "Hands-on" instruction is favored over classroom teaching. Scannapieco et al. (2016) found that as the amount of time given to classroom instruction increased, youth involvement in educational programs decreased. What did increase involvement in ILS was giving time to future-oriented activities such as educational and career planning.

Kroner and Mares (2011) provide evidence on the importance of extending foster care. Barnow and colleagues (2015) reported that giving job preparation services over an extended period led to better outcomes in a number of areas including employment. Mares and Kroner (2011) found that being older when receiving services and having had longer lengths of time in an independent living program were both associated with better independent living outcomes. Extended periods of participation enable youth to develop relationships with program staff, who later can become role models, mentors, and sources of support. A number of the studies reviewed in this chapter emphasized the importance of relationships with staff in youth's assessment of their ILS experience.

Routes to ILS

Brown and Wilderson (2010) suggest two routes by which EFY enter ILS programs. The first is a referral for service as part of the planned process of exiting care. Another pathway is for youth to encounter a crisis after leaving care, such as homelessness, that causes them to seek services, or perhaps an outreach effort on the part of a program reaches them while they are in crisis. Because of the many crises that discharge brings, youth may be more receptive to ILS training after leaving care. Crisis theory would suggest that youth are open to services at that point. The danger of entering services after a crisis is that youth enter with more cumulative risks than those who entered through a referral prior to leaving care. Thus, giving services before discharge is an important prevention strategy.

One particular problem with beginning programs in early adolescence is that the learning may be forgotten after emancipation. Youth also may not be listening given other issues in their adolescent lives. Some of the information, especially hard skills, are difficult to teach in a manner that engages students. McMillen et al. (1997) hypothesized that the enthusiasm of EFY for financial skills training came after encounters with the reality of life after foster care, so EFY were willing to receive and absorb the lessons about money management. Iglehart and Becerra (2002) suggest a need for refresher courses postemancipation to help cope with the challenges of independent living.

Practical Suggestions for Improving Independent Living Programs

Empirical Evidence about What Works Is Needed

ILS providers appear not to have received the memo about the importance of evidence-based practice. The methodologies used in most evaluations were weak. Therefore, the positive assertions about ILS programs must be viewed with caution. The MEFYP was a limited examination of four programs across the country whose purpose was to give a picture of existing programs, not to provide demonstrations of innovative, effective programs. As noted earlier, the best that can be said about the programs evaluated is that the results were mixed. Demonstrations are needed that would allow innovative programs to establish their efficacy. This research should be disseminated to relevant audiences. We also need to know how programs can engage these youth in services both prior to and after emancipation.

The Lessons of Successful Programs

The lessons from the one study that demonstrated a cause and effect relationship between ILS participation and a Chafee outcome (education), suggest that ILS programs should operate on the principle of self-determination. Furthermore, they should feature aggressive outreach, intensive casework, individualized transition case plans, a relationship-based approach, and assistance for youth in connecting with and navigating the various bureaucracies that are needed for a successful transition (Courtney, Dworsky, & Peters, 2009; Courtney et al., 2011a, 2011b).

The most successful ILS programs address multiple needs that youth have: housing, daily living skills, education, employment, social support, and preventative services (to avoid drug use, early parenthood, and criminal justice involvement) (Burt, 2002; Osterling-Lemon & Hines, 2006; Rashid, 2004). These services should not mimic EFY former bureaucratic service contacts, but should as much as possible replicate what a parent should do for their child (Packard, Delgado, Fellmeth, & McReady, 2008). Services should be provided on a continuum from a period of preparation before leaving care, during the actual transition, and a period of after-care services (Iglehart & Becerra, 2002).

Finding Better Ways to Teach Independent Living Skills

Courtney, commenting on the lack of success of the Los Angeles-based portion of the MEFYP, suggested that classroom-based instruction might not work for some ILS content, and other means of engaging youth are needed (U.S. Department of Health and Human Services, 2008a). Finding alternatives to classroom instruction has been a frequent request by youth in qualitative studies. Youth reported receiving the bulk of independent living training from sources outside of the classroom; including learning from the biological family, foster parents, teachers, schools, and social workers (U.S. Department of Health and Human Services, 2008a, 2008b). Training should give youth an opportunity to practice skills in the real world (Mares, 2010; Scannapieco, Connell-Carrick, & Painter, 2007; U.S. Department of Health and Human Services, 2008b).

A number of studies have revealed the importance of foster parents in the teaching of independent living skills. Geenen and Powers (2007) and Mares (2010) reported that youth said home-based daily living skills training provided by their foster parent was a more naturalistic way of teaching these skills. Foster parents can model skills and provide explanations of them as the teaching occurs. The importance of foster parents should be recognized, and to solidify their role they should be trained and integrated into the youth's independent living program. Independent living specialists should coordinate the delivery of ILS with group home personnel, as some evidence suggests that group homes are deficient in teaching independent living skills.

Iglehart and Becerra (2002) suggest recruiting FFY with successful emancipation experiences to teach, act as role models, and be peer counselors in independent living programs. They assert that EFY would be seen by youth still in care as presenting a more realistic picture of foster care. They report instances of FFY receiving pay to act as teachers in ILS programs, but no evaluation of their effectiveness is available.

Keeping Youth Connected to Sources of Social Support

A different dialogue should permeate ILS and transitional services. Self-sufficiency is one aspect of that dialogue. However, students must also understand interdependence and connectedness, and get the message that reliance on others, rather than being a sign of failure during the transition to adulthood, should be viewed as a strength in gathering resources to meet the challenges of emerging adulthood (Propp, Ortega, & NewHeart, 2003). An additional need identified by Scannapieco et al. (2007), which fits the interdependence concept, is connecting youth with at least one support person or network prior to leaving care. Social connectedness is discussed in Chapter 13.

The *Take Charge* intervention described by Powers et al. (2012) emphasized mentoring and coaching to provide the skills for achieving self-identified goals. The effectiveness of this promising approach was demonstrated in a clinical trial by Powers and colleagues (2012) and seemed to have youth more engaged in the ILS program.

Group work experiences with similar youth would also enable youth to break out of their isolation as they interact with people who have had experiences similar to their own. Youth in a Missouri study said ILS programs were places where they could connect and form relationships with other EFY (McMillen et al., 1997). Nixon and Jones (2000) suggest a variation of peers as teachers in the formation of self-help groups for former foster youth. These groups would help with skill building but would also enable youth to share solutions to real-world problems, which can be empowering for participants. Rice and McFadden (1988) suggest that "forums" be held at regular intervals for FFY as well as youth about to leave foster care, to help break them out of possible isolation, continue their independent living training, and assist them in establishing sources of social support. Forums could take the form of conferences; regular, ongoing support groups; picnics; and/or dinners for youth with nowhere to go for the holidays. These efforts are also seen as "destigmatizing" because youth meet people in circumstances similar to their own.

Leaving Care with Needed Documents

A Casey program recommendation for youth is that before they leave care they be provided with a "toolbox" of needed personal documents (birth certificate, driver's license, Social Security card, state-issued identification), and referral sources should they encounter difficulties (e.g., housing assistance, health care access, substance abuse treatment, legal assistance, etc.) (Havalchak et al., 2008).

CHAPTER FIVE

Research on Life after Foster Care

This chapter reviews the methodologies used in the research on youth leaving foster care and their adaptation to emerging adulthood. It is necessary to consider the strengths and weaknesses of the research before conclusions can be drawn about the status of former foster youth (FFY) during emerging adulthood. The intent of this chapter is to prepare readers to interpret the data presented in this book. Readers can refer back to this chapter to assess the empirical strength of a study and its findings discussed in upcoming chapters. An additional aim of this chapter is to give the reader a snapshot of the state-of-the-art of research on FFY, and the subset of this group, emancipated foster youth (EFY).

Since the passage of the Independent Living Initiative in 1986, numerous studies have been published about how well FFY are faring during the transition from adolescence to emerging adulthood. These studies are reviewed in this book, and are summarized in Appendix B. These studies provide a picture of foster care after federal involvement in 1986, and thus this book can be seen as an evaluation of sorts of the efforts to improve the conditions of youth aging out of care.

A Critique of the Studies

These studies, if taken in total, have multiple limitations. Most of the studies are descriptive with little attention given to identifying variables that might contribute to better outcomes (Daining & DePanfilis, 2007). The most salient weaknesses of these studies are that they often have small, purposive, unrepresentative samples collected at a single site, with one data collection point in time, and in many instances the studies do not have comparison groups. Even when samples are large, they may be confined to a single state or geographic region. Because of differences in policies, the degree of support provided to EFY, differing eligibility criteria for services, and the number of and type of services provided by the state, it is often difficult to compare findings. Sometimes these service delivery differences are found between counties within states. Nevertheless, we can make inferences about specific policies by comparing outcomes among the states. For example, the effects of extending foster care can be estimated by comparing states that have done so with states that have not.

Research methodology issues, such as differing ways of operationalizing variables (including measures used), can make it difficult to compare outcomes across studies. Many of the studies relied on self-reports from youth, or others in their social networks such as social workers or caretakers, for data. In addition, reports are often retrospective. Therefore, we cannot be certain that the information provided is accurate. In addition, complicating the comparisons of findings is that studies collect data from youth of different age ranges. Studies in which the mean age of the sample is older are more likely to show more FFY with a high school diploma or GED than are the studies that used younger youth as informants.

In addition, most of the studies are cross-sectional, which limits the ability to establish cause and effect between variables. The longitudinal studies, while a vast improvement over the cross-sectional efforts, also have some difficulties. Economic conditions and social policies shaping programs and services for youth change over time, which can affect outcomes. In addition, this population is very mobile and difficult to locate for follow-up interviews. The frequent moves may not only be an indicator of housing instability but also make retaining youth in studies challenging. It is possible that those youth who elect to continue receiving services from agencies are more stable than youth who choose not to receive services, and are thus easier to find for continued data collection.

All of these limitations call the validity and generalizability of the findings of many of the studies into question. Nevertheless, despite significant limitations in the research, a review of the cumulative research on outcomes for transitioning youth provides us with an opportunity to identify their needs, and gives us some idea of the effectiveness of federal and state policies meant to improve outcomes for discharged foster youth.

Noteworthy Studies

This section describes some of the more important and methodologically strongest studies that constitute the knowledge base regarding the transition from foster care to adulthood. Other studies not included in this section are described in subsequent chapters if they are important in the specific domain discussed in that chapter.

Midwest Evaluation of the Adult Functioning of Former Foster Children (Midwest Study)

Probably the most important study to date in establishing what we know about youth discharged from foster care is the *Midwest Evaluation of the Adult Functioning of Former Foster Children*. This study is often called the *Midwest Study*, as it will be referred to in this book. This study, led by Mark Courtney, was the first large-scale investigation of what happens to youth after they leave care. The Midwest Study spawned a series of published secondary analyses of the data (seventeen by my count). This study began collecting data after the federal Title IV-E Independent Living Program was fully implemented, and so it has been described as an evaluation of those efforts (Courtney & Barth, 1996; Courtney, Piliavin, Grogan-Kaylor, & Nesmith, 2001; McDonald, Allen, Westerfelt, & Piliavin, 1993). The Midwest Study was a longitudinal panel study that began in 2002 and interviewed 732 out of the eligible 758 foster youth from Illinois (n=474), Wisconsin (n=195), and Iowa (n=63). The initial response rate was an impressive 97 percent. The three states in the study contained a rural, urban, and suburban mix and thus are broadly representative of the United States.

All transitioning youth in Iowa and Wisconsin, and a random sample of two-thirds of the foster youth in the much larger state of Illinois, made up the study participants. Interviews began at age 17 or 18 while youth were still in foster care. Youth were then interviewed four times at approximately two-year intervals until age 25 or 26 (Courtney, 2009). Data were collected about a variety of different domains that were defined by Congress in the Foster Care Independence Act of 1999 (FCIA) as information needed for accountability. These domains included: education, employment, finances, physical and mental health, social support, family relationships, criminal justice involvement, delinquency, victimization, sexual behavior, parenting, public assistance receipt, substance use and abuse, and independent living training experiences. Each interview sought to update the experiences from the previous interview (Courtney & Dworsky, 2006). Of the original sample, 596 youth were interviewed at age 26 (81 percent retention rate). Females and residents of Iowa and Wisconsin were more likely than males or participants from Illinois to be retained in the study.

A unique feature of the study was that Illinois chose to extend foster care until age 19, but the other two states continued to discharge foster youth at age 18. Therefore, the Midwest Study provided an opportunity to examine the effect of remaining in or leaving care. The Midwest Study also utilized the nationally representative National Longitudinal Study of Adolescent to Adult Health as a comparison group with the EFY in its sample. This research is also described in this chapter.

One limitation of the study was that EFY in psychiatric hospitals, in prisons or jails, who had physical or mental disabilities, or who had run away from placement were not included in the sample (Keller, Cusick, & Courtney, 2007). Many subsequent studies used the same or similar exclusion criteria as used in the Midwest Studies. These criteria excluded youth who may be the most disconnected from society and the child welfare system, and who have the most difficulties with transitioning from care to adulthood. We are lacking information on their post–foster care experience.

National Longitudinal Study of Adolescent to Adult Health (ADD Health)

ADD Health, as the National Longitudinal Study of Adolescent to Adult Health is usually called, is a longitudinal study of a nationally representative sample of youth in grades 7 through 12 begun during the years 1994 to 1995, and is the largest and most comprehensive survey of adolescent health completed to date. However, it should be noted with both this study and most of the other secondary data analyses of nationally representative samples that exist in the literature, that they are not representative of the foster care population. ADD Health was also not designed as a child welfare study, but it has an adequate subset of former foster youth for analysis. What it does not have is the precision of child welfare-designed studies in describing the circumstances of foster care. For example, it is not possible to distinguish between FFY and EFY. This study was used as a comparison sample in the Midwest Study and other studies. It has also been used on its own to investigate the experience of FFY. Singer and Berzin (2015) used this data set to compare the pace at which FFY and youth in the general population emerge into adulthood. The database was also used by Greeson, Usher, and Grinstien-Weiss (2010) to examine mentors, social support, and asset accumulation among FFY.

Multistage stratified sampling procedures were used to identify the ADD Health participants. First, the researchers constructed the sample frame using every high school and middle school in the United States. The researchers then used region of the country, location (whether the school was rural, suburban, or urban), whether the school was public or private, racial composition of the school, and school size to select a representative sample of 80 high schools and 52 middle schools for the first wave of data collection. The initial data collection efforts at these schools began with the administration of an in-school questionnaire. Youth who completed the questionnaire were then selected for in-home interviews. The ADD Health sample was interviewed four times in their homes when they were between the ages of 18 and 26 about their health and other factors that might affect their health status. The initial in-home interview had a 78.9 percent participation rate (n=20,745; mean age of 15.75). The Wave II interviews included 88.2 percent of the individuals who had completed the initial interview. Wave III had 77.4 percent of eligible participants take part, and the final wave at age 26 had a sample of 15,197 (77 percent retention rate). A large number of youth (n=10,828) participated in all four waves (Chantala & Tabor, 2010; Harris, et al., 2009).

Casey National Foster Care Alumni Study (Casey National Study)

The Casey Family Program is a privately endowed, not-for-profit, high-quality, long-term family foster care agency. Casey is based in Seattle, Washington, but has field offices throughout the United States in 23 communities in 13 states. Casey takes seriously the imperative to evaluate its services, and has developed a number of important outcome studies on FFY. These studies have particular relevance for transitioning youth because children who receive services from Casey are not likely to be reunified or adopted but will stay in foster care until emancipation. A stable family life is provided for these youth through a long-term foster family. Casey targets 10- to 17-year-olds for services. Because youth are expected to stay in foster care until emancipation, the length of stay in care at Casey is longer than most agencies. Casey also seeks to help the youth maintain or develop healthy relationships with the family of origin. Preparation for independent living is an underlying theme of the program. Casey financially supports youth participation in a variety of enrichment activities that youth in public care often do not have the opportunity to experience. These activities include such things as art, sports, and hobbies. Youth are encouraged to cultivate developmentally appropriate social skills through participation in community activities, such as church, scouting, and summer camps (Harris, Jackson, O'Brien, & Pecora, 2009). Youth are also encouraged to work part-time or volunteer as a preparation experience for leaving care.

Casey has developed a measure, the Ansel-Casey Life Skills Assessment, which allows staff to evaluate youth progress on specific skill development. Youth also engage in "capacity enhancing advocacy" by learning specific skills such as negotiating various bureaucracies and finding housing (Kerman, Wildfire, & Barth, 2002, p. 326). Support continues for youth after emancipation through case management. Casey also provides scholarship support for youth pursuing further education (college, vocational, professional certifications, and graduate school) (Harris, Jackson, et al., 2009).

The high quality of services is made possible by the small caseloads social workers have (16 youth for one social worker). This small caseload enables workers to devote considerable time and energy to each youth in their caseload. The turnover rate at Casey for social workers and foster parents is low. Social worker turnover rate was reported at 8.2 percent during the period data were collected. In comparison, a study by the American Public Human Services Association found that 43 states reported an average annual worker turnover rate of 22 percent and a job vacancy rate of 7 percent (Cyphers, 2001). Low turnover is an indicator of both high worker job satisfaction and that an agency has the human capital to deliver high-quality services. Social workers with experience are essential to ensuring that abused and neglected children and their families are getting the support they need.

Data for the alumni study were collected from the abstraction of case records and interviews. Information was gathered about their foster care and subsequent life experiences, educational and employment attainments, and social functioning. The sample drawn from Casey Family Programs across the United States consisted of 1,087 alumni who had received services for at least one year. The proportion of the alumni interviewed was 73.6 percent. Respondents ranged from ages 20 to 51. Youth not interviewed included those who were incarcerated (3.4 percent), in psychiatric facilities (0.7), or deceased (3.9 percent). Youth were matched on age, gender, and ethnicity with 3,547 young adults drawn from the National Comorbidity Study, a nationally representative study that collected data between 1995 and 1998 (Merikangas et al., 2010; Pecora, White, Jackson, & Wiggins, 2009).

One feature of the Casey studies that is both a strength and a weakness of the research is many studies collect data at a single agency, which limits the generalizability of findings. However, they give us an idea of what high-quality foster care can do for improving outcomes. Casey has had particular success with educating foster youth, which will be discussed in the next chapter.

Casey Young Adult Survey (CYAS)

The CYAS was a cohort study that collected outcome data from 19-, 22-, and 25-year-olds who had received foster care services for at least one year from Casey Family Programs. To be included in the sample youth had to be mentally competent to complete a phone interview. Data were collected through an approximately one-hour telephone interview from 557 young adults who received services from field offices in 12 states. Interviews were conducted on an annual basis during the years 2004 to 2006 by professional interviewers from the University of Pittsburg. The overall response rate was 48.2 percent. Only 2.5 percent of youth approached for an interview refused to participate. The low participation rate is an indicator of the problems of completing research studies with this mobile population since most of the youth not included were not locatable for interviews. More women (65 percent) and whites (51.2 percent) participated than males or minorities, and thus data were weighted on these demographic variables to adjust for response bias (Havalchak, White, & O'Brien, 2008).

Northwest Foster Care Alumni Study

The Northwest Foster Care Alumni Study (NFCAS) was a collaborative effort between the University of Washington, Harvard Medical School, the University of Michigan Survey Research Center, Casey Family Programs, and the state public child welfare agencies in Oregon and Washington. The NFCAS is distinguished from the earlier Casey alumni study in that only Casey agencies in Washington and Oregon participated. The primary purpose of the study was to evaluate the intermediate effects of family foster care on adult outcomes, with an emphasis on mental health functioning. The study assessed the lifetime and 12-month prevalence of mental health problems (Pecora, Kessler, et al., 2006).

Data were collected from 659 youth who had been in foster care for at least one year at some point between 1988 and 1998. Case records of all 659 FFY were abstracted for relevant data, and 479 of these youth were interviewed as adults by professional interviewers from the University of Michigan. The Casey NAS sample was between the ages of 20 and 33 at the time of the interview. The difference between the number of record reviews and interviews was that many of the alumni could not be located (n=154) for an interview. An additional 26 youth were not "eligible" to participate because they were deceased, or because they were incarcerated or in a psychiatric facility. The participation rate was 76 percent (Pecora, Kessler, et al., 2006). The record reviews were used to describe their foster care experience, and the interviews gathered information about educational attainments, employment, finances, mental health, independent living services usage, and social support after leaving foster care.

The Missouri NIMH Study

This study funded by the National Institute of Mental Health recruited youth between May 2001 and December 2003 from eight counties in Missouri surrounding the city of St. Louis. The research was completed with the assistance of the Missouri Division of Family Services. Youth were interviewed at ages 17, 18, and 19. The youths' caseworkers screened the youth for participation. Youth with an IQ below 70, who had moved more than 100 miles from the study location, or who were runaways were excluded from the study. Thus, 515 youth were initially eligible. The final sample comprised 404 youth.

At age 19, 325 of these youth (80 percent) were interviewed. Youth were not interviewed for a variety of reasons, including: unable to locate (n=63), refused interview (n=7), incarceration (n=7), overseas military service (n=2), and deceased (n=1). In addition, the researchers completed a logistic regression to predict retention. Being male, having a history of juvenile detention, having a post-traumatic stress disorder diagnosis, and leaving care at age 18 were all associated with sample attrition. Data were collected about demographics, maltreatment history, experiences in foster care, service utilization, substance use and abuse, legal involvement, mental health diagnosis, and living arrangements.

A unique feature and strength of this study was that data were gathered from youth several times at four-month intervals during the period of 2001–2003. Youth were interviewed by trained professionals at a time and place of the youth's choosing. Phone interviews were used in the latter interviews if in-person interviews were not possible (McCoy, McMillen, & Spitznagel, 2008; McMillen & Raghavan, 2009). The researchers assert that the Missouri child welfare system is comparable to the rest of America (Vaughan, Shook, & McMillen, 2008). Like both the Midwest study and the Casey efforts, this study has spawned a number of secondary analyses.

National Youth in Transition Database (NYTD)

The Foster Care Independence Act required the Administration for Children and Families (ACF) in the U.S. Department of Health and Human Services to develop a database for which all states, the District of Columbia, and Puerto Rico would be required to deposit data on defined outcomes to determine the effectiveness of independent living programs. Outcome data included employment (status and skills), education, and support from adults, homelessness, substance abuse, incarceration, pregnancy, and ILS receipt.

Two methods were used to gather data. The first method was to track the delivery of services in 14 independent living skills areas that are collected as part of the administration of programs. Second, outcome data were collected directly from youth. States had a choice of collecting data from youth in person, by phone, or by computer. Youth participation in the study was voluntary (Shpiegel & Cascardi, 2015). These data collection efforts allow us to determine how foster youth compare in the transition to adulthood with other young people in the general population, as well as help us gain a better understanding of the challenges that EFY encounter when they leave care.

The states began collecting data in October 2010, and the ACF initially reported data for 2011. In 2014, the ACF began reporting data. Fifty-three percent of eligible youth provided data. Problems have been identified with the data collection. Variations were noted among the states in youth participation rates at age 17 (12 percent to 100 percent). Interviews with eligible 19-year-olds in 2013 showed a respectable 69 percent participation rate (n=7,845). However, variations were still evident in the state's participation rates (26 percent to 95 percent), with one state not reporting outcome data

(National Youth in Transition Database, 2014a, 2014b). A large number of nonresponses also raises questions about the representativeness of the sample, about how responders might differ from nonresponders. Furthermore, the study also collects data at only three data collection points ending at age 21. Extending data collection until later ages would allow us to gain a greater understanding of what happens to EFY during emerging adulthood.

Some of the problems in completing research with this population are evident in the reasons given for the relatively low level of participation. Eighteen percent of youth could not be located, 12 percent refused permission to be interviewed, 5 percent had run away from placement, 2 percent were described as incapacitated, and 2 percent were incarcerated. No demographic differences were noted between participants and nonparticipants (National Youth in Transition Database, 2014a, 2014b).

This database may in the future provide a means of evaluating whether the Fostering Connections to Success Act (FCSA) has improved outcomes for foster youth. Suggestions for improvement include requiring the states to improve response rates, which may mean eliminating the online option for responses. In addition, adapting a panel approach to data collection may help us determine the temporal relationships between the various types of problems youth encounter (Shpiegel & Cascardi, 2015).

California Youth Transitions to Adulthood Study (CalYOUTH)

The CalYOUTH study is being conducted by Mark Courtney, the principal investigator of the Midwest Study. This investigation is a collaboration of Chapin Hall Center for Children at the University of Chicago, the California Department of Social Services, and the California County Welfare Directors Association. The California welfare directors have the public child welfare agencies under their purview, as the California child welfare system is run by the counties rather than the state. CalYOUTH is an evaluation of the effect of the California FCSA on the transition to adulthood by California's EFY. This investigation is important because California has the nation's largest foster care population, and was an early adopter of the extension of foster care. Youth in California can remain in care until age 24.

This study is being carried out over a five-year period (2012–2017). Youth are to be interviewed in person at ages 17, 19, and 21. The quantitative interview instrument uses many questions drawn from the ADD Health study, which will aid in future comparisons of EFY and the general population on outcomes (Courtney, Charles, Okpych, Napolitano, & Halsted, 2014). Some of these youth will remain in extended care, which will provide an opportunity for comparisons with youth who left care.

So far, data have been reported on the interviews with 17- and 19-year-olds. Seven-hundred-twenty-seven youth completed the first interview, which represented 95 percent of eligible youth. Six-hundred-eleven youth took part in the second interview (84 percent of eligible youth). The sample was stratified in order to reflect the county-administered system, and to ensure that small counties were represented. Therefore, the sample is representative of California's foster children. In addition, an online survey of 232 child welfare workers was completed to get their perceptions of the key characteristics of service delivery in the context of extended foster care. Lastly, qualitative interviews were completed with EFY and staff in a variety of living arrangements to get their perspectives on extended care and their current living situations (Courtney et al., 2016).

National Longitudinal Survey of Youth 1997

A number of researchers have used large-scale data sets that were representative of the national youth population. These studies were not developed to examine the experiences of foster youth, but because they contain some foster youth, they have been used to investigate what happens to these youth in comparison to nonfoster youth during the transition. For researchers interested in the transition, these data sets provide large representative samples with which the experiences of FFY can be compared against youth in the general population. However, they also have some limitations. Most of these data sets used a single variable to identify foster youth in their sample and do not distinguish between EFY and FFY. Generally, no data are available to describe the youth's maltreatment, placement history, length of time in foster care, or service history.

Berzin (2008, 2010) and Berzin, Rhodes, and Curtis (2011) used the National Longitudinal Survey of Youth, a data set collected by the U.S. Office of Management and Budget, the U.S. Bureau of Labor Statistics, and the U.S. Census Bureau. Youth interviewed in this study were born between the years 1980 and 1984. Youth and a corresponding parent or parent-type person (the biological mother was preferred, but if the mother was not available, 12 other possible parent-type relationships in a descending order of preference) were interviewed 11 times between the years 1997 and 2007. Youth were chosen for participation in a multistage sampling process in which sampling units, defined as regions with 2,000 housing units, were selected to be representative of the U.S. population on key demographic variables. A subset of units was selected and screened for the presence of youth between the ages of 12 and 16. This procedure yielded 9,806 eligible youth, of whom 8,994 were interviewed. African American and Hispanic youth were oversampled to assure the representativeness of the sample (U.S. Bureau of Labor Statistics, 2003). One-hundred-thirty-six FFY were identified who had not been adopted. These youth were then matched using propensity scoring (PS) with nonfoster youth in the sample. The PS is a device for constructing matched sets when there are a large number of covariates of interest on which the researcher wants to match groups. PS uses those covariates to predict the likelihood that a person has the characteristics of someone who might have been in foster care (Rosenbaum & Rubin, 1983). PS relies on a linear combination of the potentially confounding variables that differentiates foster youth from youth never in foster youth. An odds ratio was computed for each youth in this study that reflected the probability or "propensity" of that youth receiving foster care services. A single score was the result of the procedure, which was used to link to foster youth with their nonfoster peers who had similar scores. For Berzin's (2008) research, this yielded a sample of 458 youth matched with the 133 FFY. Only 50 percent of the FFY had been in care after age 17, but 88 percent had been in foster care as a teen. The strategy is considered superior to matching, but less powerful than using random assignment in establishing causal relationships.

Administrative Databases

A number of studies have used administrative databases to examine the experiences of FFY. Some researchers combined databases across states and/or combined data from different service sectors such as child welfare, education, criminal justice, and income maintenance. These studies yield large samples and provide nonfoster comparisons, but researchers must limit their investigation to what is in the database. Therefore, researchers do not learn as much as they would like about how being in foster care might affect adult outcomes. One example of the use of administrative data is Macomber et al.'s (2008) effort, which combined data from TANF and unemployment insurance departments in three states (North Carolina, California, and Minnesota). Findings from this study are reviewed in Chapter 7.

Needell, Cuccaro-Alamin, Brookhart, Jackman, and Shlonsky (2002) combined public sector databases in California (child welfare, prison, health, medical, and community colleges). The resulting database linked records from various state agencies for 11,060 youth exiting foster care during the years 1992–1997. Dworsky (2005) did the same in Wisconsin where she compared both EFY and FFY, who were reunified with their parents, on the receipt of public assistance and unemployment insurance. Goerge et al. (2002) used similar databases in California, Illinois, and South Carolina. They compared EFY with reunified FFY, and low-income with youth on public assistance receipt, income, and labor market participation. Shook et al. (2013) used databases from a variety of public agencies in Alleghany County, Pennsylvania, to construct three groups of a system involved youth to compare on outcomes. These groups were composed of children (1) who received services in their home; (2) who went into placement but left care prior to turning age 17; and (3) who left placement at age 17 or later. They also used the subset of EFY to determine youth patterns of system involvement in mental health, substance abuse, criminal justice, and food and housing agencies (n=1,365) (Shook et al., 2011). The unique features of these studies were the size of the data base, which is one of the largest to date of FFY (n=42,375), and the inclusion of youth who received child welfare services, but who were not in out-of-home care, to determine the effects of child welfare involvement.

Future Research Needs

Classical experimental designs that utilize random assignment are the acknowledged means in the sciences of examining cause and effect relationships. These types of studies would help us understand what interventions work with FFY. They would also help answer the question of how being in foster care affects outcomes in emerging adulthood. Such investigations are not possible under most circumstances in child welfare agencies. In the place of random assignment, matching or comparison group strategies should be used. Matching and its improved counterpart, propensity matching, involve finding youth with similar characteristics as foster youth to compare on transitional outcomes. Using comparison samples as done in many studies is another alternative, but this strategy has its limitations. Many of these comparisons are not representative of foster children, so it is difficult to untangle issues such as poverty from foster care in determining outcomes. However, large samples of foster youth are needed (not always guaranteed by the large nationally representative samples) for researchers to use in multivariate statistical analyses to try to control for some of the variables that would give greater clarity to findings.

Longitudinal cohort research utilizing representative samples that also have comparison groups are needed to move us closer to determining causal relationships between a successful transition and having resided in foster care. Questions that need to be addressed by this research include how well are youth being prepared for life after foster care and what is the best method or methods of providing this preparation. We also need to know what in the post–foster care environment contributes to or hinders adult development. It would be beneficial to gather data from multiple informants: youth self-reports, administrative data, observation, and data collected from others in a youth's social network including family and social workers. The use of standardized measures and common definitions of outcomes would allow for a more valid comparison of findings across studies. Most studies end data collection shortly after a youth leaves care with a few studies extending their efforts to the midtwenties. Research is needed that extends this age range in order to learn more about how the experience of foster care affects a person across the life cycle.

Most of the research has focused on the poor outcomes in early adulthood shown by FFY. However, even these studies show some youth as having a healthy and productive adaptation to emerging adulthood. Data on the experience of these youth would give policy and program planners insight into the types of interventions that would lead to successful outcomes.

CHAPTER SIX

Education Outcomes and Challenges for Foster Children

The research tells us that youth leave foster care with considerable educational deficits, and that these deficiencies have significant detrimental impacts on the transition to adulthood. Entering emerging adulthood with a high school diploma is essential. Most studies report that youth leave care with low levels of educational attainment, and many without completing high school. Former foster youth (FFY) fare poorly when compared to their peers in the general population in attending postsecondary education, and in graduating when they do attend college. Social policy, as evidenced by the Promoting Safe and Stable Families Amendments Act (2001), and the Fostering Connections to Success and Increasing Adoptions Act (2008), emphasizes the importance of education for foster youth. These two pieces of legislation provided additional support for postsecondary education for emancipated former foster youth. Education is viewed as essential to meet the demands of a changing job market, and the policy emphasis on self-sufficiency for emancipated foster youth (EFY). Completing their education positions youth to meet one of the markers of adulthood; being financially self-supporting. Table 6.1 describes the financial rewards for increased educational attainments.

Table 6.1 shows that completing high school can add $180 to a person's weekly income and reduce the chances of being unemployed by 50 percent. A person who attains a college degree has the potential to earn $403 more per week than a worker with only a high school diploma. A college degree also opens up the possibility of pursuing professions that are well paid and provide satisfying and meaningful work (Baum, Ma, & Payea, 2013).

Table 6.1   Median Usual Weekly Earnings of Full-Time Wage and Salary Workers Age 25 and Older by Education Attainment in 2014

Educational Level	Unemployment Rate	Earnings
Advanced degree	2.0	$1,386
Bachelor's and higher	2.8	$1,193
Bachelor's only	3.5	$1,101
Associate's degree	4.5	$792
Some college	6.0	$741
High School diploma only	6.0	$668
Less than high school	9.0	$488
Total Average	5.0	$839

Source: Bureau of Labor Statistics (2015)

In addition to the financial rewards, the college degree provides a number of other nonmonetary benefits: the conferring of social status, including socioeconomic status; an association with better health for the worker and his or her family, including longer life spans (Porter, 2002); increasing the likelihood of marriage and parenthood within marriage (Cherlin, 2010); making it more likely that one's children will be educated, and is associated with more leisure time (Perna, 2005). Benefits accrue not only to the individual but also to society. An increase in college graduations means more tax revenue from increased earnings, and a corresponding reduction in the use of public benefits (Packard, Delgado, Fellmeth, & McReady, 2008; Peters, Dworsky, Courtney, & Pollack, 2009). College graduates also tend to have more active engagement within their communities. For instance the college-educated population is more likely to vote, volunteer in community activities, and hold leadership positions in civic organizations (Tierney, Bailey, Constantine, Finkelstein, & Hurd, 2009).

The benefits of a college education are not distributed equally in society. Historically, minority student enrollments have been low, although, recently minority students have been narrowing the attendance gap between them and whites of the same age. However, college graduation rates for students of color still lag those of white students—a point that is particularly noteworthy for the disproportionately minority foster care population (Casselman, 2014).

High School Completion

High school graduation rates for FFY range from 33 percent to 85 percent for youth leaving care. Notably, among foster youth in special education, the rate of high school completion was only 16 percent (Smithgall, Gladden,

Yang, & Goerge, 2005). Research from California that matched 4,000 foster youth with an equal number of youth without foster care experience on selected educational variables found that the graduation rate for foster youth was 45 percent compared with 79 percent for the general-population sample (Frerer, Sosenko, & Henke, 2013). McMillen and Tucker (1999) gathered data from EFY in Missouri and found that only 33 percent of their sample had finished high school.

A study that linked statewide education and child welfare data in California found that children in foster care had higher dropout rates and lower graduation rates than did students in the general population (Wiegmann, Putnam-Hornstein, Barrat, Magruder, & Needell, 2016). Reilly (2003) found a 50 percent graduation rate among former foster youth in Nevada. These two studies examined youth within a year or two of leaving care. Courtney, Dworsky, Brown, Cary, Love, and Vorheis (2011) found in a longitudinal study that 83 percent of females and 77 percent of males had a high school diploma (HSD) or a general equivalency diploma (GED) at age 26. At age 19, the percentage of graduates in the Midwest Study was 66 percent for females and 58 percent for males. By ages 25 or 26, 63.7 percent of the youth in that study had obtained a high school diploma and another 10.8 percent had earned a GED (Okpych & Courtney, 2014). The Midwest Study used ADD Health, with its nationally representative sample, as a comparison group. In contrast to Midwest youth, 87 percent of the ADD Health 19-year-old respondents had completed high school. Forty-five percent of the 17-year-old CalYOUTH EFY had earned an HSD. At age 19, 66 percent of these California foster alumni had earned an HSD. An additional 2.8 percent of the sample had earned a GED (Courtney et al., 2016). The Northwest Foster Care Alumni Study, which examined adult outcomes for FFY who had received foster care from three agencies in Washington and Oregon, reported an 85 percent graduation rate among foster care alumni, which is close to the national rate (Pecora, Kessler, et al., 2006). The longitudinal Casey Young Adult Survey reported an 83 percent graduation rate (Havalchak, White, & O'Brien, 2008). In both Casey studies, youth had been out of foster care for some time before they gave interviews for the research. The mean age of a respondent in the Casey Alumni Study was 30, with some respondents having been out of foster care for as long as 32 years. These persons are much older than is found in the typical study of former foster youth, which may account for the high level of high school completion by Casey alumni. These last four studies suggest considerable improvement in high school completion as youth age. However, FFY studies show that these youth still lag their general population counterparts in high school completion.

The U.S. Department of Education reported that in academic year 2011–2012 the national graduation rate for public school students was 81 percent. Since the passage of the independent living legislation, the national rates of high school completion ranged from 74 percent in 1990–1991 to a low of 71 percent in 1995–1996. Beginning in 1998, graduation rates began a slow climb to the 81 percent rate (National Center for Education Statistics, 2015).

Buehler, Orme, Post, and Patterson (2000) used a nationally representative sample to identify three comparison groups of adults to isolate the long-term effects of foster care. One group consisted of youth who had any foster care experience, not just youth who had been emancipated from foster care. The second group was selected randomly from among adults in the sample who had never been in foster care. The third group comprised adults who had socioeconomic characteristics similar to the FFY but did not have foster care experience. This last group was then matched on selected variables with the FFY. These researchers found that graduation rates were significantly lower for the FFY when compared to the random sample (58 percent versus 71 percent), but no differences in school completion rates were found with the FFY and matched group. Buehler and colleagues concluded from this last finding that the poor results seen in high school completion rates among foster youth could possibly be a reflection of impoverished backgrounds rather than being due to contact with the child welfare system.

Many studies in reporting graduation rates lump completion by diploma and GED together. Data suggest that these two indicators of high school completion are very different from one another. Pecora, Williams et al. (2006) report that former Casey clients were four times more likely than youth in the general population to have GED as evidence of high school completion. Almost one in five Casey alumni had a GED. In fact, the Casey Foundation researchers caution that the relatively high graduation rates seen in their report relative to other studies should be considered in light of the large number of GEDs in their samples. Havalchak et al. (2008) reported that the graduation rate without the GED in the Casey Young Adult Survey was closer to 74 percent. Needell, Cuccaro-Alamin, Brookhart, Jackman, and Shlonsky (2002) used administrative data drawn from a variety of California State databases to examine GED completion among FFY. These researchers found that about 6 to 7 percent of California's FFY have a GED, which is far below the rate reported by the Casey studies, but still slightly above the national average. However, more recent data suggest that the GED completion rate in California is about 3 percent (Courtney et al., 2016). The national average of high school completion via a GED, reported by Pecora, Williams, et al. (2006) was 5 percent. Leathers and Testa (2006) found a low high school graduation rate of 42 percent in Illinois, with 5 percent of youth earning a GED. They also found that males were less likely to complete high school than females, and when males did finish high school, they did so through the GED in greater numbers than did females.

The limitation of a GED compared to an HSD is evident in both the chances of proceeding on to a college or university and future income derived from work. Seventy-three percent of individuals with an HSD went on to postsecondary education. Correspondingly only 43 percent of the GED holders did so. About one-third of HSD holders have a bachelor's degree (BA), whereas only 5 percent of GED recipients earned a college degree. High school graduates had an income that was $1,600 per month greater than individuals with a GED. Differences on income were noted even for GED recipients who went on to earn a college degree. They still earned $1,400 less a month than other college graduates (Ewart, 2012). Okpych and Courtney (2014) found that at age 25 or 26 EFY with a GED did not have any more earnings than EFY without anything to indicate high school completion. Though, both Pecora, Kessler, et al. (2006) and Ewart (2012) argue that having a GED is better than not having any evidence of completing high school. Ewart's data indicate that a GED will add $300 a month to a person's income. Nevertheless, the high school diploma should be encouraged for foster youth rather than the GED, given the benefits and advantages of the diploma over the GED.

Hispanics in the Midwest Study completed high school (77.3 percent) in greater numbers than either whites (70.4 percent) or African American youth (65.7 percent), and they were more likely than were the other groups to do so with a diploma rather than a GED (Dworsky, White, et al., 2010). African Americans were more likely than other ethnic groups in the Casey Northwest Alumni Study to complete high school, but they were more likely to finish with a GED than were the youth in the general populations. The difference in graduation rates between African Americans and whites was not significant (Harris, Jackson, O'Brien, & Pecora, 2009). Data from the Casey National Alumni Study showed that American Indian/Alaska Natives graduated at the same rate as other ethnic alumni, but they were more likely to have a GED than an HSD (O'Brien et al., 2010).

Postsecondary Attendance and Completion

Most studies find that EFY are less likely than their peers in the general population to proceed on to postsecondary education or training after high school (Courtney, Dworsky, Cusick, et al., 2009). A study of Michigan's FFY that utilized ADD Health as a comparison group found that 7.7 percent of the foster alumni had a BA versus 24.7 percent of the ADD Health sample with that degree (White, O'Brien, Pecora, & Buher, 2015).

The initial conclusion one might reach from the data on EFY and postsecondary education is that it is not surprising that the number of EFY proceeding to college is small, given their low high school graduation rates. Nevertheless, Pecora, Williams, et al. (2006) using data from the Casey Alumni study, which gathered data from FFY who had been in Casey placements nationally, found that 49 percent of their alumni had some college, which was comparable to rates in the general population (51 percent). As with data on high school completion, these researchers gathered data about postsecondary education from an older group of FFY than is found in the typical study of foster youth. This difference may account for the high level of college attendance by Casey alumni. Many of the other studies of FFY or EFY examined these youth when they were ages 19 to 20. The long view of the Casey study provides a different perspective on college attendance. Simply put, youth graduate high school or college when they do, and that is not always on the expected schedule of adolescence and young adulthood. Previous difficulties that foster youth encountered may mean a delay in educational attainments. Foster youth might have shown better education outcomes if more data were available that covered a longer period.

Despite the low levels of college attendance by FFY, several studies indicate that foster youth express a strong interest in attending college. Courtney, Terao, and Bost (2004) reported that 88 percent of their sample of 17- and 18-year-olds said they wished to attend college. McMillen, Auslander, Elze, White, and Thompson (2003) said that 70 percent of the 15- to 19-year-old independent living program participants they interviewed said they aspired to earn a college degree. Nineteen percent of that sample said they wished to go beyond college and seek further education. However, not all studies report the same high level of academic aspirations. Forty-nine percent of Blome's (1997) sample indicated a desire to attend college, which was less than the level expressed by a comparison group of nonfoster peers. Kirk, Lewis, Nilsen, and Colvin (2013) examined educational aspirations of low-income youth participating in a program meant to encourage college attendance among disadvantaged youth in Kansas. They found that only 43 percent of foster youth aspired to attend a four-year college. In comparison, 67 percent of the nonfoster teens in their sample wanted to go to a four-year school.

Kirk and colleagues explain the gap between foster youth and other youth by suggesting that foster youth experience lower levels of parental support for education, have a more critical view of their academic abilities, and are hindered by the effects of trauma of abuse and foster care on their ability to learn. McMillen et al. (2003) found that youth with low aspirations for college in their sample were male, had more negative peers, had a present rather than future orientation, and were more likely to have been hospitalized for psychiatric reasons. Among all youth with low levels of college aspirations, the perception that college was unaffordable was a major factor in their view of whether or not they would attend college.

Kirk and colleagues limited their questioning to an interest in attending four-year colleges, which may underestimate actual levels of postsecondary aspirations in their foster care sample. Data from two different sources in California suggest that FFY may favor two-year colleges because of monetary concerns, and a perception that those institutions' admission criteria are less stringent than the policies at four-year institutions (Courtney et al., 2016; Needell et al., 2002).

Researchers have studied this gap and noted a difference between aspirations, the ideal level of education desired, and expectations of what youth think they can achieve (Beal & Crockett, 2010; Boxer, Goldstein, DeLorenzo, Savoy, & Mercado, 2011; Kirk et al., 2013). McCarron and Inkelas (2006) studied high school students who said they wanted to go to college and would be the first person in their family to do so. They found that 62 percent of these youth had not done so two years later. These researchers note that teachers and parents are important in setting a youth's educational aspirations. In the absence of parents, child welfare workers need to play a large role in setting these expectations (Boxer et al., 2011). However, there is some evidence to suggest that social workers and child professionals are not encouraging college attendance by foster youth. Rios and Rocco (2014) reported that only 11 of the 24 EFY in their qualitative sample said their social worker was actively involved in their college application process.

Gender is an important factor in college attendance of FFY, just as it is in other sectors. In the general population, the female-to-male ratio has been shifting in favor of females since the 1970s, with females now outnumbering males on college campuses nationally (Lopez & Gonzales-Barrera, 2014). Foster youth follow this trend as well, but with even a greater gender imbalance in favor of females. Seventy-six percent of the FFY students in the California State University system were female (Merdinger, Hines, Lemon, Osterling, & Wyatt, 2005). Leathers and Testa (2006) report similar findings from Illinois that female FFY attended college in greater proportion than males. Young women in the CalYOUTH study were more likely than males in that sample to say they expected to gain a college degree and seek additional education (Courtney et al., 2016).

In the Midwest Study, African Americans were the least likely group to complete high school, but they were more likely to go on to college if they had an HSD than were white or Hispanic EFY (Dworsky et al., 2010). Research that has investigated ethnicity/race has not found differences between whites and African Americans on school completion (Harris et al., 2009; Villegas, Rosenthal, O'Brien, & Pecora, 2014). Most differences on African American ethnicity found in bi-variate analysis disappeared in multivariate analysis when other variables were considered. Whites had a slightly higher near significant chance (p<.07) of graduating when compared to Hispanics (Villegas et al., 2014). American Indian/Alaska Natives had only a 2.8 percent college completion rate (O'Brien et al., 2010).

Educational Problems While in Care

Burley and Halpern (2001), using administrative data from of the state of Washington, found that youth with short stays in care had the same educational deficits as youth with long-term stays in care. This finding is a cause for concern, as it suggests either that these problems preceded foster care, or that even a small dose of care carries additional educational risk for all foster children.

Poverty and Low Income

Researchers have found that foster youth have considerable difficulties with their educational experience while in care. However, the foundations of these problems are set well before youth entered care. Many foster youth have grown up in impoverished environments and must deal with all the correlates of poverty. For example, 71 percent of Utah's foster children were classified as low-income students by the schools (Barrat & Berliner, 2016). One of those correlates of poverty is that children are likely to be enrolled in poorly performing schools before entering care (Frerer et al., 2013; Lee & Barth, 2009; Okpych, 2012; Smithgall, Gladden, Howard, Goerge, & Court-ney, 2004). Wiegmann and colleagues (2016) found foster youth, along with other low socioeconomic status (SES) students, are more likely than the general student population to be attending low-performing schools, as measured by California's Academic Performance Index. Thus, according to results from statewide testing, by the time they enter foster care they are academically behind. The documented achievement gap widens as length of stay in foster care increases.

Berzin (2008) used a nationally representative data set to identify FFY and then match them with youth never in foster care but with similar socioeconomic backgrounds. Berzin found no differences in high school and college graduations between the two groups. This finding was unusual; most studies of foster youth show them having deficits in relation to comparison groups, but Berzin explains the findings as resulting from the fact that both groups had similar economic backgrounds. Therefore, poverty is more likely the reason for the educational deficits noted, rather than the foster care experience. Just as Buehler et al. (2000) found, poverty that preceded foster care may account for adverse findings as much as child welfare involvement.

Mental Health

Foster children also arrive in the system with the mental health and behavioral problems associated with maltreatment, which complicate and diminish their ability to focus on their education. These problems may be exacerbated by the experience of foster care (Burns et al., 2004; Smithgall et al., 2004). A number of studies reviewed in Chapter 10 document the high prevalence of mental health problems found among foster children. Foster children exhibit mental health problems that range from relationship and coping difficulties to emotional and behavioral disorders that caused moderate to severe impairment (Needell et al., 2002).

These mental health problems can carry over into the classroom and interfere with student learning (Smithgall et al., 2005; Zima et al., 2000). Clausen, Landsverk, Ganger, Chadwick, and Litrownick (1998) used a standardized measure for identifying behavioral problems to establish the link between exhibiting clinical levels of behavioral problems in increasing the chances of school expulsion or suspension. McMillen et al. (2003) extended these links to find that behavior problems were also associated with a child having to repeat a grade. Mental health difficulties frequently required that youth be taken from regular classrooms and be placed in alternative schools. Wiegmann and colleagues (2016) reported that about one in five of California's high school age foster children were attending a nontraditional school. This rate of placement in these types of schools was much higher than their nonfoster peers. The most frequently given reason for this placement was an emotional disturbance.

A number of additional challenges face foster children in their educational program. Vandivere, Chalk, and Moore (2003) reported that almost 60 percent of children age two and under in foster care were at a high risk for a developmental delay or neurological impairment. Therefore, it is not surprising that foster youth are more likely than their nonfoster peers to be diagnosed with a learning disability and be placed in special education classes. In California the rate of disability among foster children was double that of children who were never in foster care. Almost 40 percent of foster children had a disability, which limited foster students' cognitive, reading, and math abilities. Nine percent of California's students were eligible for gifted and talented services; only 2 percent of foster children received those services. Six percent of the state's low-income students received those same services. However, foster youth were much less likely to be diagnosed with autism, speech, and language disorders than their nonfoster peers (Wiegmann et al., 2016).

In addition, experiencing child abuse can leave a child with cognitive skill deficits that limit their ability to learn. They may not have had parents who were involved in their schooling and thus did not stress education's importance to their children (Stone, 2006).

Measures of Educational Outcomes

Foster children also lagged behind their peers without foster care experience on measures of educational outcomes. Foster children did poorer on standardized tests, were behind on reading levels, and they were more likely to fail a grade, when compared to these peers. Foster youth were also twice as likely to be absent and/or truant from school, and they are more likely than nonfoster youth to face school expulsion or suspension. They were also more likely to repeat a grade (Choice et al., 2001; Conger & Rebeck, 2001;

Courtney et al., 2004; McMillen et al., 2003; Merdinger et al., 2005; Smith-gall et al., 2004; Sullivan, Jones, & Mathiesen, 2010; Zima et al., 2000).

Placement Change and School Mobility

Throughout this book we will see that placement change carries significant risks for youth. Placement change is often accompanied by a transfer to a new school. School change has been found to cause difficulties for a child's educational program (Conger & Finkelstein, 2003; Courtney, Piliavin, Grogan-Kaylor, & Nesmith, 2001; Smithgall et al., 2004). The negative effects of placement change on a child's academic functioning have been established with foster youth (Altschuler, 1997; Ayasse, 1995; Barth, 1990; Conger & Rebeck, 2001; Eckenrode, Rowe, Laird, & Brathwaite, 1995; Zetlin, Weinberg, & Luderer, 2004). Foster youth were twice as likely to experience a school change as were students not in foster care (Eckenrode et al., 1995; Pecora, 2010). Almost 33 percent of Casey's foster children said they had attended 10 different primary, middle, and high schools by graduation. Most of the remaining Casey FFY had numerous placements and school changes (Pecora, Williams, et al., 2006). The high rates of placement change have been noted by other researchers. A study that used administrative data containing all of California's foster children found that one-third of the children experienced five or more placement changes (Needell et al., 2002). Wisconsin's foster youth children had a mean of four to six different placements (Courtney et al., 2001). One study that used administrative data from California compared school change rates between children who had at least three years of foster care experience, and nonfoster children, found much higher rates of school mobility among the foster youth. The foster children had attended a mean of three schools in the previous year. Youth in this study who had stable placements were less likely to drop out of school and were more likely to earn a high school diploma.

Two Casey studies also linked placement stability to completing high school. Casey youth who were moved less frequently than the total Casey sample had nearly double the chance of graduating high school (Pecora, 2012; Pecora, Kessler, et al., 2006). Merdinger et al. (2005) found this stability during the high school years translated into proceeding on to college. Fifty-one percent of the California youth attending college in this California sample had attended only one high school. Another 22 percent had attended only two high schools.

School mobility has also been shown to adversely affect standardized test scores (Cochrane et al., 2001). Placement change has also been correlated with lagging behind expected reading levels and failure to earn a high school diploma (Rumberger, Larsen, Ream, & Palardi, 1999). Placement change has also been linked to truancy problems (Conger & Rebeck, 2001; Eckenrode et al., 995). School mobility can carry a risk to a student's academic progress for a number of reasons. Changing schools disrupts a student's daily routine and places demands on their social workers to coordinate the transfer. Many researchers have commented on the lack of coordination between child welfare agencies and the educational institutions. The importance of a timely transfer of youth's academic records has been emphasized. These records are necessary for teachers and school staff to assure that youth receive the proper academic placement. School records document the course work completed as well as a student's proficiency by reporting their academic grades. They also contain behavioral information, attendance, and education plans (particularly special needs). Often records do not arrive with the student at their new school (or they might not arrive at all) (Blome, 1997; Choice et al., 2001; Eckenrode et al., 1995; McMillen et al., 2003; Powers & Stotland, 2002; Smithgall et al., 2004). If records are not available youth may be placed in inappropriate classrooms. They may lose credit for courses already completed and thus may have to repeat coursework, or even a grade level (Kerbow, 1996). Zetlin et al. (2004) noted that children with serious educational and behavioral problems had less accurate and complete records than other youth. Group home residents seem particularly vulnerable for record problems. Sixty-eight percent of California's group home providers said that records not arriving with students could result in group home residents not having appropriate classroom placements (Parrish et al., 2001).

Independent of the record problems, children may be stressed by the move and need help adjusting to a new educational setting (Yu, Day, & Williams, 2002). Youth who have frequent placement changes are hindered in establishing the support networks that might assist in achieving school success, as well as coping with the challenges of foster care. Foster children may have been participating in after-school and extracurricular activities at their old school. Children may have lost a teacher who was a source of emotional and academic support. They must adjust to new teachers and staff and a different curriculum. They may have lost friendships as a result of the move (Sullivan et al., 2010). They must fit into a new classroom and establish new peer connections. They must worry about who will associate with them on the playground, and who will eat with them during lunch (Stott & Gustavsson, 2010). All of these are sources of stress that have outsized importance for children and adolescents. These activities may not be available at a new school, which may further isolate youth (Day, Riebschleger, Dworsky, Damashek, & Fogarty, 2012).

It should be noted that in addition to adapting to a new school, youth are also coping with adjusting to new caretakers and a new home. Wolanin (2005) has noted that each placement change may be a reminder of the emotional trauma of abandonment and separation that occurred in the removal from their family of origin (Wolanin, 2005). The school mobility after a time may make youth hesitant to commit to their educational program in their new school. After all, they may think the current stay is also temporary.

Child welfare workers have suggested that the frequent school change that foster children experience may make them also appear temporary to teachers and staff. The suspicion of child welfare workers is that if educational staff does view the child's stay as temporary, they might be reluctant to invest the time, energy, and resources to assess the child's needs and provide the services that are needed. However, educational personnel insist that foster children are given the same services and effort as other children (McMillen et al., 2003; Stone, D'Andrade, & Austin, 2007).

The research summarized in this section shows that youth in care have substantial academic (as well as other) problems that are likely to present challenges to them as they seek a successful transition to emerging adulthood. These problems are a barrier to completing high school, and without a high school diploma one cannot move on to the next level of education—college or university postsecondary education.

College-Related Problems

Sixty-four percent of a sample of FFY attending college said the foster care system had not prepared them for college (Merdinger et al., 2005). About 32 percent of America's high school students enrolled in courses aimed at preparing them for college, whereas only 15 percent of foster children had taken such courses (Sheehy et al., 2001). Foster youth are much less likely than their nonfoster care peers to have taken advanced or college preparatory classes (Blome, 1997). Students who are in foster care are not encouraged by their teachers, social workers, and other adults to attend college (Davis, 2006). Given the litany of problems foster youth have with primary and secondary education, it is not surprising that if they arrive at college at all, they are unprepared to succeed. In comparison to other students, FFY are more frequently required to take college remedial courses without credit to address academic deficits (Dworsky & Perez, 2010).

Unrau, Font, and Rawls (2012) provide evidence of this lack of preparation in their comparison of FFY freshmen with their peers in the general population. FFY were more likely to drop out of school than other freshmen (21.4 percent versus 13 percent) and had lower grade-point averages than other first-year students (2.34 versus 2.85). Forty-seven percent of foster youth had withdrawn from a course during their first semester in college compared to 18 percent among all students. Despite these poor numbers, these researchers report evidence from a college engagement measure that the FFY expressed a stronger intensity to finish college than their peers who had never been in foster care.

Needell et al. (2002) found that 55 percent of FFY attended a community college. Forty percent of those youth at two-year schools did not earn any credits because they were enrolled in noncredit remedial classes. Frerer et al. (2013) found that foster youth were less likely than other community college students, including a matched group of students with similar SES and educational characteristics, to return to school for a second year or to graduate. Needell and colleagues further report from their data that only 2 percent of the FFY graduated with an associate's degree and another 2 percent transferred to a four-year institution. By comparison, nationally 37 percent of youth who attended a community college complete a degree and 19 percent transfer to a four-year college.

FFY have a multitude of needs and problems that compete and interfere with their educational careers and aspirations. Many former foster youth who attend college need to work in order to cover living expenses, housing, fees, and tuition (Day, Dworsky, Fogarty, & Damashek, 2011; Merdinger et al., 2005). Merdinger and colleagues studied a sample composed of FFY attending universities in California. They found that 76 percent reported they had to work. Students who work more than 15 to 20 hours a week are less likely to succeed academically (Pike, Kuh, & Massa-McKinley, 2009). Salazar (2012) described hours worked as the most salient factor in determining whether a youth would drop out of school. Money difficulties is one of the most frequently given reasons for dropping out of school (Batsche et al., 2014; Courtney, Dworsky, Lee, & Rapp, 2010; Hernandez & Naccarato, 2010).

Although most foster youth can partially offset this disadvantage with larger financial aid packages than other students, they may not have access to financial support from families when a crisis strikes. In fact, they may feel obligated to use financial aid to assist their financially stressed families (Hernandez and Naccarato, 2010; Kendig, Mattingly, & Bianchi, 2014). Furthermore, not all eligible FFY receive the available aid. A report from California showed that 84 percent of the states' FFY who attended college received a Pell Grant, 17 percent received a state Cal Grant, and just 9 percent received an educational training voucher (ETV). Only 4 percent of students received all three types of aid (Cochrane & Szabo-Kubitz, 2009). Additionally, African American and Latino FFY were less likely than white or mixed-race FFY to have received financial aid (Courtney et al., 2016).

In addition to finances, there are other barriers to remaining in college. Both Salazar (2012) and Hernandez and Naccarato (2010) identify housing difficulties (see Chapter 8) as a major reason for students dropping out of their academic program. Parenting teens note the difficulties of balancing the demands of school and home (Courtney et al., 2016). See Chapter 11 for a discussion on parenting and its effect on the transition to adulthood.

As discussed earlier in this chapter FFY also have more mental health issues, behavioral difficulties, and substance abuse problems than youth in the general population. The increased stress faced in college can exacerbate many preexisting problems (Hernandez & Naccarato, 2010; Hines, Merdinger, & Wyatt, 2005). Salazar (2013) found a history of severe maltreatment or a positive screen for post-traumatic stress disorder to be associated with drop-ping out of college (prevalence of this diagnosis among FFY is discussed in Chapter 10). Other mental health problems show similar effects on a youth's postsecondary academic career, particularly if the need was not treated while the youth was in school. Data from interviews with program coordinators of college support program show that drug use and abuse were major prob-lems for FFY in college (Hernandez & Naccarato, 2010). Previous research has indicated that substance use increases in this age group, particularly among those youth in college (Larimer, Kilmer, & Lee, 2005). College stu-dents confront many new interpersonal, academic, and social demands. The lack of social connections and supports to cope with these challenges is one possible explanation for the high college dropout rate found among FFY (Day et al., 2011). Substance use may help students cope with these demands in the short term, but in the end, it inhibits their successful adaptation to college and young adulthood. Youth also report that teachers and administrators do not understand the unique needs of FFY or they are not prepared to address these needs (Dworsky & Perez, 2010).

Although there has been a proliferation of on-campus programs to support FFY in college, students often report not being aware of them when available, or not having a desire to avoid them because of a perceived stigma of being a former foster child (Merdinger et al., 2005). About one-half of California's foster youth who attended a college or university said they used the services of one of these programs. Another one-fifth of respondents reported being aware of the program on their campus but never used their services (Court-ney et al., 2016). Some students who were aware of the presence of such pro-grams on campus did not use them because they did not perceive that those programs provided the services they need (Dworsky & Perez, 2010).

College Is Not a Magic Bullet

Moving a youth through school to a college education still leaves many problems unresolved. Foster youth's problems are multifaceted, and solving these problems requires action in a number of areas. Salazar (2013) com-pared FFY who were college graduates with their peers in two nationally representative population studies, the General Social Survey and the Panel Study of Income Dynamics. She found similar rates of employment between groups. However, FFY had lower household incomes when employed.

FFY youth have many other problems that go beyond educational deficits. Okpych and Courtney (2014) compared the Midwest Study sample at ages 25 or 26 with their peers in a Bureau of Labor Statistics survey, and found some-what different results. Each level of educational attainment (as described in Table 6.1) showed larger gains in income and the likelihood of employment as EFY progressed through the educational levels than for the youth in the comparison sample who were making similar educational advancements. The largest gain for the EFY was in the completion of a BA/BS degree. However, the EFY still lagged their peers in earnings until they earned either an associate or bachelor's degree. Less than 10 percent of the Midwest Study youth had a degree beyond a high school diploma. Overall earnings between the two samples show Midwest Study youth having about one-half the income of their peers ($14,148 vs. $28,105).

It should be noted most EFY are more likely to pursue vocational training than college. Villegas et al. (2014) report that Casey alumni were choosing professional certification programs rather than college (26.8 percent vs. 8.8 percent). Encouraging the pursuit of these certificates may help some youth without the interest or ability to pursue college to prepare for better-paying jobs, and may expose these youth to the culture of continued education beyond high school. This exposure may help some youth develop an interest in obtaining additional education.

Practical Recommendations for Improving Educational Outcomes for Foster Youth

Ensuring educational success has always been part of the job of the child welfare social worker. Foster youth are expected to attend school while they are in care. Social workers, and in many cases foster parents, are supposed to be educational advocates for youth. The process of placing a child in care and moving a child among placements requires a social worker to ensure that children are enrolled in school and that their academic records accompany them. Social workers are also responsible for monitoring progress and connections between educational personnel and caregivers, and the resolution of any problems between the two. As mentioned earlier, federal policy has emphasized the importance of education in achieving a successful transition to adulthood.

A successful transition to emerging adulthood requires youth to gain an education. Given that most foster youth come from low-income backgrounds and reside in areas with substandard, underperforming schools, improving the educational deficits of EFY will be difficult to impossible unless the overall educational inequities plaguing poor children are addressed and rectified by a larger society. The United States must address these problems for all its citizens by assuring its poor children have adequate schools. The absence of such an effort means the school-related problems of foster youth are bound to continue. Because of the changes to the economy, foster youth need to be encouraged and be given the resources to proceed educationally beyond high school. Too few EFY are gaining the type of human capital that would allow them to thrive in today's technological economy. Without additional education beyond high school, EFY will be at high risk of finding only low-paying jobs that provide little security and few benefits. Hence, and in light of the educational difficulties outlined in this chapter, the following recommenda-tions are made for those who work with foster children and transitioning youth. These recommendations are divided into two types: before college (primary and secondary schooling), and while attending college.

Primary School through High School

Lessons from an Exemplary Program

Casey Family Programs, a nationally known, high-quality foster care agency, has reported relatively good results on educational outcomes for its alumni. These results suggest that Casey provides a model on how to improve educational attainments for foster children. Casey staff and foster parents use advocacy, integrated social work and education case management, and con-tinuous monitoring of educational progress to address educational deficits in the youth whom they serve (Dworsky, White, et al., 2010; Pecora, Williams, et al., 2006).

Foster children's educational careers needs to be better supported by child welfare agencies. Blome (1997) reported that only 35 percent of his sample of foster children said that a parent or guardian had ever attended a parent-teacher conference. Educational advocacy needs to be part of a foster parent's job description. Foster parents should be expected to regularly monitor a child's academic progress, help with homework, meet with teachers, encour-age and assist the birth-parent's engagement in their child's educational pro-gram, and allow youth to participate in extracurricular and after-school activities. Most of the qualitative studies reviewed in this point emphasize the need for youth to have caring and helpful adults to assist them with their academic programs. One suggestion, from Michigan's Kidspeak Program that gathers input from current foster youth and FFY, is that youth should be matched with adult mentors who would provide advocacy, guidance, and support (Day et al., 2012). Ideally, this relationship would continue beyond case closure. Provision of mentors might increase the likelihood that pri-mary, high school, and college students would reach their educational aspi-rations and goals (Haussmann, Schofield, & Woods, 2007).

Making Schools Responsive to Foster Youth

Schools, especially those with significant numbers of foster children, should have educational staff designated as a foster care liaison to encourage collaboration with child welfare agencies. Part of the job of liaison would be to educate school personnel about the needs and barriers that hinder educa-tional achievement of foster children. The liaison would also be charged with informing foster children who are students about the availability of services, such as tutoring and counseling, and would work with social workers to get mental health referrals when necessary.

Educational personnel and child welfare staff need cross-training to develop awareness of the kinds of educational challenges that foster children face. Teachers, administrators, counselors, and other school staff must be educated about issues of child maltreatment, trauma, separation from the family of origin, and the dynamics of school and placement change in order that they can respond in a manner that best meets the needs of foster children

Minimize Placement Mobility

The research reviewed in this chapter described how school change can adversely affect students' educational progress. Social workers must take the risks of school mobility into consideration when considering a placement change. Social workers must consider how educational continuity can be maintained, and they must be reluctant to disrupt an environment where a foster child has found supportive foster parents, teachers, and peers. If a change of placement is necessary, workers must help a child cope with feelings of loss and anxiety that accompany the move to a new situation. School change should be recognized as a risk to foster children who are already beset by problems that might require mental health intervention. If a new foster home is needed, efforts should be made to maintain a child in the same school. Perhaps thought should be given to delaying a needed placement change to the end of school year or semester (Pecora, 2012; Pecora, Kessler, et al., 2005). If that is not possible, social workers should consider what efforts could be made to keep the child connected to friends and other supportive persons in their previous environment. When moves are necessary child welfare workers should make every effort to ease the transition. One of the most obvious efforts in this area is to assure that academic records accompany students. They might also accompany the foster child student to the new school prior to placement in an effort to help their student become comfortable with their new academic setting (Stott, 2012).

Washington State has a "Foster Care Passport Program." This passport is a file that contains the medical, dental, behavioral, and educational records of a foster child. The passport is presumed to aid youth undergoing placement and school change by easing the record transfer problems that have affected foster children (Choice et al., 2001).

Lastly, research is needed to determine whether frequent placement change is a reflection of a child's individual characteristics or instead actually reflects the child welfare system's inability to provide consistent care for many of the children for which it is responsible.

Preparing Foster Youth for College

Youth should understand both the process of applying to college or other postsecondary programs and the intricacies of financial aid. Social workers should also receive in-service training on these issues so that they can assist their charges with college applications, financial aid, and so on. This content should be part of any independent living program in order to help youth prepare for postsecondary education.

The Higher Education Opportunities Act (Public Law No. 110–315) was amended in 2008 to make foster children eligible to participate in federal TRIO programs. TRIO programs are "educational opportunity outreach programs designed to motivate and support students from disadvantaged backgrounds" to aspire and go on to postsecondary education. Examples of these programs are Talent Search and Upward Bound (Okpych, 2012). These programs get foster youth used to the idea that college is a realistic possibility for them, and that they belong on campus.

A Radical Suggestion for Improving Educational Outcomes

San Pasqual Academy (SPA) in San Diego County, California, is a radical response to the dismal educational outcomes noted in the literature for former foster youth. The residence is an innovative residential placement option for adolescent foster youth who do not have a reunification or adoption permanency plan. SPA is expected to provide a long-term, stable living arrangement, along with a quality educational program where the student completes their high school education in preparation for discharge from foster care. SPA differs from other congregate placement options by having an education rather than treatment focus. Most treatment programs are temporary placements where a youth's mental health symptoms are stabilized in order that they might be moved to a lower-level group home or foster care. SPA has a public high school on-site that residents are expected to attend until graduation. Thus, students avoid school change and its disruptive effects that were discussed earlier in this chapter. Youth have the possibility of developing long-term relationships with teachers and other staff. Thus, teachers have more time to know their students, and they have a greater opportunity to respond appropriately to youth needs. Youth who are assured that this will be their home until they leave care may have a greater willingness to invest their best efforts in their education than they might if they perceived the stay was temporary. Graduates can choose to live in transitional housing located on campus and continue to receive independent living services for up to one year after discharge (Jones & Landsverk, 2006).

SPA reported a 76 percent graduation rate and said that 43 percent of its early cohort's graduates attended college or vocational school (Jones, 2008).

For youth who remained at SPA until age 18 or older the graduation rate was 92 percent; furthermore, 56 percent of these youth who graduated had some sort of postsecondary education (Lawler, Sayfan, Goodman, Narr, & Cordon, 2014). These graduation rates exceed those in most published studies of FFY, and the rate for those who remain in care until age 18 exceeds both California and national averages for completing high school (Frerer et al., 2013). As of yet, however, SPA has not released a rigorous evaluation of its program. Therefore, we cannot say that residential education is a solution for poor educational outcomes for EFY.

Recommendations for Improving College Outcomes

Extending Foster Care

CalYOUTH respondents who remained in care were more likely than those who left to have earned a high school diploma (70.2 percent versus 51.8 percent), and a vocational certificate or license (16.8 percent versus 8.0 percent). They were also more likely if they went on to college to have received financial aid than those EFY who left care, but were attending college (65.6 percent versus 33 percent) (Courtney et al., 2016). Extending the time that states can claim Title IV-E federal reimbursement for EFY to age 25 and/or continue with independent living services would provide more assistance for the educational preparation needed for future self-sufficiency. EFY students are on average older than traditional college students because they are more likely than nonfoster students to have repeated a grade. They are often in need of remedial work that is taken without credit, which extends their college experience. EFY are often forced to go to school part-time because of financial and other factors. Thus, EFY may need more time to complete school. This extension would put EFY on the same footing as nonfoster youth given the societal trends discussed in Chapter 2. For college students, the extended funding would be in line with recent data. The U.S. Department of Education data says it takes a little over six years to complete a BA degree (Kertscher, 2013).

A cost-benefit analysis that used the Midwest Study data examined the effect of extending foster care to age 20. Those researchers estimate that an extension would cost $38,000 per foster child, but would provide twice that amount in benefits. These benefits would be delivered in the increased educational attainment that would lead to better jobs, less reliance on public benefits, and higher tax revenues that would result from higher incomes. The researchers estimate a return of $2.40 on every public dollar expended on transitioning youth. They cite data that shows that if a youth earned a BA degree, that youth would earn $92,000 more income over his or her work life. Remaining in care until age 20 and having at least some college would result in an additional $84,000 in benefits. Other nonmonetary benefits were identified at the start of this chapter. Therefore, results regarding benefits would probably be greater if one could monetize these more intangible benefits (Peters et al., 2009). Barnow et al. (2015) report data from a longitudinal database with a large sample that showed that the longer youth stayed in a transitional program, the better their education and employment outcomes.

Making the Campus FFY Friendly

Campus-based support services for FFY (possibly paid for from FCIA funds) to address the high dropout rate of foster youth attending college should be established. Campus-based programs can provide coordination, information, and referral services for housing, financial assistance, tutoring, guidance, child care, mental health services referrals, advocacy, curriculum advising, and possibly a support community on campus. The goal of these programs is to assist youth to graduate.

Such programs are relatively new and are clustered in California and Washington. These types of services could be helpful because they are located on the campus where students spend considerable time. Personnel in these programs understand the college or university bureaucracy and requirements, and they employ staff who have knowledge of the specific needs of FFY (Dworsky & Perez, 2010; Okpych, 2012). The Higher Education Opportunities Act (P.L. 110–315) supports these sorts of programs. That act requires postsecondary institutions to recruit and serve former foster youth and to develop an institutional climate that is supportive of former foster youth (Okpych, 2012). Federal and/or state funding for implementation and evaluation can be assessed for these programs as an investment strategy. The costs would be offset by the benefits of a college degree described earlier in this chapter (Pecora, Williams, et al., 2006).

An alternative approach that is both simple and effective, and appropriate for small campuses that have few FFY students, is to designate an existing student services staff member to be the primary support person for FFY. This person would be responsible for seeing that the FFY were aware of the institutional resources including financial aid, tuition waivers, scholarship opportunities, and mental health and other support services on campus (Batsche et al., 2014). Whatever is done, rigorous evaluation of these programs is required to determine their effectiveness.

More efficient and effective coordination needs to occur among child welfare agencies, high schools, colleges, and universities to facilitate the transition from foster care to postsecondary education. Youth need help in navigating the often bewildering tangle of agencies and programs meant to help students get into and stay in college. Posting personnel from these different service sectors in satellite posts at the other agencies would also aid students (Day et al., 2011).

One way EFY college students may differ from their nonfoster peers is that they may not have places to go on holidays and breaks like other college students. Alternative housing, year-round financial assistance, and employment options must be a consideration for these students who do not have ties to parents or others (Pecora, Williams, et al., 2006).

Meeting Youth's Financial Needs

ETV funding should reflect true college costs. College tuition and fees have been escalating steadily, and ETV grants have not kept pace. Okpych (2012) presents data showing that the 2003–2004 grant covered about 51 percent of college costs. Because of increased costs, this same grant covered only 31 percent of costs in 2011–2012. EFY may also benefit from the College Cost Reduction Act of 2009, which allows youth in foster care to claim independent status when applying for financial aid (Fernandes, 2008). Both social workers and FFY need to be aware of this information. The states could also consider providing tuition waivers for current and former foster youth at public universities (American Bar Association Commission on Youth at Risk, 2011).

Because larger numbers of EFY work while attending college, mostly out of necessity, they should receive preference in work-study slots. Work-study positions more easily fit into the academic schedule, and thus are less likely to adversely affect an EFY's education (Day et al., 2011).

The Casey Family Foundation reports that one need met by its aftercare program is connecting youth with income support services such as TANF. This connection improved educational and employment outcomes. This linkage helps youth secure basic concrete needs (Barnow et al., 2015). Single-stop centers are needed to allow students to use all possible social benefits. EFY also need continued financial management training and assistance.

Goldrick-Rab and Broton (2015) investigated hunger and homelessness among college students, particularly community college attendees, and they urge changes to the social and educational polices regarding the provision of food and housing assistance for students. They give as one example the School Lunch Program, which feeds school children but not college students. Subsidized housing and transportation given to students also ends with high school. As a part of rethinking emerging adulthood, these researchers urge continuing such programs for low-income college students as an investment strategy.

Low-income students are particularly vulnerable to the for-profit, predatory educational enterprises. Efforts must be made to keep EFY away from these institutions, because the outcome of contact with these institutions is burdensome debt and degrees or certificates that do not help much in the job market.

ILS Programs May Improve Educational Outcomes

Youth should be encouraged to participate in ILS programs, presumably with content that focuses on application procedures, financial aid, study skills, and so on. There is some evidence from nonrandomized studies that ILS programs contribute to better educational outcomes for EFY (Montgomery, Donkoh, & Underhill, 2006; Naccarato & DeLorenzo, 2008). An education-focused evaluation that used random assignment (Courtney et al., 2011a) found that youth formerly in intensive foster care who took part in an extended foster care program that had case management as a core feature were more likely than the control group to attend and persist in college. However, without more randomized studies, we cannot assert with certainty that ILS programs provide a benefit to EFY.

One evidence-based program for helping FFY with mental health challenges prepare for college was the Better Futures Program. Sixty-seven youth were randomly assigned to a treatment or control group. The intervention involved participation in a Summer Institute, postsecondary education preparation, individual peer coaching, and mentoring workshops. Significant gains were found in postsecondary participation and mental health empowerment. Positive trends were noted in high school completion, mental health status, and quality of life (Geenen, Powers, Phillips, Nelson, & McKenna, 2015).

Research Needs

Youth who enter college should be tracked until they complete their programs (or drop out). Such data might help us understand the needs of youth who pursue secondary education, and thus we may be able to design programs that more closely meet their needs.

CHAPTER SEVEN

Self-Sufficiency

*Employment, Earnings, and Receipt
of Public Benefits*

An important task of emerging adulthood is making a successful transition from schooling to work. This transition is also a major concern of social policy as expressed in the legislation discussed in Chapter 3 that emphasizes self-sufficiency. The collective research notes that many youth are discharged from care without employment or, as discussed in Chapter 6, an educational program. When youth find employment, it is often in low-income work. Earnings from these jobs are not enough to meet basic needs and leave many youth mired in poverty. These poor outcomes are linked to the educational difficulties discussed in the last chapter. In addition, many emancipated foster youth (EFY) have problems such as mental health difficulties and substance use and abuse issues that cause them employment problems (Lenz-Rashid, 2006).

Most of the former foster youth (FFY) studies reviewed in this chapter report that about one-half of EFY were working when interviewed. The Midwest Study, and other studies, used the ADD Health nationally representative sample (described in Chapter 5) as a comparison, and found that EFY consistently lagged the ADD Health youth in employment rates and earnings. In contrast to the FFY, 80 percent of the ADD Health respondents were employed (Courtney, Dworsky, et al., 2011). Most of the research suggests that females were more likely to have work than males unless pregnancy intervened (Courtney, Dworsky, et al., 2011; Dworsky, 2005; National Youth in Transition Database, 2014). Most of the research indicates that unemployed EFYs do report that they had worked at some point after discharge. Their work histories consist of cycling in and out of low-income work (Courtney, Dworsky,

Lee, & Rapp, 2010). Thus, they have employment histories, but staying connected to the labor market appears to be difficult for these youth. The employed FFY were not only working in low-income jobs, but they also felt less secure about their work, when compared with youth who had never been in out-of-home care (Salazar, 2013).

A number of researchers have used state-level administrative databases as a means of investigating the work and income trajectories of FFY. Findings from these studies mirror those research efforts that collected data directly from youth. Macomber et al.'s (2008) secondary data analysis is an example of this type of research. This study linked child welfare databases and unemployment insurance wage records from California, Minnesota, and North Carolina, and tracked youth longitudinally. These researchers found that only between 16 percent (North Carolina) to 25 percent (California) of FFY were working consistently between their discharge from care and age 24. Twenty-two percent of North Carolina youth, and 33 percent of youth in California never had a job. These researchers contrasted these findings with the results from the nationally representative sample, the National Longitudinal Survey of Youth. This comparison showed that youth never in care were more likely to be working and had much higher incomes than the FFY, well into emerging adulthood.

Another example of this type of research was conducted by Goerge et al. (2002). These researchers combined administrative data from Illinois, California, and South Carolina. Three groups were identified from the data for analysis: youth who left care via emancipation, FFY who were reunited with their family before emancipation, and low-income youth without foster care experience. Less than one-half (45 percent) of the EFY group, and the youth who went to live with their families before emancipation, had income in more than 3 quarters of the 13 quarters investigated. The low-income youth group did slightly better having income in a little over 50 percent of the quarters. This finding suggests that youth without foster care experience but with backgrounds similar to those foster youth were doing slightly better economically than the FFY. Most foster youth come from low-income (if not poverty) backgrounds and thus could be assumed to be much like the low-income youth except for out-of-home care experience. What foster youth have that the low-income group does not have is access to child welfare services (including a social worker) that are supposed to ameliorate some of the disadvantages that come from being low income.

A nationally representative survey, the 1988 National Survey of Households and Families (NSHF), suggests more positive employment findings for FFY than reported in most studies (Buehler, Orme, Post, & Patterson, 2000). As did Goerge and colleagues (2002), these researchers using the NSHF identified three groups for analysis from this dataset. First, they identified youth who had been in out-of-home care. Second, they identified a group from among the remaining sample composed of low-income youth. This group was matched with the foster youth on selected variables. The last group was randomly chosen from the remaining sample to represent youth in the general population. Buehler et al. (2000) found that more than 90 percent of adults in the survey were working. Significant statistical differences on employment were not observed between the three study groups. As with the Casey data reported in Chapter 6, the FFY in this database were older than in most studies of EFY, which may be the reason that more youth were working. The FFY group was also composed of not just EFY, but any youth with foster care experience. However, results were not all positive. Despite the lack of differences in the rate of employment, the FFY were more likely to have earnings that put them below the poverty line, when compared to the randomly chosen group. Both the matched group and the FFY group had similar poverty rates, but the FFY's income lagged the matched group by $2,000 a year. Their explanation for their findings is that spending time in foster care while a child may pose a risk to future economic well-being. These researchers also conclude with regard to economic well-being that foster youth are much more like poor children who were never in out-of-home care than they are like children from the general population.

Researchers who have followed FFY over time do note that income increases over time, but income often lags what is needed to stay out of poverty (Courtney, Dworsky, et al., 2011; Dworsky, 2005; Goerge et al., 2002; Naccarato, Brophy, & Courtney, 2010). The Casey Youth Survey found 36 percent of the sample was living below the poverty line, and 84 percent of the youth had incomes that the Casey researchers defined as less than a living wage, that is, an income that was below three times the poverty line (Havalchak, White, & O'Brien, 2008).

Thirty-eight percent of the Midwest Study's 26-year-olds did not earn at least $5,000 a year. The overall sample said their median yearly income was $8,950 (Courtney, Dworsky, et al., 2011). Nineteen-year-old EFYs in Los Angeles reported median yearly earnings of $4,000 (Pergamit & Johnson, 2009). Dworsky (2005) followed FFY in Wisconsin for two years in order to track their income and their usage public benefits. She found a cyclical pattern of employment/unemployment over time. She also found that the cumulative income over the entire period did not equal what a full-time worker would earn if employed continuously over the two-year period. The ADD Health comparison sample had a median income of $27,310 a year. Salazar (2013) contrasted Casey alumni who were college graduates with a sample of similar degree holders from the nationally representative General Social Survey (GSS) that is used as a comparison in Casey studies. Individual income reported by the two samples was similar, but GSS household incomes were $15,000 to $25,000 higher than the amounts reported by the Casey youth ($40,000 to 49,000 versus $25,000 to 29,999). About 30 percent of residents of a statewide transitional housing program in California did not have any income at all. Those residents with an income reported a median yearly income of $8,724 (Kimberlin & Lemley, 2012). Courtney, Zinn, et al. (2011a) also reported that EFY were less likely than the ADD Health comparisons to be working in jobs that included benefits such as health care or vacations with pay. Seventy-seven percent of ADD Health youth had jobs that provided them with the benefit of a paid vacation. Only 52 percent of the Midwest Study youth were working in positions that had paid vacations as a benefit. Having this benefit is important, not only for having the ability to take a vacation, but to also for having the option to take a day off to address an out-of-work concern, such as taking care of a sick child.

Midwest Study researchers identified that employment during adolescence was positively associated with increased earnings and chances of employment. The likelihood of having income derived from work increased if the youth had employment in the last quarter of the year prior to turning age 18. Not being employed in that quarter was associated with a lack of income through age 20 (Courtney, Dworsky, Cusick, et al., 2009). Macomber et al. (2008) also found that if youth were employed between ages 16 and 18, they had a greater chance of working consistently to age 24. They note that the relationship between early working and future employment might be unrelated to child welfare intervention, but instead was a byproduct of the youth's characteristics, such as their desire to work or be self-sufficient. Nevertheless, many foster youth do not have the opportunity to work before leaving care. Data from the National Youth in Transition Database suggest only about one-third of 17-year-old foster adolescents had a job (National Youth in Transition Database, 2014b).

In Chapter 6, we saw that some youth were able to show resilience by graduating high school or going on to postsecondary education and earning a degree at that level. Other youth also exhibited resilience by working, increasing their income over time, and earning enough money to meet their basic needs. The characteristics of these resilient youth were that at discharge from care, they had employment, were more likely to extend their stay in care, were older when they left care, were disproportionately female, and had a high school diploma (Barnow et al., 2015; Dworsky, 2005; Fallesen, 2013; Pecora, Kessler, et al., 2006).

Mental health problems were associated with lower incomes in the Midwest Study. Surprisingly, alcohol and drug use were associated with an increase in earnings. The researchers' explanation for this finding was that work provided the money necessary to purchase alcohol or drugs. An alternative explanation is that youth when interviewed had met the study's operational definition for alcohol and drug use/abuse but had stopped using when they were working (Naccarato et al., 2010). Other studies have contradicted this finding and report drugs or alcohol use/abuse has negative impacts on employment and income (Lenz-Rashid, 2006).

Vulnerable Groups

It should not come as a surprise that studies report employment and earnings for African Americans lag behind other groups. Among 24-year-old Midwest Study African American youth, 40 percent were without work. Sixty percent of white youth were working at that age (Courtney, Dworsky, et al., 2010). Dworsky (2005) also reports that the following variables predicted decreased earnings in her sample: being African American or Hispanic, voluntary placement, running away from placement, or having had an institutional placement. However, African American youth who were working had higher wages than working white youth. This difference may mean employed African Americans had higher levels of human capital than did the white youth. Findings on ethnicity vary across studies. Goerge and colleagues' (2002) findings were mixed on race, ethnicity, and gender in the three states they examined. In South Carolina no effect was observed with these variables on employment. However, in the other states African Americans were less likely to be working than other youth. African Americans who were working had lower earnings than the other FFY in all three states investigated. Hispanic youth in California were more likely to be employed than youth from other ethnic groups (Courtney et al., 2016). African Americans were less likely than other racial/ethnic groups to have a job in Illinois. Leathers and Testa (2006) reported similar findings in their survey of Illinois caseworkers who said that their African American former clients were more likely than the other groups to be unemployed. Macomber et al. (2008) found that whites had more employment stability and higher earnings than the other ethnicities investigated.

Lenz-Rashid (2006) compared the experiences of homeless FFY with homeless youth who had never been in foster care. She found Hispanic FFY had higher earnings than nonfoster Hispanic youth. Lenz-Rashid concludes that the independent living services (ILS) available to foster youth may have given them opportunities to learn job readiness skills and other skills necessary to find employment, such as how to search for a job. Hispanic youth in Texas who had been through an ILS program were more likely to be working than non-Hispanic youth who never had ILS training (Scannapieco, Smith, & Blakeney-Strong, 2016). ILS programs may have allowed foster youth to add to their human capital. More research is needed in determining how ILS contributes to helping youth become part of the labor force.

Eighty percent of African American Casey alumni reported earnings that placed them below the poverty line. In sharp contrast one-third of the white alumni had incomes that put them below the poverty line. When impact of race on income was considered in multivariate analysis, race/ethnicity's effect on earnings was no longer significant. Other variables were more important in determining income than race, such as the age when interviewed, being learning disabled, not receiving support services before or after leaving care, and the relationship with foster parents (Harris, Jackson, O'Brien, & Pecora, 2010).

Most researchers support the assertion that African Americans are handicapped in finding employment during the period of emerging adulthood. Specifically, they are subject to racial bias in looking for work. Some research suggests that African American adolescents put more effort into job seeking than do white adolescents, but despite these efforts, they are less likely to find work (Entwisle, Alexander, & Steffel-Olsen, 2000). They are also likely to reside in communities with high unemployment levels. The lack of jobs results in heavy competition for what work is available.

Data from the Casey National Alumni Study found that two-thirds of American Indian/Native American alumni lived in a household that had an income below the poverty line, and only one-fifth of these FFY had Casey's living wage. This rate was far worse than other groups. They were also less likely to work than were white alumni (60 percent versus 77 percent) (O'Brien et al., 2010).

The variations in employment findings across states and communities are a result of economic conditions (such as the number of jobs available and labor force participation rates), demographic and socioeconomic variations among FFY studied, independent living preparation policies of the state in which the youth was in foster care, age when they left care, and how the individual is helped to prepare for the transition to independent living.

Dworsky (2005) reported that female FFY were more likely to be working, had higher incomes, and were less likely to be incarcerated than were their male counterparts. They were also more likely to be collecting public benefits, because the presence of children made them eligible for assistance (Dworsky, 2005). Dworsky notes (2005) that the higher incomes and employment rates found among females when compared to males was a result of their higher educational attainments when compared to their male counterparts (discussed in Chapter 6). However, gender differences in income were not found in Illinois (Goerge et al., 2002), but in the other two states these researchers investigated they found that males had higher earnings than females. Their study was somewhat different than many of the studies reviewed in this book because in addition to EFY, their sample contained FFY who had been reunited with their families or had been adopted. These youth were more likely to be working than EFY. It is possible that parents or other family members helped youth find jobs. An alternate explanation is that families placed pressure on youth to look for work, and when found, would not allow them to quit that job.

Types of Capital and Work Earnings

One means of examining the employment and income deficits of FFY is to use capital theory. *Human capital* refers to education and the job skill set that a person might possess that equips them for success in the labor market, and is a determinant of their future income. Chapter 6 demonstrated that human capital of FFY is quite low. *Personal capital* consists of behavioral and personal characteristics that would help them find and maintain employment (Hook & Courtney, 2011). Courtney, Hook, and Lee (2010), after combining the Midwest Study sample with data from the National Youth in Transition Database (2014, September) for analysis, gave us an illustration of how *personal capital* works against employment. These researchers found that male EFY have significant involvement with the criminal justice system, including incarceration, that limits their job prospects. Specifically, incarceration reduced the chances of employment by 25 percent among Midwest Study youth. In Chapter 12 the problem of the disproportionate involvement of African American EFY in the criminal justice system is discussed. This involvement explains at least some of the employment problems for this group that were discussed earlier. In contrast, pregnancy and parenting create problems for female EFY who are seeking work (a topic in Chapter 11). However, parenting females can be partially compensated for not working by utilizing public benefits. Mental health and behavioral problems, which are highly prevalent in FFY populations (discussed in Chapter 10), have been shown to be a major factor in determining whether someone was working (Lenz-Rashid, 2006).

Social capital is the relationships that person has that can assist them in finding employment opportunities. For example, persons in a youth's social network can identify work vacancies that a youth could apply to fill, or put in "a good word" for them with a potential employer. Growing up in care may isolate youth from developing these types of contacts that they might have found in their family or neighborhood. Placement mobility or residing in group care may be a barrier to forming close relationships with these supportive adults who could help youth make those social connections.

Hook and Courtney (2011) provide evidence of the damage that placement change could have for earnings. They report that each move a foster child experienced was associated with a 7 percent loss in future income. They do think it is possible that the behavioral problems that may have triggered the move were responsible for findings on income. Behavioral problems may inhibit job finding, and if working could cause problems with holding that job. These researchers also report that youth residing in a group home or institution were less likely to be working after leaving care than youth who had been in family or kin foster care. Youth who had been in kinship care were 30 percent less likely to be working after discharge than youth coming from family foster care.

Receiving Public Benefits

In addition to employment, the receipt of public benefits has been used by many researchers as an outcome measure in determining whether a youth is self-sufficient. Most researchers define the collecting of government benefits negatively, that it indicates that an FFY is not meeting the Foster Care Independence Act's goal of self-sufficiency. The available evidence suggests many FFY are not meeting this goal.

Seventy-seven percent of Midwest Study females and 48 percent of the males were recipients of at least one of the following benefits in the previous year; Unemployment Insurance, Temporary Assistance for Needy Families (TANF), Supplemental Security Income (SSI), food stamps, public housing or rental assistance, or Women, Infants, and Children (WIC, a supplementary food program for low-income mothers and their children). Sixty-eight percent of females and 41 percent of males received Food Stamps, which made it the most frequently used benefit in that study. At age 26, 56 percent of Midwest Study youth were collecting Food Stamps. In 2012, the national rate of Food Stamp use was 13.4 percent. Of Midwest Study youth, 15 percent of the females and 2 percent of males received TANF, a cash assistance program. Only 1 percent of the general population collected TANF in 2012. Similarly, the reliance by EFY on housing assistance was twice the rate found in the general population (9.3 percent versus 4.2 percent); SSI was received at almost 5 times the rate in the nonfoster population (14.4 percent versus 3 percent) The reliance on government benefits had declined by age 26, but it was still higher than what is found in the general population (Courtney, Dworsky, et al., 2011; Irving & Loveless, 2015). The other EYF studies that have examined the reliance on public support programs support the Midwest Study findings, and suggest that 30 percent to 40 percent of youth rely on these benefits (Cook, Fleishman, & Grimes, 1991; Dworsky, 2005; Goerge et al., 2002; Havalchak et al., 2008; Kimberlin & Lemley, 2012; Needell, Cuccaro-Alamin, Brookhart, Jackman, & Schlonsky, 2002).

Analysis of Wisconsin administrative data revealed that in the first two years after leaving care one-third of FFY received TANF or food stamps (Dworsky, 2005). Youth who avoided the reliance on these two types of assistance were male, white, and had longer stays in foster care. Having employment on discharge was strongly predictive of future work and earnings; not having work upon leaving care did not automatically mean that one collected public cash assistance. Dworsky's analysis was done at a time (1992–1998) that was noted for its relative prosperity. The economy was generating jobs that youth could fill. TANF also replaced Aid for Dependent Children during this period. It should have been expected that TANF rolls would have dropped because of the increased number of jobs available. TANF participation rates have always lagged those of the AFDC program. TANF also had much more strict work requirements on its participants than did AFDC, which made it a more unattractive option than its predecessor. TANF, like the old AFDC program, tended to place its participants in low-income work. The Wisconsin data suggested that FFY who were unable to find work were more likely to rely on the Food Stamp program than they were to participate in TANF. This trend was observed in the general population. The utilization of Food Stamps rose dramatically in the United States over the last two decades, with some observers suggesting Food Stamps had become the new safety net replacing TANF in that role (Yu, Lombe, & Nebbit, 2010). In support of this assertion see earlier in this chapter for data on the receipt of these two programs. It should be expected that minority youth were more likely than whites to be recipients of public benefits, because of widely acknowledged problems of racism and discrimination that handicaps their participation in the work force. As discussed earlier, the greater prevalence of females collecting benefits, as opposed to males, is explained by the fact that females are more likely than males to be a sole custodial parent. Dependent children made them eligible for benefits.

The unmistakable conclusion is that EFY are much more likely to rely on government assistance than other youth. Dworsky (2005) notes that youth leave care with the assumption that they will live independently, but in reality they quickly again are dependent on the same government that they had relied on while in foster care. However, the collection of public benefits need not be viewed solely as a deficit. Seeking and then receiving benefits could be viewed as a strength because it may mean youth are demonstrating the ability to meet their basic needs, which in some cases means they can continue their education or take care of their children.

Home Ownership and Other Assets

The process of building up assets is an important part of transition and becoming a self-sufficient adult. Assets provide the financial means to reach a person's goals for themselves, as well as help them become a contributing member to a larger society (Greeson, Usher, & Grinstein-Weiss, 2010). In Chapter 2, it was noted most youth can expect their parents to help with transitioning into emerging adulthood, which includes giving monetary assistance, and assisting youth to develop assets (sometimes referred to as wealth). These assets include houses, cars, academic degrees, savings, 401(k)s, and maybe a small business. Accumulating assets is not only how a person accomplished their financial goals; research indicates reaching these goals has positive psychosocial benefits. These benefits include enhanced life satisfaction, fewer episodes of depression, decreased alcohol abuse (Rohe & Stegman, 1994; Yadama & Sherraden, 1996), improved health status (Robert & House, 1996), more civic engagement (Van Zandt & Rohe, 2006), and better mental health not only for the person but also for their children. Their children also attain higher levels of education and avoid teenage pregnancy. Asset development should be given attention during the period of emerging adulthood because of its importance in obtaining self-sufficiency, promoting the well-being of EFY and their families, and enabling youth to reach their life goals.

An anecdote from 2012 demonstrated the lack of understanding of the reality of disadvantaged youth exhibited by many policy makers. Presidential campaign candidate Mitt Romney urged a group of college students to ask their parents for loans to start small businesses as an answer to the economic recession that was occurring at the time. Romney told the college students a story regarding a son of a friend who received a loan from his parents to open a Subway sandwich shop that would have required an $80,000 investment (MSNBC, 2012). Some youth have families able to provide this level of financial assistance for their offspring, but this level of support is not the reality of former FFY. The reality for EFY leaving care is illustrated in Nevada, where many youth discharged from care had just $250 (Reilly, 2003). This amount of money is insufficient for funding a youth effort to become independent.

It is widely acknowledged that the home is a person's largest asset. Available data suggest that FFY lag the general population in homeownership. The twenty-six-year-olds in the Midwest Study had 9 percent of the EFY as homeowners. In sharp contrast, 30 percent of the ADD Health comparisons own a home at age 26 (Courtney, Dworsky, et al., 2011). This difference between the two studies in homeownership was found even with youth who had finished college. Data from two Casey Family studies (Pecora, Kessler, et al., 2006; Pecora, Williams, et al., 2003) found homeownership was about one-half of the rate of their comparison group, the General Social Survey (Salazar, 2013). Buehler et al. (2000) found that foster youth were less likely to own a home than the group chosen to represent the general population (40 percent versus 64 percent). They also had a lower home ownership rate than did the low-income matched group (40 percent versus 54 percent). Both the Casey and Buehler et al. samples were composed of youth who were older than the Midwest Study sample. This age difference may have accounted for the divergent findings between these studies on home ownership. Buehler et al.'s FFY were more likely to be apartment dwellers than live in a house.

Salazar (2013) examined other assets among Midwest Study youth, and reported that only 47 percent of the EFY owned a car and less than one-half of youth had a bank account (48 percent). Similarly, Pergamit and Johnson (2009) found EFY in Los Angeles had similar rates of having bank accounts as the Midwest Study youth. Possessing a bank account alone can be misleading on how well you are doing in acquiring assets. The Los Angeles EFY, including those with bank accounts, said the median amount of money they had available to them at the time of the interview was $100. In contrast, 73 percent of the ADD Health Study comparisons owned an automobile, and 82 percent of youth in that study had a bank account. The lack of a bank account by EFY suggests they might not have cash available to cope with a crisis they might have. Not owning a motor vehicle is likely to be a hindrance in keeping connected to the labor market.

Economic Hardships and Well-Being

Low incomes and insufficient savings make many EYF vulnerable to crises caused by something like an unexpected bill or a rent increase. The Midwest Study examined this vulnerability by querying respondents about five possible economic hardships. These hardships included not having the money to cover the rent, being unable to pay a utility bill, having experienced a utility shutoff for nonpayment, losing their telephone service, or suffering an eviction from their domicile. At each wave of the study, 50 percent of the Midwest sample said that they had experienced at least one of these economic hardships, which was always at least twice the rate of the ADD Health comparisons (Courtney, Dworsky, et al., 2010).

At ages 23–24, about a third of the youth had lost their phone service at some point in the previous year, which was the most frequently occurring hardship. Not having a phone would be a handicap in a job search. A little over one-quarter of the sample (27 percent) were evicted from an apartment because of nonpayment of rent. A similar number of youth reported that they did not have the money to pay a gas or electric bill (Courtney, Dworsky, Cusick, et al., 2009). Housing problems are taken up in the next chapter. Once again ADD Health respondents were much less likely to report similar problems. Only 9 percent of that sample reported an inability to pay rent and 11 percent were unable at some point to pay an electric or gas bill (Courtney, Dworsky, et al., 2010). These types of problems would make youth vulnerable to credit problems that can adversely affect job search when they fail an employer's credit check.

Twenty-one-year-olds in the sample said they were food insecure. At age 24, the number of Midwest Study youth reporting food insecurity had risen to 29 percent. *Food insecurity* means a person does not always have access to enough food for an active healthy life and may mean youth are skipping meals because of a lack of money. Thirteen percent of a sample of Los Angeles EFY said they had experienced hunger because they did not have the money to purchase food (Pergamit & Johnson, 2009). The U.S. Department of Agriculture regards hunger as a more serious problem and byproduct of food insecurity (Feeding America, 2016). We can compare the experiences of Midwest Study 19-year-olds who exited foster care versus those who took advantage of extended foster care. Youth in care were less likely to experience any of the material hardships than youth who left the system. Four percent of the youth who took advantage of extended care said they were food insecure, whereas 12 percent of youth who had left care reported food insecurity (Courtney & Dworsky, 2006). This analysis provides even more evidence for the advisability of extending foster care.

Practical Recommendations for Improving Employment Outcomes

Extend Foster Care

Data showing that youth can benefit from an extension of foster care continues to accumulate. Length of time in care has been positively associated with likelihood of employment and higher earnings (Barnow et al., 2015, Courtney, Dworsky, et al., 2011; Fallesen, 2013; Hook & Courtney, 2011; Kerman, Wildfire, & Barth, 2002). In the previous chapter, additional time in care was shown to improve high school completion and college attendance rates. Youth need services after age 18 over an extended period. Specifically, Courtney, Hook, and Lee (2010) assert from their cost-benefit analysis that each additional year in care increases the likelihood of employment by 18 percent.

Minimum Provisions That Youth Need on Leaving Care for Employment

It is essential on discharge that youth have either an educational program or a career-oriented job. Follow-ups with youth should ascertain how well youth are doing with their employment career trajectories, and if barriers are identified, youth should be provided assistance to eliminate these barriers. This help should be included in their individualized independent living plan. Career planning should begin in independent living programs. Careers mean students have a path to employment that provides for an increase in earnings over time, as well for advancement. Researchers have noted that the cyclical pattern of employment is a problem associated with low-income work (Macomber et al., 2008). Working in better paying positions that have advancement potential would contribute to both financial security and job stability. However, it should be recognized that locating better paying positions for this group is difficult. One-half of America's minimum wage workers are ages 16 to 24 (Silver, 2014). If youth are to go beyond minimum wage work, they need to acquire more human capital through further education. A high school education may not be enough. Other alternatives to college such as vocational training ought to be considered. College is not for everyone. Some youth may not have the skills to succeed or the inclination for education at that level. It should be noted that many careers do not require college and can provide good salaries.

ILS Programs May Improve Employment Outcomes

ILS programs should provide employment and vocational training services, job placement, and financial literacy components. Evidence presented in this chapter points to the benefits of early work experiences. Beginning at age 16, youth ILS programs should be helping youth with obtaining these experiences. These experiences include part-time work, summer employment, internships (paid if possible), and apprenticeships. These opportunities would give foster youth the chance to earn money, accumulate savings, and practice managing finances prior to having to do these things on their own. Classroom instruction may not help youth acquire the job-related skills that are needed. These types of experiences will aid foster youth to gain work experience that they can use to build a résumé, and it will help them acquire job maintenance skills like punctuality and maturity. These types of skills may be essential to breaking the cycle of being in and out of work. Leathers and Testa (2006) report that the child welfare case workers they interviewed said foster youth lack job-retention skills. Youth not only need training that makes them job ready but also need to know how to keep any job they find (Barth, 1990; Lenz-Rashid, 2006). ILS funds could be used to pay for these efforts (Dworsky, 2005).

Two strategies to help youth with adapting to the work world are mentoring and job coaching. Mentoring is discussed in Chapter 13. In the employment sphere, mentoring entails providing youth with the knowledge regarding the pathways to desirable job opportunities and is seen as a crucial part of career development. If the mentor is someone from a similar socioeconomic background, the youth could also gain a role model. Job coaching is similar, but seeks to help deal with issues specific to a particular job. Mentors focus on broader issues of career development (Lenz-Rashid, 2006).

Youth would also be eligible for employment and training services funded under the Workforce Investment Act of 1998 (U.S. Department of Labor, 2000). The use of tax credits as incentives for the hiring of FFY is another route to job creation for FFY that should be considered (Atkinson, 2008). States might also consider providing stipends for ILS participants, who on average have little or no income after leaving care.

The ILS evaluation literature is not definitive on their effectiveness with helping youth obtain better work and income outcomes. A systematic research review of ILS evaluations reached the conclusion that ILS do contribute to more positive work outcomes for youth participants of those programs (Montgomery, Donkoh, & Underhill, 2006). However, the Multi-Site Evaluation of Foster Youth Program (MSEFYP), which used random assignment, found no relationship between ILS participation and more positive economic outcomes (Courtney, Zinn, et al., 2011a). Okpych and Courtney (2014) also reported, with some surprise, that the Midwest Study youth who had participated in an

ILS program at age 17 were less likely than those EFY who had not taken part in ILS to be employed at age 25 or 26. Courtney, Zinn, and colleagues thought they might have found more positive findings in MSEFYP had they not been conducting the research during the Great Recession in an area that already had high unemployment. Also, many of the ILS evaluations reviewed by Montgomery and colleagues (2006) were done in a time of relative prosperity. It is to be expected that youth entering the labor market at a time of economic downturn would find it more difficult to secure work. Courtney and fellow researchers also criticized the program for not being more aggressive in its efforts to help youth find jobs, which these researchers thought was needed as a way of improving employment outcomes with EFY.

Evaluations of programs using experimental designs are a must in order to identify interventions that are effective with improving FFY employment prospects. The data presented in this chapter suggest many youth are not well prepared for the labor force. Okpych and Courtney (2014) speculated that maybe ILS participants are youth with more challenges than youth who do not take part in these programs, or that ILS training as it currently exists is just not very good.

Despite the mixed findings on the effectiveness of ILS on improving the economic prospects for EFY, these programs do have a place in preparing youth for discharge, given the public policy emphasis on self-sufficiency. In order to be effective, this training needs to have the hands-on experiences described earlier in this chapter (Iglehart, 1994). ILS programs are a vehicle for preparing youth to interview for jobs, construct a résumé, learn work retention skills, and teach them financial literacy skills.

EFY also need to know how to budget a limited income, and should be aware of some traps that low-income workers can fall into. These include predatory payday or title loans. Child welfare social workers also have to be educated about these issues. This content might not have been part of their MSW or BSW program. Some social work educators have given attention to what social workers need to know when working with low-income clients. These educators have developed curriculum on financial literacy and management that are meant to provide social workers with the skills they need to effectively help youth. These curricula could be viewed as a start toward more extensive training for intervention in this area (Jacobson, Sander, Svoboda, & Elkinson, 2011).

Assisting Vulnerable Groups with Employment

The research does identify a number of vulnerable groups within the larger community of FFY who need special attention. Naccarato et al. (2010) reported that mental health problems, particularly post-traumatic stress disorder, were associated with lower incomes among Midwest Study youth. The need for mental health services, both before youth leave care and after, is a subject in Chapter 10. Specialized ILS programs must be developed that respond to the needs of youth with mental health problems. Because of the vulnerability revealed in the research regarding FFY of color, particularly African Americans, additional efforts must be made to prepare youth for work or school in a culturally appropriate manner (Hook & Courtney, 2011).

An overlooked group who often do not receive ILS are those FFY who reunite with their families (or are adopted or go to a guardianship) before emancipation. Public policy assumes that their families are providing the preparation for emerging adulthood. Available data indicates theses youth also have poor employment and earnings outcomes. These youth ought to be offered these services if needed (Dworsky, 2005).

Tangible Needs on Leaving Care

One way to prepare youth to leave care and begin the process of asset accumulation is to have youth develop Individual Development Accounts and Youth Opportunity Passports. This is a strategy developed by Casey Family Programs. Casey establishes a bank account for youth when they turn age 14. Youth savings are matched by Casey. Casey also provides the youth a financial literacy program. These services aid youth in developing a financial cushion that enables them to move toward independence on leaving care. Alleviating some of their financial worries may enable youth to focus on their continued education and/or work program (Pecora et al., 2006; Peters et al., 2016).

Casey Family Services provides additional tangible resources for their alumni up to age 26. These resources include such things as housing support, in the form of household items necessary to establish a household or equip a dorm room (mattresses, kitchen wares, security deposit, first and last month's rent, and so on), clothing vouchers to purchase a wardrobe needed for a job search or employment, and financial help with school tuition and book costs. Youth are also assisted in making connections to family (Pecora et al., 2006; Peters et al., 2016). Mares (2010) noted in his qualitative study that youth were specifically requesting these types of tangible assistance. Kerman et al. (2002), who completed a cost/benefit analysis of the Casey effort, note that expenditures on tangible resources are associated with fewer after-care problems. They estimate that an expenditure of about $4,000 a year for two to eight years would have long-term payouts. If such support could stop a youth from dropping out of school or becoming homeless, it would be worth the monetary expenditure.

Transportation problems are often cited as barriers to school attendance, and in both finding and retaining work (Jones, 2014a). In most places in the United States, public transportation options are limited. Thirty-five California

EFY in an extended foster care program were interviewed by Napolitano and Courtney (2014). Only two of these youth indicated that they had access to a car. Keeping a work or school schedule without a car can be difficult to impossible. Most of the youth working and/or attending school said that they had a two-hour daily commute. Foster youth need to be assisted, perhaps with public and private funds, with getting financial assistance to buy a car, obtaining insurance for that vehicle, and having access to emergency funds when car repairs are needed. This effort would also help the student in begin asset accumulation.

CHAPTER EIGHT

Housing and the Dangers of Homelessness

A stable domicile is almost a prerequisite for self-sufficiency. A fixed address is needed to secure employment, receive public benefits, attend school, and gain a sense of security. Unstable and/or unsafe housing can result in negative consequences for physical and mental health (Crowley, 2003; Leventhal & Newman, 2010). Establishing an independent household is also one of the markers of a successful transition to adulthood. A task of emerging adulthood is to secure a safe, stable, and affordable place to live (Mech, 2003).

Foster youth face steep challenges in this area. Housing instability accompanies economic problems discussed in Chapter 7. The lack of a dependable monthly income makes it difficult to pay rent. This income deficit is a major factor contributing to the high rate of homelessness found among discharged foster youth (Barth, 1990; Berzin, Rhodes, & Curtis, 2011; Cook, 1994; Courtney, Piliavin, Grogan-Kaylor, & Nesmith, 2001; Merdinger, Hines, Lemon, Osterling, & Wyatt, 2005; Rashid, 2004). Because they may not have relationships with their parents, or because their parents do not have resources, former foster youth (FFY) often do not have anyone who can cosign a lease, which results in them not being able to obtain safe and secure housing (Unrau, Font, & Rawls, 2012). As discussed in Chapter 2, emancipated foster youth (EFY) may not have a family home to return to upon discharge, and/or they cannot depend upon the family home as a fallback position when other arrangements do not work out. EFY are less likely than youth in the general population to live with parents or other family members, which may be indicative of strained family relations (Berzin et al., 2011; Iglehart, 1994). They may also leave care unprepared for the process of finding and keeping a residence, and they often receive little support in securing housing (Courtney et al., 2001; Reilly, 2003). They may also be young parents, or they may have criminal records. Youth formerly in care, as we will see in later chapters, often have considerable problems with mental health and substance abuse that make finding stable housing even more difficult.

The housing market also presents barriers. One estimate is that there are only 30 low-income residences for every one who needs them (Baker, 2014). The lack of affordable housing, racial discrimination, and lack of a rental history because of their young age all contribute to FFY's problem of finding secure housing (Dion, Dworsky, Huff, & Kleinman, 2014). Thus, assistance with housing is crucial in helping this group complete the gradual movement toward adulthood described by Arnett (2000).

Homelessness

The most serious problem noted with FFY in regards to housing is homelessness. Studies reviewed in the chapter that have examined FFY post–foster care adaptation give a range of homelessness among FFY from 9 percent to 36 percent. The incidence of homelessness in the U.S. population is about 1 percent (Berzin et al., 2011; Kushel, Yen, Gee, & Courtney, 2007).

The variations in estimates of homelessness reflect differences in ages of the youth included in a study sample, the area of the country from which the sample was obtained, how long the youth had been out of care, the representativeness of the subjects, and how the researchers defined homelessness (Dion et al., 2014). Most studies define homelessness as being without a place to sleep for one night. The Midwest Study considered youth to be homeless if they were "sleeping in a place where people were not meant to sleep, or sleeping in a homeless shelter, or not having a regular residence in which to sleep" (Dworsky, 2010, p.3). Merdinger et al. (2005) reported that in their sample homeless youth were without housing for an average of 75 days, with a median of 30 days on the streets. Data from the National Youth Transition Database (2014, September) found that 34 percent of the youth who had experienced homelessness at age 19 also reported being homeless at age 17.

Other studies of homeless shelter populations reveal that about 20 percent of the residents of shelters are FFY (Park, Metraux, & Culhane, 2004; Roman & Wolfe, 1997). Park and colleagues also found that homeless EFY had longer stays in shelters than FFY who went to live with a parent. According to Stoner (1999), 15 percent to 39 percent of the nation's homeless are FFY. A national survey of homeless reported that 40 percent of the homeless population had been in the foster care system (Aran, Valente, & Iwen, 1999). Piliavin, Bradley, Wright, Mare, and Westerfelt (1996) found that 39 percent of 331 homeless adults in Minnesota had been in foster care. At the time of this study, 2 percent of the general population had been in foster care. Roman and Wolfe (1997) assert that homeless FFY are more likely than nonfoster youth to have their children placed in foster care. Park, Fertig, and Metraux (2014) say that child welfare involvement, incarceration, or mental health hospitalization pose similar risks for becoming homeless. They make this connection because prevalence rates among shelter populations are similar for criminal justice, mental health, and child welfare involvement.

Homeless adolescents have problems that may make it more difficult to remain housed. They have extensive substance abuse problems (Van Leeuwen et al., 2004; Shah, Albrecht, & Felver, 2013), engage in risky sexual behavior (Ensign & Santelli, 1997), and are prone to more physical and sexual victimizations (Fowler, Marcal, Zhang, Day, & Landsverk, 2017; Kipke, Simon, Montgomery, Unger, & Iversen, 1997). They also have more unplanned pregnancies (Green & Ringwalt, 1998; Kushel, Yen, Gee, & Courtney, 2007), mental health difficulties (Kipke et al., 1997; Shah et al., 2013), and health problems (Kushel et al., 2007) than their housed counterparts in the general population do. A Washington State study of 1,100 EFY found that youth who experienced homelessness were 42 percent less likely to be employed than youth who had stable housing in the first 10 months after discharge. Even when employed, homeless EFY had lower incomes than EFY without identified housing needs (Shah et al., 2013).

In the Midwest study, 54 percent of EFY experienced unstable housing or homelessness (Kushel et al., 2007). At age 19, one year out of foster care, 14 percent of the Midwest Study sample had experienced homelessness. Two-thirds of these youth who had experienced homelessness did so in the first six months after leaving care. The Midwest Study youth who had never been homeless had experienced, on average, three housing moves in the first 14 months after discharge (Courtney & Dworsky, 2005). Even they do not experience homelessness; frequent moves and/or "couch surfing" are the reality for many EFY (Courtney, Dworsky, Brown, et al., 2011; Dworsky & Courtney, 2009a; Perez & Romo, 2011). Couch surfing is sleeping on the couches of friends temporarily when one cannot afford one's own fixed address; this, along with moving frequently, is often seen as a precursor to homelessness (Perez & Romo, 2011). At age 26 approximately 31 percent of Courtney and colleagues' sample had been homeless or couch surfed in the past year or two (Courtney, Dworsky, Brown, et al., 2011). At ages 23–24, nearly 40 percent of the Midwest Study sample had either couch surfed or been without their own housing (Courtney, Dworsky, Lee, & Rapp, 2010).

The overrepresentation of FFY among the nation's homeless population is explained in several ways. Most economists agree that a person's largest expenditure is housing. The average American spends 36 percent of their income on housing. Poor Americans spend a larger proportion of their income (56 percent) on housing (Scopelliti, 2014) which makes them even more vulnerable to crisis because they do not have the wherewithal to build up savings to cope with an unexpected crisis. According to the National

Housing Coalition, there is not a single state where a minimum-wage worker could afford a one-bedroom apartment if he or she spent no more than the recommended 30 percent of their income on rent. If the minimum wage was increased to $15, the outer range suggested in the most recent attempts to raise that wage, a one-bedroom apartment would be affordable in only 21 states. Most of these states are located in the South, Midwest, Great Plains, and Mountain West regions of the country (Zeeshan, 2015).

Federal housing assistance is available for low-income people. However, it is not an entitlement, and has never reached more than a small portion of eligible persons (Park et al., 2014). The search for public housing or vouchers can mean encounters with long waiting lists or residences in undesirable housing. EFY often lack the skills to search for an apartment, the money to pay deposits and move-in costs, and the funds to stock an apartment with the necessities (Duke-Lucio, Peck, & Segal, 2010).

Living Arrangements after Leaving Care

A California Department of Social Services (2002) needs assessment reported that 65 percent of youth emancipating from foster care in 2000–2001 were in need of safe, affordable housing. County public child welfare agencies assisted about 38 percent of those youth in finding housing. One year later, they were still working with 41 percent of the youth on finding them a suitable place to live. How the other youth fared with housing is not known. The CDSS estimated that the state needed to develop another 3,762 additional suitable living arrangements for youth. However, dividing the state allocation for EFY needing housing by the amount available came to only $1,266 a year per youth, which would seem inadequate to address the housing needs of EFY in California.

Kroner and Mares (2011), among other researchers, note that EFY's preferred living relationship is to live on their own rather than returning to the family home. The Midwest Study found that at age 19, those youth who left care were most likely to be living on their own (29 percent). Less rigorous research has reported higher rates of youth living independently at age 19 or 20 than did the Midwest Study (a range of 36 percent to 82 percent) (Georgiades, 2005; Kroner and Mares, 2011; Lindsey & Ahmed, 1999; Scannapieco, Schagrin, & Scannapieco, 1995). Most of these studies examined youth participating in or leaving independent living programs, whom you would expect to have more stable housing. The second largest group of Midwest Study EFY left care to live with relatives other than parents (18 percent), followed closely by living with their parents (17 percent). About one-half of those 19-year-olds who remained in care were in supervised settings (Courtney & Dworsky, 2005). These patterns held true at ages 23 and 24, but about one-half of youth were living "in their own place" (Courtney, Dworsky, et al.,

2010). At age, 26 about two-thirds of the Courtney, Dworsky, et al. sample (2011) were living independently by themselves or with a spouse or partner. Four percent of the sample was living with their parents at that age. Seventeen percent of the ADD Health sample was living with their parents at age 26 (Courtney, Dworsky, et al., 2011). Berzin et al. (2011), who used the National Longitudinal Survey of Youth data, found that FFY moved out of the home at similar rates as nonfoster youth, but they were less likely to return home once they had left. Forty-three percent of foster youth never returned home once they left care versus 33 percent of nonfoster youth. Foster youth were also more likely to live in public housing (7.5 percent) than a matched group of nonfoster care low-income youth (3.5 percent), or a representative group selected at random (2 percent).

Housing Instability

During the transition period, housing can be in flux for most youth who are waiting for careers and incomes to develop and grow. Youth can expect a period of frequent moves (housing instability), apartments with a shifting cast of roommates, and lower-quality housing. Some of these moves, as discussed in Chapter 2, include cycling in and out of the parental home. Housing situations will improve and become more stable if income grows. The impact of these moves on a youth is influenced by the reason for the change of residence. A move driven by a desire for a safer neighborhood, better apartment, or having a desired roommate has a different effect on a person than a move dictated by an eviction. EFY are more likely to move because they are forced to do so by others, and thus residential mobility is likely to be viewed negatively by EFY (Curry & Abrams, 2015).

At ages 23 and 24, two-thirds of the Midwest Study youth had moved three times since leaving care, and almost one-third had moved five times (Courtney, Dworsky, et al., 2010). This instability continued at age 26. About 37 percent of the sample had been living at their current address for under a year. Another 28 percent had been in the current residence for less than two years (Courtney et al., 2011c). Thirty-five percent of Nevada FFY who had been out of care for at least six months had moved at least three times (Reilly, 2003).

Housing instability has an effect on outcomes. Fowler, Toro, and Miles (2011) note that about 41 percent of their Detroit-based sample were classified as *Stable-Engaged*: they had relatively few housing moves, were never homeless, and were able to maintain an educational program and/or employment. Another 30 percent, the *Stable-Disengaged*, despite having similar housing experiences as the prior group, still had problems with maintaining work and school connections. This group had low levels of human capital on leaving care. Only about one-third had a high school diploma, which suggests that providing housing is not a panacea for other problems. Deficits in other domains also need to be addressed. A final group, *Unstable-Disengaged*, experienced chronically unstable housing, and thus were unable to maintain an educational program or employment. This group had fewer familial connections, and was younger when they left care than the other two groups.

Several studies have linked placement changes and/or level of placement restrictiveness while in care with housing instability after discharge (Brown & Wilderson, 2010; Fowler, Toro, & Miles, 2009; Kroner & Mares, 2011). Park et al. (2005) suggest that having the experience of multiple out-of-home placements leaves youth unprepared for living independently. The transience begun in foster care with frequent changes in residence may carry over into adulthood. These frequent moves may cause FFY to have only fragile connections to their communities and other adults. Other researchers suggest that youth with multiple placements are likely to have mental health and behavioral problems that are the reason for the frequent moves as caretakers cannot meet their needs. Fowler et al. (2009, 2011) found these problems continue after these youth leave care, and may make it difficult for these youth to maintain stable housing.

Contributing to housing instability is the range of difficulties encountered after leaving care. Other problems such as pregnancy and criminal justice involvement were associated with youth living in continuously unstable situations (James, 2004; Newton, Litrownick, & Landsverk, 2000; Wulczyn, Kogan, & Harden, 2003). In turn, the lack of stable housing may contribute to the mental health difficulties of FFY (Fowler et al., 2011). Fowler and colleagues' (2011) Detroit investigation found that EFY who maintained stable housing had better mental health than youth in unstable housing. The direction of this relationship is unclear. Resolving mental health problems prior to leaving care would certainly increase the likelihood of maintaining stable living situations. A study by Buehler, Orme, Post, and Patterson (2000) found both FFY and a matched group of low-income nonfoster youth in their study were less engaged with their community than the group chosen at random to represent the general population.

Chafee and Housing Support

In 1999, the Chafee Foster Care Independence Program allowed the expenditure of 30 percent of a state's funding for housing support until age 21. Dworsky and Havlicek (2009) reported that 44 states were using Chafee funds for housing. Pergamit, McDaniel, and Hawkins (2012) found that 17 states in their sample spent most of their Chafee housing funds for one or more of three basic expenditures: apartment start-up costs (security deposits, utility turn-ons, and purchase of household goods), ongoing financial support, and emergency uses such as one-time rental assistance. The provision of ongoing rental assistance is usually limited to a year or less, and some states gradually phase out their contribution toward rent, thus requiring the youth to increase their share of the rent over time.

There is a clear gap between need and available funds for housing support. Pergamit et al. (2012) estimated the available funds for housing (30 percent of $140 million dollars or $42 million) were divided among the EFY who exited care in a year, and each youth would receive $456 a year or $38 per month. Although these researchers noted that not all youth need housing support, they project that if you spent a minimal $300 per month on those youth with a presumed need for housing assistance, the allocation is only enough to cover one-eighth of needy eligible youth.

Vulnerable Youth and Housing Problems

Two studies examined homeless shelter populations in San Francisco (Lenz-Rashid, 2006) and New York City (Nolan, 2006). Both studies found FFY overrepresented in their studies. About one-half of the residents in these studies were FFY. In the San Francisco sample, 34 percent of the FFY identified themselves as lesbian, gay, bisexual, transgender, or questioning/queer (LGBTQ) at intake. In New York, 92.5 percent of the youth said they were LGBTQ. These studies are important because they are the only FFY studies that have focused on an LGBTQ FFY population. The samples are small and nonrandom, so caution is urged in drawing conclusions about the makeup of shelter populations. Nevertheless, Lenz-Rashid raises questions about how well these LGBTQ youth are supported during the transition to adulthood. She suggests that these youth may have fewer housing options than FFY who achieved reunification with their families or those who were adopted by new families. Nolan (2006) found that foster youth were more likely to exit the shelter to live independently. Nonfoster youth exited more often to family, a fact suggesting that many EFY family relationships may be broken. EFY may have families who might not be willing or able to take them back into the home after they exit care. Otherwise they might have been reunited earlier.

Running away from placement is a form of instability, and is a behavior linked to future homelessness and other housing problems (Dworsky & Courtney, 2009a). The states reported to U.S. Department of Health and Human Services (2014b) that 4,500 youth had run away from care. Most of these youth ran away from care in their late teens prior to emancipation, and for the most part these youth are not eligible for transition services. They also are disproportionately LGBTQ. A study in Los Angeles County found that youth who identify as LGBTQ were also more likely than other youth either to have run away from foster care or to have been told to leave a placement (Wilson, Cooper, Kastanis, & Nezhad, 2014). Research findings on youth who run away from foster care are generally consistent with findings relating to the broader runaway and homeless youth population. These youth frequently have problems with substance abuse and mental health issues. Running away from foster care is often both a sign and a result of problems, such as unstable placements, undiagnosed mental health difficulties, unresolved issues with the family of origin, and possibly a desire to stay connected to that family (Courtney, Skyles, et al., 2005). Dworsky and Courtney (2009a) found that Midwest Study youth who had run away from placement had an 800 percent increased chance of being homeless. They also found that having had a group home placement increased fourfold the likelihood of being without a place to sleep. Delinquency was also predictive of homelessness. In addition, Dworsky, working in conjunction with Casey Foundation researchers, reported that African American FFY were more likely to live in public housing, live in poor-quality housing, and experience homelessness than other ethnic and racial groups (Dworsky, White, et al., 2010). The National Youth in Transition Database (2012) concluded that youth who entered care with a family history of homelessness were also at risk of homelessness when discharged from care.

Practical Recommendations for Improving Housing Stability

Extend Foster Care

Homelessness and the associated negative outcomes could be prevented by extending foster care (Fowler et al., 2009, 2011). Allowing young people to remain in foster care until age 21 would prevent a great deal of homelessness in an otherwise vulnerable population. These youth would continue receiving housing from the state while in extended care (Dworsky, 2010). Two studies, one using Midwest Study data and the other using National Youth Transition Database (NYTD) data, both found that extending care until age 19 reduced homelessness among those youth (Dworsky, 2010; Prince, Vidal, & Connell, 2016). However, extending foster care is not a cure for homelessness. The Midwest Study data suggests that a foster care extension would not prevent homelessness after age 23 (Dworsky, 2010). Youth would continue to need services and support even after they left care at that age, and assistance with problems other than homelessness.

Youth Need Individualized Housing Plans When They Leave Care

Youth must not leave foster care without an individualized housing plan, and they should not be discharged without a stable living situation. Parenting EFY need housing that accommodates their child. This type of housing may not be part of many transitional housing options. Youth with mental or physical health needs also need special assistance and support with housing. The literature indicates that youth who experienced placement instability are vulnerable to becoming homeless, and this is just one more reason that care needs to be taken with placement moves. Fowler et al. (2009, 2011) argue that a stable housing situation is a protective mechanism against many of the problems encountered by foster youth and would increase the likelihood that youth would persist in an educational program or maintain employment. Child welfare, independent living, and transitional personnel must be aware of the risks of homelessness so that they might address these risks.

The Need for Transitional Housing

Rashid (2004) suggested that a period in transitional housing would provide needed stability and aid youth in building up savings to meet some of the challenges of early adulthood. Transitional housing should be part of a strategy to expand housing stock for FFY. The best transitional living programs combine subsidized housing with case management, and continued independent living services (ILS) (Gardner, 2008). The time in transitional housing might be viewed as a means of gaining additional services such as mental health assistance, completing an education program, and/or finding stable employment. A recent evaluation that utilized randomized assignment examined the effectiveness of the National Youth Villages Program. The treatment group received intensive case management, support services, and counseling. The control group received referrals to nonprofit service providers from their social worker. The treatment group did better one year after discharge than the control group on employment earnings, housing stability, mental health outcomes, and avoiding intimate partner violence. However, no differences between groups were observed on educational attainments, criminality, or social support (Valentine, Skemer, & Courtney, 2015).

Another example of providing stable housing after age 18 is California's Transitional Housing Program for Emancipated Foster/Probation Youth (THP-Plus). This program provides a structured housing environment for youth ages 18 to 24. Forty-eight percent of the youth served were ages 21 to 24. Under state law, California counties have the option to extend care to age 25. Support services include case management, home visiting, ILS, counseling, educational services, and employment support. To be eligible for services, youth must also be participating in an ILS program. The housing model includes apartments, single-family dwellings, condominiums, college dormitories, and host families (which sometimes means living with people the foster youth knows). Much of the housing provided by THP-Plus is supervised by child welfare staff. Shelters or temporary accommodations with friends are not considered to be acceptable housing under THP-Plus (Lemley & Sepe, 2014).

An evaluation of the THP concluded that 50 percent of EFY were in need of housing on entry into the program. Almost all youth exited to stable housing, and small gains were noted in employment, income, and education during the course of the program (Kimberlin & Lemley, 2012). The critique of the program spurred the development of four suggestions to strengthen future interventions. First, the THP needs to be funded at levels high enough to reach all of California's EFY (Atkinson, 2008; Brown & Wilderson, 2010). Second, even though youth had stable housing on exit, the average rent paid consumed 43 percent of their income. This level of expenditure for housing suggests that housing costs represent a burden that may be difficult to sustain over the long run. This issue needs addressing. Third, the 24-month program may be insufficient given the continued vulnerability to housing instability that EFY experience, and should be expanded to meet the needs of youth. Finally, 41 percent of program participants had to be asked to leave the program because they failed to follow rules or meet program expectations. The program subjects its participants to more stringent rules and restrictions than the typical emerging adult would experience at home. Transitional housing programs often have curfews, substance use restrictions, and various program attendance requirements. Developmental expectations of this group suggest that we should expect some level of noncompliance from this group, particularly from young people who are leaving the highly structured environment of foster care. Some youth would prefer life on the streets where they perceive they have more freedom. It is a challenge in dealing with this population to help them develop adult notions of accountability and to conform to the sort of rules they will find in a landlord/tenant relationship. Previous studies of youth in transitional housing programs suggest the need for flexibility in service rules and requirements (Ryan & Thompson, 2013). Programs should provide second chances for youth who leave the program prematurely. The youth asked to leave programs because of noncompliance are still likely to encounter housing difficulties. Just as youth in the general population return home after a crisis, many of these EFY who encounter the reality of life after foster care may be willing to return to the program and comply with requirements after a crisis (Kimberlin & Lemley, 2012).

Other states have housing support efforts similar to California. Kentucky's child welfare agency formed a partnership with the state housing agency that funds short-term rental vouchers and uses the housing authority's existing expertise and infrastructure in managing the program. The program functions like a short-term Section 8 voucher program. Two states, Delaware and New Mexico, contract out services to community agencies to provide transitional living programs. In New Mexico, youth live either in group homes or in their own apartments, and receive a range of services such as life skills training, financial literacy instruction, education assistance, and employment services. Michigan provides assistance to youth who become homeless after leaving care by contracting with transitional living programs to reserve slots for homeless FFY. All of these efforts are paid for primarily using state, rather than federal, funds and typically their use is limited to youth who were in the foster care system in the state providing the assistance (Pergamit et al., 2012).

Innovative Solutions—Housing Vouchers for FFY

Dworsky (2010) suggests amending the Foster Care Independence Act to include a housing voucher that would be similar to the ETV for education needs. She also suggests expanding the number of foster youth eligible for housing and services under the Family Unification Program. Dworsky further recommends increasing or eliminating the 18-month time limit under that program as being insufficient to meet the needs of FFY. The length currently allowed does not match most landlord/tenant rental agreements, which are usually 12 months in duration. The base period of any voucher program should cover the time it takes to complete an associate or baccalaureate degree. Families receiving these vouchers face no such limits, and over time these relatively scarce vouchers end up in the hands of families. Only 20,500 are available and youth who need them often cannot obtain them. Just about one-third of the providers of vouchers set aside any vouchers for FFY, and about one-half said they could not serve all FFY referred to them. Some providers thought the requirement of providing supportive services to FFY was a disincentive to providing assistance that could be eliminated by increased funding (Dion et al., 2014). The overall goal of any rental subsidy program would be to have FFY spend no more than 30 percent of their income on rent, which would meet one of the critiques of THP-Plus. This income limit is comparable to what is provided for HUD's Housing Choice Program (HCP) (formerly known as Section 8). This limit on spending would also make rent payments sustainable for these youth. The HCP is another possibility for FFY, but the program only reaches a fraction of need, waiting lists are long, and the vouchers do not come with the supportive services youth need (Park et al., 2014).

ILS Participation and Improving Housing Outcomes

In Chapter 4, the research reviewed suggested that ILS participation could contribute to better housing outcomes. This research conclusion should be accepted with caution because of the methodological weaknesses of many of those studies. Nevertheless, such programs would seem to be appropriate venues for teaching about tenant responsibilities and rights, where to find housing resources, locating and maintaining an apartment, and basic housekeeping skills.

The Housing Needs of College Students

The housing problems can be linked to EFY problems with persisting and completing school. Berzin et al. (2011) asserts that helping a student prepare for college should include efforts to seek safe and secure housing for college-bound youth. North Carolina's NC Reach pays for the cost of college, including housing, for up to four years at the state's public universities and colleges. This program uses Chaffee funding to cover housing for the summer months when the youth are not attending school. Texas now requires state colleges and universities to assist FFY, and if funds are available to pay for housing during the summer and winter breaks for FFY. Existing dorm facilities that are vacant during the summer months may be a possible source of housing for these youth (Pergamit et al., 2012). This housing is important for youth who do not have families to go home to on holiday or summer breaks.

Developing Social Support Systems

Youth should be encouraged to develop long-term relationships with foster parents and other supportive adults in order that they might have a place to go in a crisis or for special holidays (Pecora, Kessler, et al., 2006). California recruits "host" families as a housing option. These hosts are often families known to the EFY. This type of housing might provide youth with some semblance of family support (California Department of Social Services, 2002).

Choca et al. (2004) suggest considering such options as intergenerational housing. Seniors may have housing with extra space and might be willing to provide mentorship as well as lodging in exchange for extra money. Youth might be able to provide help with housekeeping and errands in exchange for a reduced rent.

Assisting Homeless Youth

Homeless FFY need specialized services and shelters designed for their needs. It is inappropriate to house youth with adults and subject vulnerable youth to additional risks. Most shelters are designed to service families or single adults, and thus may not be appropriate for FFY. Housing First is a model with empirical support for its effectiveness in providing homeless youth with services. This approach aims at providing permanent and affordable housing as rapidly as possible for persons experiencing homelessness, and then supplying the supportive services and connections to the community-based supports that people need to keep their housing and avoid returning to homelessness. The philosophy of the model is that a homeless individual's primary need is to obtain stable and affordable housing, and any other issues an individual has can be more effectively assessed and treated once housing is secured.

The traditional way of addressing homelessness is to resolve the other issues that may have caused the homeless spell prior to getting the person housing. For example, a homeless person must resolve a substance abuse issue prior to being housed. Culhane, Metraux, & Hadley (2002) tested the Housing First model and found that providing housing and other assistance to the homeless is a cost-effective way to address their other problems as well. The researchers tracked mentally ill homeless people between 1989 and 1997 and found that each permanent supported housing unit saved $16,281 a year in public costs for shelter, health care, mental health care, and criminal justice, offsetting most of the $17,277 cost of housing and other services. Note that the program was not specifically developed for EFY and might have to be tweaked to meet the needs of emerging adults.

Collaboration with Housing Providers on Behalf of FFY

Housing is an area not within child welfare purview, and thus collaboration with agencies that have expertise and resources in this area is obviously necessary. Child welfare agencies should work directly with public housing agencies and the private sector to identify apartments for EFY. Casey staff work as a liaison between property owners and FFY tenants. Property owners might be willing to house EFY if the youth received subsidies and case management to help them with any housing difficulties. Napolitano and Courtney (2014) noted that one of the difficulties in developing housing for EFY was the reluctance of property owners to rent to former foster youth. The Casey Foundation describes a model in which they work with nonprofit builders, HUD officials (to provide technical assistance), local housing authorities, ILS and other youth services providers, interested foundations, and public child welfare staff (Choca et al., 2004).

An Empirical Base for Practice Is a Necessity

Data are lacking that would guide policy makers and program planners on how to design interventions and deploy the limited resources that will address the housing needs of FFY. The federal government is addressing this data deficit. In addition to the NYTD outcomes survey, a second evaluation of federally funded independent living efforts is underway: the United States

Interagency Council on Homelessness. This study will develop steps that local stakeholders can take to end youth homelessness. Planning grants will be made available to enable program developers and researchers to define core components of a program model and test it in rigorous evaluation for the purpose of developing programs to end youth homelessness (Dion et al., 2014).

CHAPTER NINE

Health Outcomes

For youth leaving foster care, health problems and lack of access to health care presents a serious challenge to achieving a successful transition. One of the abrupt losses upon leaving care for many youth is health care coverage. About 50 percent of youth in foster care have chronic medical problems (Rubin, Halfon, Raghavan, & Rosenbaum, 2005). These conditions include asthma, severe allergies, atopic dermatitis, dental decay, cognitive abnormalities, and visual and auditory problems (Jee, Barth, Szilagyi, Szilagyi, & Davis, 2006; Kruszka, Lindell, Killion, & Criss, 2012). The research also shows a high prevalence of physical disabilities in the foster care population when compared with youth in the general population (U.S. Department of Health and Human Services, 2004). These health problems follow a youth into adulthood. Data from the California Health Interview Survey (n=70,456) said that adults who had been in foster care were more likely than individuals without foster care experience to have a chronic health problem that limited their physical activity at least one day a month. Adult former foster youth (FFY) were more likely to have asthma, diabetes, hypertension, or epilepsy, or be a current smoker than individuals in the general population who had never been in foster care. FFY were also more likely than the general population to have missed at least one year of work due to a physical disability as measured by the receipt of social security disability insurance (Zlotnick, Tam, & Soman, 2012). Thirty percent of Reilly's (2003) Nevada sample (n=100) who had been out of foster care at least six months had health problems. In an earlier study, Barth (1990) reported that 44 percent of his sample of 55 FFY said they had a serious medical problem of which 38 percent went untreated.

Health Care While in Foster Care

Despite a high rate of health care needs, youth in foster care often do not receive appropriate medical care (O'Sullivan & Lussier-Duynstee, 2006). Foster children experience more discontinuities in care than children in the general population. They also have more health problems than children not in foster care but who receive Medicaid (DiGiuseppe & Christakis, 2003). The federal government reported that 40 percent of the nation's public child welfare agencies did not consistently provide preventive health and dental care. This deficit in care is attributed to various barriers to care within a complex system, and to the failures of social workers, foster parents, and health care providers to identify problems, particularly when these problems require specialized care (American Academy of Pediatrics, 2002). The inadequate preparation of youth leaving foster care to address their own health care needs increases the risk of exacerbating the already poor health and is the reason why these risks and problems extend into adulthood (Massinga & Pecora, 2004; Zlotnick et al., 2012). The system barriers include placement changes and worker turnover that disrupts the continuity of care with health care providers, the reticence of providers to render services to Medicaid recipients because of the low level of reimbursements, and abuse reporting requirements that may place additional demands on a provider's time. These barriers may lead health care providers to avoid providing services to these youth. Similar to the problem with educational records, medical histories are often unavailable, which further complicates the delivery of care (Simms, Dubowitz, & Szilagyi, 2000). Rubin, Alessandrini, Feudtner, Localio, and Hadley (2004) found an overreliance by former foster children on emergency rooms (a sign of lack of continuity of care that increased with the number of placements while in care). Youth at this stage of life may not understand why they may need ongoing health care. One of the fears discussed in the debate over the Affordable Care Act (ACA) was that the so-called "invulnerables," young healthy adults, would not see the need for health insurance because they thought their good health negated the need for medical care.

It is important to note that the conditions in which youth lived prior to foster care have an adverse effect on health. Many of these FFY grew up poor and struggle with the correlates of poverty: lack of access to health care, low birth weight, lead poisoning, unstable neighborhoods, and food insecurity, to name a few. They also suffer from the health and trauma effects resulting from maltreatment (Gerber & Dicker, 2006).

General Health of Former Foster Youth

One study that used a nationally representative study found that foster youth were not different from their nonfoster peers in exhibiting health problems (Buehler, Orme, Post, & Patterson, 2000). As expected with this age group, FFY generally self-reported good to excellent health (Barth, 1990). However, emancipated foster youth (EFY) give poorer assessments of their health status than do youth in the general population in describing their own health (Courtney et al., 2005). Two advantages FFY may have over many of their nonfoster care peers, particularly low-income ones, is that they have access to health insurance through Medicaid (Courtney & Dworsky, 2006), and they generally receive more social services to address any problems they might have. However, the cumulative disadvantages experienced before and during foster care may make them more at risk than their nonfoster peers, even those from similar socioeconomic backgrounds (Berzin, 2008; Buehler et al., 2000; Kerman, Wildfire, & Barth, 2002; Mech, 2003).

Youth in the Midwest Study reported levels of good health similar to those of the ADD sample at age 17 just prior to discharge. Eighty-six percent of the foster youth and ADD Health respondents reported their health as good to excellent, and 63 to 66 percent in both samples said health problems never caused them to miss school. However, 22 percent of the foster sample and 14 percent of the ADD Health youth said they had experienced at least one serious injury in the past year. The U.S. Census Bureau (2009) reported that 30 percent of youth ages 18 to 24 were without health insurance. On leaving care, white youth said they had poorer health than African American youth, while African American EFY said their health status was similar to their non-foster peers (Courtney, 2009). The Midwest Study EFY also had more emergency room visits and were hospitalized more often than the ADD Health comparison sample (Courtney, Dworsky, Ruth, Keller, Havlicek, & Bost, 2005). Another study conducted by Courtney and colleagues collected data similar to the information gathered in the Midwest Study from a sample of California's EFY. California EFY reported the same good health (88 percent) as well as the same propensity for injury (23 percent) as their Midwestern counterparts. However, 47 percent had missed at least some of the school year due to health problems, which was more than the Midwest Study youth (Courtney, Charles, Okpych, Napolitano, & Halsted, 2014).

Nineteen-year-old Midwest youth reported they had at least good to excellent health, but they begin to lag the ADD Health sample (88 percent to 95 percent) in assertions that they are in at least good health. The EFY also reported that they were more likely to have limited engagement in moderate activity due to health concerns than were their peers in the representative national sample. It is also possible to use the 19-year-old Illinois youth who remained in care as a comparison for youth in the other two states in the Midwest Study that did not extend care. Youth self-reports of their health status at that age were similar in all three states. However, the youth who had left care were more likely to report specific health problems such as stomach aches, skin problems, muscle and joint aches, sleeping problems, moodiness, and having trouble relaxing. At age 21, 86 percent of the Midwest Study respondents were at in at least good health, while 95 percent of the ADD

Health sample described their health in that manner. The EFY sample was also more likely to say they had a disabling condition that limited their daily activities than the ADD Health participants (11 percent versus 5 percent). At ages 23 or 24 and 26 the responses are somewhat similar, though they showed a slight decline from age 21 in claiming their health was either excellent or good by the EFY (82 percent versus 84 percent) (Courtney, Dworsky, Cusick, et al., 2009). ADD Health self-reports of health status showed an improvement over the same period (91 percent versus 96 percent saying their health was good to excellent). FFY youth were also more likely than ADD Health respondents were to report an inability to engage in moderate and vigorous activity. Courtney and colleagues speculated that these health concerns might be a reaction to the transition to independent living (Courtney & Dworsky, 2005). The limiting conditions most reported were asthma, attention deficit hyperactive disorder, or disability (Courtney, Dworsky, Brown, et al., 2011; Courtney, Dworsky, Lee, & Rapp, 2010).

In longitudinal studies, a general pattern emerges of heath worsening over time. Additional health problems were noted in the Multi-Site Evaluation of Foster Programs in Los Angeles. One-fifth of youth in that study were obese, and another quarter of the youth were overweight. These reported rates were above what was to be expected for similarly aged youth nationally (Pergamit & Johnson, 2009).

Access to Health Care by Former Foster Youth

A consistent finding of the cumulative research on former foster youth is that they have problems with access to health care. Studies report that anywhere from 30 percent to 63 percent of former foster youth lack health care insurance (Courtney et al., 2001; Courtney & Dworsky, 2005; National Youth in Transition Database, 2012, 2013, 2014a, 2014b; Pecora et al., 2003; Raghavan, Shi, Aarons, Roesch, & McMillen, 2009). In the Midwest Study sample, about one-half of EFY reported that they had been without insurance at some point in the previous year (Kushel, Yen, Gee, & Courtney, 2007); the corresponding rate of noncoverage in the general population was 30 percent (Park, Mulye, Adams, Brindis, & Irwin, 2006). The high end report is from the National Youth in Transition Database, which has more recent data and reflects the impact of the Fostering Connections to Success Act (FCSA). Nevertheless, 19-year-old youth who had left care were less likely than youth who remained in extended foster care to receive Medicaid (85 percent versus 63 percent). Not surprisingly, youth reported in corresponding percentages that they were unable to access needed care (Barth, 1990; Courtney, 2009; Courtney, Dworsky, Ruth, et al., 2005). Reilly (2003) said that one former foster youth in his small sample (n=100), a diabetic, died because he was unable to obtain care. About one-quarter of the youth in Los Angeles participating in the Multi-Site Evaluation of Foster Youth Program Study said they had not sought health care when needed, and the most frequently given reason for not seeking care was inability to pay (Pergamit & Johnson, 2009). Lack of income means that health care must compete with the need the youth has to pay the month's rent or have money to buy food. This population may not see health care needs as a priority if the need is not acute or immediate.

Because of the documented problems that foster youth have, both prior to coming into the child welfare system and while in care, transitioning youth need continuity of care (Raghavan et al., 2009). Most youth get their health care coverage through their employed parents' health plans (assuming that is a benefit provided by their parents' employers), or they obtain a job with health insurance as part of its compensation package. When Midwest Study EFY have health insurance, they are more likely to report that they had coverage through Medicaid. The ADD Health comparison group was more likely to say they received their health care coverage under their parent's insurance (Courtney, Dworsky, Cusick, et al., 2009; Courtney, Dworsky, et al., 2010). EFY may find that obtaining insurance through their parents' plan is not a viable option, either because their parents are not employed in covered jobs or because relationships with parents have been severed. Even when youth do secure employment, frequently the jobs do not provide health care coverage. FFY may be caught up in a larger societal trend of a decline in the number of employers that provide health insurance as part of a benefit package (Skidmore, 2010). Or when health coverage is provided, deductibles, copayments, and the cost of premiums make coverage unaffordable. In contrast, Raghavan and colleagues (2009), in a secondary analysis of the Missouri data, found that employment was associated with health coverage, but student status was not. However, only 50 percent of their sample was employed. Their findings suggest vulnerability with health care access among youth pursuing further education.

Health care has been provided to children in foster care for decades. States are required to provide their charges with Medicaid. Libby, Kelleher, and Leslie (2007) estimate that 99 percent of foster children receive Medicaid. It is only since the passage of the Foster Care Independence Act of 1999 that federal policy has addressed health care coverage for youth leaving care. However, states had showed a reluctance to extend benefits to transitioning youth, until nudged by the federal government through the passage of the FCSA in 2008. Prior to that, only 17 states provided Medicaid to EFY in 2007 up to age 21, leaving an estimated 25,000 EFY without health insurance (Child Welfare Information Gateway, 2009). Some of these states provided coverage to youth who were in certain programs, such as in school or taking part in independent living activities (Schelbe, 2011). Even after passage of the FCSA, many EFY were without insurance.

One consistent finding from the research is that dental care access is somewhat lower than FFY access to obtain physical health care. In the Midwest

Study, youth were less likely to have dental insurance than the general population comparison, the ADD Health Study. Not surprisingly, the EFY were less likely than the comparison sample to have sought dental health care, and the reason most often given for lack of treatment was the cost of such care.

In the Midwest Study, being male, alcohol abuse, being unstably housed, and reporting good health were all associated with lacking health insurance (Kushel et al., 2007). Females have a higher rate of health care coverage than males because of the high incidence of pregnancy among EFY (discussed in Chapter 11). Pregnancy makes these low-income women eligible for public benefits. Also, the good health enjoyed by this group may lead them to think they are not vulnerable to illness, and thus they may feel they need not incur the extra expense of health insurance coverage.

The Impact of the Affordable Care Act and Its Replacement on the Health Care of Former Foster Youth

At the time this chapter was written, the Patient Protection and Affordable Care Act (ACA, Public Law No. 111–148) had survived a Republican attempt at repeal, but it still faces hostility from President Trump, who has vowed to repeal it. The Republican replacement, the failed Affordable Health Care Act (AHCA), carried considerable risks for foster children and FFY. The ACA said all EFY, regardless of income, would be eligible for Medicaid, until they reached age 26. FFY who left care prior to aging out were not covered by the mandate for Medicaid. However, the states were given the option of covering these youth. The ACA mandated that as of January 1, 2014, any youth who had been in foster care for at least six months would be eligible for Medicaid benefits up to age 26 and beyond if the state so chose. The mandatory coverage did not begin until 2014, which means there is a cohort of EFY who may not have any insurance coverage. The provision is mandatory and is not affected by the Supreme Court decision that made the ACA's expansion of Medicaid by the states voluntary.

However, the Department of Health and Human Services (DHHS) issued a regulation saying that Medicaid coverage was only mandatory for youth living in the state where they had been in foster care. If FFY were residing in a state where they had not been in foster care, Medicaid coverage is optional and left up to the state where youth are in residence. As of October 2016, only 13 states had elected to extend coverage to EFY from other states (Mailman School of Public Health, 2016). Lack of availability of Medicaid could affect a youth's decision about where to go to school or get a job. The AHCA had placed EFY access to health care through Medicaid in doubt. The AHCA would have allowed young adults to remain on their parents' health insurance to age 26, but the proposed law did not have parallel language that would have allowed FFY to retain their Medicaid coverage to age 26 (Houshyar, 2014).

Medicaid, or any other coverage, will help transitioning youth emerge successfully into adulthood. Coverage would remove barriers to success in college and employment that can result from unexpected health problems, unmet medical needs, and unaffordable insurance premiums or copayments.

Prior to the ACA, eligibility for Medicaid was limited to custodial parents, pregnant women, or disabled individuals. The ACA widened Medicaid coverage to include single adults whose incomes do not exceed 133 percent of the poverty line (Bagley & Levy, 2014). It is important to note that the ACA provides not only access to physical health treatment, but also to mental health and substance abuse services (ACA, 2010). Chapter 10 discusses the need for these services. A repeal of the ACA would threaten the states' ability to provide those services both for children in care and for youth who are transitioning to emerging adulthood. It is Speaker of the House Paul Ryan's goal to change Medicaid's structure to a block grant, which means the states will receive a capped amount of money to serve the needs of everyone in the state. Federal funding will be cut $800 billion over 10 years. No specific service would be mandatory by the federal government, which means nothing is guaranteed. States would have to meet a multitude of needs within a fixed budget for everyone currently helped by Medicaid, including low-income seniors, adults, persons with special needs, and children. The cap on Medicaid funding would be fixed despite any increase in needs caused by changes in the number of youth entering foster care or the intensity of needs of youth in care. The historical record regarding block grants suggests that funding drops over time. An example is the TANF block funding grant, which has declined by 30 percent since its inception. Things will probably get worse with Medicaid (Biallas, 2017; Golden, 2016).

The provisions of the ACA were significant steps in moving the nation toward universal health care coverage. However, the DHHS reported in 2005 that 77 percent of the states did not have sufficient medical doctors and dentists, and 71 percent did not have enough mental health professionals who accepted Medicaid to meet the states' needs for those services. Access to care for individuals with Medicaid can still be difficult because of low reimbursement rates. Physicians may be reluctant to take on adult FFY because of these rates. Without an improvement in reimbursement rates, this service gap is likely to persist.

Vulnerable Populations

Homelessness

The lack of housing is associated with poorer health outcomes among adolescents and youth (Feldman & Middleman, 2003). They have poor access to care, do not utilize preventative care, and rely on emergency rooms for care (Klein et al., 2000). Frequent housing moves and/or paying more than one-half of their income for housing is also associated with poor access to care and a propensity to use emergency rooms for care (Kushel, Gupta, Gee, & Haas, 2006).

Kushel et al. (2007) used the Midwest Study data to find that homeless EFY were less likely to have insurance than housed EFY (53 percent homeless, 47 percent unstably housed, 77 percent stably housed), and again a lack of health care was associated with not having insurance. Homeless EFY were more likely to say they could not obtain care than were stably or unstably housed EFY (41 percent versus 24 percent versus 15 percent). Only 5 percent of youth still in care said they could not access health care when they needed it.

According to Kushel et al. (2007) the relationship between housing and ill health may be bidirectional with cost of housing limiting the ability to pay for care if uninsured; or the expense of health care and/or untreated health problems may limit EYF's ability to work or develop the financial resources to remain housed. Also, exposure to the elements that comes with homelessness may mean youth are more vulnerable to health problems.

Disabled FFY

Children in foster care have a higher rate of physical disability than do children in the general population (Lightfoot, Hill, & Laberte, 2011; Silver et al., 1999). Data from the Casey National Alumni Study found that 53 percent of the 1,087 alumni interviewed had a disability. The prevalence of disability in the general population is 18.7 percent (Stoddard, 2014). The majority of the youth had psychiatric disabilities (70.8 percent), discussed in the next chapter. Thirty-six percent had learning disabilities, 19.8 percent had attention deficit/hyperactivity disorders, and 3.2 percent had mental retardation. A smaller number had other disabilities: visual (2.8 percent), auditory (2.7 percent), and physical limitations (2.8 percent). (Note, a youth could have more than one disability [Anctil, McCubbin, O'Brien, Pecora, & Anderson-Harumi, 2007].) About 9 percent of the representative California sample of FFY in Needell, Cuccaro-Alamin, Brookhart, Jackman, & Shlonsky (2002) received Medi-Cal for a disability.

Anctil et al. (2007) found youth with disabilities had worse outcomes than nondisabled Casey Alumni on educational attainment, quality of life, and in financial management. Disabled males fared worse than disabled females. Because of the general persistence of disabilities from early childhood into emerging adulthood we should expect poorer health and more psychiatric problems among youth who leave foster care (Kendall-Tacket, 2003). However, Anctil and colleagues found that this was not true across the board, and they argue for research to identify protective factors that might account for good outcomes for disabled youth. Such research could aid in the designing of interventions and programs that would lead to a more successful adjustment to emerging adulthood.

Practical Recommendations for Improving the Health Status of Former Foster Youth

Extend Foster Care

As was stated in previous chapters, foster care should be extended to age 25 and include eligibility for Medicaid regardless of income up to that age. This provision puts FYY on a par with youth who have eligibility for health insurance through a parent's insurance policies, and reaffirms the state's duty as corporate parent. Youth need to be assisted in finding alternative access to health care at age 26 since medical needs will not stop at that age. As stated earlier, many of these youth are most likely working in jobs that do not provide health insurance. Although the ACA had moved us toward the goal of universal health care coverage, it does not reach that goal. The Republican plans would move us away from that goal. The Congressional Budget Office (2017) estimated that 23 million Americans would lose their health insurance if repeal occurs. An incremental step toward protecting EFY that is in line with the corporate parenting concept is providing FFY such coverage without regard to income eligibility after age 26, in much the same way as veterans are entitled to U.S.-supplied health care.

The low reimbursement rate for Medicaid services needs to be addressed. One concern raised by the American Academy of Pediatrics (2016) is that physicians who specialize in adult medicine will be reluctant to provide care to FFY because of the low payment rate for these services. This reluctance may place further pressure on pediatricians or family physicians to fill this service gap. Medicaid reimbursement rates need to be raised for all recipients, but incremental steps of higher reimbursements for Medicaid could be given to these former wards of the state on a par with veterans and Medicare recipients. Higher reimbursements would help FFY find and maintain health care providers.

Collaboration with Pediatricians and Other Physicians

Child welfare workers, independent living specialists, and physicians need to work collaboratively to help plan for the EFY's transition to adulthood. Child welfare agencies should provide opportunities for training of pediatricians and other physicians to learn about the health needs of foster children, particularly those at the transition points where they are aging out of foster care. Pediatricians who are the primary source of health care for foster children need to teach youth who are "aging out" of foster care the skills needed to navigate a health care system designed for adults. Social workers and pediatricians should aid EFY in transferring their health records, assisting youth to understand their own health care needs and learning how to tell others about those needs. Youth need to be educated about their eligibility for Medicaid and other health services, and helped to navigate protocols for service utilization (Pergamit, McDaniel, & Hawkins, 2012). Finally, each EFY should be linked to a new physician; in short, we need to help them find a new medical home.

Advocacy at the State Level

Child welfare and state Medicaid agencies should designate a person who would be responsible for verifying former foster care status for another state, and allow for electronic submission for Medicaid eligibility. The Medicaid eligibility documents must be a component of any packet of documentation a youth takes away from care (Houshyar, 2014). These documents, described as a health passport by some, include a Social Security card, birth certificate or any record showing age, residential address, and bank statement or record of employment or income, as well as medical records. These records must include both physical and mental health. A youth's social worker should link the youth with Medicaid prior to discharge (Kruszka, Lindell, Killion, & Criss, 2016). Texas is a state model that could be copied where youth are automatically enrolled in Medicaid before they leave care (Patel & Roherty, 2007).

Research is needed to discover how to hold states accountable for providing Medicaid coverage. This research must track youth both before and after they leave care, and afterwards to identify rate of coverage among these youth. Also, access to and utilization of health care could be fruitful subjects of investigation for the purpose of examining the adequacy of health care efforts on behalf of these youth.

Health Homes: Integrated Care Models

The ACA had encouraged the states to deliver benefits through integrated care models. EFY are a group with many needs that can be quite costly to serve. Integrated care models may offer opportunities for case management and integrated health and mental health services that would help transitioning youth with medical needs. In addition, Medicaid has permitted states to cover targeted case management services, which may include coordination of both health care and non-health care services. Integrated approaches may be particularly appropriate to aid FFY because they emphasize coordination that allows for increased continuity of care over time, and strong links between physical and behavioral health services (Shirk, 2008).

The provision of coordinated services can yield fiscal savings over the long term by improving patient health and reducing the need for costlier health care and social services later. Health homes are a prime example from the ACA. States can apply for health homes that are targeted towards serving specific groups of Medicaid patients such as EFY or FFY. Health and mental health services that are designed for the needs of FFY would mean FFY are able to receive more comprehensive care. Under the ACA states that choose to implement health homes receive short-term access to 90 percent federal matching funds (Enam & Golden, 2014).

Enroll Eligible Youth Who Aged Out of Care before 2014, but Who Are under Age 26

Eligibility for Medicaid must be extended to the cohort of foster youth who were in foster care prior to 2014, because the FCSA did not address their medical needs. Child welfare officials must take the lead in finding these youth by using their own administrative records and the networks and community partners that work with youth. Medical personnel should inquire about foster care status of any youth they encounter.

Keeping What We Have as a Start to Something Better

Republican plans would reverse many of the health gains for American children. The rate of children without health insurance was at an historic low of 4.8 percent in 2015, and has been reduced 68 percent since passage of the Clinton-era Children's Health Insurance Program. We should not step back from these gains. Republican plans for health care are a serious threat to America's poor and low-income children, including foster children, and would seriously threaten the health and well-being of FFY (Biallas, 2017).

CHAPTER TEN

Mental Health Outcomes

Foster children are more likely than children in the general population to have a physical health problem, a learning disability, and/or a mental health disorder that limits their functioning (Kortenkamp & Ehrle, 2002). They are also more likely than children who have never been in care to receive services for a mental health problem (Harman, Childs, & Kelleher, 2000). The cumulative research suggests that foster children have more psychological, emotional, and behavioral problems when compared to community samples (Clausen, Landsverk, Ganger, Chadwick, & Litrownick, 1998; Harman et al., 2000; Kortenkamp & Ehrle, 2002). A number of studies cited in Chapter 6 have reported a range of 27 percent to 80 percent of foster youth exhibited behavioral problems that fall into the borderline or clinical ranges. Vandivere, Chalk, and Moore (2003) reported that almost 60 percent of children age two and under in foster care were at a high risk for a developmental delay or neurological impairment.

One would expect an increased vulnerability to mental health and substance abuse disorders in this population, given their prior history of adverse experiences. Data from the National Survey of Child and Adolescent Well-Being (NSCAW), the largest nationally representative sample of youth served by the child welfare system (n=6,321), found that 45.7 percent of these youth had scores on a standardized measure of cognitive, behavioral, and social skills that would have qualified them for early intervention services. Twenty-five percent of children age six and under had scores that placed them at risk of behavioral problems (Stahmer, Hurlburt, Barth, Webb, & Landsverk, 2005). Interviewers in the Missouri study used the Diagnostic Interview Schedule for the DSM-IV to gather data from youth at age 17 prior to discharge and found that 37 percent of those youth had met the criteria for a psychiatric diagnosis in the preceding 12 months. Sixty-one percent of the youth met the conditions for a lifetime mental health diagnosis. The most common types of problems were conduct disorders, oppositional defiant disorders, major depression, and attention-deficit-hyperactivity disorder (ADHD). The lifetime prevalence for conduct disorders was 40 percent among Missouri's 17-year-old foster youth, and the past-year prevalence for conduct disorders among those youth was 20.7 percent. Additionally, 94 percent of these youth had received mental health services. Sixty-six percent of the Missouri sample were recipients of services at the time of their interview (McMillen et al., 2005). The rate in the general population for conduct disorders for 17- and 18-year-olds was 10 percent (McMillen et al., 2005; Merikangas et al., 2010). The National Survey of Children's Health, (n=85,116 children aged 3–17 years) provides another comparison for foster children and the general population on mental health problems. This survey indicated that about 20 percent of U.S. children have a mental health disorder (Houtrow & Okamura, 2011).

Casey studies utilized the National Comorbidity Study (NCS) as a comparison sample, and used the Composite International Diagnostic Interview (CIDI) to assess youth mental health status. The CIDI is a standardized instrument developed by the World Health Organization for use by trained lay interviewers to collect data for a comprehensive assessment of mental disorders. The CIDI required a respondent to identify past year and lifetime prevalence of particular psychiatric symptoms. The Casey Field Office Mental Health Study (CFOMH) administered the CIDI to 188 14- to 17-year-olds served by Casey Family Services. Sixty-three percent of Casey youth had at least one lifetime mental health diagnosis, and 22.8 percent of respondents had at least three of these diagnoses. The most common problems observed in the sample were similar to those found with the Missouri youth, and included oppositional defiant disorders (29.3 percent), conduct disorders (20.7 percent), major depressive disorders (19 percent), and ADHD (15 percent) (Pecora, White, Jackson, & Wiggins, 2009). CFOMH youth had higher past-year and lifetime rates than NCS adolescents on conduct disorders, mania, and post-traumatic stress disorders (PTSD). The Casey respondents also had higher lifetime prevalence rates than NCS youth for ADHD, bulimia, panic disorders, social phobias, major depressive disorders, and separation anxiety disorders. A review of Casey National Alumni Study case files found that 11 percent of youth preparing to leave care had a current diagnosable mental health condition, and one-half had at some point been diagnosed with a psychological disorder. Mental health and employment services were the most commonly provided services in this study (Pecora, Williams, et al., 2006).

The Midwest Study found that 16.1 percent of the 17-year-olds waiting to exit foster care had a diagnosis of PTSD and 2.9 percent were clinically depressed. About 36 percent had received psychological counseling, 23 percent were on psychotropic medication, and 7 percent had been in a hospital at some point for a psychiatric problem (Courtney, Terao, & Bost, 2004).

Fourteen percent of the Missouri sample had a diagnosis of PTSD at age 17 or 18 (McMillen et al., 2005). The rates of PTSD in both of these samples were over twice the expected rate in the general population (6 percent) (Merikangas et al., 2010).

Explanations for the High Incidence of Mental Health Problems among Foster Youth

Previous discussions in this book have identified the reasons why foster youth are vulnerable to mental health and behavioral problems. Just to reiterate, using cumulative disadvantaged theory, we can see that before these youth entered foster care they had experienced the trauma of abuse in their own homes. Much evidence is available to suggest that childhood traumatic events can have physical and psychological effects that carry over into adulthood.

A study by Bramlett and Radel (2014) found that foster youth, on average, had experienced four or more potentially childhood traumatic events, which made them vulnerable to adverse outcomes as both a child and an adult. The removal from the home and birth parents and placement into foster care also leads to the loss of siblings, extended family relationships, and familiar environments. The foster care system presents new demands and challenges that might compound the trauma. In foster care, youth must adjust to new caretakers who may or may not meet their needs. Frequent placement change is the lot of many foster children when the new caretaker does not work out. They may also face the stigma of being in care, which marks them as different from their peers. The stigma may contribute to a foster child feeling isolated and perhaps leads to differential treatment of foster youth by teachers. This reaction by teachers accounts for some of the school difficulties discussed in Chapter 6.

Mental Health Needs of Transitioning Youth

The previous section discussed problems that youth had prior to leaving care; some of these problems preceded entry into the child welfare system. This section reviews the research on youth mental status after leaving care. The research reviewed in this chapter generally shows that youth emancipating from the child welfare system have much higher rates of mental health disorders than do their peers in the general population. Evidence to support these conclusions come from standardized mental health assessments administered to former foster youth (FFY), and the widespread documented use of mental health services. Results from the California Health Interview Survey (n=70,456) reported that adults with a history of foster care were 1.62 times more likely to report at least one mental health problem in the previous month than were individuals without foster care experience (Zlotnick, Tam, & Soman, 2012).

Merdinger, Hines, Lemon, Osterling, and Wyatt (2005) reported that 35 percent of their college-attending sample had accessed mental health services. These researchers suggest that the services helped youth remain in college, but having a mental health or substance abuse disorder can interfere with youth continuing their education, finding and maintaining employment, and/or developing positive supportive relationships with others. Kroner and Mares (2011) found that having mental health problems at age 19 reduced the chance of achieving successful outcomes in education, employment, and independent living by one-half. The high rate of mental health problems found among FFY is an important factor in their difficulties in the transition to adulthood outlined throughout this book. The behaviors exhibited as a result of these disorders, as discussed in Chapter 8, may also exclude FFY from participating in programs meant to help transitioning youth.

Three Casey Studies of FFY—the National Casey Alumni Study (NCAS), the Casey Young Adult Survey (CYAS), and the Northwest Alumni Study (NAS)—all found that FFY were twice as likely as the general population to have a mental health problem. On leaving care, Casey alumni showed an increasing rate of psychological distress. One possible reason for the deterioration in mental health status is the loss of the protective features of foster care such as services and social workers to provide support.

The NCAS study found that CIDI diagnoses were three to five times more likely in FFY than among youth in the CFOMH, which assessed mental health status prior to leaving care. These data suggest that mental health status worsens after leaving care. For example, the rate for PTSD among youth in care in the past year was 9.3 percent, but the lifetime prevalence for PTSD was 30 percent. Among the general population the PTSD yearly rate is 7.6 percent (Pecora et al., 2009; Pecora, Williams, et al., 2003; White, O'Brien, White, Pecora, & Phillips, 2008). The CYAS sample was an annual cohort survey that interviewed youth at ages 19, 22, and 25. The 41.1 percent lifetime prevalence rate of PTSD expressed among alumni was also almost twice the rate in the general population (21 percent) (Pecora et al., 2009). The PTSD incidence among the alumni was comparable to that experienced by Vietnam veterans for whom the diagnosis was initially identified, and exceeded the rate for recent American war veterans (Kulka, Fairbank, Jordan, & Weiss, 1990).

Youth in the CYAS had symptoms of mental health disorders at a much higher rate than the general population. Symptoms of psychoticism were 2.8 times higher, paranoid ideation was 2.5 times more common, obsessive compulsive symptoms were 2.4 times greater, and the Casey alumni were 2.1 times more likely to suffer depression than what one would expect in a general-population sample. One in five of the respondents (21.4 percent) met the diagnostic criteria for a psychiatric disorder (Havalchak, White, & O'Brien, 2008). In the NAS, 11.3 percent of the alumni met the criteria for a diagnosis of a lifetime prevalence for an alcohol use disorder, and 21 percent met the criteria for lifetime diagnosis of substance abuse. The corresponding rate in the national comparison sample was 7.1 percent for alcohol and 4.5 percent for drugs. However, the 12-month rate for alcohol dependence was similar for Casey alumni and the CMS comparison, but rates of drug dependence for alumni were substantially higher than in the comparison sample (8.0 percent versus 0.7 percent). The young adults in the CYAS survey were reporting rates closer to the general population for experiencing PTSD symptoms in the previous year (6.4 percent).

The CYAS examined recovery among alumni by comparing lifetime prevalence with the past year incidence of a specific mental health diagnosis on the CIDI. They found that large numbers of youth recovered from drug (67.9 percent) and alcohol dependence (61.8 percent), but mental health problems showed more resistance to change. Low recovery rates were noted for generalized anxiety disorders (39.6 percent), social phobias (26.6 percent), bulimia (25.8 percent), and PTSD (15.7 percent) (Havalchak et al., 2008).

The Casey Alumni studies examined racial and ethnic differences in the mental health functioning of transitioning youth. The sole difference found was that white youth had more social phobias than did their African American counterparts (Harris, Jackson, O'Brien, & Pecora, 2010).

The Midwest Study used the same mental health measure as the Casey studies, the CIDI. In that study, the most prevalent diagnoses at age 19 were PTSD (12.5 percent), major depression (10.3 percent), alcohol dependence (6.2 percent), and drug dependence (5.3 percent). About one-third of the young adults in that study had a mental health or a substance abuse problem, including an alcohol disorder (Courtney & Dworsky, 2005). One in five alumni had three or more mental health diagnoses. Females had nearly twice the rate of depression and three times the rate of PTSD as males in the sample. Nearly 100 percent of females had more than one diagnosis. No ethnic differences on diagnoses were noted. Rates of disorders were lower in the Midwest Study than noted among the Northwest alumni. Casey researchers' explanation for this variation in rates was that it was an artifact of the age differences between these two samples (Pecora et al., 2009).

Midwest Study youth show a pattern of mental health and substance abuse symptoms (behavioral health) declining over time, but their symptoms are always much higher than the general population. At age 17, 70 percent of the sample had at least one behavioral symptom indicating a problem, but the percentage of youth with such symptoms had declined to 40 percent at age 23–24 (Brown, Courtney, & McMillen, 2015).

At age 26, one-third of the Midwest Study sample reported a social phobia, which was defined as an unusually strong fear of social situations. Females were more likely than males to experience such feelings. On all measures, women were showing more mental health problems than males.

For example, at age 21, females had a greater prevalence of depression or PTSD (14 percent versus 5 percent) than did young men of the same age. Almost 60 percent of the overall sample had experienced an extremely stressful event in the previous year. Fifty-seven percent of the sample reported at least one symptom of PTSD with males and females experiencing those symptoms at equal rates (Courtney, Dworsky, Cusick, et al., 2009).

Over half of the CalYOUTH participants at age 17, and again at age 19, had a mental health disorder (53 percent). This study selected questions from the CIDI, and the Mini International Neuropsychiatric Interview for Children and Adolescents for a mental health assessment. As with the other studies reported upon in this chapter, the diagnoses with the highest prevalence were major depression, dysthymia, mania, hypomania, psychotic disorders, substance abuse and dependence, and alcohol dependence. Females were more likely than males to report symptoms of major depression (25.2 percent versus 13.5 percent), dysthymia (9.4 percent versus 4.9 percent), and PTSD (10.6 percent versus 2.9 percent). LGBTQ youth were much more likely than youth who identified exclusively as heterosexual to have a mental health or substance abuse problem (73.7 percent versus 47.1 percent) (Courtney, Okpych, et al., 2016).

Foster youth and alumni are particularly vulnerable to suicide. Forty-four percent of the California's former foster youth reported suicidal ideation and 26.3 percent of those youth said they had attempted suicide. Females and LGBTQ youth were the most likely groups in the sample to report both suicidal ideation and attempts at suicide. African Americans were the least likely group to do so (Courtney & Charles, 2015). This rate of suicidal ideation was much higher than you would find in the general population. A Centers for Disease Control (2016) national survey of U.S. high school age adolescents found that 22.4 percent of females and 11.6 percent of males reported having seriously thought about attempting suicide. The rate for completed suicides among youth in the general population age 15 to 24 was 9.9 per 100,000 (Debski, Spadafore, Jacob, Poole, & Hixson, 2007). A large representative study of Sweden's population found that adults with foster care experience were four to five times more likely than the country's general population to have been hospitalized for a suicide attempt (Vinnerjung, Hjern, & Lindbald, 2006).

Resilience in Transitioning Foster Youth

Despite these alarming findings on the mental health status of FFY, many youth showed encouraging signs of resilience. Lee, Festinger, Jaccard, and Munson (2017) noted that about 56.1 percent of 19-year-olds in the NSCAW showed minimal symptoms. Most of the 17-year-olds in the CalYOUTH study said that as they left care, they were optimistic about the future and they had high aspirations for their emerging adulthood. The Midwest Study asked three questions that could be interpreted as inquiries about mental health status. One question had youth report on their satisfaction with life; another item asked if they thought their life was better since leaving care; and the final query asked about their of level optimism for the future. At ages 23–24 and 26, about two-thirds of the youth said they were at least satisfied with their lives. Eighty-nine percent of the sample reported feeling "fairly optimistic" to "very optimistic" about their future. The optimism about the future and satisfaction with their life seem to be an indicator of resilience in the sample. However, Midwest study respondents were less optimistic about the future than the ADD Health youth (Courtney, Dworsky, et al., 2011; Courtney, Dworsky, Lee, & Rapp, 2010). In addition, when Midwest Study youth responded to the Life Orientation Scale, a standardized measure of locus of control, most youth indicated that they felt in control of shaping what happened to them in the future. They maintained resilient feelings despite not receiving the supports they needed to emerge as successful adults. In contrast, about one-half of the respondents reported that foster care provided a better quality of life than they had on their own after leaving care (Courtney, Dworsky, et al., 2011).

The findings of poorer mental health among FFY are not universal. Buehler, Orme, Post, and Patterson (2000) used the National Survey of Families and Households to investigate FFY's adjustment to life after care. They did not find differences on depression, self-esteem, or life satisfaction between FFY and youth who had never been in foster care. This study contained an unknown number of emancipated foster youth (EFY), and most of the sample was probably composed of FFY. No data were available to describe how these FFY exited or on how long they had been in care. These differences from EFY studies may account for these divergent findings.

Mental Health Treatment for Transitioning Youth

Prevalence of Treatment

Despite the high level of need exhibited by foster children, questions have been raised about whether they are receiving all the mental health services they need while in care (Bergman, 2000; Landsverk, Burns, Stambaugh, & Reutz, 2006; Shin, 2006). Lack of treatment for mental health problems is something that FFY's share with nonfoster youth. Only 25 percent of America's children get the mental health care they need (RAND, 2001). Leaving problems unattended can have an adverse effect on future life chances. Mental health problems are chronic conditions and follow youth into adulthood. CalYOUTH study participants reported that they were seldom involved in their mental health treatment decisions while in care, and they were not prepared to manage their health care after discharge (Courtney, Opkych, et al., 2016).

We know that over time the use of mental health services declines for youth leaving care (Brown et al., 2015; Havlicek, Garcia, & Smith, 2013; McMillen & Raghavan, 2009). McMillen and Raghavan's (2009) analysis of the Missouri Study data provides support for the suspicion that that some youth's mental health needs may go untreated after they leave care. They reported a sharp drop-off in the usage of mental health services between the ages of 17 and 19. Thirty-five percent of 17-year-olds used mental health services, whereas only 10 percent of 19-year-olds were receiving mental health services. The decline in mental health service receipt was most evident in the 30 days prior to discharge, and 30 days after leaving care. A decline in the use of psychotropic medication and outpatient treatment was noted even among those still in care at age 19. Cost was the reason most frequently given by youth for not using mental health services. The Midwest Study reported a similar decline in service usage between ages 17 and 21; 36 percent of youth reported receiving mental health services at the initial interview. This number had declined to 10 percent at age 21. However, the Midwest Study reported that transitioning youth still received mental health services at twice the rate (21 percent versus 9 percent) of the general population and were twice as likely to have received substance abuse treatment than their nonfoster peers (8 percent versus 3 percent) (Courtney & Dworsky, 2006). At age 21, they were more likely than the ADD Health sample to have received counseling or psychotropic medication (11 percent and 13 percent versus 7 percent and 2 percent) (Courtney, Dworsky, Cusick, et al., 2009). About 20 percent of the sample was receiving mental health services at age 26, and 12 percent of the sample received psychological counseling, which was about the same rate as the ADD Health sample (Courtney, Dworsky, et al., 2011). Young women were more likely than males to have received counseling and medication. Only 4 percent of the sample said they could not access mental health care.

Fifty-four percent of the CalYOUTH sample had received counseling, which was three times the rate of treatment in the general population. Females were more likely than males to have received treatment (60.3 percent versus 44.8 percent). LGBTQ youth received counseling (68.2 percent versus 48.8 percent) more often than did heterosexuals. Ten percent of the sample had been in a hospital for psychiatric reasons, and 29 percent received psychotropic medications. No gender differences were noted regarding these treatments, but LGBTQ youth were more likely than heterosexuals to have been the recipient of both (Courtney & Charles, 2015).

Both the Midwest and Missouri Studies observed a reduction in the use of psychotropic medication after leaving care (Courtney et al., 2004; McMillen et al., 2005). Nevertheless, data indicate that a substantial number of FFY received mental health services, if not medication. A California investigation that linked records of 11,060 former foster youth from the child welfare system with the state's Department of Mental Health database found that 53 percent of the sample had received mental health services (Needell, Cuccaro-Alamin, Brookhart, Jackman, & Shlonsky, 2002). Eighty-four percent of FFY in Allegheny County, Pennsylvania, had received mental health services, and 39 percent had been recipients of substance abuse treatment. Sixty percent of the sample had received an appointment for medication management. A little more than a third of the sample had received outpatient services. The median cost per youth of these services was $7,000. Many of the mental health services provided were mandatory psychological assessments. The receipt of this assessment did not necessarily mean that youth received additional services. The high percentage of youth receiving services in that study may have been the result of youth undergoing that assessment (Shook et al., 2011, 2013).

Raghavan et al. (2005), using a nationally representative database, reported that the use of psychotropic medication in a child welfare population was two times the rate of use found among other children eligible for Medicaid. Thirty-six percent of the Missouri sample was taking psychotropic medications. Thirteen percent of the youth were taking two medications, and 22 percent of these youth were using more than two psychotropics. Youth who had a history of physical or sexual abuse were the most likely group to be taking multiple psychotropics (Raghavan & McMillen, 2008).

Courtney and Charles (2015) reported that 30 percent of the Midwest EFY expressed concern about taking psychotropic medication. Most youth conceded some benefit from taking medications, but they were concerned about side effects. Courtney, Dworsky, Cusick, et al. (2009) noted that in the Midwest Study youth often stopped taking the drugs on their own without a physician's advice. They raise questions about whether this decision was a good one, or whether youth were being overmedicated. Raghavan and McMillen (2008) expressed concern about the number of youth in their sample taking multiple medications, which is a risk to their health. They suggest the high degree of externalizing disorders in their sample may result in overmedication as an attempt to get youth behavior under control. However, they also suggest that some youth with mental health problems in their sample were underutilizing medication.

Why the Reduction in the Use of Mental Health Services?

The reduction in the receipt of mental health services for this age group is also found in the general population (Pottick, Bilder, Stoep, Warner, & Alvarez, 2008). Despite the decline in FFY utilization of mental health services in their twenties, it may still be greater than the general population. At least part of the diminution in the utilization of mental health services may be the result of maturation, which could eliminate some of the problems that had caused them to seek services earlier. Youth reports noted in Chapter 9 detailed some of the problems that transitioning youth have in accessing health care. Available data supports the notion that youth discontinue mental health services because of lack of perceived need or belief in the effectiveness of treatment (McMillen & Raghavan, 2009; Munson, Scott, Smalling, Kim, & Floersch, 2011). A qualitative study of FFY reported that some participants said the reason that they discontinued use of mental health services was that they were no longer mandated to receive such services. They were also not "forced" to use services by social workers, foster parents, or other child welfare personnel (Munson et al., 2011). These access problems occurred mostly because of a lack of insurance and/or inability to pay for services (Courtney, Dworsky, et al., 2011). The Affordable Care Act had provided some remedy for the problem of lack of access because of an inability to pay for services by expanding Medicaid to cover single low-income persons. However, not all states have taken advantage of this expansion. This remedy, as discussed in the last chapter, is now in jeopardy.

Transitioning youth also have the same problem for mental health as they did for physical health difficulties. This problem involves moving from a system geared to treating children and adolescents to one that treats adults. Therefore, when they do seek help, they may encounter health care providers who do not understand their needs.

Substance Abuse While in Care

Foster children come from an environment in which parental substance abuse is more common than it is in the general population (Jones, 2004; Sun, Shillington, Hohman, & Jones, 2001). Data from the Casey Alumni study found that 64.6 percent of the parents and 45.1 percent fathers of the alumni had a substance abuse problem, suggesting substantial risk factors for FFY (Aarons et al., 2008; AFCARS, 2015; Pecora, Williams, et al., 2006). Parents who use drugs put their children at risk of a number of problems, including developmental and health difficulties, hazardous living conditions, inconsistent parenting, and increased exposure to violence. Parental drug use thus exposes children to the conditions for abuse and neglect, and indeed may be the cause of a child's entry into the foster care system (U.S. Government Accountability Office, 1994; White et al., 2008).

Late adolescence and continuing into young adulthood is a time when alcohol and marijuana use increases in the general population (Johnston, O'Malley, Bachman, & Schulenberg, 2012; SAMSHA, 2013). The evidence on whether foster youth are more likely to use or abuse substances and/or alcohol is mixed. The inconclusive findings can be traced to researchers inquiring about the extent of the problem in different time frames (30 days, 6 months, 1 year, and lifetime use), the use of different measures, having informants of differing ages, and relying on self-reports. However, data on the usage of alcohol and substances indicates something other than experimentation by foster youth both before and after they leave care.

Kohlenberg, Norlund, Lowin, and Treicher (2012) matched a group of foster youth with a random sample of children not in foster care in the same state. They found that foster youth were more likely than the matched group to have used alcohol and drugs at least one time, and tended to have begun using alcohol and drugs 18 months before the nonfoster comparisons. However, adolescents living in their family home were more likely than foster youth to have used opiates, cocaine, and hallucinogenics in the past 30 days. The two groups looked similar in the use of alcohol and marijuana, including heavy use of these intoxicants in the previous month. Using the Diagnostic Interview Schedule, these researchers found that 9.6 percent of their foster youth versus 6.2 percent of the general sample met the DSM-III-R criteria for a substance use disorder in the previous six months. Pilowsky and Wu (2006) investigated FFY use of alcohol and drugs by using the National Household Survey on Drug Abuse, which included 464 foster alumni among its representative sample of 19,430 12- to 17-year-olds. These researchers found that FFY were more likely to use alcohol (40 percent versus 32.9 percent), be alcohol dependent (6.5 percent versus 1.9 percent), have used illicit drugs (34.2 percent versus 18.1 percent), and be drug dependent than were their nonfoster peers (9.8 percent versus 2.2 percent).

NSCAW data showed that among youth age 15 and under, lifetime use of alcohol and marijuana was similar to national norms or slightly below, while the use of crack cocaine and heroin was higher than found in same-age peers in the general population (Wall & Kohl, 2007). However, the current use of alcohol (31.2 percent) among 14- and 15-year-olds in the NSCAW was two-and-a-half times the national rate (Cheng & Lo, 2010; Johnston et al., 2012). The Midwest Study reported a lower lifetime rate of 14 percent for alcohol disorders and 7.3 percent for substance abuse disorders among 17-year-olds than ADD Health respondents (Courtney et al., 2004). Rates of alcohol abuse and dependence were the same for both Midwest Study EFY and the general population at 14 percent (Keller, Salazar, & Courtney, 2010). Merikangas et al. (2010) said the rate of abuse and dependence on drugs in the general population at that age was 22 percent. Thompson and Auslander (2007) found similar rates of alcohol use between youth in care and youth never in foster care at ages 15 to 18. However, they found marijuana use was higher among foster youth than the other youth. Thirty-seven percent of the 17-year-olds in the Missouri Study had used alcohol in the last 6 months, and 26 percent had used marijuana during the same time. The reported rates in this study for use in the last year were similar to the general population. In contrast, the lifetime prevalence for a substance abuse disorder in the Missouri sample was 37 percent (Vaughan, Ollie, McMillen, Scott, & Munson, 2007), which was much higher than the general population. Youth in the CYAS had more life-time issues (14.1 percent versus 8.1 percent) with substance abuse than did their nonfoster peers, but youth in the general population (National Comor-bidity Study) had more past-year problems than the Casey alumni had. The lifetime rate for alcohol abuse was also higher than the general popula-tion (3.6 percent versus 1.1 percent) for this population (Havalchak et al., 2008). This rate is consistent with findings from studies that indicate that foster youth have higher rates of lifetime prevalence of substance abuse disorders than the general population (Aarons, Brown, Hough, Garland, & Wood, 2001; Courtney et al., 2004; Wall & Kohl, 2007). Aarons and col-leagues' (2001) study found 11.2 percent of the San Diego foster children they investigated met the criteria for substance abuse in the previous year, with 19.2 percent having met the criteria for a lifetime diagnosis. At age 17, 28 percent of youth in the National Youth in Transition Database (2014b), reported receiving drug treatment at some point. The rate of alcohol use among 12- to 17-year-olds was 11.6 percent in 2013. Youth binge and heavy drinking rates in 2013 were 6.2 percent and 1.2 percent, respectively. FFY who responded to the National Household Survey on Drug Abuse met the criteria for drug abuse in the past year at five times the rate of the general population (10 percent versus 2 percent) (Pilowsky & Wu, 2006). Data on the general population shows lower use rates by youth who had never been in foster care when compared to FFY. Almost 9 percent of a representa-tive sample of America's youth aged 12 to 17 used an illicit drug in 2013 (SAMHSA, 2013).

Risk Factors for Developing a Substance Abuse While in Care

Risk factors for developing an alcohol and/or drug disorder while in care included being male (Aarons et al., 2001); presence of an externalizing or behavioral disorder; having a history of physical abuse (Aarons et al., 2001; Vaughan et al., 2007; Wall & Kohl, 2007); being a victim of peer or sibling abuse (Aarons et al., 2001; Thompson & Auslander, 2007; Wall & Kohl, 2007); being white; truancy; being a victim of neglect; and having a PTSD diagnosis (Vaughan et al., 2007). Rubin, O'Reilly, Luan, and Localio (2007) suggest that instability in care as experienced through placement change can exacerbate drug problems. Comorbid anxiety and behavior disorders often follow the abuse of alcohol (Rhode, Lewinsohn, & Seeley, 1996). A national survey of adolescents (n=4,023) found the risk for substance abuse to be increased among those youth whose family had a history of alcohol abuse and/ or among those who had been the victim of or a witness to family violence (Kilpatrick et al., 2003). The finding on independent living environments has special relevance for those youth transitioning out of care. These youth are leaving structured environments where they are under the supervision of adults. When they leave care, they are out from under that scrutiny and have more opportunity to use substances and alcohol without detection (Narendorf & McMillen, 2010). Child welfare supervision may be one of the reasons that some studies find that youth in the general population use more drugs than youth in foster care.

Substance Use and Abuse among Transitioning Youth

While the evidence that FFY have more mental health problems than their nonfoster peers is abundant, the empirical support is less clear on whether former system-involved youth have more problems with substance abuse than youth in the general population. Nevertheless, many youth leaving care use substances in ways that interfere with the transition (Keller et al., 2010). The federal government's Substance Abuse and Mental Health Administration (SAMHSA) National Survey on Drug Use and Health 2002 and 2003 reported that 34 percent of FFY had used illicit drugs in the previous year versus 22 percent of youth who had never been in foster care (SAMHSA, 2005). The Midwest Study found that the abuse and use of alcohol and drugs increased as youth left care. At age 19, 8 percent of youth were abusing substances and 3 percent were dependent on alcohol, but at age 26, 16 percent of these youth were alcohol abusers and 13 percent were alcohol dependent. The corresponding rates for substance abuse disorders at ages 19 and 26 were 16 percent and 13 percent. The rates of substance abuse and dependence at age 26 were 23 percent and 20 percent, suggesting that EFY have a different pattern of abuse and dependence than the general population, where abuse and dependence peaks at around age 19 and then decreases. EFY increase their use of substances throughout their twenties (SAMHSA, 2011).

The Missouri study showed that substance abuse disorders were more frequent in that sample than the general population, and as shown in other studies, increased after a youth left the child welfare system. This study also showed a steady increase in "getting drunk" between the ages of 17 and 19, from 18 percent to 31 percent. Self-reported use of drugs increased from 2 percent to 6 percent during the same period. For those who exited at age 18, the biggest jump in usage occurred in the year after the youth left care. This increase in substance abuse was not as pronounced with those who remained in care until age 19. Missouri youth were more likely to use substances or get drug treatment at age 17 if they lived in an independent living situation compared to those who stayed in care. After that age, the living situation of the youth does not appear to make a statistical difference in substance usage rates (Narendorf & McMillen, 2010).

In a national evaluation of independent living programs, Cook, Fleishman, and Grimes (1991), found that rates of alcohol consumption were lower among FFY, but substance use rates were similar to use in the general population. In contrast, Casey Alumni experienced more than seven times the rate of drug dependency, and almost two times the rate of alcohol dependency as their peers in the National Comorbidity Study who had never been in out-of-home care (Pecora, Kessler, et al., 2003). Casey alumni reported substance dependency at greater rates than the general population, but these respondents reported no greater dependency on alcohol than youth in the general population (Pecora, Kessler, et al., 2005). About one-quarter (25.8 percent) of CalYOUTH FFY at age 17 had a diagnosable substance abuse disorder, with 13.6 percent having a mental health problem also. At age 19 about 15 percent of youth had a substance abuse diagnosis, with about 33 percent having either a substance abuse or mental health disorder. About one-fifth of the sample reported being in a substance abuse treatment program (18.8 percent), with males being more likely than females to receive those services (23.4 percent versus 15.6 percent). About three-quarters of youth who self-reported substance abuse problems received services. Youth who left care were more likely to screen for substance abuse treatment than youth who remained in care (Courtney & Charles, 2015; Courtney, Opkych, et al., 2016).

At age 21, 23 percent of Midwest Study males and 9 percent of females had a drug or alcohol diagnosis. About one-quarter of the sample said they had used substances in the last year. About 6 percent of the sample met the diagnostic criteria for substance abuse and 5 percent were drug dependent (Courtney, Dworsky, Cusick, et al., 2009). The only gender differences on the use of drugs were that males were twice as likely as females to use marijuana, and they were more likely than females to report that the use of drugs gave them problems in other areas of their life primarily through involvement with the legal system.

Sixteen percent of the Midwest Study's 26-year-old youth met the criteria for alcohol abuse, and 13 percent of participants were alcohol dependent. The most frequent indicator of abuse was being drunk in situations where it was potentially harmful to them, such as driving a car. Dependence was partially determined by youth saying they drank more than they should, and wanted to cut down on their drinking. Males were more likely than females to report an arrest for driving under the influence, and to say that they "wanted a drink so badly they could not think of anything else." Males in the Midwest Study were more likely on all measures to report abuse and dependence problems with alcohol than were females (Courtney, Dworsky, et al., 2011).

Despite the high level of need for treatment services, the National Youth in Transition Database (2014, September) shows a drop in referrals for drug or alcohol services between ages 17 and 19. At age 19, 15 percent of FFY reported receiving a referral for substance abuse. At age 17, 28 percent of youth had received such a referral. Either some youth have recovered, or some youth are not receiving needed services.

In both the Midwest and Missouri Studies, youth who remained in care had fewer substance disorders at age 19 than youth who had left the system (Courtney & Dworsky, 2005, 2006; Narendorf & McMillen, 2010). In the Missouri study, 41 percent of youth who left care "got drunk" in the previous month versus 21 percent of those who remained in care. At age 18, the same pattern was found for marijuana; 31 percent of youth who left care reported using versus a 9 percent usage rate for those remaining in care, providing further evidence on the benefits of extended foster care (Narendorf & McMillen, 2010).

Risk Factors for Mental Health and Substance Abuse Problems among Transitioning Youth

Risk factors for substance use found in the Missouri study were being male, having a conduct disorder, and having peers who used substances. Females and males with sexual abuse histories were more likely to use alcohol than those without that type of maltreatment history (Vaughan et al., 2007). Other risk factors for alcohol and drug use noted for youth that have been identified in the literature include mental health problems, particularly a PTSD diagnosis; low educational attainments; delinquent behavior; lack of positive social role models (Traube, James, Zang, & Landsverk, 2012); and poor social environments (Braciszewski & Stout, 2012; Stott, 2012). A number of studies indicate that a predictor of drug use was having peers who were involved with drugs (Kohlenberg et al., 2012; Narendorf & McMillen, 2010; Thompson & Auslander, 2007). Keller et al. (2010), using Midwest study data, found that white youth were more likely to use substances and alcohol than were African American youth. African Americans were the ethnic group least likely to have abused or be dependent on alcohol. Youth in kinship care were less likely than youth in other types of care to meet any diagnostic criteria for substance abuse or alcohol disorder. These researchers note that the most vulnerable living relationship for developing a disorder was to live independently.

Fowler, Toro, and Miles (2011) used latent class analysis with 265 Detroit EFY to identify subgroup adaptations to the transition. Twenty-nine percent of youth were in a group called *Instable-Disengaged*. This group had more mental health problems, substance abuse disorders, and other accompanying problems than the other identified groups. This group had chronic housing problems, high unemployment, and low levels of educational achievement.

The *Stable-Engaged* group not only had fewer mental health problems but also had stable housing and higher levels of employment. They were also more likely to have completed high school. Kushel, Yen, Gee, and Courtney (2007) used the Midwest Study data to identify that homeless youth had more drug and alcohol problems than stably housed youth (46.3 percent versus 23.5 percent). These findings are in congruence with ecological theory that suggests the environmental context and its supports are important in determining adaption to any situation such as the transition period (Belsky, 1993; Bronfenbrenner, 1979). However, it is not clear whether drug and alcohol problems preceded housing difficulties or came afterward.

A number of studies have examined how the conditions of foster care affect risk for mental health and substance abuse disorders. A familiar risk discussed in earlier chapters is that frequent placement changes aggravate behavior problems and are associated with substance abuse (Jonson-Reid & Barth, 2000; McCoy, McMillen, & Spitznagel, 2008; Reilly, 2003; Ryan & Testa, 2005; White et al., 2008; Zima, Bussing, Freeman, Yang, Belin, & Forness, 2000). Both Narendorf and McMillen (2010) and Stott (2012) found as the number of placement changes increased while in care, the likelihood of substance abuse also increased. Stott asserted that frequent placement changes disrupted social networks and sources of social support, made it difficult to make friends, and resulted in foster youth drifting toward high-risk relationships. Similarly, school mobility has been identified as a risk factor for alcohol and drug problems, perhaps because school change is also disruptive of support systems (White et al., 2008). Other studies have shown that youth in congregate care generally have more behavioral and mental health problems than youth in family or kin foster care (Barth, 2002; Hook & Courtney, 2011; Ryan, Marshall, Herz, & Hernandez, 2008). The findings that youth in congregate care are more prone to problems is not surprising given these placements are for youth with more difficult behaviors.

Shook et al. (2013) used their large data set from Alleghany County, Pennsylvania (n=42,375), to determine that youth who "aged out of care" had more mental health problems and substance abuse disorders (84 percent and 41 percent respectively) than youth who left care prior to age 17 (70 percent and 26 percent). These EFY also had worse mental health than other system-involved youth who had never been in out-of-home care (37 percent and 10 percent). These findings are not surprising given the long stay in foster care without a permanency plan. The time in care may have exacerbated problems that existed before care. These problems may have been the reason for the removal of the youth from their original home when they were a child.

Youth in the Northwest Alumni study were more likely to have an alcohol and drug dependence problem if they had parents with such dependency problems and/or did not know their parents prior to being removed and going into care. Youth who entered foster care with a diagnosed behavior problem were more likely to develop a drug dependence problem as a young adult. Frequent placement changes, with an accompanying high rate of school change, were both associated with higher levels of alcohol dependence. Placement with kin was associated with lower levels of alcohol dependence. Alumni who perceived foster parents to be very helpful were less likely to be alcohol or drug dependent than youth who thought their foster parent was "somewhat" or "less" helpful. Youth who received educational support services were less likely to have drug dependence problems. Casey alumni who left care with the tangible resources described in Chapter 7 (driver's license, kitchen utensils, and $250 in cash) were less likely to be drug dependent (White et al., 2008).

Practical Recommendations for Improving the Mental and Behavioral Health of Former Foster Youth

Chapters 9 and 10 summarize the evidence that adverse childhood experiences are associated with adult physical and mental health status and morbidity, and confirm that maltreatment and placement into foster care is a risk. Public health epidemiology uses the concept of a *sentinel event* to describe an injury or worse that arises from a preventable event. These events require an immediate evaluation of the event and a response to guarantee patient safety. Zlotnick et al. (2012) assert that foster care is such an event that signals an opportunity. At-risk youth enter into a system where they can potentially receive the assistance needed to reduce the likelihood of experiencing the kind of health problems outlined in this and the previous chapter.

Evidence-Based Services

The research on brain development and neuroscience suggests that the period of adolescence and into the midtwenties provides a "window of opportunity" for improving developmental outcomes (Masten, 2006; Schulenberg, Sameroff, & Cicchetti, 2004). It follows then that youth at this age may benefit from well-designed, evidence-based programs while they are in care, and continuing services when they leave.

Evidence-based treatment programs are a necessity for youth. These treatments are especially important for PTSD, depression, and conduct disorders, given their high prevalence with foster youth, both while in care and after discharge. Family-based interventions with the involvement of caregivers have sufficient empirical support for their effectiveness with conduct disorders. The family-based requirement may be a limitation for foster youth, particularly those without permanency plans (Chambless & Ollendick, 2001; Chambless

& Reid, 1998). The evidence also suggests that cognitive behavioral treatment is effective for trauma (Cohen, Berliner, & Mannarino, 2010). Evidence on what works for substance abuse disorders is more mixed. Clarity is needed on this matter given the prevalence of these disorders among FFY. Youth who do not receive mental health treatment might turn to drugs as means of self-medication to cope.

Riggs and Davies (2002) describe a promising approach for treating depression and substance abuse in FFY that combines assessment, the development of client-created goals, psychotherapy, pharmacology if needed, and frequent toxic screening for substance abuse. Treatment that addresses both mental health and substance abuse at the same time is a critical need for many FFY.

Child welfare personnel (social workers and foster parents) and collaborating staff from other agencies should have knowledge about how trauma affects a child's or adolescent's developmental trajectory. Personnel should also understand how maltreatment and systems and services characteristics, such as frequent placement changes, contribute to trauma. Workers need not be trauma intervention specialists, but they should be trauma informed. They should at least be able to assess for the presence of trauma and make appropriate referrals (Jim Casey Opportunities Initiatives, 2011). Similar training for professionals should be done for substance abuse. Foster parents need to know the risks for and warning signs of substance abuse.

Screening and Assessment

Routine periodic screening for mental health and substance abuse problems should be a part of the child welfare system's services. At a minimum, assessments should be part of the intake process for foster care, and at exit from care. Substance abuse treatment is likely to be most effective when it is available before a youth leaves care, when she or he is a captive audience and not worried about gathering the basic needs for survival (Braciszewski & Stout, 2012).

Extend Foster Care

Both the Midwest and Missouri studies present data that shows youth who remain in care past age 18 will more likely utilize mental health services than youth who leave care to live independently. Courtney and Dworsky (2006) report that youth who remained in care until age 19 were twice as likely to receive mental health or substance disorder services. Perhaps the continued supervision by social workers is a factor here. These studies also indicate that extended foster care would reduce alcohol or substance abuse and/or dependence (Brown et al., 2015; McMillen & Raghavan, 2009). Illinois case-workers reported that youth who remained in care had fewer behavioral problems, educational deficits, and job skill deficits than youth who opted out of care (Leather & Testa, 2006). However, some researchers suggest that high-risk youth are more likely to leave care, which may mean there is some sort of self-selection process underlying these data. Youth with difficulties may actively seek to disengage from care. This extension is crucial for youth with substance abuse disorders or conduct disorders, as these problems require longer periods of treatment. Relapse is an expected part of substance disorder recovery and treatment, and thus youth with these problems may need more time in care in order to be treated successfully. It may be difficult for youth with mental health and substance abuse problems to meet the employment and educational requirements to continue to receive services when they turn 21; this highlights a need for states to develop programs that meet the specific needs of substance-abusing transition-age youth.

Aftercare Planning Must Include Mental Health and/or Substance Abuse Treatment for Those Who Need It

Youth should leave care with a plan for transfer to the adult health and behavioral health systems in order to avoid gaps in care that could lead to more severe problems later. Youth must exit with the medical passport discussed in Chapter 9.

Educating Foster Youth about Substance and Alcohol Use and Abuse

Data from the National Survey on Drug Use and Health 2002–2012 indicate that foster youth ages 12 to 17 were less likely than those children never removed from their homes to discuss with a parent or guardian the dangers of drug and alcohol use. Adolescents in foster care were also less likely to report seeing media messages about the dangers of substance use and to report participating in school-based prevention programs during regular class compared with adolescents who were not in foster care. However, foster youth were more likely than other youth to have participated in drug and alcohol prevention programs outside of school. Foster youth, foster parents, and the biological families of the youth should have access to evidence-based substance abuse prevention programs that they can utilize with their charges. Certainly such education should be part of any independent living program. Transitioning youth also report not knowing about mental health care or the services that are available to them when they leave care (Havlicek, McMillen, Fedoravicius, McNelly, & Robinson, 2012).

Reduce Placement and School Change

Casey Alumni Study data suggests that youth who see their foster parents as "very helpful" are more likely to resist drug and alcohol use and abuse. Youth need time to build support from foster parents, which is difficult when frequent placement change makes it difficult to build relationships with their caretakers (White et al., 2008). See Chapter 6 for further discussion on the effect placement changes on youth.

Collaboration Between Child Welfare and Substance Abuse Treatment Agencies

Greater access to treatment for alcohol, drug, and substance abuse for transitioning youth is a need that must be met. The sharp drop-off in treatment for substance abuse is an area of concern that needs examination. Child welfare professionals and mental health providers including pediatric mental health specialists need to do a better job at coordinating services in order to insure a smooth transition to adult care. Close collaboration between the child welfare, health, behavioral health, and educational systems needs to occur before and after discharge to ensure that the behavioral health needs of youth are not overlooked. Identification preceded treatment. This is particularly important when alcohol and substance abuse are co-occurring in FFY because treatment of these problems often occurs in separate agencies. Unfortunately, mental health treatment has not been integrated well with other services youth need (Miller & Brown, 1997). An important factor in the success of programs developed for FFY is how well these programs recognize and integrate mental health and substance abuse treatment services. Havlicek et al. (2013) suggests a program called Partnership for Youth Transition, a federally funded and tested program that integrated support and services to engage transition age youth with serious mental health disorders with adult serving organizations (Davis, Koroloff, & Ellison, 2012). We should recognize that providing mental health treatment in itself might reduce substance abuse.

Independent Living Services

Georgiades (2005) presents some evidence that youth who take part in independent living services (ILS) are less likely to be depressed and have fewer anger management issues than youth who do not participate in ILS programs. However, the direction of the relationship is unclear. More stable foster youth may seek out ILS, so a self-selection process may be at work. As stated in Chapter 4, stronger tests of the efficacy of ILS programs should occur so that we may determine what works.

Additional Research Needs on Mental Health and Substance Abuse

We need to know what types of treatments would be most beneficial in addressing mental health and/or substance abuse disorders for EFY. This means identifying what type of programs would help the adolescent transition more successfully to emerging adulthood. Data should describe the trajectories of disorders (onset, severity, co-occurrences with other conditions) and identify risk factors that predict the use of substances among foster children in order to develop preventative interventions. Given the drop-off noted in the use of mental health services by EFY, we might consider whether youth avoid these services because they do not meet their needs or because they do not have a means to access services.

Monitor the Use of Psychotropic Medication

Research has indicated that between 13 and 40 percent of foster youth use psychotropic or prescription medication (Leslie, Raghavan, Zhang, & Aarons, 2010; McMillen, Zima, Scott, Ollie, & Munson, 2004). At the low end, this rate of usage is twice the rate in the general population (6.7 percent) (Zito et al., 2008). Youth need to have some choice and/or input as appropriate for the use of psychotropic medications and other mental health services. Social workers need to recognize the short- and long-term risks associated with psychotropic medication use. Despite these risks, social workers should also recognize that proper psychotropic medication use could help alleviate suffering in children and youth who are battling psychiatric conditions and must take the necessary steps to find resources that will help ameliorate this distress appropriately (Ramirez, 2015).

CHAPTER ELEVEN

Pregnancy, Sexuality, and Parenting

In 2014, there were 24.2 births for every 1,000 U.S. adolescent female ages 15–19. Almost 89 percent of these births occurred to single women. The 2014 teen birth rate had declined to 17.7 percent from 2012, when the birth rate was 26.5 per 1,000 adolescent females. Despite this decline, young women in America are at a high risk of an early, unplanned teen pregnancy compared with their counterparts in the developed world (Kost, 2016).

The risk of adolescent pregnancy is even greater for foster children. They are two or three times more likely to become pregnant than teens in the general population (Boonstra, 2011; Oshima, Narendorf, & McMillen, 2013; Shaw, Barth, Svoboda, & Shaikh, 2010). Midwest youth had children at over twice the rate of the ADD Health sample. Data from the National Youth in Transition Database (2014a, 2014b) found that at age 17, 17.7 percent of the former foster youth (FFY) had a child. A Maryland study found the rate for adolescent pregnancy among foster youth was 92.7 per thousand compared to 32.7 per thousand in the state's general population (Shaw et al., 2010). California researchers who used a probability sample of adolescents found the rate of pregnancy for 15- to 17-year-old females in foster care was 30.2 per thousand, while the state's rate for girls of the same age who had never been in care was 20.0 per thousand (King, Putnam-Hornstein, Cederbaum, & Needell, 2014). In Arizona, Stott (2012) found that 17.4 percent of the 18-year-olds in her sample were currently pregnant, and 22.2 percent of the 19-year-olds were pregnant. The state's pregnancy rate at the time of her study was 10.5 percent for 18-year-olds and 13.9 percent for those youth age 19. Gotbaum (2005) found approximately 16 percent of New York City females in care (ages 13 to 21) were pregnant. About 17 percent of young women served by Casey Family Programs had at least one child while in care (Pecora, Williams, et al., 2003). Seventeen percent of the young women in the National Youth in Transition Database (NYTD) sample had birthed a child while they were 18 or 19, and 6 percent of males in that data base had become fathers. Twelve percent of the overall sample had become parents (National Youth in Transition Database, 2014a, 2014b).

The Casey Young Adult Survey (CYAS) reported that by age 25, 38 percent of the sample had given birth or fathered a child. Twenty-six percent of the pregnancies were planned (Havalchak, White, & O'Brien, 2008). Singer (2004) reported that 31 percent of females who emancipated from Utah's foster care system had become pregnant by age 24. Both Berzin (2008) and Buehler, Orme, Post, & Patterson (2000) used nationally representative samples to compare the experiences of former foster youth (FFY) with the general population. They also selected a low-income matched group that was similar to the FFY except for the experience of being in out-of-home care for further comparisons. Berzin (2008), using the National Longitudinal Survey of Youth, found that foster youth had higher pregnancy rates than youth in the general population, but they had the same rate as a matched group of youth with similar socioeconomic characteristics. Buehler et al. (2000) reported data from the National Survey of Families and Households that FFY had more unintended children than both the general population and a low-income matched group. However, these researchers found no difference in family size between groups, but both the FFY and low-income groups reported less satisfaction with their role as parent than did parents in the general population. Schmitz (2005), using the same data set as Berzin, found youth who had been in foster care had more children in their twenties than did youth who were never in care.

The Midwest Study provided further evidence that as young women leave care, they become vulnerable to pregnancy. Pregnancies were more common among youth who left care than among those who chose to remain in extended foster care. One-third of the females had been pregnant prior to their first interview at age 17 or 18. In contrast, just 13.5 percent of the ADD Health sample had been pregnant by those ages. About two-thirds of these women said the pregnancy was unwanted. For 23 percent of these women this pregnancy was a repeat (Courtney, Terao, & Bost, 2004). Repeat pregnancies were common at all measures. At age 19, half of the Midwest young women (51 percent) had been or were pregnant versus 27 percent of the same age females in the ADD Health comparison group. Forty-seven percent of these Midwest pregnancies were a repeat pregnancy. At age 21, 71 percent of the Midwest Study's young women had been pregnant, and 62 percent of these pregnancies were, at least, their second pregnancy. In comparison, only one-third of the young women in the ADD Health sample had been pregnant more than once (Courtney, Dworsky, Cusick, et al., 2009). The Los Angeles

Multi-Site Evaluation sample had similar rates of pregnancy (Pergamit & Johnson, 2009).

By age, 23–24, 75 percent of the Midwest young women and 61 percent of the young men had become a parent (Courtney, Dworsky, Lee, & Rapp, 2010). More than 50 percent of these women were parenting a child at the time of the interview. Fifty-five percent of the Missouri Study females had been pregnant by age 19, and 23 percent of the males had fathered a child by that age (Oshima et al., 2013). Similar results were obtained in the CalYOUTH sample, where one-half of the young women were pregnant, and about 65 percent of these young women had already given birth (Courtney et al., 2016). At the final Midwest interview at age 26, 80 percent of the young women had been pregnant versus 55 percent of the females in the ADD Health Study. Forty-four percent of the pregnancies had occurred since the last interview (ages 23 or 24) (Courtney, Dworsky, et al., 2011).

Pregnancy and the Transition

Pregnancy presents a barrier to achieving self-sufficiency. The cumulative research on the topic indicates that adolescent mothers face many challenges in moving into emerging adulthood. Early parenting adversely affects educational progress, employment prospects, and financial stability (Boden, Fergusson, & Horwood, 2008; Mares & Kroner, 2011). In addition, pregnancy complicates the problem of finding affordable housing (Dion, Dworsky, Huff, & Kleinman, 2014), results in more mental health difficulties (Barnet, Liu, & DeVoe, 2008), increases substance abuse, enhances the possibility of victimization (Jaffee, 2002), and heightens the risk of being a perpetrator of child maltreatment (Goerge, Harden, & Lee, 2008). Fifteen percent of the CalYOUTH sample who had dropped out of high school said having a child was their reason for quitting school (Courtney et al., 2016). Difficulties have been noted with the children of these mothers well into early adulthood including a higher risk of infant and perinatal mortality (Mathews & MacDorman, 2013), behavioral problems, school deficits (Jaffee, Caspi, Moffitt, Taylor, & Dickson, 2001), and involvement in risky sexual behaviors (Levine, Emery, & Pollack, 2007).

Chapter 3 reported on the use of latent class analysis to classify the Midwest sample into distinct groups. This analysis found that the youth who most resembled Arnett's *Emerging Adults* were also the youth most likely to have avoided becoming parents. These young adults were attending school and/or were employed, and did not have the kind of difficulties that most EFY were encountering. Those in the *Accelerated Adults* category had experienced an event like a pregnancy, which rushed a youth into adulthood before they were ready. Youth were struggling economically, but they were working and parenting their children, and sometimes continuing their own education. However, they needed more support than the Emerging Adults. *Struggling Parents* were those having more employment problems and difficulties continuing their education. Pregnancy had happened before they finished high school, which made it difficult for them to find work, and without assistance, they were having trouble meeting their child's needs. The final group, *Troubled and Troubling*, had a range of problems (mental health, substance abuse, housing), that made them unable to raise their children, and in some instances their children had entered the child welfare system (Cusick & Courtney, 2007).

Leaving care pregnant or with a child presents a serious additional challenge that must be addressed (Courtney, Hook, & Lee, 2010). The experience of Emerging and Accelerated Adults suggests that this is not impossible, though it is certainly difficult.

Risk and Protective Factors for Pregnancy

Previous chapters of this book have identified risk factors that the literature indicates would increase the likelihood of an early pregnancy. These include factors such as depression and conduct disorders (Barnet, Jaffee, Duggan, Wilson, & Repke, 1996; Jaffee, 2002), substance abuse problems (Stott, 2012), academic difficulties (Moore, Manlove, Glei, & Morrison, 1998), minority ethnic status (Thompson, Bender, Lewis, & Watkins, 2008), and being a victim of maltreatment (Francisco et al., 2008). Factors associated with avoiding pregnancy included staying in school (Dogan-Ates & Carrion-Basham, 2007), having strong religious beliefs (Rostosky, Regenerus, & Comer-Wright, 2003), not having criminal justice or juvenile delinquency involvement (Stott, 2012), and staying in care past age 18 (Courtney & Dworsky, 2006; Stott, 2012).

A secondary analysis of the Midwest data found 53.3 percent of homeless EFY females became pregnant versus 38.4 percent of the total sample. The pregnancy rate among youth who remained in extended foster care was 31.5 percent. Young women who became pregnant were more likely to have left care (44 percent versus 31 percent). Dworsky and Courtney (2010b) explained this finding in a number of ways. First, pregnancy may be the reason why these young women left care, or it may be that foster care exerts a protective effect for those who remain within the child welfare system. Perhaps foster parent supervision reduces opportunities for pregnancy for those still in care. Foster youth may also receive more information about birth control and risky sexual behavior. However, an unexpected finding from this research was that women who left care were more likely to describe the pregnancy as wanted and they sought prenatal care more often than young pregnant women who remained in foster care. Another surprise finding was that women in care were more likely to end a pregnancy through an abortion than were young emancipated women (22 percent versus 3 percent). This finding makes sense in light of the claim that the pregnancy was more likely to be unwanted if the young woman had not left the child welfare system (Courtney & Dworsky, 2006). Midwest Study young women at age 26 were less likely than ADD Health respondents were to report the use of birth control. They were also more likely than the comparison sample to say a pregnancy was unplanned (73.3 percent versus 51.3 percent) (Courtney, Dworsky, et al., 2011).

Homelessness was associated with pregnancy, but only at a level approaching significance. The researchers said their small sample size might have interfered with finding a significant difference. If the EFY was homeless, the chance that the EFY's child would enter the foster care system increased (Kushel, Yen, Gee, & Courtney, 2007). The same analysis found young women without insurance were more likely to be pregnant than those with insurance.

Data from the NYTD suggest that adolescent mothers in foster care were more likely to be nonwhite and Hispanic (Shpiegel & Cascardi, 2015). In Illinois, a randomly selected sample of social workers of EFY were interviewed (n=416) about their perceptions of how well they thought their former foster care clients would do in the transition. These social workers reported that African American adolescent females were three times more likely than white girls to have had a baby (Leathers & Testa, 2006). This finding parallels other published reports on higher rates of teen pregnancy comparisons between white and African American teens. Some research is available to suggest that African American adolescent mothers are more resilient than either Hispanic or white mothers (Wiltz, 2015). A survey of 17-year-old or younger mothers found that the African American mothers were more likely to persist in school than were mothers from other racial groups (Testa, 1992). According to the caseworkers, the African American mothers were also less likely than the young white mothers to be delinquent, engage in risky behavior, and be a victim of domestic violence (Leathers & Testa, 2006). Brubaker and Wright (2006) maintain the high value placed on mothering and children in the African American community can bring recognition and status to these young mothers. Nevertheless, African American mothers aging out of foster care reported financial difficulties, stress from trying to manage multiple roles and responsibilities, often without the support of the father, and having anxiety about losing their children to child protective services (CPS). They also struggle with loss of autonomy and further stigma if there is CPS involvement with their children (Courtney, Dworsky, & Pollack, 2007; Haight, Finet, Bamba, & Helton, 2009).

Motivations for Child Rearing among Current and Former Foster Youth

One-third of the Midwest women who became pregnant by age 19 said the pregnancy was "definitely" or "probably" wanted (Dworsky & Courtney, 2010). Qualitative studies of young mothers at emancipation suggest a number of reasons why adolescent females might choose to become pregnant. These young mothers report that having a child, even when the pregnancy was unplanned, gave them an opportunity to create a meaningful relationship that included a permanent family. A child also gave the young women someone to love, provided them with hope for the future, and gave them a sense of purpose. A child was a means of metamorphosing from a problem teenager or daughter into a mature adult and "good mother." These mothers also claimed that having a child gave them an incentive to succeed in education and/or employment, and provided them with status and respect in their community (Haight et al., 2009; Love, McIntosh, Rosst, & Tertzakian, 2005; Pryce & Samuels, 2010). Other research studies suggest that youth see motherhood as a way to regain the family they lost or never had, and to fill an emotional need that comes from the instability of many placements (Boonstra, 2011; Connolly, Heifetz, & Bohr, 2012). Data are available that suggest low-income status may lead adolescents and their families to view an early pregnancy more positively than higher income persons (Vespa, Lewis, & Kreider, 2013). This sentiment does not mean these mothers do not feel initial shame, and they may feel a sense of loss that their educational or other plans may have to be put on hold. They do experience the pressure of having to perform multiple roles and continued stigma. The positive features of parenting identified in qualitative studies may often be undermined as youth encounter the financial and environmental stress of motherhood.

Parenting Behavior after Leaving Care

Most of the mothers in the Midwest and CalYOUTH studies had their child living with them. At age 19, 31.6 percent of the Midwest Study females and 13.8 percent of the males were parents. No differences were noted between the two EFY samples of 19-year-olds and the comparison group on whether children were living with their mother or not. Three-quarters of parents reported that their child lived with them. Female parents were more likely than males to say that their child was residing with them (93 percent versus 18 percent). Similar rates of Midwest Study and ADD Health parents lived with their children at age 19. After age 19 fewer of these children lived with their mother than did children in the ADD Health sample (Courtney & Dworsky, 2006). At age 21, over one-half of the females and almost one-third of the males had a child. Two-thirds of the mothers were a custodial parent. Females were much more likely than males to be raising their children (32 percent versus 14 percent at age 19, and 91 percent versus 24 percent at age 26) (Courtney et al., 2005; Courtney, Dworsky, et al., 2011). Therefore, these young women bear the disproportionate challenges of parenting. They must secure the resources needed to sustain a young child as well as meet their own needs. Midwest Study youth who remained in care were less likely than those who had left care to have their child living with them (Courtney et al., 2005; Courtney, Dworsky, et al., 2011).

Only 15 percent of the Midwest Study fathers were living with their child. Among the noncustodial parents at age 21 similar monthly visiting rates with their children were observed for females and males (73 percent versus 69 percent), but more females than males said they never saw their child (31 percent versus 13 percent). Both the Midwest Study and CalYOUTH fathers who remained in care were more likely to have contact with their children than fathers who had left care (Courtney et al., 2016; Hook & Courtney, 2011). Noncustodial children of the Midwest parents were likely to be in foster care or were adopted. The ADD Health parents' nonresident children were more likely to be living with relatives, most often a maternal grandmother.

Forty-three percent of the 19-year-old CalYOUTH fathers of a child lived with the mother. Mothers reported that each custodial parent spent about equal amounts of time with the child, but about two-thirds reported that the noncustodial parent only rarely or never visited the child. Whether a non-resident parent spent time with their child was partially contingent on whether the fathers had a romantic relationship with the parent who lived with the child (Courtney et al., 2016).

Twenty-six-year-old noncustodial Midwest males visited their children more often than did noncustodial mothers. Almost a quarter of these males reported daily visits with their child, versus 13 percent of the noncustodial mothers who said they saw their child daily. Nearly 30 percent of the mothers and 15 percent of the males with nonresidential children said they never visited their child (Courtney, Dworsky, et al., 2011).

Positive aspects of FFY becoming parents were identified by Leathers and Testa's (2006) sample of case workers. These workers reported that only 8 percent of the parenting youth had "very much a problem" with parenting, and another 30 percent had somewhat of a problem with the parenting role. These findings suggest that social workers think that the bulk of these young mothers can do a "good enough" job of parenting. Midwest custodial parents at ages 25 and 26 did not report high levels of stress from parenting, but they did say raising a child was more difficult than they had expected (Courtney, Dworsky, et al., 2011; Courtney, Dworsky, Cusick, et al., 2009).

NYTD data provides significant descriptive data about these parents. Most of these parents reported being in an educational program (91 percent). Thirteen percent of the youthful parents said they were working, and 95 percent said they had at least one adult they could rely on. On the negative side, 16 percent had been homeless, 28 percent had been referred for substance abuse assessment or treatment, and 35 percent had been incarcerated. Only on educational involvement, (95 percent versus 91 percent) and incarceration (35 percent versus 25 percent), did these parents differ statistically from nonparenting foster youth. These negative outcomes were more apparent with adolescent fathers than with the mothers. Fathers were more often than the mothers to be homeless, to have used substances, and to have been incarcerated. Finally, pregnancy or parenting did not affect independent living services receipt. No ethnic or racial differences were found for male parents in the NYTD sample on any of the above variables (Shpiegel & Cascardi, 2015).

The Involvement of the Children of FFY in the Child Welfare System

Prevalence of Child Welfare Involvement by the Children of FFY

Fifteen percent of the parents in the CalYOUTH study had at least one child who was a dependent of the court (Courtney et al., 2016). At age 23–24, 22 percent of the Midwest mothers gave as a reason their child was not residing with them was that the child was in foster care (Courtney, Dworsky, et al., 2010). Eight percent of the youth in the Northwest Alumni study had a child in foster care (Pecora, Williams, et al., 2003). Goerge and colleagues (2008), using administrative data from Illinois, found the chances of child abuse or neglect were elevated 2.7 times if the mother was under age 18, and 2.3 times greater if the mother was age 19 or 20. The elevated risk in this study continued until age 22.

Dworsky (2015) also utilized Illinois child welfare administrative data to find that 39 percent of children of mothers who had previously been in foster care were the subject of at least one child abuse investigation by the time the child reached age five. The chance of having an "indicated" child maltreatment report, which means at least some credible evidence of maltreatment was found, was elevated 2.8 times if the mother was a foster alumnus. The likelihood of being the subject of a child abuse investigation was increased by 1.5 times if the parent of that child had been in foster care. The mean age of the child at the investigation was 18 months. About one-third of the mothers were still in care, and 14 percent of the mothers had exited at the time of the report. Eighty-five percent of these investigations were for allegations of neglect, 45 percent were for physical abuse, and 11 percent were for possible sexual abuse. Forty-five percent of these investigations resulted in an indicated report (17 percent of the sample).

Risk Factors for Child Welfare Involvement

Youth not only leave care with limited support and a host of problems but they may also lack parenting skills and knowledge of child development. The impact of their own abuse, combined with their own lack of consistent stable parenting, may result in them being less able to parent than adolescents who had never been abused or in foster care (DePaul & Domenech, 2000;

Dworsky, 2015; Valentino, Nuttall, Cmoas, Borkowski, & Akai, 2012). In addition to maltreatment, before going into foster care they may have been exposed to domestic violence, parents with both substance abuse, and mental health problems. In care, frequent placement change, and possible poor care-taking by foster parents, may further exacerbate behavioral problems. They may lack the proper role models for becoming a good parent, and they may not have the social support that one needs to raise a child at such a young age. We have already noted in previous chapters the numerous problems that FFY have with adult functioning, which also interferes with parenting.

A study with a robust methodological design that linked birth records in Los Angeles with statewide databases found the strongest predictor of mater-nal maltreatment of children to be whether the mother had been abused prior to age six. This history was stronger than other variables, such as the age at which she gave birth, the birth weight of the child, and the presence or absence of prenatal care, in predicting whether or not she would abuse her child (Putnam-Hornstein, Cederbaum, King, & Needell, 2013). Data from a small convenience sample (n=60) of adolescent mothers participating in a home visiting program found that the risk of maternal child neglect increased by four times if the mother had been physically abused in her own child-hood. Eleven percent of the children of FFY were removed from their paren-tal home prior to their fifth birthday. The most common reason for removal was neglect. Caution should be exercised in interpreting these results because of the small sample size and missing data (Bartlett & Eastbrooks, 2012).

Early motherhood and parenting is a known risk for child maltreatment. The lack of knowledge of parenting and child development, and their own normal adolescent egocentric perspective, means that young mothers might not see their own child's needs or they may have unrealistic expectations of their child (Borkowski et al., 2007; Keogh, Weed, & Noria, 2007). Methods of discipline put youth at risk of a CPS investigation. Forty-five percent of mothers and 49 percent of fathers reported what Courtney, Dworsky, et al. (2011) characterized as minor physical assaults (spanking, hit with belt, slapped, pinched, shook the child) as a disciplinary tactic with their chil-dren. About 1 percent of females and 3.3 percent of males reported "severe" disciplinary tactics (beatings, choking, deliberate burnings, threatening with a gun).

Young Fathers

Prevalence of Fatherhood

Research on adolescent fathers is much harder to come by than the research on adolescent or young adult mothers. Possibly this is because males are much less likely than females to be custodial parents and may have little contact with their children (Jaffee et al., 2001). However, some of the FFY studies do provide some data.

Seven percent of the Midwest Study males were fathers at age 17 (Courtney et al., 2004). In Arizona, males who remained in foster care at age 19 were less likely than young men who left care to have fathered a child (Stott, 2012). Fourteen percent of the Midwest males had fathered a child by age 19. By age 21, almost one-third of the Midwest young men were fathers. This rate was two times the rate found for fatherhood found in the ADD Health sample (Courtney, Dworsky, Cusick, et al., 2009). At ages 23 or 24, almost 61 percent of the young men reported that they had impregnated a female versus 28 percent of the ADD Health males (Courtney, Dworsky, et al., 2010). By age 25 or 26, the final interview in the Midwest Study, 38 percent of males reported they had made a partner pregnant since the interview at age 23 or 24. One-third of the fathers lived with their child, and another 10 percent had daily contact with their child. Twenty-five percent of the children saw their father at least once a month. Overall, 67 percent of youth said they were a father versus 39 percent of the ADD Health males who were a parent. Midwest Study males were also less likely than ADD Health young men to say that they had used birth control or were married to their partner. The Midwest young men said 60 percent of the pregnancies were unplanned (Courtney, Dworsky, et al., 2011).

Contact with Children

Hook and Courtney (2011) reported that adolescent fathers were more likely to live with their offspring if they remained in foster care past age 18, cohabitated with or married the mother, were employed, and avoided a criminal justice conviction. The factors dictating a father's involvement with their child included his relationship with the mother and his ability to support his child financially. Fathers are more likely to be involved with the children if they had a romantic relationship with the mother, or if not romantic, at least a relationship with the mother that could be described as good (Ryan, Kalil, & Ziol-Guest, 2008; Tach, Mincy, & Edlin, 2010).

An analysis of the Midwest Study data found younger and African American fathers were more likely than other fathers were to maintain frequent contact with their child. With the other ethnic groups what determined the frequency of contact was whether a father lived with a child and the amount of income he had. Income was a key determinant of a father's involvement with all groups. Fathers with an average income of $8,000 a year saw their children less than once a month. Young men with an annual income of more than $23,000 saw their children daily. Men who are unable to provide financially for their children may withdraw from other aspects of parenting (Bunting & McAuley, 2004). The child's mother may also restrict a father's involvement with their child if he is not meeting what she sees as his financial obligations to provide for the child's support (Johnson, 2001). Noncustodial parents may face child support obligations.

In addition, fathers who were involved with their children had the following characteristics. They left care after age 18, had lower levels of posttraumatic stress disorders, had not exited care from a group placement, and had avoided criminal justice entanglement. Nonresident fathers who had lived with the mother at some point or who had a legal custody or a child support agreement also had high levels of contact with their children (Hook & Courtney, 2011).

Marriage and Other Relationships

Youth in the Midwest Study sample favored cohabitation over marriage, which parallels the behavior of youth of the same age, educational backgrounds, and socioeconomic status in the general population (Vespa et al., 2013). Findings from the Fragile Families Study, which investigated family formation among a mostly poor and urban sample of parenting couples, showed that relationships between partners with low socioeconomic status were fluid over time. Even when couples were cohabitating at the time of the pregnancy, the relationships often did not last and only rarely resulted in marriage. Even though marriage was not the likely outcome for these couples, they did express a desire to marry at some point (Osborn, Manning, & Smock, 2007). Perhaps marriage rates would be higher with this population if economic prospects in this population were better.

ADD Health youth were more likely to be married, but less likely to cohabit with someone than were the Midwest sample (Courtney, Dworsky, Cusick, et al., 2009). This pattern continued at all measures in the Midwest Study. The available evidence suggests that at least for of EFY ages 18–24, marriage rates lag those of the general population. About 1.7 percent of the Midwest and 1 percent of the CalYOUTH samples were married at age 19. Midwest EFY 19-year-olds were much less likely than the ADD Health comparison sample to be married or cohabitating (8 percent versus 16 percent) (Courtney & Dworsky, 2006). The CYAS found that at age 25, 23.5 percent of the Casey alumni had been married at some point. Eighteen percent of the sample was married at the time of their interview (Havalchak et al. 2008). About half of the respondents said they were in a romantic relationship, with 90 percent of those relationships being described as serious. Females were more likely than males to report they were in a relationship of at least two years' duration, and to report that they were cohabiting (55.7 percent versus 28.8 percent). Latino (58.1 percent) and white youth (57.4 percent) were more likely than mixed-race (37.6 percent) or African American (36.7 percent) youth to report that they had a romantic relationship. In two-thirds of these relationships, the partner was the parent of their child (Courtney, Dworsky, Cusick, et al., 2009; Courtney et al., 2016). The marriage findings were similar to those reported by Buehler et al. (2000). Those researchers reported that FFY and a matched low-income group were more likely to cohabit than to marry, and to live with their spouse prior to marriage, than were a random sample meant to represent the general population from the National Survey of Households and Families. However, no statistical differences were found between study groups on whether they were married. Seventy-nine percent of the FFY, 82 percent of the low-income group, and 84 percent of the randomly chosen group that represented the general population were married. The FFY and low-income group were less likely than the random sample to endorse marriage as preferable to being single. The low-income group had responses on marriage that were similar to those of the foster care alumni. Forty-seven percent of the FFY were currently married versus 51 percent of the low-income group and 53 percent of the randomly chosen group.

The available data on divorce for FFY are sparse and dated. These data suggest divorce rates do not differ that much from the general population. Reported divorce rates among FFY ranged from 7 percent to 30 percent (Alexander & Huberty, 1993; Festinger, 1983; Zimmerman, 1982).

Sexuality

Sexual Intercourse and Birth Control

A national survey conducted in 2011–2013 found that among unmarried 15- to 19-year-olds in the general population, 44 percent of females and 49 percent of males had engaged in sexual intercourse. Seventy-one percent of women in the general population had engaged in sex. These percentages have not changed since 2002 (Martinez & Abma, 2015). The proportion of women in the general population not using a birth control method is highest among 15- to 19-year-olds (18 percent) (Jones, Mosher, & Daniels, 2012). About 85 percent of the 18-year-old young women in Stott's (2012) nonrandom sample from Arizona said they had engaged in consensual intercourse. Twenty percent of these sexually active young women were using birth control methods other than condoms. Young men who were formerly in foster care were less likely than males who had never been in foster care to have used condoms (29 percent versus 36 percent). Females in foster care were twice as likely as the general population to have had sex by age 15 (54 percent versus 26 percent). Eighty-five percent of youth from the Los Angeles sample of the Multi-Site Evaluation of Foster Programs reported at age 19 that they had engaged in sexual intercourse, and 75 percent had sex in the last year. Twenty-nine percent of those who were sexually active in the past year had at least two partners. The former California foster youth were more likely to have had sexual intercourse than the ADD Health youth. These youth used birth control in less than 50 percent of sexual episodes (Pergamit & Johnson, 2009). CalYOUTH females had more lifetime partners than the ADD Health females. Males self-reported more partners in the past year than ADD Health males. At age 19, more than 80 percent of the CalYOUTH sample had engaged in intercourse. Among the sexually active youth, the average number of sexual partners was 6.1 with a medium of 3, with a mean 2.3 partners in the previous year with the medium being 1. White (mean=8.0) and African American (M=7.5) youth claimed more partners than did either Hispanic youth (M=4.6) or the youth in the other ethnic category (M=3.4). CalYOUTH males reported more sexual partners than their comparisons (about three more lifetime partners), but the difference was not statistically significant.

Foster youth tend to become sexually active at earlier ages, and they are more likely to engage in risky sexual behavior than the general population. About 25 percent of the CalYOUTH sample reported having had intercourse by age 13, and they were more likely than ADD Health youth to report having had sexual intercourse between the ages of 10 and 12 (16.5 percent versus 1.5 percent) (Courtney et al., 2016). Obviously postponing the onset of sexual activity will reduce the risk of pregnancy. Early sexual activity exposes one to higher risks of pregnancy, sexually transmitted disease, and exploitation (Stott, 2012).

At age 21, 90 percent of the Midwest youth had experienced sexual intercourse with 70 percent having had sex in the previous year. Only 60 percent of youth said they had used birth control during sex in the last year. About 50 percent of the youth who engaged in sex in the previous year had used a condom all the time in the past year (Courtney, Dworsky, Cusick, et al., 2009).

Risky Behavior

About 10 percent of the CalYOUTH sample had contracted a sexually transmitted disease (STD) in the past year, and 14.1 percent had an STD at some point in their life. Females were more vulnerable to STDs than males (19.3 percent versus 5.2 percent). Only a third of youth who had sex in the previous year said they always used condoms. Another third did not use birth control, and the remainder of the youth said they used protection "some of the time" (Courtney et al., 2016). Females in the Midwest Study were more likely to report engaging in risky behavior that would result in pregnancy or contraction of an STD than were the ADD Health females. Six percent of the CalYOUTH participants reported receiving money to have sex, which far outpaced the ADD Health report of the same behavior (1.9 percent). The "other" ethnic and African American categories, and youth who had left foster care early, were more likely to have had sex for money than other youth in the sample. Males in both the CalYOUTH and Midwest Studies were more likely than females to have paid for sex. Five percent of the EFY in these samples said they had sex with an intravenous drug user, which placed them at risk of a sexually transmitted disease (Courtney et al., 2016; Courtney, Dworsky, Cusick, et al., 2009).

LGBTQ Youth

Data about LGBTQ FFY is scarce, but it is an issue that the Courtney-led studies have addressed. In the Midwest Study, 7 percent of the responding 19-year-olds described themselves as "bisexual," "mostly homosexual," or "100 percent homosexual." Males were more likely than females to report themselves as 100 percent heterosexual (84 percent versus 74 percent) (Courtney, Dworsky, Cusick, et al., 2009). Eighty percent of the CalYOUTH respondents said they were "100 percent heterosexual." More females than males were likely to report that they were "bisexual" or "mostly homosexual." ADD Health youth were more likely than the CalYOUTH to say that they were "100 percent heterosexual" (90.3 percent versus 80.0 percent) or "bisexual" (8.6 percent versus 1.6 percent). The difference on bisexuality was most pronounced with females with more CalYOUTH young women saying they were bisexual than did the ADD Health females (13.4 percent to 1.9 percent).

Practical Recommendations for Reducing Pregnancies and Improving Parenting

Extend Foster Care

Courtney, Dworsky, and Pollack (2007), using the state comparisons available in the Midwest Study, estimated that keeping youth in care until 19 would reduce pregnancies by 38 percent. Reductions continued after age 19, but the differences were not statistically significant. Hook and Courtney (2011) identify an additional benefit of extended care that fathers are more likely to remain in contact with their children than youth who leave care at age 18. Dworsky (2015) asserts that an extension of foster care may mean that the number of children of foster alumni who go into the child welfare system may increase because of the continued scrutiny by child welfare workers. Nevertheless, she notes that the additional services may help a young parent avoid being a perpetrator of abuse or neglect. A gap in the research that begs for attention concerns identifying the effect of keeping parenting youth in care, and their subsequent child protective service involvement.

Sex and Relationship Education

One of the best ways to ensure foster alumni are able to accomplish the tasks of early adulthood and keep their children out of the child welfare system is to help these young adults delay parenthood. Peters, Dworsky, Courtney, & Pollack (2009) note that the monetary benefits for society associated with preventing pregnancy stem from stopping early parenting before age 18, which means that, from a strictly fiscal standpoint pregnancy must be prevented prior to emancipation.

Only one-third of Midwest Study 21-year-old females, and one-fifth of the same age males, reported that they had received family planning information in the past year (Courtney, Dworsky, Cusick, et al., 2009). Pergamit and Johnson (2009) reported that just one in six EFY in their Los Angeles sample had received family planning services in the previous year. They found only a slight, nonsignificant difference between sexually active and not sexually active youth on whether they had received family planning information in the previous year (18 percent versus 16 percent). To address this deficit in family planning information, the John Burton Foundation is collaborating with the National Campaign to Prevent Teenage Pregnancy and the American Public Human Services Association to adapt *Making Choices*, an evidence-based sex education curriculum for foster youth. The program is currently undergoing pilot testing in six California counties (California Pregnancy Institute, 2013).

Social workers, foster parents, and relative caregivers need to be educated on topics related to adolescent pregnancy and parenting. These groups are currently not getting this training (Love et al., 2005). Training should be aimed at helping these potentially supportive adults be comfortable about discussing pregnancy prevention with youth.

Family planning is not a panacea. In fact, Dworsky and Courtney (2010b) found that young women who received family planning services were more likely to get pregnant than women who did not receive these services. One explanation they have for this finding is that more sexually active females seek out birth control information. Perhaps the information they receive is not enough, or is delivered too late, or they still do not know how to use birth control effectively after receiving the information. It is assumed that if youth have the knowledge of how to use birth control then they would contraceptive effectively. The knowledge and skills of safe sex are needed by FFY, but these skills may not be used without including relationship-based competencies in educational programs. Youth need to know how to negotiate the use of birth control with a partner. Stott (2012) and Pryce and Samuels (2010) critiqued independent living programs' approach to family planning as being heavy on techniques of birth control but light on the relationship training necessary for emerging adults to develop the social and emotional competency necessary for effective contraception.

Another faulty assumption is that these pregnancies are largely unintentional. Independent living staff who are preparing youth for emerging adulthood have to recognize why a young woman might want to have child. A belief must be challenged is the perception that the benefits of child bearing at such a young age always outweigh the costs. Helping youth in other domains such as education and work careers may empower them to reduce risky sexual behavior.

Revisit the Foster Care Connections Act

The Foster Care Connections Act should be redrawn to consider the circumstances of pregnant and parenting emerging adults, which are not currently addressed in the law. Many struggling parenting youth may lose eligibility for continued services as they are unable to balance work and education requirements imposed by the law because of parenting demands. This loss will harm both the parents and their children. The states must then develop programs that meet the specific needs of pregnant and parenting transition-aged youth (Courtney, Hook, & Lee, 2010).

Evidence-Based Practices

Multidimensional Treatment Foster Care was shown to reduce pregnancy among foster youth in a randomized clinical trial in Oregon. Twenty-seven percent of the treatment group became pregnant versus 47 percent of the control group. The model provides a behavioral treatment in a structured environment with clear reinforcers and consequences, is linked with supervision, and provides the skills to maintain positive peer relationships. Youth have mentors to give guidance (Kerr, Leve, & Chamberlain, 2009).

When pregnancy does occur, early intervention efforts such as the State of Illinois' mandated home visiting and assessment of mothers with newborns program show promise in improving outcomes. Specialty workers make one or two visits and provide an assessment that identifies needs, safety and risk concerns, parenting skills, and service needs (Dworsky, 2015). Home visiting as an effective strategy to improve the parenting skills of new mothers has been rigorously studied and validated (Coalition for Evidence-Based Policy, 2009; Geeraert, Noorgate, Grietens, & Onghena, 2004; Sweet & Appelbaum, 2004). However, it is less well established as a strategy to reduce child maltreatment (Lowell, Carter, Godoy, Paulicin, & Briggs-Gowan, 2011). Studies have demonstrated home visiting benefits in improving parenting knowledge, attitudes, and behavior; reducing a young mother's own reluctance to seek services; and engaging other caretakers, including foster parents, in providing a model of good parenting (Wagner, Iida, & Spiker, 2001).

Young Mothers

New parents need life skills and parenting training, as well as assistance with seeking public benefits (cash assistance, food stamps, and Medicaid). They should also receive family planning services to both enable them to avoid repeated pregnancies, and to maintain an educational or employment program leading to future self-sufficiency. They need help in securing safe and affordable housing where they can either reside with the child or maintain contact with their nonresident children.

Haight et al. (2009) argues for support groups based on their experiences with young mothers who are eager to talk about their mutual issues and engage in mutual self-support. They also argue for education interventions with social workers to change negative attitudes that social workers displayed toward adolescent parenting that youth reported they encountered while in care.

Young Fathers

Without the provision of appropriate services, some fathers may be a risk to their children. The culture of child welfare agencies, which has been reluctant to engage fathers, must be changed. High levels of unemployment and/or substance abuse among fathers may be a cause in conflict with mothers that can lead to violence and/or mental health problems among mothers and children. Chapter 12 discusses their high rate of incarceration, which makes some FFY fathers unavailable for parenting.

Social workers should actively engage with the fathers of the children of young mothers who were formerly in foster care (Jackson Foster, Beadnell, & Pecora, 2015). Some group work interventions (support, educational, etc.) have been shown to encourage more positive father involvement with their children and to lower the risk of repeated abuse and neglect (Bronte-Tinkew, Carrano, Horowitz, & Kinukawa, 2008; Coakley, 2008; Huebner, Werner, Hartwig, White, & Shewa, 2008). Providing adolescent fathers with education and employment services may address poverty, which is an identified factor in the development of child abuse. Becoming a father may be the motivation that young men need to get serious about education and employment. Work may also reduce criminal justice involvement. Interventions may also help fathers develop a better relationship with the child's mother, which may improve the mother's economic well-being and reduce her role strain. Research is needed to determine the effectiveness of these and other programs. The child welfare system should assist fathers in accessing mental health services and/or drug or alcohol treatment as a means of improving child well-being and reducing the burden on young mothers.

Research Needs

Few states are tracking young parents and children in their care. No federal mandate exists to collect this type of data. These data should be collected as a first step toward assessing what types of services these youth need, and if what is provided is meeting their needs. One improvement in this area occurred with the passage of the Preventing Sex Trafficking and Strengthening Families Act of 2014. The U.S. Department of Health and Human Services will now have to report state-level data on pregnant and parenting youth. These data will be a source of information about unanswered questions about pregnant and parenting FFY.

Longitudinal studies with representative samples would allow a prospective view on the needs of young adult parents when they leave care, and may help us understand the relationship between adolescent parenthood and their problems and needs. These data will contribute to the development of more relevant programming.

CHAPTER TWELVE

Criminal Justice Involvement

Criminal justice involvement (CJI) presents a serious challenge to youth attempting to make the transition to adulthood. The Juvenile Justice Division of the Child Welfare League of America reported that involved children in the child welfare system had a 55 percent increased risk of arrest and a 93 percent increased probability that the arrest was for a violent crime when compared with their peers in the general population who have not spent part of their childhood in out-of-home care. Once former foster youth (FFY) are in the justice system, they receive harsher sentences and remain in the system for longer periods than youth without foster care experience (Hertz et al., 2012). It is important to note that an arrest without a conviction still means the person has a criminal record that can affect other areas of life such as limiting their employment chances (McGinty, 2015). The National Institute of Justice reported that childhood maltreatment increased the chances of juvenile or CJI by age 26 by 29 percent. An extension of this study followed the sample until the youth were 32.5 years old. The researchers matched FFY who were involved with juvenile justice with a comparison group of youth juvenile delinquents who had never been in the child welfare system. They found that the FFY were vulnerable to arrest at an early age and had more CJI as an adult than the comparisons. However, adult FFY were no more likely to be arrested for a violent offense than the nonfoster care group (63 percent versus 61 percent) (Widom & Maxfield, 2001).

The transition age is a time when the risk of legal of involvement increases (Hirschi & Gottfredson, 1983). Ages 20 to 25 are the peak time for involvement in violent crimes (Widom & Maxfield, 2001). Eighteen- to 24-year-olds make up 10 percent of the population, but they account for 28 percent of all arrests (Requarth, 2017). There is also evidence of a strong association between mental health, substance abuse problems, and the likelihood of running afoul of the law (Davis, Banks, Fisher, & Grudzinskas, 2004; Pullman, 2010). The high occurrence of these problems among FFY was a topic in

Chapter 11. Many of the other problems discussed earlier in this book are also associated with CJI such as poverty, poor bonding to parents, lack of parental supervision, peer-related difficulties, and residing in high-crime areas (Caspi, 1993; Pullman, 2010; Sampson & Laub, 1990). In addition, FFY come from poor families and are likely to have grown up in neighborhoods struggling with the correlates of poverty such as little economic opportunity, social disorganization, drugs, substandard schools, and high crime rates (Courtney & Heuring, 2005; Kozol, 1991). Strong correlational evidence has linked maltreatment with future delinquency (Ryan & Testa, 2005). Youth often live in neighborhoods that do not provide them with sufficient employment opportunities. These neighborhoods are likely to have heavy police surveillance, which places youth, particularly minority youth, at risk. The social disorganization found in impoverished neighborhoods increases the likelihood of contact with deviant peers involved in illegal activities (Bursik & Grasmick, 1993; Elliot, Huizinga, & Ageton, 1985). Youth leave care without the means to obtain employment that provides sufficient income needed to survive. Working is not only associated with a successful transition; it is also associated with avoiding delinquent behavior (Sampson & Laub, 1992). Some youth may resort to illegal means to support themselves when employment is not available to them. All of the above increases the likelihood of ensnarement in the criminal justice system.

Prevalence of Juvenile and Adult Criminal Justice Involvement by Former Foster Youth

Table 12.1 contains data from the Midwest Study, and shows a high degree of CJI at each data collection point. The majority of youth will engage in delinquent activity at some point during their adolescence. It is important to note that this does not mean an arrest for that behavior. However, data collected from Midwest youth caused the researchers to conclude that these

Table 12.1   Criminal Justice Involvement in the Previous Year for the Midwest Study

Age Cohorts	Arrests		Convictions		Incarcerations	
	Males	**Females**	**Males**	**Females**	**Males**	**Females**
17*	61%	41%	28%	15%	43%	33.5%
19	41%	20%	19%	7%	33%	11%
21	43%	18%	22%	6%	43%	16%
23 or 24	41%	17%	22%	8%	44%	17%
26	38%	16%	22%	8%	40%	10%

*Youth were asked at age 17 not only for the previous year, but also at any point previously.

youth's behavior exceeded the national norms for delinquency; 61 percent of the Midwest Study males and 45 percent of females had already been involved in the legal system prior to leaving care.

Another conclusion that can be drawn from the longitudinal Midwest data is that the vulnerability to arrest, conviction, and incarceration is highest at age 17 and lowest at age 26, suggesting many youth "age out" of criminal activity (Courtney, Dworsky, Brown, et al., 2011). Some youth who leave care at 18 might have trouble adapting to life after care without supervision, support, and services. Perhaps the risk of arrest dissipates because youth are beginning to make positive adaptations to life after foster care (Lee, Courtney, & Tajima, 2014).

Midwest Study youth were also compared with their ADD Health peers on their involvement in illegal activities during the transition. At all measures, emancipated foster youth (EFY) were found to be involved in more criminal conduct (damaging property, theft, selling drugs, group fighting, and assaultive behaviors) than their nonfoster care peers. They were also more likely than the ADD Health sample to have been engaged in theft, fighting with weapons, injuring other people, and running away from where they lived (Courtney, Terao, & Bost, 2004). CJI rates for EFY are always high relative to their nonfoster care peers at each measure, but differences narrow over time (Cusick & Courtney, 2007). The greatest differences were present at the initial interview when the youth were still in care and under system supervision.

About one-half of the women and 60 percent of the men had an arrest after leaving care (Lee et al., 2014). At ages 23 or 24, 28 percent of the Midwest Study females had a conviction for a crime at any time versus 2 percent in the comparison sample. Fifty-nine percent of Midwest Study males had a criminal conviction, whereas only 10 percent of the ADD Health males had a criminal conviction. Seventeen percent of the females and 40 percent of the males had been in jail at some point in the previous year (Courtney, Dworsky, Lee, & Rapp, 2010). Twenty percent of the youth in the Missouri Study had an arrest by age 20. The same percentage of Missouri Study youth said their means of making money was illegal (Vaughan, Shook, & McMillen, 2008). These emerging adults were disproportionately male.

Jonson-Reid and Barth (2000) used administrative data from the California State child welfare databases combined with data from the California Youth Authority (CYA). The CYA is a division of the state's correctional system that provides education, training, and treatment services for California's most serious young offenders. The researchers found that 7 out of every 1,000 foster children would later enter the CYA. These researchers estimate the number would be closer to 8 or 9 per thousand if Los Angeles County did not have an alternative to the CYA. Los Angeles, which is home to 40 percent of the state's foster children, has a network of county-run juvenile camps where they can send offenders for incarceration in lieu of the CYA. Furthermore, they found that 1.1 percent of the FFY were under probation supervision. Pergamit and Johnson (2009) reporting from Los Angeles said that 22 percent of 19-year-olds participating in the Multi-Site Evaluation of Foster Youth Programs said they had been arrested, and 14 percent had been incarcerated. Shook et al. (2011), using administrative data from Allegheny County Pennsylvania, reported that 24 percent of the youth in their large sample had both juvenile and adult criminal justice involvements. Nineteen percent of that sample had adult CJI. Seventeen percent of the sample had spent time in jail at some point. Males were overrepresented among those entangled with the criminal justice system. An examination of 13,000 preadjudication juvenile detention decisions between 1997 and 1999 found that child welfare system–involved youth were 10 percent more likely to be detained for a first-time delinquent offense than were nondependent delinquent youth (Conger & Ross, 2001), which suggests a vulnerability regarding foster youth encounters with the criminal justice system.

The Effect of Criminal Justice Involvement on the Transition

One conclusion that can be drawn from the data is that females, as discussed in Chapter 11, face a great challenge to successful negotiation of the transition from the risk of a too-early pregnancy and parenting. Males have a corresponding challenge in trying to cope with demands of early adulthood in having more entanglements than females with the legal system. Midwest Study young men were more likely than their female counterparts to report that they had been arrested, convicted, and incarcerated at all interviews (Cusick & Courtney, 2007; McMahon & Fields, 2015).

This vulnerability to CJI is a concern because an arrest and conviction during the transition can seriously alter a person's life chances. An arrest record can affect one's employment prospects, and with some felony convictions the consequences could be permanent (Pager, 2003). Youth may not be able to receive federal housing benefits such as public housing if they have a criminal record. Raphael (2007) reported research findings that youth with a history of incarceration are less likely to be working or married. Researchers assert that youth with criminal justice involvement do not achieve the educational attainments, forge the social bonds, or develop the social support necessary for the successful transition to emerging adulthood (Chung, Little, & Steinberg, 2005; Holzer, Raphael & Stoll, 2003; Uggen & Wakefield, 2005).

Theories to Explain Criminal and Juvenile Justice Involvement

Ryan and Testa (2005) used social capital and social control theory to explain why FFY youth might be at risk to increased juvenile justice involvement. Our *social capital* is the consistent relationships a person has that entail commitment, trust, and obligation that bind people together and facilitate the exchange of resources (Coleman, 1988). *Social control*, a concept also used by Lee, Courtney, and Hook (2012), is a form of social capital that refers to socialization agents such as parents who make considerable investments in the care, education, and supervision of their offspring. These efforts result in a child developing a sense of attachment, commitment, and obligation that binds the child to family and community and gives them a stake in conventional behavior. Youth bond to society through family, school, and society, which are the mechanisms of social control (Sampson & Laub, 1990).

Research shows that engagement with institutions such as family, school, peers, and religious communities is crucial in mediating the relationship between experiencing child maltreatment and future criminal activity, particularly violence (Herrenkohl, Huang, Tajima, & Whitney, 2003). Hirschi (1969) notes that through the process of living we acquire material possessions, a reputation, and a sense of the future, and fear of jeopardizing any of these assets acts as a deterrent to violating societal rules. When youth have this type of social capital, they are more likely to reject opportunities to engage in nonnormative or illegal behavior, because their actions might jeopardize their social relationships. Good relationships with foster parents are essential for youth in the absence of other significant adult social ties. Foster care may also act as an agent of social control for youth when bonds to family are strained or severed. Child maltreatment is a form of disinvestment by parents that does not allow the development of healthy social capital. When attachments to family and caregivers are strained and bonds to the community are weak, youth may feel their behavior to be less bound by social constraints, or they may be less likely to deter their negative actions by of the feelings of others (Bowlby, 1988; Durkheim, 1951). The greater the feeling of disconnection, the more likely it is that one will engage in delinquent or criminal behavior (Hirschi, 1969).

Crossover Youth

Shook et al. (2011) describe a porous boundary between child welfare and juvenile justice where foster youth "drift" toward juvenile correction involvement and have a dual engagement with both systems. Drift occurs when a child in foster care breaks a law and the court adjudicates them as delinquent; it can also occur when a child reunifies with their family and later commits a crime. Because of this behavior, such children reenter public care, but this time they are in the juvenile justice system. Child welfare workers do not always view "drift" as a negative, because they may consider the treatment-oriented mission of the juvenile court as a means of getting help for troubled youth. This aid might be something the youth might not have been willing to accept without the coercion that the court provides.

Youth involved in both systems are referred to as *crossover youth*. However, these systems have separate administrations, which means that without collaboration and coordination, youth may "fall between the cracks" between systems (Davidson, 2008). Based on their data, Hertz et al. (2012) assert that crossover youth are twice as likely to be recidivists and have more behavioral problems than their peers had in the juvenile justice system without child welfare involvement. Many youth may transfer to the juvenile justice system as they age out of the child welfare system (Wylie, 2014). About 2 percent of the youth who left care in 2013 were transferred "to another agency" (AFCARS, 2016). Presumably, many of these youth end up in the correctional system.

The states handle *crossover youth* in one of three ways. *Concurrent jurisdiction* has each system maintain involvement with the youth but assigns one system (usually the child welfare system) primary responsibility for the youth. *On-hold* refers to a suspension of dependency system involvement while the juvenile justice issue is being resolved. Other states terminate the child welfare system's role with the child and have the juvenile justice system assume responsibility for the youth. According to a report from the federal Office of Juvenile Justice and Delinquency Prevention, the first option provides for better outcomes and management of the youth. One reason for this belief is that the child welfare system has more resources and expertise in helping youth with the transition. Placement in the child welfare system may not carry as much stigma for youth as being labeled a "juvenile delinquent" (Brown, Herz, & Ryan, 2008).

Type of Criminal Activity in Which FFY Are Involved

At ages 19 and 21, the Midwest Study youth were more likely than their ADD Health peers to be engaged in violence. The FFY report more often than the ADD youth that they had used or threatened to use a weapon in a fight, belonged to a gang, took part in a gang fight, had damaged property, dealt with stolen property, or injured someone badly enough that the person required medical attention. Most of these differences were due to a heavy degree of male involvement in these activities. Gang affiliations were substantial for these foster alumni. Eighteen percent of Midwest Study youth said that at age 26 they had belonged to or were currently part of a street gang (Courtney, Dworsky, Brown, et al., 2011). Eight percent of the CalYOUTH sample were, or had been, a gang member (Courtney et al., 2016).

McMahon and Fields (2015) identified four clusters of criminal activity among Midwest youth at age 17 or 18. Only 27.9 percent of youth reported "no criminal misconduct." This group was disproportionately female. The "heavy criminal conduct group" (11.9 percent of the sample) was involved in violent crimes. About 90 percent had pulled a gun on someone, 79.3 percent had hurt someone badly enough that the person needed medical care, 65.5 percent were involved in gang fighting, 62.1 percent had taken something that did not belong to them worth more than $50, 58.6 percent had dealt drugs, and 37.9 percent had shot or stabbed someone. Another category of youth, "group fighting" (19.0 percent), had gang involvement as its distinguishing feature. This group was also involved in criminal activity, but not in the same proportions as the first group. One in five youth in this group sold substances, a quarter were involved in minor theft (the item taken was worth less than $50), and a little over one-half said they had hurt someone badly enough that the person needed medical attention by that person. The largest group consisted of "moderate offenders" (41 percent). These FFY were much less likely to engage in violence than the other groups, but 45.7 percent of this group said that they had hurt someone badly enough that the person needed medical attention. They had more criminal conduct than the "group fighting" youth, except for the group altercations. They were mostly engaged in minor theft (60.7 percent), and about one-quarter sold drugs.

The young women in the Midwest Study had fewer contacts with the justice system. However, females were more likely than their peers are in the general population to belong to a gang, or to have pulled a knife or gun on someone (Courtney & Dworsky, 2005; Courtney, Dworsky, Cusick, et al., 2009). By age 26, fewer statistically significant differences were observed on reports of illegal activity between the Midwest Study and ADD Health samples. Again, this reduction of problematic behavior between groups may suggest youth may diminish their propensity to engage in criminal acts as they age. Nevertheless, the EFY still tend to be more involved in violent crime than their same-age peers. However, the Midwest Study youth were more likely than their nonfoster peers to have damaged property and taken part in group fighting (Courtney, Dworsky, Brown, et al., 2011). Courtney et al. (2016) reported that both the CalYOUTH and the Midwest youth engaged in more illegal activity than did the ADD Health comparisons. The illegal activities most frequently engaged in by youth were damaging property (15.5 percent), engaging in group fighting (10.3 percent), selling marijuana (10.8 percent), and stealing something worth more than $50 (8.1 percent). A property crime was the most likely offense committed that led to a conviction.

Needell and colleagues (2002) used administrative data in California to find that the high incarceration rates found among foster youth was a result of engaging in serious criminal behavior. They discovered that 30 percent of the incarcerated FFY in California had committed a robbery. A little over 18 percent of these youth had a conviction for assault and battery and/or weapons charges. About 7 percent of youth had a sex crime conviction. Males were jailed more often than females (38 percent versus 7 percent).

Youth in the Missouri Study self-reported much lower rates of criminal conduct than did the Midwest Study participants. At age 19, 20 percent of the youth said they had done something illegal for money. Six percent said they had assaulted someone. Another 6 percent said they had sold drugs. Sixty-nine percent of youth were classified as low risk for legal involvement (Vaughan et al., 2008). They suggest differences with the Midwest Study may have to do with how these two studies defined key variables. It also may be due to the limits of self-reports to get accurate information on these matters.

Predicting Juvenile or Adult Criminal Justice Involvement

Characteristics of EFY Engaged in Heavy Criminal Conduct

Cusick and Courtney (2007), who used latent class analysis with the Midwest Study sample, found that chronic violent offenders were disproportionally male, had experienced frequent placement changes, had substance abuse disorders, and had low levels of social support. Nonoffenders were more likely than offenders were to be attending school at ages 19 and 21. McMahon and Fields (2015) found that those with heavy criminal conduct had at least five foster care placements (56 percent versus 45 percent for the rest of the respondents) and were more likely to have been placed in congregate care (28 percent versus 18 percent). In addition, they were more likely to have an alcohol or drug disorder (52 percent versus 20 percent), did not have a living mother or stepmother (22 percent versus 12 percent), were more likely to live independently (23 percent versus 15 percent), had low rates of school enrollment (71 percent versus 82 percent), and were less likely to be employed (22 percent versus 35 percent). This group was also more likely to have been a victim of physical abuse and was not close to caretakers (32 percent versus 21 percent).

Conditions in Care

The Midwest Study researchers found each placement change a youth experienced was correlated with a 4 to 6 percent increase in the odds of being arrested, convicted, or incarcerated (Lee et al., 2012, 2014). Widom and Maxfield (2001) found that children who had three or more foster care placements had twice the arrest rates as both juveniles and as adults than youth with more stable placement histories. These researchers noted that youth with frequent placement changes also had significantly more behavioral problems than other youth. Needell et al.'s (2002) findings from an analysis of a large database in California suggest that frequent placement change is associated with incarceration in the CYA. In Shook and colleagues' (2011) Pennsylvania sample, youth who had experienced stable placements were more likely to be in the low criminal justice involvement group. In a later study, they reported each placement change increased the likelihood of

CJI by 7 percent. These researchers leave open the possibility that the youth's behavior problems were the cause of the placement move, rather than placement instability that caused the behavior difficulties (Shook et al., 2013).

Running away from placement was also predictive of juvenile justice involvement. Youth who left care prematurely by running away were prone to engaging in criminal behavior such as prostitution as a means of making money (Shook et al., 2011). According United Nations conventions codified in U.S. law, if trafficking is involved, the authorities should treat youth as victims and not as perpetrators. Running away from placement and receiving drug and alcohol treatment increased the possibility of juvenile justice involvement. Once in the juvenile justice system, the chances of entering the adult correctional system increased 3.5 times (Shook et al., 2013). Widom (1996) found that multiple spells of child welfare involvement were predictors of juvenile justice involvement, suggesting instability in living arrangements was the risk for CJI. These youth also had higher rates of incarceration than those who had avoided reentry into the child welfare system after exiting (Courtney & Barth, 1996).

Reunification

Ryan, Perron, and Huang (2016) used State of Washington child welfare and criminal justice (both adult and juvenile) records to compare arrests of those in out-of-home placements versus youth who received child welfare services in their own home. Surprisingly, those in out-of-home placement had fewer arrests than those who received services in their own homes; however, the overall risk of arrests was high for both groups when compared to the general population. Reunification with the family is the preferred outcome for youth in foster care. It appears reunification seems to make former foster youth vulnerable to criminal justice involvement. Ryan and Testa (2005) also found that reunification with their families actually doubled the chance that African American and Hispanic youth would have a future entry into the CYA (Needell et al., 2002). Courtney and Barth (1996) suggest the arrest risk may be greater for youth living in their own homes because their neighborhoods may be high-crime areas with greater police scrutiny. Ryan et al. (2016) point out that we do not have much data on adult outcomes of system-involved youth who received services in their own home. Finding answers to these questions requires more research. Obviously, the removal from high-risk homes and neighborhoods did not provide a protective buffer from delinquency. Jonson-Reid and Barth (2000) also found that system-involved youth who received services in their home had higher arrest rates than youth in out-of-home placement. These researchers suggest even if given sufficient services while in care, the home environment with its risks may overwhelm the gains derived from being in care.

Youth involved with either the justice or the child welfare systems were likely to have spent half their time in care in congregate care. They found only about one-half of those youth received mental health or substance abuse treatment services. However, youth with longer stays in care were less likely to have legal problems than youth with short stays. This finding suggests another benefit to extending care (Shook et al., 2013).

Race and Ethnicity

Numerous studies show African American youth to be at greater risk of CJI involvement regardless of their child welfare system status. About 9 percent of the U.S. adult population has a felony conviction compared with one-quarter of the U.S. adult African American population (Suede, 2014). African American youth face greater surveillance from authorities and experience harsher treatment at each stage of contact with the justice system than do white youth (Marshall & Haight, 2014). Some researchers note that the self-reports of illegal activities show few differences between minorities and white youth (Elliott & Ageton, 1980). Nevertheless, whites face less scrutiny from authorities than minorities. They must engage in more serious illegal behavior before they come to the attention of law enforcement. Widom and Maxfield (2001) found that African American and white FFY were more likely to have an arrest record than a comparison group of youth without dependency system involvement. Differences between maltreated and non-maltreated youth were greatest for African Americans. Although white FFY were more likely to have an arrest record than their non-FFY comparisons, differences were not observed between them on arrest for violent crimes. Maltreatment predicted a greater chance of arrest for violent crimes when compared with nonmaltreated youth for all youth, regardless of ethnicity. Needell et al. (2002) reported that while African Americans made up 29 percent of all EFY in their sample, they made up 60 percent of the entries into the CYA. Both whites and Hispanics were less likely than other FFY to enter the CYA.

Vaughan et al. (2008) used latent class analysis with the Missouri Study sample to classify youth into five groups. The group that had a *low risk* for legal involvement was disproportionally female and African American. Youth in this group were more likely than the other groups to report high levels of family support, were less likely to be polysubstance abusers, and had fewer externalizing problems. However, they had more internalizing behaviors (depression). This group also had the highest percentage of employed youth relative to the other groups. The researchers suggest that this low-risk group was more likely to internalize problems than act out in delinquent or criminal activity. The *moderate-risk group* was the only group with a majority of white youth (55 percent) and had the highest percentage of youth living in nonurban areas. Two high-risk groups were identified. The *externalizing group* exhibited a high degree of externalizing behaviors and had the most arrests. The *drug-selling group* had fewer arrests than the *externalizing group* but had more arrests than the other groups. Minority members were over-represented in the low-risk and drug-selling groups.

In the Midwest Study, African Americans, both males and females, were more likely than white participants to report engagement in violent crimes (Lee et al., 2012). The disproportionate problems with employment and income experienced by African Americans, described in Chapter 7, may result in youth undertaking illegal activity such as selling substances as a survival strategy. African American youth in Pennsylvania were twice as likely as other youth to have CJI (Shook et al., 2011, 2013). Fifty-six percent of the African American males in that study had such involvement, with 44 percent of the involved youth being in jail or prison at some point. Twenty-six percent of the African American females had CJI. Forty-four percent of young white men and 23 percent of white females had CJI. Despite being more likely to be in the low-CJI group than were whites, African Americans were more likely to have been in jail than white youth. This finding may indicate vulnerability based on racism.

Shook and colleagues (2011, 2013) note that the African Americans in their study had some protective features for avoiding CJI. They were more likely to be in kin placement, spent less time than white youth in congregate care, had fewer out-of-home placements, and spent more time in care.

Age

Youth who entered the child welfare system between ages 11 and 14 were the most vulnerable age group for developing criminal justice problems. These vulnerabilities may have their root in that this age is a time for transition filled with many stressors, such as the move into middle school. Students may be moving from a neighborhood school into a situation where they must adapt to new peers and teachers. They may have multiple teachers rather than the single teacher found in a primary school, which may result in children receiving less attention from educators. They may have been more vulnerable to placement change at this age because of behavioral problems that make them more difficult to manage (Jonson-Reid & Barth, 1990).

Gender

Males had more juvenile and criminal justice involvement than females, which at least in part was due to their problems with alcohol and substances described in Chapter 11 (Courtney, Hook, & Lee, 2010; Shook et al., 2011).

Pergamit and Johnson (2009) found that males in Los Angeles were 3 times more likely than females to have CJI and 4 times more likely to be in jail. Males who reported alcohol or substance abuse at age 21 were 1.8 times more likely to have an arrest record than males who did not drink or use drugs. For males, enrollment in school also reduced the likelihood of illegal involvement (Lee et al., 2012). However, female FFY criminal justice involvement was still greater than it was for women in the general population (37.6 percent versus 21.9 percent). In California, female FFY were more likely to have been in jail or prison than females who had never been in out-of-home care (11 percent versus 4 percent). Young women with foster care experience had a 10-times higher chance of incarceration than young women without that experience. Male FFY were 5 times as likely as males who had never been in foster care to enter the CYA (Jonson-Reid & Barth, 1990).

Females who lived with their own child had the lowest risk of criminal activity. However, child rearing by FFY is not necessarily preventive against CJI. Shpiegel and Cascardi (2015), using data from the National Youth in Transition Database, found that male and female parents were more likely than nonparents to have been in jail (75 percent, 35 percent, versus 46 percent, 25 percent). These researchers do point out that they do not know whether the incarceration came before or after child bearing, or whether the child was living with the parent at the time the offense was committed that led to the FFY being in jail.

For females, placement in a group home predicted an increase in CJI. Fathers who lived with their child were less likely to be involved in criminal activity than males who did not reside with their offspring (Lee et al., 2014; Widom & Maxfield, 2001).

Type of Abuse

Lee et al. (2012) reported that neglect as an abuse type was associated with a greater likelihood of involvement in property or drug crimes for women. The cycle of violence hypothesis suggests that victims of physical abuse would be more vulnerable to committing violent acts. They found that youth who were victims of physical abuse and/or neglect were about equally likely to enter the CYA. Having been a victim of physical abuse and neglect, but not sexual abuse, was associated with an increase in violent crime. Experiencing physical abuse was also associated with a reduced length of time between leaving care and an arrest (Lee et al., 2014). Widom and Maxfield (2001) suggest that the link of violence and physical abuse is a cycle. Youth learn violent behavior in their childhood that they repeat as adults. Jonson-Reid & Barth (2000) did not find support for this conclusion for youth entering the CYA. They also found neglect predicted movement into the CYA at 2.5 times the rate of victims of sexual abuse. The explanation given is that sexual abuse victims are overwhelmingly female, who, as it has been noted, are less likely than males to have legal problems.

Mental Health

The externalizing high-risk group in Vaughan et al.'s (2008) study exhibited a high prevalence of characteristics indicating externalizing pathology. They were four-and-a-half times more likely than the low-risk group to have a conduct disorder, twice as likely to have attention deficit disorder hyperactivity, and 69 percent more likely to live in highly disorganized neighborhoods. This high-risk group had lower levels of family support and higher levels of unemployment. They also had more social workers than system-involved youth in the other groups, which was an indicator of relationship instability. High-risk groups in this study had more deviant peers than the other groups. However, the type of abuse experienced did not predict assignment to any group.

The drug-selling group in that study was 2.5 times more likely to have a conduct disorder than the low-risk group. Youth in the drug-selling group reported more stress than the other groups, possibly because of the dangers of selling substances. They said they carried a gun more often than the other groups. An interesting note is 7.7 percent of the ADD Health sample owned a gun versus 3.1 percent of the California EFY (Vaughan et al., 2008).

Social Support

Vaughan and colleagues (2008) found a small but statistically significant relationship between youth's perception of their social support and the risk for arrest. However, this relationship was not in the direction expected. Youth who perceived that they had *high* levels of social support had a higher probability of arrest. Having support from social workers or former foster parents had no effect on arrest risks. This finding indicates either that youth have deviant peer groups that encourage offending behavior, or social support a youth receives is not enough to avoid problems. According to emerging neuroscience research, adolescent and transition-age youth have undeveloped parts of the brain that make them highly susceptible to risk taking and thrill seeking that is attenuated by the presence of peers (Steinberg, 2007). Youth leaving foster care have many cumulative disadvantages and continue to accumulate problems after they leave care. The time between discharge and first arrest was brief if the youth had an alcohol or drug problem.

Cusick, Havlicek, & Courtney (2012) also found that closeness to biological parents or other substitute caregivers did not predict CJI. However, not having a living biological mother increased the risk of arrest by 64 percent. Cusick and colleagues note that this is a puzzling finding because many transitioning system-involved youth do not have parents able or willing to provide support; they speculate that the mere fact of having parents may provide emotional and concrete benefits to youth.

Factors Protective against CJI

Hirschi (1969) has proposed that delinquent behavior stems from damaged or broken social bonds. Social capital theory has been extended into social bond theory to include its focus on social support systems acting as an informal means of social control to protect youth from CJI (Sampson & Laub, 1992). For example, the connections that children and adolescents have with their parents and schools may protect them from such involvement (Hirschi, 1969; Sampson & Laub, 1990). We already know that these bonds are weak for transitioning youth in general. Employment and marriage have also been shown to discourage criminal activity (Horney, Osgood, & Marshall, 1995; Sampson, Laub, & Wimer, 2006). Marriage rates are low among transitioning youth and may come later in life for FFY. However, women and men who had a child living with them were less likely to engage in criminal activity. Family formation seems to have a protective effect.

Cusick, Havlicek, and Courtney (2012) used hazard rates to test social bond theory with the Midwest Study data by linking those data to official arrest records. Hazard analysis is a statistical analytic technique initially used in medical research to test whether new procedures or medications contribute to the duration of patient survival. This technique has been used in the social sciences as well; Cusick and colleagues used it to identify what factors might extend the time after discharge before a youth was arrested. They found that aspiring to earn a bachelor's degree and/or having employment reduced the hazard rate for arrest by 24 percent and 32 percent respectively. However, attending school at the time of discharge was not significantly associated with the timing of an arrest. Ryan, Hernandez, and Herz (2007) found attending school, along with having housing stability, was associated with avoiding an arrest before age 16.

Among Midwest Study youth, placement with kin was protective of CJI, but arrest chances increased if the youth had a placement in a group home or had frequent placement changes. Group home placement increased the hazard rate of arrest by 58 percent compared to a foster home placement, and each placement change increased the hazard rate for arrest by 4 percent (Cusick et al., 2012). Munson and McMillen (2009) found that having a mentor at age 18 and 19 reduced the chance of arrest. A number of studies have highlighted the importance of youth having a sense of "giving back" to the community through volunteer activities. This feeling is thought to be a buffer against negative outcomes such as CJI (Allen, Kupermine, Philliber, & Herre, 1994).

Victimization

FFY not only had a high degree of CJI as perpetrators but also had a heightened risk of being a victim. The Midwest Study addressed this issue. Rates of victimization for the male FFY were much greater than they were for males in the ADD Health sample. Midwest Study males reported 2 to 3 times the rate of victimization of the young women in that study. However, females reported being sexually victimized at twice the rate of males until age 26 (Courtney, Dworsky, et al., 2010). At age 26, males reported victimization at 2.5 times the rate of females (21.8 percent versus 8.2 percent). Both males and females were reporting the most frequent crime committed against them was having a gun or knife pulled on them (13.8 percent versus 3.6 percent). Women were more likely than men were to report that they were "beaten up" (6.1 percent versus 4.0 percent). At age 26, both genders reported about equal amounts of sexual victimization (females 5.9 percent; males 5.5 percent). Four percent of females and 1.6 percent of males reported being raped (Courtney, Dworsky, Brown, et al., 2011). Differences with the comparison sample females were less pronounced, but Midwest Study females were more likely than the ADD Health women to have had a gun pulled on them (Courtney, Dworsky, Cusick, et al., 2009). Reilly (2003) reported that youth who had more placement changes were more likely to have been in romantic relationships where violence between partners was an issue.

Pergamit and Johnson (2009) also reported that males were more likely than females to report victimization. The most common forms of victimization were being robbed (15 percent), having a gun or knife pulled on them (10 percent), being beaten up (11 percent), and being shot or stabbed (3 percent). Data from Baltimore showed 33 percent of respondents had been a victim of intimate partner violence. On the other hand, 42 percent of the respondents said they had hit, slapped, kicked, or beaten up a partner (Benedict, Zuravin, & Stallings, 1996). These data from the Midwest and Los Angeles studies suggest youth have considerable and alarming exposure to violence.

Practical Recommendations for Reducing Criminal Justice Involvement or Ameliorating Its Effect

Extend Foster Care

Social control theory would suggest that continued system involvement would reduce legal problems. Data from the Midwest and CalYOUTH studies found that remaining in care until age 19 reduced the risk of arrest and incarceration for both men and women. Thirty-four percent of Midwest Study youth had an arrest after leaving care and 24 percent had spent at least one night in jail. In contrast, 22 percent of the youth who had remained in care had an arrest and 14.4 percent had been in jail (Courtney & Dworsky, 2006; Courtney et al., 2016). CalYOUTH study participants who took advantage of extended foster care were less likely than those who left care to be arrested (25.1 percent versus 11.6 percent), convicted of a crime (20.2 percent versus 4.9 percent), or incarcerated (24.2 percent versus 9.7 percent). Similarly, the National Youth in Transition Database (2014a) reports that at age 19, youth who remained in care had one-half the incarceration rate as youth no longer in care (26 percent versus 13 percent). Youth who left care were also more likely to have an arrest for a drug-related problem. However, findings in the Midwest Study, which collected data over a longer time, revealed that the data are not as strong in suggesting a reduction in CJI for those who remain in the system after age 19. The protective features of foster care for avoiding legal entanglements appear to dissipate. It is important to note that even a one-year extension of care protects youth during a period when they are most vulnerable to engaging in illegal activity. Allowing youth to remain in care until age 25 would take youth through the period of the highest risk for CJI. Remaining in care would encourage a commitment to society by helping youth finish school and find employment where they can build bonds with society (Lee et al., 2012). Data from the Midwest Study showed that for males, attending school or finding employment reduced legal involvement; this result provides support for social bonds theory as a framework for reducing criminal justice problems.

Data from the Midwest Study suggest that for women, remaining in care lessened the likelihood of arrests and involvement in property crimes, and marginally reduced incarceration. The same held true for men, but not after age 19. These researchers noted that, as with any secondary data analyses, they could only use the variables available. The dependent variables for criminal justice outcomes and the variables for measuring involvement with social institutions were dichotomous and may not have provided the amount of information that continuous variables would have provided. They state that further investigation should examine the effects of extended care in reducing CJI as well as examining the relevance of social control theory for preventing criminal activities (Lee et al., 2012).

Rethinking Permanency

Reunification may mean returning a youth to a high-risk environment, which is a significant barrier to a transition to a healthy emerging adulthood. If this is the case, child welfare workers and policy makers must weigh the costs and benefits of returning youth to their home or allowing those youth to remain in care. Jonson-Reid and Barth (2002, p. 512) ask, "What is the public responsibility in cases where the youth is not in life-threatening danger, but is left in an environment of relative neglect and impoverishment, and is likely to fail to reach a productive adulthood?" Perhaps something like the residential education facility discussed in Chapter 6 could be an alternate approach to stability and permanency.

Substance Abuse and Mental Health Treatment May Help Youth Avoid Criminal Justice Involvement

See Chapter 10 for interventions and strategies in this area.

Early Intervention

Problematic pathways embarked upon in adolescence can be difficult to correct in adulthood. We need a prevention strategy that identifies problems early. The later the intervention, the more difficult it is to interrupt youth early in their offending careers. Teachers, health care professionals, police, and social workers should know how to identify abuse and neglect, because maltreatment is a precursor to many other problems including CJI. Early identification could trigger the beginning of intervention.

Employment and Education

Lee et al. (2012) provide evidence to support the claim that employment or educational involvement at discharge from care onset may reduce FFY's exposure to deviant peers and high-risk environments. Low levels of both employment and educational attainment were noted earlier in this book as significant problems for these emerging adults. Youth in school may learn new skills, develop a sense of personal efficacy, and connect to a larger social structure (Caspi, 1993; Cusick et al., 2012). The increased human capital from education may pay off in lessening the need to engage in illegal activities. Employment may also occupy their time reducing the opportunities for illegal behavior.

Collaboration with the Criminal Justice System

Many EFY have been or are involved with other systems of care, which increases the risk of involvement with other systems. Mental health and drug and alcohol agencies should work collaboratively with criminal justice and child welfare systems. Youth need to retain access to child welfare services and support if they enter the juvenile justice system. It may be difficult for youth with CJI to meet the employment and educational requirements to continue to receive services until they turn age 21. As discussed in other chapters, policies that deny youth services because of past transgressions need to be revised. In the long term, neither society nor youth are going to benefit from a denial of services. The loss of access to after-care support services could hinder their attempt to make a favorable adaptation to emerging adulthood.

Title IV-E foster care payments may be made to state agencies for cross-over youth if they are in a "qualified" placement and "shall not include detention facilities, forestry camps, training schools, or any facility operated for children who are determined to be delinquent" (Wylie, 2014).

Wylie (2014) suggests that the child welfare system should have the task of independent living preparation, as most correctional system personnel do not have training in this area. She suggests amending the Fostering Connections to Success Act to make it possible for this to occur. Youth who cross over into the juvenile justice system may need assistance to reenter the dependency system in states where that is possible. Youth and correctional staff must be made aware of their ability to do so where that is possible.

Before collaboration, these child welfare and criminal justice systems need to resolve cultural differences in how they approach clients. Probation officers see their primary job as protecting the community. Child welfare workers see their core duty as providing the youth with needed services (Osgood, Foster, & Courtney, 2010).

Supporting Young Families

Data from the Midwest Study suggest that youth who are living with and raising children are more likely to avoid CJI. The needs of their children and the greater society would be met by providing greater support to these young families. A crime prevention activity might be to reach out to parenting youth with support services including employment services (Lee et al., 2012).

Young Adult Courts

A number of jurisdictions around the country (San Francisco, Idaho, Nebraska, and New York) have developed young adult courts. Based on the science of brain development, these courts recognize that the immaturity of the young adult brain diminishes youth's capacity to make good decisions, which can lead to CJI. These courts extend the treatment orientation of the juvenile court until a youth's midtwenties. The services are given to correct problems, and enable the youth to avoid the types of labeling associated with the criminal justice system that can adversely affect their opportunities for life. As yet, there are not any evaluations to tell us how successful they are at helping young people avoid additional legal problems (Requarth, 2017).

Limiting the Damage from Criminal Justice Involvement

Legislators and private-sector employers are recognizing how counterproductive it is for society to hold prospective employees' past mistakes against them, and are beginning to adopt reforms in this respect. The *ban the box* or *fair chance movement* has led 12 states and more than 150 municipalities to adopt laws that bar a private employer from asking about a criminal justice conviction history on a job application and delay the background check until later in the hiring process (Rodriguez & Avery, 2016). Bipartisan efforts are under way to clear barriers to employment for ex-felons. In March 2016, Senators Rand Paul (R-KY) and Cory Booker (D-NJ) introduced the Redeem Act, which would allow some nonviolent criminal and juvenile offenses to be sealed or expunged. President Obama established the National Clean Slate Clearinghouse, a collaboration between the Labor Department and Justice Department, to help with record cleaning and expungement (Freidman, 2015) and "banned the box" for federal jobs. The Department of Housing and Urban Development released guidelines that told landlords and home sellers that turning down applicants on the basis of CJI may be a violation of the Fair Housing Act, which would make it easier for the formerly incarcerated to find housing (Domonoske, 2016). These sorts of efforts are essential so that FFY and 70 million other Americans are not hampered in their bids to become responsible members of society because of the mistakes made in their youth. It is unclear whether either of these efforts will ultimately come to fruition given the change in federal administrations. The Obama administration initiated reforms that actually reduced the prison population for the first time since 1980. Trump declared himself the "law and order" candidate and warned that crime was "out of control." The new attorney general, Jeff Sessions, has indicated he does not regard the current large prison population as a problem and favors more and longer incarcerations (Lichtblau, 2017).

CHAPTER THIRTEEN

Family and Other Social Support Networks

Youth need to leave care with permanent connections to supportive persons, both inside and outside the child welfare system. They need a social network where they have relationships with people who can provide an emergency loan, a place to stay when needed, dinner and companionship during the holidays, a sympathetic ear in times of trouble, guidance around crucial decisions, connections to possible jobs, and advice on child rearing if needed. All of this support is preferably available for a crisis that occurs in the middle of the night (Stott, 2013).

It is a challenge for many foster youth to establish these types of relationships. They are victims of abuse and neglect from their birth families, which is why they are not in their own homes. However, the process of being in care may have also harmed them. First, the removal from home often disrupts family, peer, and neighborhood supports. Subsequent placement changes after the initial removal are often accompanied by a change in schools, as discussed in Chapter 6. These changes can disrupt existing relationships, or create barriers to developing new supportive relationships (James, Landsverk, & Slyman, 2004). Chapter 6 discusses how placement change can have a detrimental effect on relationships with teachers and others. Youth might also find it difficult to develop relationships with social workers because of frequent job turnover, which has been noted as a problem in child welfare agencies.

Samuels (2009) has stressed how former foster youth (FFY), because of their previous history of relationship instability, develop a reluctance to become dependent on others. She described the "psychological homelessness" that foster youth experience because they know they cannot expect the same level of supports from their families that most youth can expect and depend upon. Similarly, Barth (1990) reports that about one in six youth in his California sample felt that they did not have a "psychological parent," a person who could provide them with help and guidance.

Because of their traumatic relationship histories, many youth may leave care without the social support they need. They might not have a family that they perceive as a safe base from which they can explore the world of emerging adulthood. It is the responsibility of child welfare agencies to prepare youth for leaving care by enabling them to develop the social support they will need during the transition (Antle, Johnson, Barbee, & Sullivan, 2009; Arnett & Tanner, 2006). Data suggest either that this responsibility is taken seriously by agencies or youth are good at developing relationships without assistance. Ninety-four percent of youth participating in the California Transitional Housing Program reported both at entrance and exit from this one-year program that they had a caring adult "who could provide support, advice, and guidance" (Kimberlin & Lemley, 2012, p. 6).

The Theoretical Framework for Social Support

Individuals exist within a web of social relationships referred to in the literature as *social networks*. These networks are possible reservoirs of social support. Networks provide the possibility for intimate relationships through which we share emotional sustenance and receive caring and tangible resources, and they give us a sense of belonging (Dean & Lin, 1977). *Social support* is defined as "the emotional, psychological, physical, informational, instrumental, and material assistance provided by others to either maintain well-being or promote adaptations to difficult life events" (Dunst & Trivette, 1988, p. 3). The stress-buffering hypothesis of social support developed by Dean and Lin (1977) asserted that those individuals who were able to access and use social support from their social networks were better able to cope with stressful life events than were those without such resources.

Courtney and Dworsky (2005) defines four different types of support; emotional (caring, listening, empathy, guidance), tangible material aid (can include such things as a spot loan, a space to sleep, a ride to a doctor's appointment), informational (defined as the type of assistance that aids problem solving), and affection. Curry and Abrams (2015) added a fifth category, affirmation support, that consists of expressions of support that we use in our self-evaluations.

Perez and Romo (2011) noted that networks are sources of *social capital*. They defined social capital as "social support relationships that facilitate needed resources or knowledge for an individual or group" (p. 240). Bourdieu (1986) notes that access to knowledge or resources are determined by "who you know." This researcher maintains we intentionally build relationships to get these resources, and we learn reciprocity as a means of assuring access to these resources. Youth may leave care with considerable social capital deficits, particularly when their relationships with parents and extended family are weak. One problem that low-income groups have in developing social support is that their networks often contain people in circumstances similar to their own. Therefore, resources in the network may be limited (McNaughton, 2008). However, many individuals in a foster youth's network share similar hardships and experiences, which makes them willing to share what little resources they might have (Bottrell, 2009). Peers are particularly important to youth who are not able to reconnect with their family, by providing resources such as a couch for sleeping that may keep a youth from spending a night on the street (Perez & Romo, 2011). Peer networks provide both tangible and emotional resources that can provide an alternative for youth who lack family and formal system supports, thereby reducing the psychological distress that youth experience and contributing to feelings of resiliency (Daining & DePanfilis, 2007).

Youth can draw support from both the child welfare or other professional service systems, and more informal sources. The child welfare system provides social workers, foster parents, and mental health professionals, and provides links to health care providers. More informally they have family members (aunts, uncles, grandparents, etc.), have friends and peers in the community, may belong to a church where they meet clergy or other church members, and teachers and other educational staff, all of whom could provide support (Collins, Spencer, & Ward, 2010). Child welfare social workers may have been a key source of social support for a youth in care. However, their formal role with a youth ends when the youth leaves care. Continued involvement with youth is not part of their job description. If they choose to maintain a relationship with a youth after discharge, they must do so while carrying out their responsibilities for the youth still in their care. Social workers who keep contact with former clients can come under criticism for what some might see as boundary violations, and/or it could be viewed as recognition that a youth is ill prepared for discharge (Mattison, Jayaratne, & Croxton, 2002). However, it should be noted that evidence is available to make the case that these social workers go beyond their legally sanctioned responsibilities by maintaining relationships and continued support for the youth formerly in their caseloads. Indeed, researchers have reported that former foster youth frequently identify a previous social worker as a source of social support (Lemon, Hines, & Merdinger, 2005; Munson & McMillen, 2009).

Eighty-nine percent of discharged foster youth in a small nonrandom sample reported they saw a former foster parent or group home provider a mean of five times a year. This contact accelerated around the holidays (Barth, 1990). One role that social workers and foster parents can play is that of a *bridging relationship* for youth leaving care. This role entails helping youth establish new sources of social support while continuing to be a resource for youth when needed (Antle et al., 2009). The expectation is that the social worker's role diminishes as the youth develops new supportive relationships.

Family Relationships of Former Foster Youth

Closeness and Contact with Family

The Midwest Study and other studies indicate that most youth thought they were receiving adequate levels of support, and that they had enough people in their networks to provide support. Differences in social support were not found between those taking advantage of extended care and those who left care (Courtney et al., 2016; Courtney, Dworsky, Cusick, et al., 2009; Courtney, Dworsky, Lee, & Rapp, 2010; Courtney, Terao, & Bost, 2004; Courtney & Lyons, 2009; Festinger, 1983; National Youth in Transition Database, 2013, 2014).

Foster youth adapt to life after foster care with its reduced system support by relying on other sources of assistance such as their families (Courtney et al., 2004; Courtney, Piliavin, Grogan-Kaylor, & Nesmith, 2001; Perry, 2006; Reilly, 2003; Samuels & Pryce, 2008). The Midwest Studies as well as other research report that despite spending years in out-of-home care, most youth maintained close ties to their family. Foster youth are particularly close to mothers, siblings, and grandparents (Barth, 1990; Collins et al., 2010; Courtney & Dworsky, 2006; Courtney et al., 2004; Reilly, 2003; Samuels & Pryce, 2008). More than 90 percent of Midwest youth at all measures described their relationships with parents as close (Courtney, Dworsky, et al., 2011). However, those relationships with parents are not as close as one might expect to find in the general population. Perry (2006) found that only 32 percent of foster youth said they thought their parents cared about them a lot. A comparison group meant to represent the general population answered the same question by saying that their parents cared about them either somewhat or a lot at three times the rate of the FFY. Buehler, Orme, Post, and Patterson (2000) found that FFY had poorer relationships with their birth mothers and fathers than either a comparison group of nonfoster youth with similar socioeconomic characteristics or another randomly selected group that represented the general population. The FFY in this sample did indicate closeness with siblings, but they were not as close to their brothers and sisters as the youth in the general population group. The FFY also reported receiving less support from siblings when compared to the general population.

Among Midwest youth, the most frequent family contact was with siblings; the least frequent contact was with their biological father. Eighty-three percent of 19-year-old youth had at least weekly contact with a family member (Courtney, Dworsky, Cusick, et al., 2009). This level of family contact is about the same at age 26 (81 percent). Dworsky and Courtney (2009a) found that contact with family is a protective factor against homelessness among FFY, particularly if they said they had at least one family adult who was close to them.

Living with the Family after Foster Care

Youth who are aging out of foster care need assistance in reestablishing relationships with their family. Social workers need to assess if biological parents who have previously been judged as deficient in providing care for their offspring are now able to provide the type of environment where youth can carry out the tasks of emerging adulthood. Despite these concerns, many youth leave care to reside with their family of origin. Estimates from a variety of studies indicate that on leaving care anywhere from 17 percent to 54 percent of the youth discharged from foster care went to live in the home of a family member (Barth, 1996; Collins, Paris, & Ward, 2008; Cook, Fleishman, & Grimes, 1991). The high-end estimate of the range of those going home on discharge from care comes from a national evaluation of independent living programs (Cook et al., 1991). Many youth in the Missouri Study went to live with their family of origin, even when their social worker recommended against them returning home (McMillen & Tucker, 1999). At age 19, the Midwest Study youth were most likely to live with a family member, most probably their mother (Courtney, Dworsky, Cusick, et al., 2009).

Reuniting with family is not always positive. In a qualitative study, Samuels and Pryce (2008) noted that although youth expressed closeness to their family, these same youth said that the relationship with their parents was fraught with problems. The researchers note the risks involved in maintaining contact with parents who may not have resolved personal issues that led to their child's placement in care. The respondents in this study told of frequent conflicts with their parents, and a role reversal in which their parent depended on them for emotional and material support. Pryce and Samuels (2010, p. 217) report from another qualitative effort that young mothers aging out of care were more likely to say their mother needed their financial assistance ("I give her money"), rather than receiving support from their parent. Chapter 6 discusses how a youth's financial aid for school might be used to cover bills for the family of origin.

A little over one-half of the respondents in a small qualitative sample (n=15) made up of African American FFY reported that family conflict caused by parental dysfunction was a problem for them after they left care (Iglehart & Becerra, 2002). Four youth said their homelessness was a direct result of this parental conflict. Other youth in the sample reported that they did not have any ties to their family.

Jones (2014b) found that youth who returned home did worse than youth who were living independently or those who went to a transitional living arrangement. His explanation was that youth might be reentering family systems that still have significant problems such as poverty, mental illness, substance abuse, and violence. Even if the family environment is pathology free, youth may be returning to neighborhoods that are afflicted with poverty, crime, and social disorganization (Sampson, Morenoff, & Gannon-Rowley, 2002).

Fowler, Toro, and Miles (2009, 2011) found that about 30 percent of their sample was in a category they called *Stable-Disengaged*. The modal living arrangement for this group was to reside with parents or relatives at discharge. Seventy percent of this Detroit-based sample went to their family on exit, and at the follow-up interview two years later, one-half of these youth were still with family. These youth were less likely to be employed or attending school than were the *Stable-Engaged group* who lived independently. However, the *Stable-Disengaged* group did much better on achieving housing stability than the *Instable-Disengaged* group, who were less likely to go to family on exit and more likely to be homeless. These researchers speculate that living independently may encourage youth to engage with larger society through work or education.

Research Findings on the Social Networks and Social Support for FFY

Yates and Grey (2012) used latent analysis with 164 emancipated foster youth (EFY) to identify resilient adaptations to the transition. They found that having intimate and reciprocal relationships with the important people in the EFY's life (including their primary romantic or platonic relationship) and having at least moderate civic engagement (registration and voting, volunteering, and organizational involvement) were associated with attending school or working.

Harknett and Harknett (2011) found that poverty was associated with weaker social networks and fewer sources of support in regards to finances, housing, child care, and emotional sustenance. The combination of poverty, depressed feelings, and low social support contributed to even worse outcomes in these areas. Data from the Multi-Site Evaluation of Foster Youth's Los Angeles site suggest that more contact with an adult family member reduced the likelihood of experiencing material hardship after discharge (Courtney et al., 2008). Won (2008) found that youth who had extensive networks while in care and maintained these networks after discharge were less likely to be affected by material hardship. Midwest Study participants who were still in care at age 19 and had a supportive relationship with an adult, when compared with those who left care at age 18, had more stable housing, received better access to health care (including for mental health services), and did not enter the juvenile justice system.

Mothers who had their children removed from the home for child mal-treatment had fewer people available to provide support or social contact. They also had more negative perceptions of the helpfulness of these networks than did the mothers who had not had their children removed (Bishop & Leadbetter, 1999). Similarly, Nair et al. (1997) noted that among mothers with substance abuse problems, the number of supportive people available to the mother was a predictor of whether their child would be removed from the home. A study that used Casey Alumni Study data revealed FFY mothers who had a poorly functioning father of their child and who had more negative than positive support from their network were in danger of having their child removed from the home (Jackson Foster, Beadnell, & Pecora, 2015).

The research of Daining and DePanfilis (2007) with 189 FFY showed that social support was associated with resilience. Their measure of resilience was a composite score of six domains (education, employment, parenthood, homelessness, health risk behaviors, and criminal activity). Katz and Court-ney (2015) found that youth who had at least one adult who was perceived as supportive were more likely than those without such an adult to say that their needs were being met (39 percent versus 22 percent).

Social Support and Mental Health

The efficacy of the buffering effect of social support has been demon-strated in the health and mental health literature. Less well established is its effectiveness with FFY or adults who have experienced abuse as a child. Babcock, Roseman, Green, and Ross (2008) did show that the effect of expe-riencing psychological abuse and post-traumatic stress disorder (PTSD) symptoms was diminished by having social support. Another study also found that social support moderated the relationship between having a his-tory of child abuse (not just psychological abuse) and PTSD, but depression was unaffected (Vranceanu, Hobfoll, & Johnson, 2007). Murthi and Espelage (2005) showed that adults who were victims of sexual abuse as a child but who perceived they were supported by others in their life did much better as adults than those adult survivors of sexual abuse who did not receive such support. Runtz and Schallow (1997), using a sample of college students, found that social support combined with positive coping strategies mediated the relationship between sexual or physical abuse experienced as a child and future psychological problems, including low self-esteem, experienced in later adulthood. Kaufman et al. (2004) reported from their study that posi-tive social supports with abused and neglected youth reduced the risks asso-ciated with depression. Salazar, Keller, and Courtney (2013) examined the buffering hypothesis in relationship to diminishing symptoms of depression in FFY. Social support was found to buffer the effect of depression in young adults, as well as moderately mediating the relationship between depression and having experienced child abuse. However, the stress buffering hypothesis was not observed with victims of multiple types of abuse. Their explanation for this finding was that the high levels of trauma associated with experiencing multiple and severe types of maltreatment overwhelmed the positive effects of social support.

Vranceanu and colleagues (2007) suggest that survivors of childhood maltreatment may avoid and have limited ability to form and maintain long-term healthy relationships, which are the type of relationships where we are likely to find consistent support.

Mentors

Describing the Relationship

Having a supportive and caring adult is something most emerging adults experience. This type of relationship is essential for buffering risk that youth are exposed to, but is also an ingredient for mastering the tasks inherent in the transitions (Avery & Freundlich, 2009; Drapeau, Saint-Jacques, Lepine, Begin, & Bernard, 2007; Hines, Merdinger, & Wyatt, 2005). The overwhelming majority of the 17- and 19-year-olds in the National Youth in Transition Database (2014, 2015) had a positive connection to an adult (89 percent and 93 percent respectively). At age 19, the percentages of youth with an adult connection were similar for those who remained in care and those who left care (93 percent versus 89 percent).

The cumulative research emphasizes that all youth leaving care must have at least one caring and committed adult in their life. This need may be more important for youth without family connections. Mentoring is identified as a way of addressing this critical need that FFY have. A mentor is a positive person in a youth's life who can be a sounding board for their difficulties and life decisions. These adults may provide the types of tangible support described earlier. They may even be able to help youth get a job.

There is strong support in the literature to indicate that youth who have had a mentor for at least one year can derive modest gains from the experience, with some evidence to suggest that such gains linger for several years (DuBois, Holloway, Valentine, & Cooper, 2002; Rhodes & Dubois, 2006). Dworsky and Courtney (2009a) assert that mentors may be even more important for foster youth than for nonfoster youth, because foster youth might be estranged from the adults in their family. The literature on resilience for children and adolescents has linked the presence of a caring and supportive adult who is not their parent with successful outcomes (Osterling-Lemon & Hines, 2006). Mentoring is thought to provide a buffering function similar to that of social networks. This buffering occurs by enhancing the mentee's social and emotional well-being, by providing a supportive trusted confidant. They contribute to positive identity development by being a role model, and by giving guidance and advice on how to negotiate the vicissitudes of the transition. They also serve as the youth's advocate (Avery, 2011; Mech, Pryde, & Rycraft, 1995).

Greeson, Usher, and Grinstein-Weiss (2010) reported that 56 percent of the FFY in the ADD Health sample said they had a mentor who gave them advice, guidance, and emotional nurturance. Only 13 percent of the respondents said this natural mentor provided practical assistance. Just 1 percent of youth thought their mentor was like a parent, and only 8 percent of them said their mentor was a role model. Fifty-four percent of the FFY said the mentor was a relative, 25 percent said it was an adult at their school, and 21 percent said the mentor was a community member. Youth had known their mentor for about 10.5 years (SD=7.89). Youth on average said they saw this person at least once a month. The FFY were more likely than their comparisons to say the mentor was a source of emotional nurturance and a role model. FFY had known their mentor for a slightly longer period (8.94 years, SD=7.07), and were more likely to have a mentor whom they met through school (33 percent) rather than family (45 percent), than were the ADD Health comparisons.

Natural versus Formal Mentors

The literature distinguishes between natural mentors who develop a relationship with the child or youth without formal system intervention and mentors assigned by programs set up for that purpose. Natural mentoring emerges from known relationships within a person's existing social network. This type of mentoring develops more slowly than formal relationships and is likely to be enduring because of the preexisting relationship between the two participants. Much more evidence is available to support the benefits of natural mentors than for formal mentors in their success with youth (Ahrens, DuBois, Richardson, Fan, & Lorenzo, 2008).

Avery (2011) warns against assuming formal mentoring programs are an answer to the many difficulties that youth have on leaving care. She also notes that the research on the effects of mentoring is weak, which limits our ability to make conclusions about how effective mentoring would be in leading to more favorable outcomes for youth. Concerns are raised that the time-limited nature of many formal mentoring relationships means they do not meet the need for relational permanence and may possibly deflect emotional resources that could be directed at building permanent relationships (Avery, 2011). Because formal mentors are usually volunteers, it is difficult to hold them accountable. Programs struggle with high turnover and inconsistency in mentors' performance (Munson, Smalling, Spencer, Scott, & Tracy, 2010).

Mentoring Outcomes: The Research Evidence

The most comprehensive evaluation of mentoring to date was done for the Big Brothers/Big Sisters programs. This evaluation found a modest effect for mentoring in helping youth avoid delinquency and/or substance abuse (Avery, 2011). Data from the ADD Health study suggested that foster youth who had a mentor for a minimum of at least two years before age 18 were more likely to finish high school and go on to a college or university, and they had better physical and mental health than youth without mentors. Mentored youth reported less suicidal ideation and fewer sexually transmitted diseases, and were less likely to engage in fighting than nonmentored youth. DuBois and Silverthorn (2005), also using the ADD Health database, found the same results on education, health, and fighting as Ahrens and colleagues (2008), but they also added that FFY with a natural mentor were more likely than those without a mentor to be employed, avoid gang membership, injure a person in a fight, and use birth control. Munson and McMillen (2009), using the Missouri study data, found that youth who had a natural mentor who was not a family member for at least one year at age 19 were not as stressed, were more satisfied with their life, and had less involvement with the criminal justice system than those youth without such a mentor. Courtney and Lyons (2009) reported that Midwest Study youth at age 21 who described themselves as being close to an adult mentor were less likely to be homeless and more likely to be working than youth without such a relationship. Having a mentor did not affect criminal justice involvement for Midwest Study youth. Collins, Spencer, and Ward (2010) found that mentored youth were more likely to finish school or a GED, and to avoid homelessness, than youth without mentors. These researchers suggest mentoring takes on added importance for youth raised in care because their relationships with families may be strained or nonexistent either because of separation brought about by removal from the home or resentments over maltreatment.

Findings on the benefits of mentoring in general are mixed. The research that is available on formal mentoring indicate that the positive effects may be small that diminish as time passes (Abbott, Meredith, Self-Kelly, & Davis, 1997; Aseltine, Dupre, & Lamlein, 2000; Harvey & Hill, 2004; Herrera et al., 2007; Shiner, Young, Newburn, & Groben, 2004). Harvey and Hill (2004) did not find positive benefits on school performance, attendance, alcohol abuse, or disciplinary problems. Efficacy studies of mentoring utilizing experimental design are few, and none have been done with transition-age foster youth.

Quality of the Relationship

A meta-analysis of existing mentoring studies conducted by DuBois et al. (2002) identified the "quality" of the mentor-mentee relationship as a crucial feature for determining if a youth would benefit from the relationship.

Quality referred to the amount of contact and perception of the degree of "closeness" of the relationship. Programs vary in quality and usually rely on volunteer mentors who may have relatively short stints as mentors before they cease participating. As such there may be risk of harm to youth who may feel they have had another relationship with an adult who was undependable (Avery, 2011). However, this research has identified a set of characteristics needed for effective mentoring. The relationship

- must be relatively long-term (Grossman & Rhodes, 2002);
- must be consistent in the amount of time and support given to youth (Herrera, Sipe, & McClanahan, 2000);
- should meet the emotional needs of FFY (Spencer, 2006);
- and the mentoring program should do what is necessary to sustain mentoring relationships (DuBois et al., 2002; Spencer, Collins, Ward, & Smashnaya, 2010).

Sixty-six percent of Collins et al.'s (2010, pp. 131–132) respondents said that they "had an adult with a special interest in them that you could count on to be there for you, and who inspires you to do your best." The mentor was most likely to be a child welfare professional or nonrelated community member. Youth in the general population are more likely to say their mentor was a member of their extended family or a community member (teacher, coach, or clergy) (Beam, Chen, & Greenberger, 2002).

Community Engagement

Along with finishing an education, developing a career, and starting a family, engagement with the community is a marker of adulthood. Involvement in the community allows youth to build sources of social support, accumulate social capital, and enable entry to educational and work possibilities. This is important not only for the well-being of communities but also for positive adult development and identity formation. Community engagement includes such activities as volunteer social service activities, church attendance/membership, participating in grassroots political movements, and involvement with FFY. Involvement in organized activities provides a person with feelings of belonging and purpose, even when the activity is not service oriented. Much of what happens to foster youth works against these connections. In addition to placement mobility, the reluctance of the child welfare system to allow its charges to engage in the full range of activities in which most adolescents actively participate limits foster children's ability to make community connections. Dropping out of school, unemployment, and criminal justice involvement have been associated with low community engagement (Flanagan & Levine, 2010).

The youth's home neighborhood may not be conducive to community engagement. Ross and Jang (2000) note that disorganized communities where individuals do not trust or feel an affinity with their neighbors have low levels of community participation. Only 27 percent of respondents said they trusted their neighbors. Thirty-one percent said they did not share the same values as the neighborhood.

Courtney, Dworsky, Cusick et al. (2009) and Courtney, Dworsky, et al. (2011) reported that Midwest Study youth maintained a lower level of participation in community organizations than did the ADD Health youth as measured by participation in volunteer service or belonging to a religious grouping. Even though Midwest youth did not attend religious services as often as ADD participants did, these young people were more likely to say religion was important to them than were the comparison sample. Another indicator of community involvement was political participation. Youth in the two samples exhibited similar behavior on voter registration and voting in presidential elections. Blome (1994) found the same level of participation between FFY and a matched group of nonfoster adults on church attendance and community involvement. Buehler et al. (2000) found that although FFY were less involved in the community than the general population group, they had similar levels of involvement as the group matched with them on SES variables. An analysis by Yates and Grey (2012) demonstrated that relational competence was not sufficient for attending school and/or working; youth also had to be at least moderately engaged in civic activities.

Could the lower levels of community participation and engagement by FFY and EFY be indicators of isolation, marginalization, and social inclusion that began even before they entered foster care that now extends into adulthood? It may be that these youth have many problems and lack of resources keeps them from participating, or that their biological and foster parents did not model community engagement behavior. In many instances, child welfare rules meant to protect foster youth may deny them the practicing behaviors that are a by-product of extracurricular activities. In addition, their multiple placements and living situations mean they do not build up the type of social investments that might make them want to engage in the community.

Predictors of Social Support

Significantly more CalYOUTH males said they had emotional, tangible advice/guidance from adults than did females. Females were also more likely than males to say their networks were a source of strain. However, the young women maintained more regular contact with people in their network than did the young men. White youth had more people they could turn to for tangible support than did the other racial groups. They also had more people to give them advice and support than either African American or Hispanic youth. Youth on average nominated 3.2 persons they could depend upon for support. Mixed-race youth had the largest social networks (3.7). African Americans had the smallest number of supportive persons (2.8). Youth who were still in care also had larger social networks than youth who had left care. Youth said 41 percent of their network members were family, 26 percent were friends, 14 percent were child welfare system employees (foster parents, group home staff, social workers, or school professionals), 9 percent were romantic relationships (including spouses), 7 percent were helping professionals (school personnel, therapists, mentors), and 3 percent were "others" (neighbors, "parent figures"). Research also indicates that considerable numbers of foster youth maintain contact with their former foster parents. Females were more likely than males to endorse romantic partners as sources of social support. Males were more likely to say their network was composed of friends or siblings (Courtney et al., 2016).

Barriers to the Development of Social Support by FFY

Placement change has been found to damage a child's social network and to be correlated with increased psychological strain (Vranceanu et al., 2007). Moving a child among placement disrupts the continuity of relationships and may make youth feel that the connections to the persons around them are tenuous and unreliable. *Continuity* in relationships is needed by youth to feel they have people on whom they can rely. Continuity occurs when the youth has interactions with others that are reliable, appropriate, and are of long duration (Wahler, 1994). This continuity is important for FFY because all they may have known are relationships that for them end too soon. The frequent changes of social workers that foster children experience may mean they are not able to experience continuous relationships with this important relationship (Salazar, 2013).

Chapter 2 emphasized that the view of independent living and self-sufficiency as a marker of adulthood and the cultural value of individualism to which foster youth are not immune may communicate to foster youth that dependence on others is undesirable. In addition, the emphasis on protection means that youth may view attempts by the child welfare system to extend supports to EFY as something to avoid because it would infringe on their independence. Because of these circumstances, as well as their situations prior to coming into care, many foster youth have experienced social support as fleeting, inconsistent, or nonexistent. The result is foster youth adopting a stance called *survivalist self-reliance* by Samuels and Pryce (2008). Youth may feel there is no pride having been in foster care, but rather take pride in surviving it and the circumstances that brought them into care. Surviving foster care and attempting to negotiate the transition without dependence on others may likewise become a source of pride. While these researchers note that although this stance may be a marker of resilience, it may also be a hindrance to FFY reaching out to or accepting help from others (Perry, 2006; Unrau, Seita, & Putney, 2008).

FFY's criminal justice involvement is a barrier to taking part in many aspects of civic life. A felony can restrict the ability to vote, serve on a jury, and hold political office. According to Uggen and Wakefield (2005) such restrictions act as clear indicators to persons who have been offenders and paid their debt to society that "they are unwanted or unaccepted as full citizens in their community." As such, it undermines the reintegration goal of having ex-felons empathize or identify with other citizens (132–133).

Practical Recommendations for Building Sources for Social Support

Network Assessment Prior to Discharge

Reilly (2003) asserts that before youth leave care, social workers should identify who the youth feels is important in their life and who might possibly be supportive after discharge and assist with making appropriate connections to these sources of social support. If deficiencies are noted, assistance needs to be given to developing alternatives. Alternatives include establishing connections to the child welfare system supports. Independent living services (ILS) programs should devote more attention to helping youth connect to various support systems needed for a successful transition (Courtney, Dworsky, Cusick, et al., 2009; Courtney, Dworsky, et al., 2011; Geenen & Powers, 2007).

Provide the Opportunities for Foster Youth to Develop Social Networks and Social Capital

Child welfare workers should give high priority to assisting foster children in building social networks as sources of social support, as a means of promoting permanency that FFY can count on throughout the life cycle. FFY may have lost or never had the support of a family or others who can provide the support necessary for a successful transition. Because of the emphasis on protection, foster youth often have not had the opportunity to develop friendships, social networks, and social capital. Youth need to be encouraged to participate in extracurricular activities, hold part-time jobs, stay overnight with a friend, or just hang out with friends during leisure time. These activities are developmentally appropriate and should be encouraged by child welfare agencies. Such facilitation includes paying fees for youth, providing transportation, buying uniforms if required for the activity, and allowing youth to go unsupervised at least part of the time, which is the normative state for adolescents. We should not expect EFY to function well independently unless they have had the freedom necessary to learn through doing and make the occasional mistake (Stott, 2013).

Daining and DePanfilis's (2007) research indicates that youth want to keep the relationships that they may have developed while in care with their former foster peers. They suggest support groups made up of FFY would give these youth an opportunity to share common problems and ways of coping with these difficulties. Support groups could be part of ILS programs in order to better prepare youth for life after foster care. Including FFY who have been successful with the transition from care might be an additional source of learning for youth on the verge of leaving.

Reconnecting with Family

Social workers need to work with youth's families to ease transitioning youth into the home (Collins et al., 2010). If reengagement with parents is not possible, efforts should be made to help youth establish relationships with other family members. Antle et al. (2009) describe a process known as *family finding*, which consists of an extensive technology-assisted search to locate family and friends who could provide housing and other types of support. The federal Administration for Children and Families had made approximately $15 million a year in Family Connection grants available to the states, to be used in a mixture of family finding and family group decision-making (FGDM) projects. Family-finding projects use computer search technology and other means to locate family of origin members for foster children/youth. Once these family members are found, social workers help youth establish or reestablish relationships, and explore ways to establish permanent family living arrangements for youth. FGDM meetings enable families to make decisions, develop plans for youth, and ensure their safety (Antle et al., 2009; Family Connections Grant, 2012).

As an example, the family-finding effort in Santa Clara established 220 connections for 8 youth initially assumed not to have such connections (Campbell et al., 2003). The Emancipated Youth Project in California worked with 20 youth who did not have an adult connection when they were preparing for discharge. Within 18 months, the project had established 191 new connections for 19 youth (Friend, 2009). These connections included both family and nonfamily adults. Campbell and colleagues claim a 98 percent success rate in finding permanent relationships for youth. As of this date, no peer-reviewed evaluations have appeared in the literature on the method. (See http://www .familyfinding.org/trainings/trainer-bios.html for further information.)

In helping youth and family connect, or easing youth back into the system, social workers need to help family members develop rules, boundaries, and expectations. McMillen and Tucker (1999), and Iglehart and Becerra (2002) recommend that ILS programs should include curriculum that prepares youth for living with families. These curricula should be available to parents and should equip parents with the knowledge to understand trauma and their youth's needs and behaviors (Jim Casey Opportunities Initiatives, 2011). When problems are noted with a youth moving back into the family home, the child welfare system should be prepared to provide services in order to alleviate those problems.

Casey provides funds to assist its alumni in making connections to family. Youth make connections by providing funds to help meet family obligations such as assistance with burial of a birth parent or to help a youth travel to get together with family at holiday breaks (Pecora, Kessler, et al., 2003; Peters, Sherraden, & Kuchinski, 2016).

A Committed Adult

Youth should not be discharged from the system without the support of a committed adult (Avery & Freundlich, 2009). Foster youth need one responsible adult who can provide guidance and assistance, particularly when youth encounter difficulties (Greeson et al., 2010). Note that this committed adult could be a biological parent or other family member if available who is willing and able to carry out the function. If parents or kin are not viable options, then other adults outside the family should be sought. The task is to find someone willing to fulfill this role over the long term if not across the entire life cycle.

The Children's Advocacy Institute of the University of San Diego School of Law suggests that every youth leaving care should choose a transition life coach (TLC) in consultation with their social worker, advocate, and attorney. The court would appoint this person to act as a trustee over a fund equivalent to the amount to those expended by an average parent on their children when they leave home. The TLC would dispense funds to the youth based on the specifications of the transition plan. Thus, the TLC would provide support and aid in the way that parents do. Disputes between the TLC and youth would be resolved by the courts (Delgado, 2013).

Formal Mentoring

The Foster Care Independence Act of 1999 calls for the provision of mentors through the "promotion of interactions with dedicated adults" to provide "personal and emotional support to youth aging out of foster care." Formal mentoring programs are frequently utilized to connect youth with a committed supportive adult (Hass & Grayden, 2009). Chafee has provisions for funding mentoring services that the states could utilize. Programs must clearly define the role and expectations of a mentor, particularly around frequency of contact, and provide appropriate supports that will enable the relationship to work. To be effective these programs must initially make a substantial expenditure of resources to screen prospective mentors to make sure that adults selected are well suited to the role, and are trained, supported, and supervised. Matching is important to ensure that mentor and mentee are compatible. A youth whose experience has consisted of inconsistent and failed relationships might experience further harm by an abrupt end to the mentor relationship. Mentors may be useful as an adjunct to other types of assistance, but may not meet the youth's need for relational permanence (Spencer et al., 2010). Avery (2011) describes mentors as a compensatory resource that can contribute to relational permanency, but a mentor is unlikely to substitute for the parental bond. It may turn out that if formal mentoring delivers only modest benefits, resources might find more productive uses elsewhere. Rigorous evaluations of mentoring programs are needed in order that we can determine their efficacy, and to ascertain whether they are the best use of scarce resources if they cannot deliver more than modest and fading benefits.

Natural Mentors

The research indicates that mentoring relationships that develop informally with nonparental adults are more likely to have a positive outcome on FFY than formal programs with adults who are not already part of the youth's lives. The child welfare system ought to encourage the type of activities through which these types of relationships can develop.

Foster Parents

Pecora, Kessler, et al. (2006) suggest that lifelong relationships should be encouraged with foster parents, group home workers, and other supportive adults as a means of giving FFY someone to turn to in times of crisis, or to just possibly have occasional companionship or to have a place to celebrate holidays. Contact with a former foster parent might also be a resource for emergency housing when needed. Such contacts have been associated with positive transition outcomes. Foster parents can give a sense of continuity that youth did not experience from their own family of origin.

CHAPTER FOURTEEN

Where Have We Been and Where Should We Go?

The rationale for removing a child from the home is that the child will have a new temporary home where circumstances will be improved. Unfortunately, the promise of an improved life for children in out-of-home care is not being met. Youth who spend at least part of their childhood and adolescence in care do not do as well as their counterparts in the general population in adapting to emerging adulthood. The research reviewed in this book suggests that many foster alumni are not adequately prepared for life after foster care. All too often they leave care without a high school diploma, job, housing, access to health care, or links to supportive relationships that would help them make a transition (Courtney, Dworsky, Cusick, et al., 2009; Pecora, Williams, Kessler, Downs, O'Brien, & Hiripi, 2003). For many youth who leave care, life is a struggle. The evidence shows that they lag their peers in reaching the milestones that indicate a successful transition to emerging adulthood. Former foster youth (FFY) continue to lag their counterparts in the general population in their mid- to late twenties, and it appears that it would be difficult for them to close the gap without considerable assistance (Courtney, Dworsky, et al., 2011). Also of great concern is that most of these youth spend their early adulthood in poverty. Many of the young men are in jail or prison, or they have legal problems. The young women in the transition phase all too often become the sole custodial parent of young children. These circumstances create difficulties for them in establishing a successful emerging adulthood.

Nevertheless, many youth demonstrate resilience after leaving foster care by avoiding some of the pitfalls that many other foster youth fall into, and they reach the milestones of a successful emerging adulthood. These emerging adults leave care with a high school education. They move on to a college, university, or vocational training program, or they work, and they avoid criminal justice involvement or early parenting. Research on these resilient young adults would enable the identification of factors that enable or contribute to their success, so that these strategies could be incorporated in programming that would help other foster youth.

Who Is Responsible for Former Foster Youth?

When a child is removed from their family home, the child welfare system assumes most of the legal obligations associated with the parental role. Chapter 1 discusses Courtney's (2009) notion of the child welfare system acting as a "corporate parent." Courtney argues that the child welfare system should regard the child as a member of a "family" with the state as "parent." Youth raised in care are entitled to have their corporate "family" render assistance with education, employment, housing, and health care. Meeting these various needs is the responsibility of any parent, the role that the system assumed when the child went into out-of-home care after being taken away from their biological family. Meeting the responsibilities and obligations of this role requires collaboration with other service systems.

Berzin (2008) and Buehler, Orme, Post, and Patterson (2000) found that FFY (not necessarily emancipated foster youth, EFY) did have poorer outcomes in adulthood than youth in the general population. However, FFY were virtually indistinguishable from youth with similar socioeconomic backgrounds who had ever been in out-of-home care. These researchers' findings suggest that the foster care system is not solely at fault for the difficulties these youth encounter during the transition. The problems FFY encounter in early adulthood are shaped by a set of family, community, and economic conditions in which the youth and their families are embedded. These conditions were present long before a youth entered foster care. At the micro level, youth enter care with the attending problems of trauma from their home life. However, at the macro level, poverty may be the prime culprit hindering youth from making a successful transition. Foster youth come from primarily poor families and are disproportionately minorities. This imbalance suggests that the youth and their families are beset by the consequences of economic inequality and racism, which they and their families had no part in creating. These social conditions are also problems that the child welfare system is ill equipped to solve. It may be that by gaining an understanding of the life course of foster care alumni, we will also learn about the difficulties of emerging into adulthood for all youth growing up with socioeconomic disadvantage.

Typologies of Adaptation

Table 14.1 describes a number of studies that have categorized adaptations to emerging adulthood. The intent of the discussion here is to examine these studies to get an idea of how well foster youth adapt to emerging adulthood, and what factors contribute to successful and unsuccessful adaptations. All but one of these studies used latent class analysis, a methodology briefly discussed in previous chapters, to construct their categories.

I have collapsed these descriptions of the adaptations of former foster youth into three categories based on the findings of these studies. The first group is called *Connected and Succeeding*, the second *Struggling but Connected*, and the last adaptation is referred to as *Problematic and Not Connected*. "Connected" refers to a youth having links to education and/or work, and having meaningful engagement with others.

The *Connected and Succeeding* category comprises about 40 to 50 percent of former foster youth. They represent a category of emerging adults moving toward self-sufficiency. They are adapting to emerging adulthood with far fewer problems than the other foster youth; their adaptation looks typical of youth in the general population. This group is disproportionately female. They have finished high school, and they may have gone on to college. They are also likely to work if they are not in school. They avoid early parenting or marriage. Generally, their mental health status is good, and they have avoided substance abuse problems and criminal justice involvement. Some youth within this category had elevated levels of depression, but for the most part their mental health symptoms were minimal. However, these characteristics do not mean that some of these youth may not have experienced problems like an episode of "couch surfing." While in care these emerging adults had relatively few placement changes. They also make connections to others, including their families. These young people have access to social support, and they can identify intimate relationships, both romantic and platonic, that they can depend on. They have reciprocal support relationships with others in these networks. In many cases, they may be living with families. They were also likely to view their overall foster care experience positively (Fowler, Toro, & Miles, 2011; Keller, Cusick, & Courtney, 2007; Yates & Grey, 2012).

Connected and Struggling describes about 25 to 35 percent of foster alumni. This group is disproportionately female. They may have moved too quickly into adulthood, perhaps spurred by a pregnancy or an ill-advised decision to leave care at emancipation age. Their adaptation to emerging adulthood is delayed. It was not uncommon for this group to be diagnosed with a mental health problem at age 19. The presence of children slowed them down in meeting the markers for a successful transition. They have lower rates of high school or GED completion than the first group. They are not likely to go on

Table 14.1 Typologies of Adaptation

	Courtney, Hook, & Lee, 2010	Yates & Grey, 2012	Macomber et al., 2008	Fowler, Toro, & Miles, 2011	Keller, Cusick, & Courtney, 2007	Lee, Festinger, Jaccard, & Munson, 2017
Study Descriptions						
	Application of Arnett's Theory of Emerging Adulthood	Profiles of Risk and Resilience	Employment trajectories through middle twenties	Housing security and transition outcomes	The Midwest Study baseline interview, just prior to leaving care	Mental health profiles of transitioning youth using NSCAW data
	Latent Class Analysis	Latent Class Analysis	Administrative records in 3 states (MN, CA, NC)	Latent Class Analysis	Latent Class Analysis	Latent Class Analysis
	Midwest Study at age 23–24	17- to 21-year-olds	17- to 24-year-olds	19- to 23-year-olds	17- to 18-year-olds	19-year-olds
	(n=732)	(n=164)		(n=265)	(n=732)	(n=1.179)
Study Categorizations						
Connected and Making It	Emerging Adults (21.1%) Accelerated Adults (36.3%)	Resilient (47%)	Consistently Connected (16% to 25%) Externally Resilient (6.7%)	Stable-Engaged (40.8%)	Competent Connected (38%)	Mental health symptoms profile (56%)
Connected but Struggling	Struggling (25.2%) Parents	Internally Resilient (30%)	Later Connected (16% to 21%)	Stable-Disengaged (30.2%)	Struggling but Staying (14%)	No diagnosed midlevel symptoms and trauma profiles (15%)
Problematic and Not Connected	Troubled and Troubling (17.5%)	Maladapted (16.5%)	Initially Connected (22% to 46%) Never Connected (22% to 33%)	Instable-Disengaged (29.1%)	Distressed-Disconnected (43%)	Multi-morbid, diagnoses midlevel symptoms, substance dependent profiles (25%)

to college even if they did finish high school, and they have erratic work histories in low-wage employment. They are less likely than the first group to live independently. Though they did not have problems with chronic homelessness, they may have had an episode of homelessness. These young people also had smaller support networks than the first category, but they were sources of social support that helped them cope. The support systems included their families. Youth in this category were generally willing to ask for support from formal service systems. Although their ability to cope with the struggle for independence shows resiliency, these youth become more stable in their later twenties, such as when they find employment that is more consistent. They may be in need of support from the formal service system, and they could benefit from extended care. Without help, they may slip into the next problematic category.

The last category, *Problematic and Not Connected*, consists of 20 to 40 percent of the former foster youth. Courtney, Dworsky, Lee, and Rapp (2010) call them "troubled and troubling." This group is mostly male. They left care at a younger age than the other groups without taking advantage of extended care. They do not have a high school diploma or GED. Substance abuse and/or mental health problems are major barriers to a successful adaptation in this group. They may have been in jail, prison, or a hospital for psychiatric or drug treatment reasons. There is a strong possibility that they will have continued criminal justice involvement, and they may have been victims of crime themselves. They have problems establishing themselves in the job market and have trouble living independently throughout their twenties. These former dependents of the system may have chronic problems with homelessness. They may be parents, but their children usually reside with others, including being in foster care. They have particular difficulties with establishing intimate relationships.

What Youth Need for a Successful Transition

A Continuum of Care

To assist in a successful transition, Iglehart and Becerra (2002) suggest a continuum of services delivered on multiple levels. The following suggestions for services are based on their specifications.

Level 1

This level occurs prior to a youth leaving care. The experiences of foster youth suggest that removal from their parent's home was counterproductive, and they did not receive a benefit from state care. Because of the experience of these youth, we must ensure that all alternatives to removal are exhausted before a child is taken into the child welfare system. The system must strengthen the checks that are in place in order to make certain that the removal decision is the correct one. It is important to note that children are more likely to be in foster care for neglect than any other reason (AFCARS, 2016). Neglect is often synonymous with poverty, and unless there is a substance abuse problem or severe mental illness, there is no reason to assume that parents could not take care of their children if they had sufficient resources. Emma Ketteringham (2017), a lawyer in New York who works to reunify foster children with their families, says we could reduce the number of neglect cases in the system by providing the parents with the payments that would have been given to foster parents. This idea is worth testing. We need to do a better job of assessing the risk for removal and reunification.

Adoption as a permanency option may not be desirable or realistic for many foster children. Legal guardianship might be more realistic for older youth. Permanence, according to some studies, is likely to come from relationships known to the youth (see discussion on natural mentors), but there is no fiscal incentive for guardianship from the federal government as there is with adoption. Developing an incentive for states to achieve permanency through guardianship is a crucial need. Given the high degree of contact that youth have with their families, and the closeness youth feel toward kin that is reflected in the research, it would seem that more could be done to achieve permanency for youth. Freundlich and Avery (2006) note the irony that many youth aging out of foster care seem to have their own goal of reunification even if their case plan does not. We need to assure that intervention is family based and provides the services that would address and ameliorate the problems that brought youth into the system (Collins, Paris, & Ward, 2008).

Youth need placement stability in order to build relational permanence and avoid the placement mobility problems noted throughout this book. Placement instability is in need of a remedy since the research reviewed in this book shows it to be a major culprit in the poor outcomes noted with transitional youth. Multiple placement changes were associated with leaving care without a high school diploma, including homelessness, behavior problems, and substance abuse (Jonson-Reid & Barth, 2000; McCoy, McMillen, & Spitznagel, 2008; Reilly, 2003; Ryan & Testa, 2005; White et al., 2008; Zima et al., 2000). Finding stable placements might lead to permanency in the form of guardianships or adoptions, or at least in life-long relationships, if youth remain in a foster home long enough to develop those relationships (Frey, Cushing, Freundlich, & Brenner, 2008).

Residing in congregate care, such as the residential education option described in Chapter 6, might challenge accepted beliefs on the negative effects of congregate care when compared to foster care. However, this type of placement may be able to provide more stability than foster care and enable youth to leave care with a high school diploma. This stability could contribute to building relationships that continue after leaving care, and encourage the continuance of a youth's education. This type of placement would run up against the requirement that youth reside in the least restrictive level of care possible. Many young people do not find stability in foster placements, and they are locked into frequent placement changes by this provision of the Adoption Assistance and Child Welfare Act of 1980. This provision should be balanced against the youth's needs for the stability in living arrangements and to obtain an education before they leave care (Stott & Gustavsson, 2010).

Youth should receive independent living services (ILS) that would provide daily skills training and socio-emotional content. Youth need assistance in developing mentors and family and friend contacts before they leave care. The system must be willing to back off from its protective stance to allow youth to engage in developmentally appropriate activities, which would help them practice independent living skills, and have the opportunity to develop community-based relationships.

Level 2

Youth should not leave care without an address where they can reside, a high school degree, a job or an educational program, access to health care, needed documents (health records, Social Security card, driver's license, etc.), and links to needed services. Discharge should not happen without becoming connected to an adult who is permanently committed to them and on whom they can count on for advice, guidance, and mentorship (Avery & Freundlich, 2009).

A strong focus on equipping youth with a high school degree upon discharge from care is essential. Youth who are able to secure a solid foundation to succeed after foster care may look back at the foster care experience more favorably. All sources of financial aid should be identified and tapped for youth in order that they may continue or complete their education.

Level 3

Contact with youth after care should continue to assure that they receive the needed services to be successful. Below I outline some steps we could take to improve outcomes after youth leave care.

A Safety Net When They Leave Care

Atkinson (2008) has suggested that youth need a universal safety net when they leave care that would be analogous to what most youth receive from their parents when they leave home. The safety net would be an answer to the critique about the abrupt discharge from the system and the accompanying lack of services. This safety net would include a guarantee to independent living skills training, assistance with housing (including transitional housing), employment, education, and access to health care.

The safety net should balance structure and flexibility. Youth need the structure that the child welfare system provides, but that structure needs to be tempered by the realization that it is developmentally expected that youth will test limits and make mistakes. The system would provide the flexibility to allow youth to recover from those mistakes. Requirements regarding school attendance, employment, or job training may mean that those young adults who are most in need of services do not receive them. This flexibility includes the right to return to foster care if they made an earlier decision to leave the system.

Extend Foster Care

A Safety Net, for How Long?

In Chapter 2, I argued that youth should remain in care until age 25. Extended time in care would provide needed stability and additional time for preparation including finishing school, and aid youth in building up savings to meet some of the challenges of early adulthood. Public child welfare agencies cannot provide support for former youth indefinitely. However, policy makers must recognize and respond to the social and economic trends noted earlier in this book. An extended period of transitional services for all foster youth might help these youth cope with the challenges of emerging adulthood. This extension would provide the same sort of supports afforded to youth in the general population and would be congruent with the normative transition to adulthood in contemporary America discussed in Chapter 2 (Osgood, Foster, & Courtney, 2010).

Staying in care for a year or two longer is not enough to assure self-sufficiency for emerging adults. Many of the gains shown for EFY in extended care had disappeared by ages 23 or 24. For example, in the Midwest Study, youth in Illinois, a state with extended care, youth who remained in care were less likely to be homeless at age 21 than youth in the two states that discharged youth at 18. However, at ages 23 or 24 youth in these three states had comparable rates of homelessness (Courtney, Dworsky, et al., 2010). Given these data, one might be tempted to assert that the extension does not prevent homelessness. However, these outcomes suggest that an extension until age 21 is not enough to resolve the challenges of emerging adulthood. Services and support need to continue. As was stated earlier, it is not any more realistic to expect someone to be self-sufficient at age 21 than it was at age 18. The extended time in care would provide youth with continued services including independent living services (Gardner, 2008). Youth might have an opportunity to receive additional services such as mental health assistance, complete an education program, and/or find stable employment.

The Benefits of Extended Care

The benefits of extended foster care are well established by the research reviewed in this book. Extended foster care is associated with finishing high school, attending college, or earning a vocational certificate or license (Courtney et al., 2016; Courtney, Dworsky, et al., 2011). FFY who remain in care were also more likely to be employed, and when working they had higher earnings relative to youth not in extended care (Barnow et al., 2015; Fallesen, 2013; Hook & Courtney, 2011; Kerman, Wildfire, & Barth, 2002). In both the Midwest and Missouri Studies, youth in extended care were more likely to utilize mental health and substance abuse services than youth who left care to live independently. These studies also indicate that extended foster care would reduce alcohol or substance abuse or dependence (Brown, Courtney, & McMillen, 2015; McMillen & Raghavan, 2009). Courtney, Dworsky, and Pollack (2007) found that keeping a youth in care until age 19 would reduce pregnancies by 38 percent. Illinois caseworkers reported that youth who remained in care had fewer behavioral problems and educational and job skill deficits than those who left care (Leathers & Testa, 2006).

The cost-benefit analyses described in this book provide evidence that the costs of the expansion of foster care will be offset as youth become taxpayers and consumers and their need of public benefits (Medicaid, TANF, SNAP, etc.) is diminished. Additional savings will be accrued as these young adults avoid mental health problems, substance abuse difficulties, and criminal justice involvement (Courtney, Dworsky, & Peters, 2009; Kerman, Wildfire, & Barth, 2004; Packard, Delgado, Fellmeth, & McReady, 2008). Courtney, Dworsky, and Peters (2009) projected a return of $2.40 on every public dollar invested on youth in extended care in just the area of future earnings. They argue the savings would be even higher if other benefits such as better health, housing stability, and reduced criminal justice involvement were monetized.

Court involvement should have a similar extension until age 25. Supervision by the court might answer the critics who would not want to extend services without it. Atkinson (2008) suggests that the courts should recognize that these youth are no longer minors and need autonomy. The structure of youth involvement with the court would be less stringent than when they were minors. Court hearings would be less frequent, and youth could miss court appearances without penalty. Atkinson suggests the use of an ombudsman or mentor appointed by the court who would act as an advocate on behalf of youth.

Do Youth Want to Stay in Care?

Leathers and Testa (2006) suggest that youth who opted to leave care without services were those with more problems, although these researchers leave open the possibility that the positive findings regarding the extension of time in care could possibly be an artifact of self-selection. Youth without major problems and who are somewhat more positive about foster care are more likely to continue in care. Youth with difficulties may actively seek to disengage from care. They also assert that it is important to engage high-risk youth with preventative services before they leave care, since they are difficult to reach once they are out of the system.

Qualitative evidence reveals that many youth want to "be out from under the thumb" of child welfare, or to "do for oneself" (Goodkind, Schelbe, & Shook, 2011; Mares, 2010; Perez & Romo, 2011). Cosner-Berzin, Singer, and Hokanson (2014) assert that many EFY view their treatment in adolescence by the child welfare system as keeping them in a childlike state. EFY may view the child welfare system as an impediment to reaching adulthood. Offers of support from the child welfare system may be interpreted as an attempt to keep them from achieving adulthood. McCoy, McMillen, and Spitznagel (2008) reported that 90 percent of the 210 EFY they interviewed wanted to leave care. Their reasons for wanting to exit care included a dislike or frustration with the system (39 percent), a desire for independence (28 percent), failure to receive services promised (22 percent), and a desire for a change of circumstances (11 percent).

The available quantitative evidence from the CalYOUTH and the Midwest evaluations paints a different picture of youth's desires to remain in care and suggests that youth would want to stay in care past emancipation if that option was available. Courtney, Dworsky, and Pollack (2007) present data showing that many foster youth will voluntarily remain in foster care when they have the choice to leave, and they do so in order to receive independent living services past emancipation age. One indicator of the popularity of extending foster care came from California where the legislature estimated that 50 percent of eligible foster youth would take advantage an extension of foster care. In fact, 80 percent of foster youth opted into the extension (Delgado, 2013). Two-thirds of the Illinois youth remained in foster care at age 20 and one-half were in care at age 21 (Courtney et al., 2007).

Does Extended Care Come at the Cost of Permanency?

One critique of the Fostering Connections to Success Act (FCSA) is that it provides incentives for youth to remain in care in lieu of reunification with family, adoption, or legal guardianship. Remaining in care did not come at the expense of legal permanence with family, but rather seems to provide an option that replaces undesirable exits. In California, only a relatively small reduction in the number of family reunifications occurred after the extension of foster care. However, the researchers note that reunifications had been declining for some time before the extension. They also make the point that youth who turn age 18 are free to return home at any time. In addition, the law did not affect the other permanency options of adoption and guardianship. The exit options most affected by FCSA were a reduction in running away from placement and youth legally emancipating prior to age 18 (Courtney & Okpych, 2015). One answer for those who are concerned with a reduction in reunifications because of FCSA is to make older reunified adolescents eligible for transition services. The data indicate that these young people could benefit from services, and it may be inaccurate to assume that their parents have the resources to assist youth with the transition. The adolescents who leave care before emancipation may also need independent living assistance. The trend with all of this legislation has been to allow the states to use ILS funds for youth at various ages and stages as they approach the transition (National Foster Care Awareness Project, 2000b).

Perhaps these youth rush through their adolescence to adulthood before they are emotionally ready. Samuels and Pryce (2008) called this phenomenon the premature conferring of adult status. Goodkind et al. (2011) also noted that this desire for independence and autonomy acted as a significant deterrent in recent efforts to extend the age eligibility for foster care assistance. Former foster youth are proud of their ability to take care of themselves and are reluctant to seek help when needed. Nevertheless, the experience of Illinois and California with extended care suggests that, given the opportunity, many if not most youth will avail themselves of the additional time and services. Youth also said they had a sense of loss concerning relationships they might have had if circumstances had not brought them into foster care. They are aware that they lacked the security and ongoing support available to many emerging adults in the general population. This loss of social relationships and its effect on their life trajectories in their early twenties is one of the strongest reasons for extending foster care support to at least age 21 if not later.

Youth Empowerment and Keeping Them in Foster Care

Scannapieco, Connell-Carrick, and Painter (2007) and Geenen and Powers (2007), in two qualitative studies that used focus groups composed of past and current foster youth, foster parents, and social workers, found that youth wanted to be involved in decision making and in the development of an individualized plan to meet their own needs. Such an approach is consistent with the assertions made by Cosner-Berzin et al. (2014) that youth want to have greater leeway in decisions in order to feel that the child welfare system is treating them as adults. Some youth may think the only way they can become adults is to sever ties with the system. Giving them more leeway in decision making might encourage them to remain in foster care.

Assuming that the qualitative researchers have a point, the system should consider providing adolescents with more decision-making opportunities commensurate with the same leeway given adolescents in the general population, in order to encourage continued use of support from the child welfare system.

A Guardian, Housing, and Stipend after Care

California has provided Chafee services to youth participating in the state's transitional housing program. Youth who opt into the program receive a stipend and services up to age 24. The stipend is $850 a month in the first year, and declines to $258 five years after discharge, the last year of eligibility. The declining amount of the stipend is predicated on the assumption that youth are making progress toward self-sufficiency and increasing their income. The juvenile court appoints a transition guardian before a youth's eighteenth birthday to assist the youth in managing money. Ideally the guardian is someone known to the youth (foster parent, adult family member, attorney, adult friend/mentor, CASA volunteer). The guardian may meet the need for a consistent, caring adult identified in the previous chapter. The court requires a progress report at six-month intervals to monitor whether youth are moving toward self-sufficiency. The youth or guardian can petition for a change to the transition plan at any point. It is important to note that California recognizes that some youth who do not wish to remain in foster care are still in need of services. Former foster youth may feel the system is stigmatizing, demeaning, and restrictive of their independence. The state continues to provide needed housing support to these youth (Packard et al., 2008). California can do this currently because this is a state-funded program. All of this presents fiscal challenges given the changed political climate in the country. The resources to fund these efforts may not be available in the future.

Develop Different Criteria for Emancipation

Emancipation need not coincide with a youth's eighteenth birthday. Could there be other considerations to take into account such as maturity, achievements of milestones like finishing school, or mental health status? The courts could decide on the basis of any of these criteria, not on an arbitrary designated age, to allow a youth to remain as a dependent and receive services. Is the ending of care at age eighteen another traumatic ending for maltreated youth, particularly if the youth does not want it?

Practice Needs

Empirical research is lacking on how to implement or deliver services for former foster youth. A number of researchers whose work was included in this book used quantitative techniques such as the previously mentioned latent class analysis to classify former foster youth (FFY). These analyses show that FFY are not a homogenous group. Their responses to "aging out" are varied, and they have different needs. Therefore, depending upon a particular youth's circumstance, that person may need a differential response. Effective assessment is required to identify both the specific needs of a youth and the package of services that would address those needs, and should be followed by a rigorous evaluation of these efforts.

Youth in qualitative studies tell us that effective programs that equip them with skills needed to live independently address multiple needs, such as housing, education, employment, and mentoring. Planners should craft programs in such a manner that they respect a youth's developmental need to break away from a system. Former foster youth perceive overregulation of their behavior as a challenge to their autonomy (Osterling-Lemon & Hines, 2006; Rashid, 2004). Programs must be flexible and recognize that mistakes are part of the territory of young adulthood.

Waivers from the federal government were utilized effectively to test innovations in welfare and Medicaid reform, and in developing innovations to moving children out of long-term foster care (Osgood et al., 2010). Just as in these cases, we need empirical tests of interventions for transition-age youth to find out what works with them.

The Need for Collaboration: Child Welfare Does Not Have Everything a Youth Needs

Meeting the many needs of youth entering emerging adulthood requires the collaboration of many service systems (education, housing, job training, health, criminal justice, behavioral health, etc.). Many of the resources that youth require to be successful are located outside the purview of the child welfare system. Youth should be assisted in accessing these resources. Ideally a partnership model would be created in which the child welfare system recognizes that the multiple and complex problems that FFY experience require a shared ownership with community partners of the responsibility to aid FFY in making the transition. Such a model would allow social workers to have access to the wide variety of services needed by youth (Packard, Jones, Gross, Hohman, & Fong, 2001).

In 2003, the federal government put together the Shared Youth Vision Initiative (SYVI) to address weaknesses noted in the White House Task Force Report on Disadvantaged Youth, which cited a lack of communication, coordination, and collaboration among federal agencies that provide services to youth. Youth aging out of care were identified as a specific group needing attention. The SYVI provides funds to enable governments at the federal, state, and local levels to develop strategic plans and coordinate initiatives at all levels to better serve disadvantaged youth, and to build partnerships and engage economic development agencies, business and industry associations, and community-based and faith-based organizations in the development and implementation of collaborative vision activities (Shared Youth Initiative, 2008).

A poorly coordinated service system hampers appropriate service delivery. Systems tend to operate in their own silos independently of one another and only rarely communicate except when they are forced to because of the needs of a specific youth. This independent operation works against collaboration in two ways. First, adult-serving agencies might not know how to serve former foster youth and may need assistance to do so. Second, youth-serving agencies may address specific functional areas. Foster youth might need help not only with continuing their education but also with housing, employment, and/or mental health. These varied needs may mean youth are required to go to multiple agencies for assistance. These agencies have separate sources of funding, differing missions, and different eligibility standards for services. This fragmentation of services can lead to gaps in the provision of services or in duplication of services (Osgood et al., 2010) and time-consuming, frustrating administrative encounters for youth. Successful collaboration with service providers from many service systems is crucial for improving outcomes. One suggestion by Osgood and colleagues is to move toward a single integrative service system at the administrative and service level. The administrative level would coordinate eligibility and financing. The service level would make sure youth receive the needed services in an efficient manner and avoid the duplication of effort. Child welfare agencies that receive Title IV-E funding for extended care can use these funds and their expertise to provide case management to integrate those services.

The various systems that serve youth (child welfare, education, juvenile justice) and those who focus on the emerging adults (postsecondary education, workforce development, housing, health, mental health, substance abuse, adult corrections) need to collaborate in the creation of state-level databases to allow for accurate data sharing on behalf of youth. Youth could move among service systems at different locations within states (Hill, 2009). One of the more interesting innovations taking place is in Alabama, which established four "one-stop" service centers throughout the state in an attempt to provide seamless service delivery for youth (Osgood et al., 2010). When a variety of different services collaborate on service delivery, cross training is needed to make sure that workers in the various service systems understand the developmental needs of emerging adults and FFY.

Amending Fostering Connections

The FCSA should be amended to widen eligibility to allow previously excluded youth to receive services. Pergamit and Johnson (2009) estimate that 67 percent to 85 percent of the Los Angeles EFY would be eligible under such an extension. Almost one-third of the California youth were unemployed, or not in school, or enrolled in a vocational training program, and therefore they were not eligible for extended foster care. Amending the FCSA should include allowing incarcerated FFY to receive transition services and assistance to return to the child welfare system to help in the transition (Wylie, 2014). The excluded youth are among the neediest of former foster youth. One policy change suggested by Courtney, Hook, and Lee (2010) that would benefit this group is changing the FCSA to include kin living relationships as supervised relationships to make sure youth would continue to receive services if they decide to stay in care.

Conclusion

The remedy for the problems identified in this book is to develop a set of social policies committed to social justice, a task that is well beyond the ability of the child welfare system. The child welfare system is designed to respond to the failures of families at the micro level; it was not developed with the intent of solving the problems of poverty and racism in America. Child welfare professionals are overmatched in this struggle. Until we have a commitment to reducing poverty in this society and to providing children with decent schools (including early childhood education), we will continue to have youth ill prepared for emerging adulthood. Berzin (2008) asserts that her findings mean that other low-income youth growing up in difficult circumstances, not just FFY, will need assistance emerging into adulthood. Their parents need educational and employment opportunities, health care that includes family planning services to ensure that more children are born wanted, and access to substance abuse or mental health services as needed. Children need to be frequently screened for difficulties that could be remedied with early intervention and thus make it easier for their parents to parent them. Parents should receive the help they need when they leave the hospital with their babies. This help should include opportunities to learn child development and parenting skills to increase their competence in caring for their child. All of these efforts would be a step toward truly assuring child welfare.

Appendices

Appendix A Review of the Research on Independent Living Programs

Author	Sample Characteristics	Geographic Region	Data Collection and Years	Outcomes
Austin & Johnson (1995)	Compared 278 youth who were in the start-up phase (1988–1991) with 255 in the fine-tuning phase (1992–1994). Shippensburg study.	Pennsylvania	1988–1994 Interviews	No differences in employment initially, but in the fine-tuning phase youth were less likely to drop out of high school and more likely to be in postsecondary education.
Barnow, Buck, O'Brien, Pecora, Ellis, & Steiner (2015)	1,058 youth in transition programs in 5 states.	5 unnamed U.S. states	Longitudinal, 2 years Data gathered from case managers	Findings described as "not overwhelmingly positive" (p. 166). 45% obtained at least 1 positive outcome with employment (full-time work, part time, apprenticeship, military service). 35% obtained employment. 23% obtained a GED or diploma. 17% enrolled in postsecondary education.
Christenson (2003)	78 pre-Chafee youth (1996–1999) compared with 164 Chafee youth (2000–2002).	Idaho	1996–2002 Record review and ILP coordinator reports	Pre-Chafee youth more likely to complete high school, be employed, and less likely to be homeless, get pregnant, or utilize social services.
Cook, Fleishman, & Grimes (1991) Westat study	1,644 at baseline. 844 youth located for a phone or in-person interview. 810 at follow-up. 57% female, 61% white. Census data were used for comparison; multistage stratified sampling with weights to assure representativeness of U.S. foster care. Compared those who used ILS with those who did not.	Title IV-E funded Independent Living Programs 8 states	18- to 24-year-olds Time 1: 1987–1988 Time 2: 1991	Found that those who used ILS did better than those who did not. The skill areas with the strongest effects were: budgeting, credit, consumer education and employment, access to health care, satisfaction with life, and self-sufficiency. ILS participation was associated with high school completion, but not employment. Describes youth after-care status as "adequate at best." (p. 217).

(continued)

Appendix A (continued)

Author	Sample Characteristics	Geographic Region	Data Collection and Years	Outcomes
Courtney, Zinn, Koralek, Bess, Stagner, Pergamit, & Johnson (2011a)	Multi-Site Evaluation of Foster Youth Programs. N=254 youth. Treatment group, n=136, control n=118. Random assignment.	Kern County, CA	Longitudinal, initial interview and 2 follow-ups	No differences noted between groups on employment. Only 40% employed at the follow-up interview.
U.S. Department of Health and Human Services (2008a)	Multi-Site Evaluation of Foster Youth Programs. N=445 randomly assigned to treatment or control.	Los Angeles County, CA	3 in-person interviews over 2 years Tutoring & mentoring	Program had no impacts on educational outcomes. Slight gains were noted in reading comprehension.
U.S. Department of Health and Human Services (2008b)	Multi-Site Evaluation of Foster Youth Programs. Life Skills Training Program. 482 17-year-olds at the time of their assignment. 234 randomly assigned to a treatment and control group, 248 randomly assigned to the follow-up.	Los Angeles	Pre- and post-test	Few impacts found on any outcome assessed (Life Skills education, employment, earnings, and avoidance of economic hardship).
Courtney, Zinn, Koralek, Bess, Stagner, Pergamit, & Johnson (2008b)	Multi-Site Evaluation of Foster Youth Programs. Longitudinal—2 years. Youth in treatment foster care. N=194 randomly assigned to a treatment or control group.	Massachusetts	Pre- and post-test	The outreach group (treatment group) more likely to enroll in college and persist than control group. Outreach youth were also more likely than controls to remain in care past 18, and were more likely to receive money management, educational and employment assistance, and financial support in obtaining housing than the control group. No differences were found on housing, delinquency, pregnancy, or self-reported preparedness for independence.

Study	Sample	Location	Method	Findings
Freundlich, Avery, & Padgett (2007)	77 respondents who represented 6 stakeholder groups (judges, agency staff that provided congregate care, attorneys, social workers affiliated with legal service organizations, youth advocacy organizations, young adults.	New York City	Qualitative	Preparation and readiness for independent living. Youth vary in their level of preparation. Agency respondents attribute part of the reason for failure to the youth themselves. However, generally programs themselves were held responsible for shortcomings of programs. Classroom-based instruction was not enough. Aging out at 21 is not sufficient for emerging adulthood. Concerns by youth and professionals about program quality.
Georgiades (2005)	49 youth in a treatment group (ILP participants) and 18 in a comparison group (non-ILP participants).	Miami-Dade & Monroe counties, Florida	Mailed questionnaire, record review. Follow-up as long as 8 years for some youth	The non-ILP group was more likely than the ILP group to lack a high school diploma or GED, be unemployed, depend upon public assistance, have been in jail, lack a driver's license.
Harding & Luft (1995)	30 former ILP participants compared with 29 non-ILP participants.	Harris County, Texas	Survey, phone, face-to-face, mailed questionnaire	ILP participants were significantly more likely than non-ILP participants to have a stable living situation and completed job corps vocational training.
Katz & Courtney (2015) Midwest Evaluation of Former Foster Youth	Secondary data analysis of the Midwest Study of former foster youth. Longitudinal (n=732).	Illinois, Iowa, & Wisconsin	Mixed methods Interview and qualitative analysis of open-ended questions on ILS	ILS participation correlated with fewer unmet needs after discharge. The most unmet need from ILS was financial skills followed by housing.
Kerman, Barth, & Wildfire (2004)	115 youth among 217 youth who were Casey Family Alumni. Sorted into 3 groups based on exit from foster care (adoption, extended foster care, and other). Cost of extended foster care. Cost Analysis.	Casey Family Program	Ages 19–26 Received services 1987–1999 Agency records	A commitment of about $14,600 over 2 to 8 years of extended foster care. Youth receiving extended care had more positive outcomes (heightened well-being and greater self-sufficiency) than those who did not.

(continued)

Author	Sample Characteristics	Geographic Region	Data Collection and Years	Outcomes
Lemon, Hines, & Merdinger (2005)	81 former foster youth with ILS participation compared with 113 former foster youth without that experience. 24.4% return rate. All were attending college. Ethnographic interviews with 9 program coordinators.	California	Mixed methods Mailed survey Semistructured telephone interview Needs assessment	The two groups of FFY had similar experiences with homelessness, criminal justice involvement, and receiving health or mental health services. ILP FFY felt their financial situation was improved, were more hopeful about their future, and maintained better contact with their former social worker than the non-ILP youth. ILP participants were more likely to be youth of color. Found mixed rates of involvement of FFY in college support programs.
Lindsey & Ahmed (1999)	44 Former Foster Youth (FFY) who had been enrolled in an ILP program compared with 32 randomly selected FFY, who had not received ILS. 24% return rate. Counties chosen by random stratified cluster sampling. Comparisons chosen at random.	8 North Carolina counties	Mailed survey one and three years after exit	ILP participants more likely than non-ILP to have completed high school, be living independently and able to manage expenses, have completed a vocational program, or be in college.
Mallon (1998)	46 participants. All participants had received independent living skills from Green Chimneys Independent Living program between Dec. 1987 and Dec. 1994; 96% of participants were of color; all participants were male; 13% were gay; 15% had an organic impairment, and 35% were learning disabled.	New York City	Case records, and survey interviews at intake (date of enrollment), exit (date of discharge from program), and follow-up (from Dec. 1994 to June 1995 after discharge)	Improvement in 14 life skills categories between pre- & post-tests. No significance levels reported.

Study	Sample	Location	Design	Findings
Mares (2010)	Self-administered survey of public and private agency ILS providers (n=83), administrative data (n=108 youth), focus groups with current and former foster youth (n=86).	Lucas County, Ohio	Needs assessment	Generated 10 recommendations for ILS practice.
Mares & Kroner (2011)	N=385 youth admitted to an ILS program.	Lighthouse Independent Living Program, Ohio	Administrative record review 2001–2005	Females more likely to be housed at discharge. No differences on housing noted with ethnicity/race.
McMillen, Rideout, Fisher, & Tucker (1997)	Focus groups completed a little over 2 years after discharge (n=25).	Missouri	Qualitative	Money management skills and the provision of stipends found important. Participation reduced stigma and isolation. The ILS caseworker, but not their social worker, was seen as helpful with the transition.
Montgomery, Donkoh, & Underhill (2006)	Review of 14 studies.	Programs scattered throughout the United States	Systematic Research Review	Studies lack empirical rigor. No randomized studies. In sum, ILP programs may improve educational, employment, & housing outcomes for youth leaving care. These findings need to be considered in light of the methodological limitations of the studies.
Okpych (2015)	National Youth in Transition Database merged with AFCARS database (n=131,204) of youth in care for at least 90 days.	49 states New York not included	Administrative record review State reports mandated by Chaffee Data from youth ages 16, 17, & 18	50.2% of youth received at least one IL service. The average number of services received was 2.31. Multiracial and Hispanic youth were most likely to receive services. African American youth, particularly those in urban areas, were the least likely to receive services. Urban youth generally received fewer services than other youth. Disabled youth received more services than nondisabled foster youth. Services aimed at secondary education, health education, home management, and financial literacy were more likely to be given than payment for housing.

(continued)

Author	Sample Characteristics	Geographic Region	Data Collection and Years	Outcomes
Powers, Geenen, Powers, Pommier-Satya, Turner, Dalton, Drummond, & Swank (2012)	Longitudinal, randomized clinical trial. N=63 youth with learning and emotional and other health impairments. Test of a self-determination enhancement intervention.	Portland, Oregon	Ages 16.5—17.5	Treatment youth more likely to use transitional services and be involved in independent living activities, and had a higher quality of life than controls. Higher employment rates and high school graduation rates reported, but no supporting statistics provided.
Scannapieco, Schagrin, & Scannapieco (1995)	44 teens who went through an ILS program & 46 foster care teen who did not participate in the program.	Baltimore, Maryland	Case record analysis 1988–1993	ILP participants were more likely than non-ILP youth to have completed high school, been employed, and had a job at discharge, and were more self-sufficient.
Scannapieco, Smith, & Blakeney-Strong (2016)	329 youth who received ILS.	Texas	Tracked on the receipt of 5 self-sufficiency services (education, employment, financial literacy, and housing)	Number of placements increased; the more negative self-sufficiency outcomes were found. Sibling placement history associated with better educational outcomes. A focus on planning and goal setting associated with better employment and education outcomes. Physical neglect history associated with poorer educational outcomes.
Waldinger & Furman (1994)	(a) 289 ILP participants vs. 65 non-participants (b) 62 in ILP & 230 in enhanced ILP.	Los Angeles	Youth assessed 6 months after the program began Interviews and case records	ILP participants had better behaviors than controls. Slightly more likely to perform above grade level. No significant differences in employment or feeling they could live independently.

(b)

Appendix B   Review of the Research on Life after Foster Care

Longitudinal Cohort Studies

Author(s)	Sample Size and Characteristics	Geographic Region	Data Collection and Years	Outcomes Studied
Barnow, Buck, O'Brien, Pecora, Ellis, & Steiner (2015)	N=1,058. 16- to 21-year-olds in transition programs. 71% of the sample were African American.	Chicago, Detroit, Houston, Los Angeles, New York City	Data collected by case managers quarterly over a 2-year period	Employment & education. ILS services provided. Housing, parent status, Criminal justice involvement.
Courtney, Dworsky & colleagues (2001, 2005, 2006, 2009, 2010, 2011). Mid-West Evaluation of Adult Functioning; Youth Outcomes at Ages 17–18, 19, 21, 23–24, 25–26 Midwest Study	Baseline interviews with 732 former foster youth. Four additional waves of interviewing. N=596 at the age 26 interview. Results were compared with ADD Health Survey sample.	Sample consisted of all foster youth eligible for emancipation in Iowa & Wisconsin, and a random sample from Illinois.	Interviews conducted 2002–2011	Living arrangements, relationships with family of origin, social support, education, employment, economic well-being, receipt of government benefits, physical & mental health, sexual behaviors, pregnancy, marriage & cohabitation, parenting, criminal justice. Data at age 19 provides a comparison between those who remained in care and those who left care.

(continued)

Appendix B *(continued)*

Longitudinal Cohort Studies

Author(s)	Sample Size and Characteristics	Geographic Region	Data Collection and Years	Outcomes Studied
Courtney, Charles, Okpych, Napolitano, & Halsted (2014); Courtney, Okpych, Charles, Dominique, Stevenson, Park, Kindle, Harty, & Feng (2016) Findings from the California Youth Transitions to Adulthood Study (CalYOUTH)	Baseline interview at age 17. Youth age 16.75 to 17.75. N=727. N=611 interviewed at age 19. Youth to be interviewed again at 21. ADD Health comparison	Stratified random sample from 51 of 58 California counties. 7 counties had 0 eligible youth. 95% participation rate.	2013–2015	Examined the impact of California's extended foster care. Foster care experience, health, social support, parenting, criminal justice, education, employment.
McCoy, McMillan, & Spitznagel (2008) Missouri NIMH study	404 formerly system-involved youth. 45% white, 52% African American. 28% depressed.	Missouri	Mixed methods. Interviewed 9 times between ages 17–19 in 2001–2003	Circumstances of leaving foster care. Where did they go, and why did they want to leave? Living arrangements. Foster care history and conditions.
Goerge, Bilaver, Joo Lee, Needell, Brookhart, & Jackman (2002)	3 groups. Aging out N=4,213. Reunification N=5,415. Low-Income Group N=247,895.	California, Illinois, South Carolina	1995–1997 Linked administrative databases in 3 states (Child Welfare System and Unemployment Wage Reporting)	Employment and earnings.

Study	Sample	Design / Time	Outcomes
Blome (1997)	167 family foster care; 167 matched on age, gender, & race. 47% female, 44% white. Randomly drawn from an existing database.	Longitudinal	High school graduation and college attendance.
Cook (1994) Westat study	1,644 youth at baseline. 810 youth at follow-up. A comparison group was used. 57% female, 61% white. Census data were used for comparison; multi-stage stratified sampling with weights to assure representativeness of U.S. foster care.	National sample	18- to 24-year-olds Time 1: 1987–1988 Time 2: 1991	Economic, education, family formation (marriage & pregnancy), employment, alcohol and drugs, housing.
Havalchak, White, & O'Brien (2008, March)	Eligibility: received foster care from the Casey Family Program for 1 year. n=557. 65% female.	AZ, CA, HI, ID, LA, MT, ND, OK, OR, SD, TX, WA, WY	2004 (n=198), 2005 (n=194), 2006 (n=166) Ages 19, 22, or 25 at interview	Mental health, health, drugs and alcohol, education, employment & finances, marriage, parenting, families, social support, community, criminal justice, independent living services.

(continued)

Appendix B (*continued*)
Longitudinal Cohort Studies

Author(s)	Sample Size and Characteristics	Geographic Region	Data Collection and Years	Outcomes Studied
Kimberlin & Lemley (2012)	Exit outcomes for former foster youth participating in California's THP Plus Transitional supportive housing programs.	California: Bay Area, Los Angeles, San Diego. 80% of California's Transitional Housing Program participants	Pre- and post-test. No comparison group. 2008–2010. Evaluation of foster connections. N=552. 82% 18–20 years old. 18% 21 to 24 years old	Employment, income, education, assets, criminal justice, social support, receipt of public benefits, parenting, housing, homelessness.
Mech & Fung (1999)	1,711 foster adolescents in Illinois preparing for emancipation.	Illinois	Interviewed at ages 18 & 21	Relationship between placement restrictiveness and educational attainment after foster care.
National Youth in Transition Database (2012, 2013, 2014b)	All youth in foster care during the years 2010–2012 (N=131, 204). Age 17: N=29,565 Age 19: N=11,712	National database (50 states)	Administrative records and interviews 2010–2012 Youth at age 17 & 19	Employment, education, connection to adults, homelessness, high-risk behaviors, pregnancy, substance abuse, criminal justice.

Cross-Sectional Survey with a Random Sample

Author(s)	Sample Size and Characteristics	Geographic Region	Data Collection and Years	Outcomes Studied
Benedict, Zuravin, & Stallings (1996)	N=214 randomly selected from cohort of 652 foster children who had been reported for abuse while in care. Mean age 23 when interviewed. 55% female. Predominantly African American.	Baltimore, MD	Interviews 1993–1994	Compared youth in kinship care with youth in non-kin care on employment, health, housing, mental health, social support, drugs and violence, domestic violence, & criminal justice involvement.
Leathers & Testa (2006)	416 randomly selected foster youth. Caseworker responded for youth.	Illinois	Interviewed the youth's social worker	Employment, pregnancy, parenting, delinquency, substance abuse.
Fowler, Toro, & Miles (2009, 2011)	Random sample drawn from all 863 youth leaving foster care in Detroit 2002–2003. N=265 who left foster care 2002–2003, ages 19–23. Both FFY & EFY.	Detroit, MI	2002–2003 2005–2006 Interviews Retrospective	Housing.
McMillen & Tucker (1999)	Missouri Alternative Care Database and record reviews (N=252). Chosen randomly during a 1 year period.	Missouri	1992–1993	Living arrangements, employment, education.

(continued)

Appendix B (*continued*)

Cross-Sectional Survey with a Random Sample

Author(s)	Sample Size and Characteristics	Geographic Region	Data Collection and Years	Outcomes Studied
Pecora, Kessler, Downs, O'Brien, Hiripi, & Morello (2003) Casey National Foster Care Alumni Study	1,082 of 1,609 eligible alumni interviewed. Covered a 32-year period. Youth interviewed had been placed with a Casey foster family for at least 12 months. Over 50% had been in care in the 1990s. Average age at interview was 30.5 years. 55% female & 65% white. Compared with youth in National Comorbidity Study (N=3,547).	23 communities across the U.S. Only one state was east of the Mississippi.	Interviews and case reviews 2000–2002	Living arrangements, education, income, health.
Pecora, Kessler, O'Brien, White, Williams, Hiripi, English, White, & Herrick (2006) Northwest Foster Care Alumni Study	659 case files renewed. 479 youth interviewed.	Sample from 4 agencies in the Pacific Northwest including Casey Family Services	In care 1988–1998	Information about educational attainments, employment, finances, mental health, independent living services usage, and social support post–foster care.
Shah, Albrecht, & Fever (2013)	1,116 who aged out of foster care and were at least 18 or older at time of exit.	Washington	2010–2011 Data collected 12 months after exit	Housing status, receipt of cash assistance, food and medical assistance, prevalence of substance abuse and mental health issues, rates of employment, criminal justice involvement, and income.

Cross-Sectional Survey Non-Random Sample with Non-Foster Comparisons

Author(s)	Sample Size and Characteristics	Geographic Region	Data Collection and Years	Outcomes Studied
Kirk, Lewis, Nilsen, & Colvin (2013)	1,377 from the Kansas GEAR UP program. Sample made up of low-income group containing both foster and nonfoster comparisons.	Kansas	Self-administered instrument	Educational goals, academic self-perception, and parental support for education.
Merdinger, Hines, Lemon, Osterling, & Wyatt (2005)	Nonprobability, purposive, N=216 (28% response rate), 77% female, 39% white, 23% African American, 22% Hispanic.	11 California State University campuses	Self-administered questionnaire Mean age 25	Current educational experiences, financial support, social support, health status, mental health, health status, substance abuse, delinquency, placement history, ILS, life satisfaction, housing.
Pecora, White, Jackson, & Wiggins (2009) Casey Field Office Mental Health Study	188 14- to 17-year-olds in Casey Foster Care.	Casey Field Offices	Administered the CIDI by trained interviewers	Mental health issues.

(continued)

Appendix B *(continued)*

Cross-Sectional Survey Non-Random Sample with Non-Foster Comparisons

Author(s)	Sample Size and Characteristics	Geographic Region	Data Collection and Years	Outcomes Studied
Roman & Wolfe (1997)	Survey of service providers (N=21). Survey of homeless individuals at 23 sites (N=1,209). 10 case studies (qualitative interviews.	Around the country	Self-administered questionnaire for survey of individuals	Foster care and homelessness.
Salazar (2013)	Study participants were all recipients of college scholarships from the Casey Family Program. N=329 responded out of 764 sent. Mean age was 25.6 years. Two studies with nationally representative samples used for comparison. These were the Panel Study of Income Dynamics & General Social Survey.	Participants located in 43 states	2010 online survey. Participants had received scholarships between the years 2001–2009	Education, health, homeownership, asset accumulation, mental health.
Unrau, Font, & Rawls (2012)	81 former foster youth admitted as freshmen to college were compared with all students entering the same university. Convenience sample.	Western Michigan University	2009–2010	Identify foster youth readiness for college engagement. Compare freshmen foster youth readiness for college with general population freshmen.

Cross-Sectional Survey with Non-Random Sample, and No Comparisons

Author(s)	Sample Size and Characteristics	Geographic Region	Data Collection and Years	Outcomes Studied
Barth (1990)	N=55 former foster youth, ages 17 to 26. 53% female, 72% white, 13% African American, 9% Hispanic.	San Francisco Bay Area & Sacramento	Interviews	Employment, contact with foster parents and birth relatives, education, life skills, health, substance abuse, criminal justice involvement, housing, income, mental health.
Brown & Wilderson (2010)	Two transitional living programs were examined. One program was specifically designed for youth leaving child welfare care (N=145). The other served homeless youth in general (N=146), which can include former foster youth.	San Francisco	2006–2009	Education, employment, mental health, substance abuse.
Daining & DePanfilis (2007)	N=100 out of universe of 189 youth age 18 or older who left foster care and did not reenter. 67% female, 26% African American; 37% white or other.	Large urban center in Maryland	Computer assisted self-administered interview 1999–2000	Resilience, education, employment, health risks, criminal activity, parenthood, social support, housing, global life stress.
Dumaret, Coppel-Batsch, & Couraud (1997)	N=63 adult former foster children.	France	Interviews and case file review	Education, employment, homeownership, housing, marital status, family formation, health, mental health.

(continued)

Cross-Sectional Survey with Non-Random Sample, and No Comparisons

Author(s)	Sample Size and Characteristics	Geographic Region	Data Collection and Years	Outcomes Studied
Dworsky & Perez (2010)	10 campus support program administrators. 98 former foster youth attending college.	California & Washington	Administrators were interviewed by phone. Students completed a web-based survey 2006–2007	Administrative data used to develop a typology of programs and identify common themes. Student perceptions and experiences with the program.
Haas & Graydon (2009)	44 youth responded to a survey sent to 146 youth. Respondents were resilient former foster youth who had completed a post-secondary educational program.	Orange County, CA	Mailed self-administered surveys	Understanding resiliency.
Havalchak, Roller, O'Brien, Pecora, & Sepulveda (2009)	N=259 young adults Casey Family Programs as a foster child who had been in care for at least one year	Seattle, WA	Telephone interviews. 54.6% response rate	High school graduation and college attendance.
Mason, Castrianno, Kessler, Holmstrand, Huefner, Payne, Pecora, Schmaltz, & Stenslie (2003)	222 youth discharged from 4 foster care agencies. 75% of alumni. Ages 11–19. Only 46 from one agency were emancipated.	Washington, DC Pittsburg, PA Seattle, WA Omaha, NE	Interviewed 6 months after discharge	Living environment, homelessness, education, employment, self-sufficiency, aggression, criminal behavior, substance abuse, relationships, community involvement, protection from harm, satisfaction, impact of services.

McMillan, Auslander, Elze, White, & Thompson (2003) Post-test only evaluation	262 youth referred for ILP preparation. Mean age of 16. 60% African American, 8% white. 80% still in high school.	Missouri	In-person interviews	Educational aspirations of former foster youth.
Osterling-Lemon & Hines (2006)	N=52 youth out of a possible 128 youth (41% return rate). Focus groups & interviews with 17 advocates.	California	Mixed methods Mailed surveys & focus groups	Description of youth participating in a mentoring program, and a description of their mentors. Experiences of both.
Pecora, Kessler, O'Brien, White, Williams, Hiripi, English, White, & Herrick (2006)	659 young adults from 2 public & 1 private child welfare agencies. Served by the agencies between 1988–1998. 60% female. 54% people of color. 16% Native American. Average age 24.	Washington, Oregon	Case record review Interviews	Educational and employment achievements.
Rashid (2004)	23 youth using transitional living programs. Homeless at intake. Ages 18–23.	San Francisco	Baseline and 6-month follow-up interview Program Evaluation	Housing, employment, income.
Reilly (2003)	N=100 youth who had been out of care for between 6 months and 3 years. 239 youth were eligible for the interview. 44% interview rate.	Las Vegas	In person interviews & review of case files 2001–2001	Employment, income, education, living arrangements, homelessness, health, criminal justice involvement, ILS participation, social support, placement history, and outcomes.

(continued)

Appendix B *(continued)*

Cross-Sectional Survey with Non-Random Sample, and No Comparisons

Author(s)	Sample Size and Characteristics	Geographic Region	Data Collection and Years	Outcomes Studied
Stott (2012)	114 former foster youth returned a survey out of 2,045 packets mailed.	Arizona	Aged out of care between July 1, 2004 & June 30, 2008	Relationship between placement changes and risky behavior (pregnancy and drug abuse).
Tyler & Melander (2010)	172 homeless young adults. 40% female, Mean age 21.45, white 80%, 9% African American.	Midwest	In-person interviews 2004–2005	Housing, mental health. Examined maltreatment histories of homeless young adults for mental health and high-risk behavior.
Yates & Grey (2012)	164 emancipated foster youth. 64% female, 34.1% Hispanic, 31.1% African American, 15.9% white.	California	In-person interviews	Latent class analysis to categorize youth as resilient or maladaptive adaptation. Education, employment, civic engagement, relational competence, self-esteem, depression, behavioral adjustment, socioemotional adjustment.

Secondary Data Analysis

Author(s)	Source of Data	Outcomes Studied
Anctil, McCubbin, O'Brien, Pecora, & Anderson-Harumi (2007)	Casey National Foster Care Alumni Study N=1,078 with disabilities	Compared disabled former foster youth with nondisabled former foster youth on mental health outcomes.
Harris, Jackson, O'Brien, & Pecora (2010)	Casey National Foster Care Alumni Study N=708 subset	Mental Health Outcomes of African American and white foster care alumni.
Harris, Jackson, O'Brien, & Pecora (2009)	Casey National Foster Care Alumni Study N=708 subset	Postsecondary education and employment outcomes of African American and white foster care alumni.
Pecora, Williams, Kessler, Hiripi, O'Brien, Emerson, Herrick, & Torres (2006)	Casey National Foster Care Alumni Study N=578 with youth disabilities	Educational attainments.
Jackson, Beadnell, & Pecora (2015)	Casey National Foster Care Alumni Study N=742	Involvement of Casey alumni's children with the child welfare system.
Kerman, Wildfire, & Barth (2002)	Casey National Foster Care Alumni Study N=115 out of a sample frame of 209. Sample in foster care 1 year, but out of care for at least 1 year. 4 groups were compared on outcomes: adoption, LTFC–left at 18, Youth in extended foster care, Other–emancipated foster youth	Assess adult developmental outcomes for youth where reunification was not possible.
O'Brien, Pecora, Echohawk, Evans-Campbell, Palamteer-Holder, & White (2010)	Casey National Foster Care Alumni Study 243 identified native American compared with other alumni experience	Education, employment, and assets.

(continued)

Appendix B *(continued)*
Secondary Data Analysis

Author(s)	Source of Data	Outcomes Studied
Salazar (2013)	Casey National Foster Care Alumni Study. N=329. Selected college graduates from the GSS, a nationally representative sample collected during 2006, and the Panel Study of Income Dynamics. Data from that study was from 2007	Value of a college degree to alumni. Employment, earnings, working conditions, homeownership, health, mental health.
Dworsky, White, O'Brien, Pecora, Courtney, & Kessler (2010)	Casey and Midwest Study Data	Racial and ethnic differences in outcomes of former foster youth.
Mason, Castrianno, Kessler, Holmstrand, Huefner, Payne, Pecora, Schmaltz, & Stenslie (2003)	Casey Alumni Survey Washington, Nebraska, Minnesota	Living arrangements, education, income, health, income, health, employment, violence, alcohol & drugs, social support, victimization, satisfaction with services.
Brown, Courtney, & McMillen (2015)	Midwest Evaluation of Former Foster Youth	Relationship between the receipt of behavioral health services and extended foster care.
Courtney (2009)	Midwest Evaluation of Former Foster Youth	Cost-benefit analysis of extending care.
Courtney, Hook, & Lee (2010)	Midwest Evaluation of Former Foster Youth	Latent class analysis to identify subpopulations in the sample.
Cusick, Havlicek, & Courtney (2012)	Midwest Evaluation of Former Foster Youth linked to official arrest records	Examine the role of social bonds in reducing criminal justice involvement at age 17.
Dworsky & Courtney (2009a)	Midwest Evaluation of Former Foster Youth	Homelessness.
Dworsky & Courtney (2009b)	Midwest Evaluation of Former Foster Youth	Pregnancy risk and extending care.

Hook & Courtney (2011)	Midwest Evaluation of Former Foster Youth	Employment.
Katz & Courtney (2015)	Midwest Evaluation of Former Foster Youth	Participation in independent living services and unmet needs after leaving care.
Keller, Cusick, & Courtney (2007)	Midwest Evaluation of Former Foster Youth	Identifying subgroups in the population. Latent class analysis.
Kushel, Yen, Gee, & Courtney (2007)	Midwest Evaluation of Former Foster Youth	Housing, homelessness, health care access.
Lee, Courtney, & Hook (2012)	Midwest Evaluation of Former Foster Youth	Criminal justice involvement.
Lee, Courtney, & Tajima (2014)	Midwest Evaluation of Former Foster Youth and official arrest records	Criminal justice involvement and extended foster care.
McMahon & Fields (2015)	Midwest Evaluation of Former Foster Youth	Criminal justice involvement.
Naccarato, Brophy, & Courtney (2010)	Midwest Evaluation of Former Foster Youth	Employment and earnings.
Okpych & Courtney (2014)	Midwest Evaluation of Former Foster Youth Bureau of Labor Statistics' NLSYB Survey made of same-age peers as Midwest Study used as comparisons	Employment, earnings, and education.
Peters, Dworsky, Courtney, & Pollack (2009)	Midwest Evaluation of Former Foster Youth compared with the 1988 National Education Longitudinal Study to estimate the graduation rate if youth allowed to remain in care until age 21	Cost-benefit analysis on extending care until age 21.
Salazar, Keller, & Courtney (2013)	Midwest Evaluation of Former Foster Youth	Social support.

(continued)

Appendix B *(continued)*

Secondary Data Analysis

Author(s)	Source of Data	Outcomes Studied
Berzin, Rhodes, & Curtis (2011)	National Longitudinal Survey of Youth collected by the Bureau of Labor Statistics. Collected 1980–1984. (N=8,894). This is a nationally representative sample that allows the comparison of youth in the general population with foster youth from Casey Family Scholarship Program.	Housing, education, substance use, child and family environment, neighborhood, teen parenting.
Berzin (2010)	National Longitudinal Survey of Youth (N=136 foster youth). Propensity scores were used to match foster youth with nonfoster youth. 50% of the FY had been in care at age 17 or above. 88% had been in care at some point in their teenage years.	Latent class analysis to identify patterns and of adaptation post-foster care. Risk and resilience.
Berzin (2008)	National Longitudinal Survey of Youth	Education, use of public assistance, teen parenthood, homelessness, drug use, criminal behavior, homelessness, substance abuse.
Buehler, Orme, Post, & Patterson (2000)	National Survey of Families and Households National probability sample of 13,017 families in 1987–1988. The response rate was 73.5%. 303 youth selected from sample. 101 reported being in foster care. 101 were chosen at random from the remainder, and who had not been in care. 101 nonfoster youth with similar characteristics to former foster youth were matched with the foster youth. Average of the former foster youth was 36.9 years. The other groups had a mean age of 39.3 at data collection.	Education, employment, alcohol and drug use, economic well-being, criminal justice, marriage, parenting, relationships with family of origin, social support, community engagement, mental health, health, life satisfaction.

Source	Data	Focus
Fowler, Marcal, Zhang, Day, & Landsverk (2017)	National Survey of Child and Adolescent Well-Being. Nationally representative survey of adolescents in foster care. Age 19 youth used in analysis	Latent class analysis used to categorize youth's housing problems.
Lee, Festinger, Jaccard, & Munson (2017)	National Survey of Child and Adolescent Well-Being. Nationally representative survey of adolescents in foster care. Age 19 youth used in analysis	Latent class analysis used to categorize youth's mental health status.
Shpiegel & Cascardi (2015)	National Youth in Transition Database. Created by the Foster Care Independence Act to assess the effectiveness of ILS programs in 50 states. 15,601 youth. 52% male, 58%. The largest minority group was African American	Pregnancy, receipt of independent living services.
Fowler, Toro, & Miles (2011)	Same as Fowler et al. (2009)	Latent class analysis to categorize EFY on mental health and housing status.
Greeson, Usher, & Grinstein-Weiss (2010)	ADD Health. National Longitudinal Study of Adolescent Health. N=15,197 Wave 3 participants	Natural mentoring, social support, asset accumulation.
Munson & McMillen (2009)	339 youth who were formerly system involved Missouri Alternative Care Database	Mentoring and its effect on employment, alcohol & substance abuse.
Narendorf & McMillen (2010)	Missouri NIMH study (N=404)	Substance abuse.
Raghavan, Shi, Aarons, Roesch, & McMillen (2009)	404 youth formerly system involved. 45% white, 52% Missouri NIMH study	Health care and health insurance coverage.

(continued)

Appendix B (continued)
Secondary Data Analysis

Author(s)	Source of Data	Outcomes Studied
McMillen & Raghavan (2009)	Missouri NIMH study (N=325; wave 2)	Mental health and service utilization.
Oshima, Narendorf, & McMillan (2013)	Missouri NIMH study (N=325; wave 2) formerly system involved	Predictors of pregnancy.
Vaughan, Shook, & McMillen (2008)	Missouri NIMH study (N=404)	Criminal justice involvement; class identification of risk (Latent class analysis); foster care context as predictors.
Raghavan & McMillen (2008)	Missouri NIMH study (N=403)	Patterns of psychotropic medication use among youth aging out of foster care.
Pergamit & Johnson (2009)	Multi-Site Evaluation of Youth in Foster Care (Life Skills Training Program) & the California Child Welfare System Case Management	Living arrangements, homelessness, education, employment, finances, health, mental health, criminal justice involvement, family planning, sexual activity, marriage and parenting, alcohol and substance abuse.
Schmitz (2005)	National Longitudinal Survey of Youth Compared youth who had been in foster care with youth raised by a biological parent, or an adoptive parent. (see Berzin)	Examine the trajectories of adult child bearing.
Zlotnick, Tam, & Soman (2012)	California Health Survey Interview. 70,456 households. Random sample of California's population. 3.4% of sample were former foster youth (N=2,355). 2003 & 2005	Health status, conditions, behavior, cancer, health care access & utilization, dental, injury, violence, employment, income, food insecurity, neighborhood, housing, public benefit use.

Administrative Data

Author(s)	Database and Characteristics	Geographic Region	Data Collection and Years	Outcomes Studied
Burley & Halpern (2001)	Administrative records in Washington (Child Welfare and Education). All foster youth compared with nonfoster youth.	Washington	2000	Educational attainment of FFY.
California Department of Social Services (2002)	Self-administered survey with all 58 county welfare directors.	California	2001	Housing needs of California's EFY.
Courtney, Charles, Okpych, Napolitano, & Halsted (2014)	California's Child Welfare Services/Case Management System. Age 17.	California	Compare youth in care 2010–2011 (N= 11,808) & 2012–2013 (N=10,076). Pre- and post-extended foster care	Early look at the relationship between extended care foster care in California and the way youth exit foster care. Does extended care discourage legal permanency?
Day, Dworsky, Fogarty, & Damashek (2011)	Michigan State University Student Information Database, N=444 self-identified former foster youth. N=602 stratified random sample of comparison MSU undergraduates.	Michigan	2000–2009	Postsecondary educational experiences.

(continued)

Appendix B *(continued)*

Administrative Data

Author(s)	Database and Characteristics	Geographic Region	Data Collection and Years	Outcomes Studied
Dion, Dworsky, Huff, & Kleinman (2014, May)	Web-based environmental scan. Survey of agencies that administer the Family Unification Program (FUP). Included visitation and in-depth interviews at the respondent's home.	National	2013	Examine housing knowledge gaps related to housing options for former foster youth, and provide policy makers with recommendations for future policy and research. Examine how communities can and do use the FUP to address the housing needs for transitioning youth.
Dworsky (2015)	Administrative data from the Illinois Department of Children and Families Services and the Teen Service Network.	Illinois	2000–2008	Examine child welfare system involvement of the children of foster care alumni.
Dworsky (2005)	3 state databases in Wisconsin were combined: Human Services Reporting System, Public Assistance Data Collection System, Unemployment Insurance Wage Reporting System. 10,183 foster youth (Both EFY and reunified youth) were in the databases. 8,511 of these youth who could be linked in all three databases. Longitudinal.	Wisconsin	1992–1998	Employment, earnings, poverty, public assistance receipt (AFDC, TANF, food stamps, SSI).

Fallesen (2013)	Danish administrative data. N=7,220 youth who had first placement after turning age 13.	Denmark	1982–1987	Health, education, social assistance, dependency, unemployment, income.
Frerer, Sosenko, & Henke (2013)	4,000 foster youth matched with 4,000 youth in the general population on education and SES variables.	California	2002–2003 2006–2007	Assess foster youth in comparison to the general population on high school graduation, community college attendance, and persistence in the second year.
Goerge, Bilaver, Joo Lee, Needell, Brookhart, & Jackman (2002)	Multi-State Foster Care Data Archive that links unemployment wage reporting data, public assistance data, and child welfare data. 3 groups were identified and compared on outcomes: aging out (4,213), reunified youth (5,415), low-income not foster youth (247,295). Longitudinal design.	California, Illinois, & South Carolina	1995–1997	Labor market participation, public assistance receipt, poverty.
Kroner & Mares (2011)	Data from administrative and clinical records of Lighthouse Independent Living Program. N=367 or 81% of discharged former foster youth.	Ohio	2001–2006	Living arrangements postdischarge. Level of restrictiveness of these arrangements.

(continued)

Appendix B *(continued)*
Administrative Data

Author(s)	Database and Characteristics	Geographic Region	Data Collection and Years	Outcomes Studied
Jonson-Reid & Barth (2000)	Child Welfare Data (N=1,753 with at least 1 foster care placement, and reentered care after discharge. These data were linked to California Youth Authority (N=213) with CYA experience.	California	1990–1995	Incarceration.
Lenz-Rashid (2006)	251 youth who graduated from job readiness program. 18- to 24-year-old homeless youth. Comparison of foster (FFY) and nonfoster youth. Asked about LGBT youth on outcomes.	San Francisco	Data gathered from staff and administrative data	Employment, earnings, education, mental health, substance abuse.
Mares (2010)	Tracking data from N=108 emancipating foster youth.	Lucas County, OH	2005–2007	Assessment of independent living need.
Macomber, Kuehn, McDaniel, Vericker, Pergamit, Cuccaro, Needell, Duncan, Kum, Stewart, Kwon-Lee, & Barth (2008)	TANF and unemployment insurance administrative databases in North Carolina, Minnesota, & California were linked. Youth were compared with the outcomes from the National Longitudinal Survey of Youth.	Illinois, Iowa, Wisconsin, North Carolina, Minnesota, & California	Not specified	Employment, earnings, & receipt of public benefits.

Needell, Cuccaro-Alamin, Brookhart, Jackman, & Shlonsky (2002)	Various State of California databases. State Prison in Base, Department of Health, Medi-Cal Eligibility Data System (N=6,661 with SSNs), AFDC-TANF codes, Department of Education, Department of Mental Health, Vital Statistics, 6,002 children with SSNs for linkage (out of 11, 408). Numbers vary by database.	California	1993–1999	Pregnancy, deaths, GED completion, community college attendance, incarceration.
Nolan (2006)	Nonprobability sample. Review of 40 case files. Compared nonfoster with foster youth, and LGBTQ with heterosexual youth.	New York City	File review	Housing.
Park, Metraux, & Culhane (2005)	11,401 young sheltered adults. Data from the Administration for Children's Services & Department of Homeless Services in New York City.	New York City	1997–1999	Examined the association between shelter use and prior child welfare services receipt.
Ryan, Hernandez, & Herz (2007)	Data from a foster care agency and arrest records from police. N=294.	Large Midwestern city	Not specified	Criminal justice involvement.

(continued)

Appendix B *(continued)*

Administrative Data

Author(s)	Database and Characteristics	Geographic Region	Data Collection and Years	Outcomes Studied
Ryan, Perron, & Huang (2016)	Washington State administrative records from child welfare and Center for Court research. Included youth in foster care for less than 1 year (N=573), in foster care for longer than 1 year (N=2,836), reunified youth (N=339), and youth who received services in-home short-term (N=2,957), in-home services long term (N=3,169).	Washington	1989–2009	Compared groups on risk of offending.
Shook, Goodkind, Pohlig, Schelbe, Herring, & Kim (2011)	The sample was made up of all 1,365 youth who had aged out of care during the study period. The database came from the Department of Human Services. This database contains data from child welfare, behavioral health, & the Office of Community Services. Also interviews were completed with 45 recent system leavers.	Alleghany County, PA	2002–2008	Explored patterns of system involvement: mental health, substance abuse, criminal justice involvement.

Study	Sample	Years	Location	Research question
Shook, Goodkind, Herring, Pohlig, Kolivoski, & Kim (2013)	All children born between 1985 and 1994 whose families received child welfare services. Three groups compared: No placement (N=33,032), Placement but not aged out (N=8,342), Aged out (N=1361).	2002–2008	Allegheny County, PA	Compared the three groups on system involvement (mental health, substance abuse, criminal justice involvement).
Widom & Maxfield (2001, February)	1,575 cases from childhood to adulthood. Included 908 substantiated cases for abuse or neglect with a comparison group of 667 nonabused children. Link records from the juvenile justice and child protective service system. NIJ.	1988–1994	Metropolitan area in the Midwest	Does childhood abuse and neglect lead to adult criminal behavior?

(continued)

Appendix B *(continued)*
Qualitative Data

Author(s)	Sample Characteristics	Geographic Region	Data Collection and Years	Outcomes Studied
Batsche, Hart, Ort, Armstrong, Stronzier, & Hummer (2014)	27 youth who made successful transitions to postsecondary education after foster care discharge.	Large urban area in the Southeast of the U.S.	Not specified	Barriers and factors in obtaining a postsecondary education.
Collins, Spencer, & Ward (2010)	96 former foster youth age 19 and older who had been in care until age 18. Mixed methods.	Northeast region of the U.S.	2007	Sources of social support.
Cosner-Berzin, Singer, & Hokanson (2014)	19 youth making the transition out of foster care. They were ages 18 to 21. 14 were male, 5 female, and 9 were African American, 4 were Hispanic, and 5 were white.	Not specified	Not specified	Subjective experiences during the transition and emerging adulthood.
Day, Riebschleger, Dworsky, Damashek, & Fogarty (2012)	Testimony of 68 high school students currently in foster care, and former foster youth in college at the Kidspeak Forum.	Michigan	2010	Needs of youth after foster care.
Geenen & Powers (2007)	10 focus groups with 88 students including youth currently in foster care (N=19), former foster youth (N=8), foster parents (N=21), child welfare professionals (N=20), educational professionals (N=9), independent living staff (N=9), other (N=2).	Not specified	Not specified	Experiences of aging out of care.

Study	Sample	Location		Focus
Goodkind, Schelbe, & Shook (2011)	11 youth interviewed individually. 34 in focus groups. 11% white, 64% African American, 62% female.	Allegheny County, PA	Not specified	The experiences of aging out of care, and the reasons they left care.
Haight, Finet, Bamba, & Helton (2009)	3 young African American transitioning mothers taking part in a writers workshop.	Illinois	Not specified	Beliefs of the mothers about parenting.
Hass, Allen, & Amoah (2014)	19 youth interviewed who had successfully completed a postsecondary educational program or had junior year college status.	Orange County, CA Orangewood Children's Foundation	Not specified	Exploration of youth in foster care account for their academic success.
Hernandez & Naccarato (2010)	A convenience sample of program coordinators from different postsecondary schools, nonprofit & public agencies that provided either scholarships or support services to foster youth in college. (N=12).	12 programs scattered throughout the country	Not specified	Inventory of services provided.
Horrocks (2002)	14 youth who left care over a 12- to 18-month period.	England & Wales	Not specified	Biographical stories constructed to consider the social developmental processes of the life course.
Kruszka, Lindell, Killion, & Criss (2016)	9 youth transitioning from foster care participated in a semistructured interview.	Indiana	Not specified	Access to health care.

(continued)

Appendix B *(continued)*

Qualitative Data

Author(s)	Sample Characteristics	Geographic Region	Data Collection and Years	Outcomes Studied
Iglehart & Becerra (2002)	The sample was made up of 10 Hispanics and 18 African Americans who had been emancipated no longer than 5 years. (N=28).	Los Angeles County	Not specified	Life after foster care from a minority perspective.
Munson, Lee, Miller, Cole, & Nedelcu (2013)	59 young adults ages 18–25.	Midwestern state	2008–2010	Examine whether foster youth's experiences with emerging adulthood differs from the general population.
Napolitano & Courtney (2014)	35 youth interviews (67% female). 61 youth in focus groups (60% female). Majority of youth from the THP plus program.	4 northern & 2 southern counties in California	Spring and summer 2013	Develop a preliminary understanding of residential settings of youth in extended foster care.
Osterling-Lemon & Hines (2006)	52 youth enrolled in a transition support program. 18 advocates.	Northern California	Not specified	Describe a youth mentoring program.
Perez & Romo (2011)	32 Hispanics ages 18 to 22 made up the sample.	A major Texas urban area	Not specified	Homelessness, housing, family relationships, education, employment.

Study	Sample	Location	Year	Purpose
Peters, Sherraden, & Kuchinski (2016)	20 high (money) savers and 10 low savers in the Operation Passport Program were compared. All were age 18.	4 unnamed sites in 3 states	2011	Financial experiences and literacy of youth aging out of foster care.
Pryce & Samuels (2010)	15 young mothers selected randomly from the Wave I survey of Midwest Study.	Illinois, Iowa, Wisconsin	Not specified	Meaning attributed to motherhood by young women aging out of care.
Rios & Rocco (2014)	24 ethnically diverse college students.	3 South Florida counties	Not specified	Describe the perceptions of college-attending former foster youth regarding educational factors related to their journey to college.
Sakai, Mackie, Shetgriri, Franzen, Partap, Flores, & Leslie (2014)	28 youth took part in focus groups.	Not specified	Not specified	Youth's perceptions of the need for mental health treatment. Perceptions of benefits of treatment versus barriers to treatment.
Samuels (2009)	29 young adults who left foster care without legal permanence, and who were participating in a program that provided support to former foster youth until age 24.	Might be drawn from across the U.S.	Not specified	Family definition and attempts at creating family.
Samuels & Pryce (2008)	44 youth in the process of aging out of foster care randomly selected from the Midwest Study.	Secondary data analysis of the Midwest Study	Wave 1 data	Explore dimensions of identity and resilience as well as the potential challenge for youth in building informal connections and mutually supportive relationships into adulthood.

References

Aarons, G.A.; Brown, S.A.; Hough, R.; Garland, A.F.; & Wood, P.A. (2001). Prevalence of adolescent substance use disorders across five sectors of care. *Journal of the American Academy of Child and Adolescent Psychiatry, 40* (4), 419–426.

Aarons, G.A.; Monn, A.; Hazen, A.; Connelly, C.D.; Leslie, L.K.; Landsverk, J.A.; Hough, R., & Brown, S.A. (2008). Substance involvement among youths in child welfare: The role of common and unique risk factors. *The American Journal of Orthopsychiatry, 78* (3), 340–349.

Abbott, D.A.; Meredith, W.H.; Self-Kelly, R.; & Davis, M.E. (1997). The influence of a Big-Brothers program on the adjustment of boys in single parent homes. *Journal of Psychology, 131,*143–156.

ACA. (2010). *Patient Protection and Affordable Care Act of 2010.* Public Law No. 111–148. 111 Congress.

Adler, L. (2001). The meanings of permanence: A critical analysis of the Adoption and Safe Families Act of 1997. *Harvard Journal on Legislation, 38,* 1–25.

AFCARS. (2015, July). Adoption and Foster Care Analysis and Reporting System. *The AFCARS Report for 2014.* Washington, DC: United States Department of Health and Human Services: Administration for Children and Families.

AFCARS. (2016). Adoption and Foster Care Analysis and Reporting System. *AFCARS Report for 2013, 21,* Washington, DC: United States Department of Health and Human Services.

Ahrens, K.R.; DuBois, D.L.; Richardson, L.P.; Fan, M.Y.; & Lorenzo, P. (2008). Youth in foster care with adult mentors during adolescence have improved adult outcomes. *Pediatrics, 121* (2), 246–252.

Alexander, G. & Huberty, T.J. (1993). *Caring for troubled children: The Villages follow-up study.* Bloomington, IN: Village of Indiana.

Allen, J.P.; Kupermine, G.; Philliber, S.; & Herre, K. (1994). Programmatic prevention of adolescent problem behaviors: The role of autonomy, relatedness, and volunteer service in the Teen Outreach Program. *American Journal of Community Psychology, 22*, 617–638.

Altschuler, S.J. (1997). A reveille for school social workers: Children in foster care need our help! *Social Work in Education, 19* (2), 121–127.

American Academy of Pediatrics. (2016). *Health care of children aging out of foster care.* www.pediatrics.org/cgidoi/10.1542/peds.2012–2063. Downloaded May 9, 2016. (AAP)

American Academy of Pediatrics, Committee of Early Childhood, Adoption and Dependent Care. (2002). Health care of young children in foster care. *Pediatrics, 109*, 536–541. (AAP)

American Bar Association Commission on Youth at Risk. (2011). *Report from a National Summit on the Fostering Connections to Success Act.* New York: Roosevelt House Public Policy Institute at Hunter College.

Anctil, T.; McCubbin, L.; O'Brien, K.; Pecora, P.; & Anderson-Harumi, C. (2007). Predictors of adult quality of life for foster care alumni with physical and/or psychiatric disabilities. *Child Abuse & Neglect, 31*, 1087–1100.

Antle, B.; Johnson, L.; Barbee, A.; & Sullivan, D. (2009). Fostering independent vs. independent living in youth aging out of care through healthy relationships. *Families in Society, 90* (3), 309–315.

Aquilino, W. (1999). Two views on one relationship: Comparing parents' and young adult children's reports of the quality of intergenerational relations. *Journal of Marriage and the Family, 61*, 858–870.

Aran, B.; Valente, D.; & Iwen, L. (1999). *Homelessness: Programs and the people they serve: Finding from the National Survey of Homeless Assistance Providers and Clients.* Technical Report, Washington, DC: Urban Institute.

Arnett, J. (1998). Learning to stand alone: The contemporary American Transition to adulthood in cultural and historical context. *Human Development, 41*, 295–315.

Arnett, J. (2000). Emerging adulthood: A theory of development from the late teens through the twenties. *American Psychologist, 55* (5), 469–480.

Arnett, J. (2003). Conception of the transition to adulthood among emerging adults in American ethnic groups. *New Directions for Child and Adolescent Development, 100*, 63–75.

Arnett, J. (2004). *Emerging adulthood: The winding road from the late teens through the twenties.* New York: Oxford University Press.

Arnett, J. & Taber, S. (1994). Adolescence is terminable and interminable: When does adolescence end? *Journal of Youth and Adolescence, 23* (5), 517–537.

Arnett, J. & Tanner, J. (Eds.). (2006). *Emerging adults in America: Coming of age in the 21ˢᵗ century.* Washington, DC: American Psychological Association.

Aseltine, R.; Dupre, M.; & Lamlein, P. (2000). Mentoring as a drug prevention strategy: An evaluation. *Adolescence and Family Health, 1*, 11–20.

Atkinson, M. (2008). Aging out of foster care: Towards a universal safety net for former foster youth. *Harvard Civil Rights—Civil Liberties Law Review, 43*, 183–212.

Austin, T. & Johnson, J. (1995). *Independent living programs: A follow-up survey report of the youth released from foster care in Nevada in 1996.* Henderson, NV: Nevada Research, Evaluation, and Planning Consultants.

Avery, R. (2011). The potential contribution of mentor programs to relational permanency for youth aging out-of-foster care. *Child Welfare, 90* (3), 9–26.

Avery, R. & Freundlich, M. (2009). You're all grown up now: Termination of foster care support at age 18. *Journal of Adolescence, 32,* 247–257.

Ayasse, R. (1995). Addressing the needs of foster children: The foster youth services program. *Social Work in Education, 17* (4), 207–217.

Babcock, J.C.; Roseman, A.; Green, C.E.; & Ross, J.M. (2008). Intimate partner abuse and PTSD symptomatology: Examining mediators and moderators of the abuse trauma link. *Journal of Family Psychology, 22,* 808–819.

Bagley, N. & Levy, H. (2014). Essential health benefits and the Affordable Health Care Act: Law and Process. *Journal of Health Politics, 39* (2), 441–462.

Baker, A. (2014). Eroding the wealth of women: Gender and the subprime foreclosure crisis. *Social Service Review, 88* (1), 59–91.

Barnet, B.; Jaffe, A.; Duggan, A.K.; Wilson, M.D.; & Repke, J.T. (1996). Depressive symptoms, stress, and social support in pregnant and postpartum adolescents. *Archives of Pediatrics & Adolescent Medicine, 150* (1), 64–69.

Barnet, B.; Liu, J.; & DeVoe, M. (2008). Double jeopardy: Depressive symptoms and rapid subsequent pregnancy in adolescent mothers. *Archives of Pediatrics and Adolescent Medicine, 162* (3), 246–252.

Barnow, B.; Buck, A.; O'Brien, K.; Pecora, P.; Ellis, M.; & Steiner, E. (2015). Effective services for improving education and employment outcomes for children and alumni of foster care services: Correlates of educational and employment outcomes. *Child and Family Social Work, 20,* 159–170.

Barrat, V. & Berliner, B. (2016). *Characteristics and education outcomes for Utah's high school dropouts who re-enrolled.* Washington, DC: U.S. Department of Education.

Barth, R. (1990). On their own: The experiences of youth after foster care. *Child and Adolescent Social Work, 7,* 419–440.

Barth, R. (1996). The juvenile court and dependence cases. *The Future of Children: The Juvenile Court, 6* (3), 100–110.

Barth, R. (2002). *Institutions and foster homes: The empirical base for a century of action.* Chapel Hill: University of North Carolina School of Social Work, Jordan Institute for Families.

Barth, R.; Wulczyn, F.; & Crea, T. (2005). From anticipation to evidence: Research on the Adoption and Safe Families Act. *Virginia Journal of Social Policy and the Law. 12,* 371–399.

Bartlett, J. & Eastbrooks, A. (2012). Links between physical abuse in childhood and child neglect among adolescent mothers. *Children and Youth Service Review, 34,* 2164–2169.

Batsche, C.; Hart, S.; Ort, R.; Armstrong, M.; Strozier; & Hummer, V. (2014). Postsecondary transitions of youth emancipated from foster care. *Child and Family Social Work, 19,* 174–184.

Baum, S.; Ma, J.; & Payea, K. (2013). *Education pays: The benefits of higher education for individuals and society.* Washington, DC: College Board.

Beal, S.J. & Crockett, L.J. (2010). Adolescents' occupational and educational aspirations and expectations: Links to high school activities and adult educational attainment. *Developmental Psychology, 46,* 258–265.

Beam, M.R.; Chen, C.; & Greenberger, E. (2002). The nature of adolescents' relationships with their very important "non-parental adults." *Journal of Community Psychology, 30* (2), 305–325.

Belsky, J. (1993). Etiology of child maltreatment: A developmental ecological analysis. *Psychological Bulletin, 114,* 413–434.

Benedict, M.; Zuravin, S.; & Stallings, R.Y. (1996). Adult functioning of children who lived in kin versus non-relative family foster homes. *Child Welfare, 75,* 529–549.

Bergman, A.B. (2000). The shame of foster care health services. *Archives of Pediatric and Adolescent Medicine, 154,* 1080–1081.

Berzin, S. (2008). Difficulties in the transition to adulthood: Using propensity scoring to understand what makes foster youth vulnerable. *Social Service Review, 82* (2), 171–196.

Berzin, S. (2010). Vulnerabilities in the transition to adulthood: Defining risk based on youth profiles. *Children and Youth Service Review, 32,* 487–495.

Berzin, S.; Rhodes, A.; & Curtis, M. (2011). Housing experiences of former foster youth: How do they fare in comparison? *Children and Youth Service Review, 33,* 2119–2126.

Biallas, M. (2017, March 7). *Medicaid, and thereby, child health coverage.* Washington, DC: First Focus: Campaign for Children, https://campaignforchildren.org/news/press-release/new-house-healthcare-bill-would-harm-medicaid-and-thereby-child-health-coverage.

Billari, F.; Philipov, D.; & Baizan, P. (2002). *Leaving home in Europe: The experience of cohorts born around 1960.* Working paper WP2001–14. Rostock, Germany: Max Plank Institute for Demographic Research.

Bishop, S.J. & Leadbetter, B.J. (1999). Maternal social support patterns and child maltreatment: Comparison of maltreating and nonmaltreating mothers. *American Journal of Orthopsychiatry, 69* (2), 172–181.

Blakemore, S.J. & Choudhury, S. (2006). Development of the adolescent brain: Implications for executive function and social cognition. *Journal of Child Psychology and Psychiatry, 47* (3–4), 296–312.

Blome, W.W. (1997). Educational experiences of a random sample of foster care youth and a matched group of non-foster care youth. *Child and Adolescent Social Work, 14,* 41–53.

Bluestone, B. & Harrison, B. (1982). *The deindustrialization of America.* New York: Basic Books.

Boden, J.; Fergusson, D.M.; & Horwood, L.J. (2008). Early motherhood and subsequent life outcomes. *Journal of Child and Psychiatry, 49* (2), 151–160.

Boonstra, H.D. (2011). Teen pregnancy among young women in foster care: A primer. *Guttmacher Policy Review, 14,* 8–19.

Borkowski, J.; Whitman, T.; Farris, J.; Carothers, S.; Keogh, D.; & Weed, K. (Eds.). (2007). *Risk and resilience: Teen mothers and their children grow up.* Mahwah, NJ: Lawrence Erlbaum.

Bottrell, D. (2009). Dealing with disadvantage: Resilience and social capital of young people's network. *Youth and Society, 40* (4), 476–501.

Bourdieu, P. (1986). The forms of capital. In J. Richardson (Ed.), *Handbook of theory and research for the sociology of education.* Westport, CT: Greenwood.

Bowlby, J. (1988). *A secure base: Clinical applications of attachment theory.* London: Routledge.

Boxer, P.; Goldstein, S.E.; DeLorenzo, T.; Savoy, S.; & Mercado, I. (2011). Discrepancies: Related to socioeconomic and academic risk factors. *Journal of Adolescence, 34,* 609–617.

Boyd, R. (2014). African-American disproportionality and disparity in child welfare: Toward a comprehensive framework. *Children and Youth Services Review, 37,* 15–27.

Braciszewski, J.M. & Stout, R. (2012). Substance use among current and former foster youth: A systematic review. *Children and Youth Service Review, 34,* 2337–2344.

Bramlett, M. & Radel, L. (2014, May). Adverse family experiences among children in non-parental care. *National Health Statistics Report, 74,* 1–8.

Bronfenbrenner, U. (1979). *The ecology of human development.* Cambridge, MA: Harvard University Press.

Bronte-Tinkew, J.; Carrano, J.; Horowitz, A.; & Kinukawa, A. (2008). Involvement among resident fathers and link to infant cognitive outcomes. *Journal of Family Issues, 29* (9), 1211–1244.

Brown, A.; Courtney, M.; & McMillen, J.C. (2015). Behavioral health needs and service use among youth who aged-out-of-foster care. *Children and Youth Service Review, 58,* 163–169.

Brown, L.; Herz, D.; & Ryan, J. (2008). *Bridging two worlds: Youth involved in the child welfare and juvenile justice systems: A policy guide for improving outcomes.* Washington, DC: Office of Juvenile Justice and Delinquency Prevention.

Brown, S. & Wilderson, D. (2010). Homelessness prevention for former foster youth: Utilization of transitional programs. *Children and Youth Service Review, 32,* 1464–1472.

Brubaker, S. & Wright, C. (2006). Identity transformation and family caregiving: Narratives of African-American teen mothers. *Journal of Marriage and the Family, 68,* 1214–1228.

Bruskas, D. (2008). Children in foster care: A vulnerable population at risk. *Journal of Child Adolescent Psychiatric Nursing, 21* (2), 70–77.

Buehler, C.; Orme, J.; Post, J.; & Patterson, D. (2000). The long-term correlates of family foster care. *Children and Youth Service Review, 22* (8), 595–625.

Bunting, L. & McCauley, C. (2004). Research review: Teenage pregnancy and parenthood: The role of fatherhoods. *Child and Family Social Work, 9* (3), 295–303.

Burley, M. & Halpern, M. (2001). *Educational attainment of foster youth: Achievement and graduation outcomes for children in state care.* Olympia: Washington State Institute for Public Policy.

Burns, B.J.; Phillips, S.D.; Wagner, R.H.; Barth, R.J.; Kolko, D.J.; Campbell, Y.; & Landsverk, J. (2004). Mental health needs and access to mental health services by youth involved in child welfare: A national survey. *Journal of the American Academy of Child and Adolescent Psychiatry, 43* (8), 960–970.

Bursik, R. & Grasmick, H.G. (1993). *Neighborhoods and crime: The dimensions of effective community control.* New York: Lexington.

Burt, M. (2002). Reasons to invest in adolescents. *Journal of Adolescent Health. 31,* 136–152.

California Department of Social Services. (2002). *Report on the survey of housing needs of emancipated foster/probation youth.* California Department of Social Services, Sacramento: Independent Living Program Policy Unit, Child and Youth Permanency Unit.

California Pregnancy Institute. (2013). San Francisco, California: John Burton Foundation. http://www.johnburtonfoundation.org/index.php/projects-a-programs/ca-foster-youth-pregnancy-prevention-institute.

Campbell, K.; Castro, S.; Houston, N.; Koenig, D.; Roberts, T.; & Rose, J.M.S. (2003). *Lighting the fires of urgency: Families lost and found in America's child welfare system.* www.senecacenter.org/perm_reports.

Caspi, A. (1993). Why maladaptive behaviors persist: Sources of continuity and change across the life source. In D.C. Funderm, R.D. Parke, C.C. Tomlinson-Keasey, & C.B. Widman (Eds.), *Studying lives through time: Personality and development* (pp. 343–376). Washington, DC: American Psychological Association.

Casselman, B. (2014, October 9–12). Race gap narrows. *538 Economics.* http://fivethirtyeight.com/features/race-gap-narrows-in-college-enrollment-but-not-in-graduation/.

Centers for Disease Control. (2016). *Suicides: Facts at a glance.* Atlanta, GA: Centers for Disease Control and Prevention.

Chambless, D.L. & Ollendick, T.H. (2001). Empirically supported psychological interventions: Controversies and evidence. *Annual Review of Psychology, 52* (10), 685–716.

Chambless, D.L. & Reid, J.B. (1998). Comparison of two community alternatives to incarceration for juvenile offenders. *Journal of Community Psychology, 19* (3), 266–276.

Chantala, K. & Tabor, J. (2010). *National Longitudinal Study of Adolescent Health: Strategies to perform a design-based analysis using ADD Health Data.* Chapel Hill, NC: Carolina Population Center, University of North Carolina at Chapel Hill.

Cheng, T.C. & Lo, C.L. (2010). The role of parenting and child welfare services in alcohol abuse by adolescents. *Children and Youth Services Review, 32* (1), 38–43.

Cherlin, A. (2010). Demographic trends in the United States: A review of research in the 2000's. *Journal of Marriage and the Family. 72,* 403–419.

Children's Bureau. (2015). *Foster Care Statistics,* Washington, DC: Child Welfare Information Gateway, U.S. Department of Health and Human Services.

Child Welfare Information Gateway. (2009). *Foster care statistics.* Retrieved http://childwelfare.gov/pubs/factsheets/foster.cfm.

Child Welfare Information Gateway. (2014). *Case planning for families involved with child welfare agencies.* Washington, DC: United States Department of Health and Human Services, Children's Bureau. http://www.childwelfare.gov/pubPDFs/caseplanning.pdf.

Choca, M.; Minoff, J.; Angene, L.; Byrnes, M.; Kenneally, L.; Norris, D.; Pearn, D.; & Rivers, M. (2004). Can't do it alone: Housing collaborations to improve foster youth outcomes. *Child Welfare, 83* (5), 469–491.

Choice, P.; D'Andrade, A.; Gunther, K.; Downes, D.; Schaldach, J.; & Csiszar, C. (2001). *Education for foster children: Removing barriers to academic success.* Retrieved March 11, 2006 from the World Wide Web, http://cssr.berkeley.edu/BASSC/pdfs/educf27.pdf.

Christenson, B.L. (2003). *Youth exiting foster care: Efficacy of foster care in the State of Idaho.* Cheney, WA: Eastern Washington University.

Chung, H.E.; Little, M.; & Steinberg, L. (2005). The transition to adulthood for adolescents in the juvenile justice system: A developmental perspective. In W. Osgood, M. Foster, C. Flanagan, & G. Ruth (Eds.), *On your own without a net: The transition to adulthood for vulnerable populations.* Chicago: University of Chicago Press.

Clark, H.B. & Davis, M. (Ed.). (2005). *Transition to adulthood: A resource for assisting young people with emotional and behavioral difficulties.* Baltimore: Paul H. Brooks.

Clausen, J.M.; Landsverk, J.; Ganger, W.; Chadwick, D.; & Litrownik, A. (1998). Mental health problems of children in foster care. *Journal of Child and Family Studies, 7* (3), 283–296.

Coakley, T.M. (2008). Examining African-American fathers' involvement in permanency planning: An effort to reduce racial disproportionality in the child welfare system. *Children and Youth Service Review, 30* (4), 407–417.

Coalition for Evidence-Based Policy. (2009). *Early childhood home visitation program models: An objective summary of the evidence of which are effective.* Washington, DC: Coalition for Evidenced Based Policy.

Cochrane, D. & Szabo-Kubitz, L. (2009). *Hopes and hurdles: California foster youth and financial aid.* Berkeley, CA: Institute for College Access and Success.

Cohen, J.A.; Berliner, L.; & Mannarino, A. (2010). Trauma focused CBT for children with co-occurring trauma and behavioral problems. *Child Abuse and Neglect, 34* (4), 215–224.

Cohen, P.; Kasen, S.; Chen, H.; Hartmark, C.; & Gordon, K. (2003). Variations in patterns of developmental transitions in the emerging adulthood period. *Developmental Psychology, 39* (4), 657–669.

Coleman, J. (1988). Social capital in the creation of human capital. *American Journal of Sociology, 94,* 95–120.

Collins, M.E. (2001). Transition to adulthood for vulnerable youths: A review of research and implications for policy. *Social Service Review, 75,* 271–290.

Collins, M.E. (2004). Enhancing services to youth leaving care: Analysis of recent legislation and its potential impact. *Children and Youth Service Review, 26,* 1051.

Collins, M.E.; Paris, R.; & Ward, R. (2008). The permanence of family ties: Implications for youth transitioning from foster care. *American Journal of Orthopsychiatry, 78* (1), 54–62.

Collins, M.E.; Spencer, R.; & Ward, R. (2010). Supporting youth in the transition from foster care: Formal and informal connections. *Child Welfare, 89* (1), 125–143.

Conger, D. & Finkelstein, M. (2003). Foster care and school mobility. *Journal of Negro Education, 72,* 97–103.

Conger, D. & Rebeck, A. (2001). *How children's foster care experiences affect their education.* New York: New York City Administration for Children's Services and Vera Institute of Justice.

Conger, D. & Ross, T. (2001). *Reducing the foster care bias in juvenile justice detention decisions: The impact of Project Concern.* New York: Vera Institute of Justice.

Congressional Budget Office. (2017). American Health Care Act. https://www .cbo.gov/publication/5248.

Connolly, J.; Heifetz, M.; & Bohr, Y. (2012). Pregnancy and motherhood among adolescent girls in child protective services. *Journal of Public Child Welfare, 6* (5), 614–635.

Cook, R. (1994). Are we helping foster care youth prepare for their future? *Children & Youth Services Review, 16,* 213–229.

Cook, R.; Fleishman, E.; & Grimes, V. (1991). A national evaluation of Title IV-E foster care independent living program for youth: *Phase 2, Final Report* (Vol. 1). Rockville, MD: Westat.

Cosner-Berzin, S.; Singer, E.; & Hokanson, K. (2014). Emerging versus emancipating: The transition to adulthood. *Journal of Adolescent Research, 29* (5), 616–638.

Courtney, M. (2009). *The difficult transition to adulthood for foster youth in the US: Implications for the state as corporate parent.* Fairfax, VA: Society for Research on Child Development.

Courtney, M. & Barth, R. (1996). Pathways of older adolescents out of foster care: Implications for independent living services. *Social Work, 41* (1), 75–83.

Courtney, M. & Charles, P. (2015). *Mental health and substance abuse problems and service utilization by transition age foster youth.* Chicago: University of Chicago, Chapin Hall Center for Children.

Courtney, M.; Charles, P.; Okpych, N.J.; Napolitano, L.; & Halsted, K. (2014). *Findings from the California Youth Transitions to Adulthood Study: Conditions at age 17.* Chicago: University of Chicago, Chapin Hall Center for Children.

Courtney, M. & Dworsky, A. (2005). *Midwest evaluation of the adult functioning of former foster youth: Outcomes at age 19.* Chicago: University of Chicago, Chapin Hall Center for Children.

Courtney, M. & Dworsky, A. (2006). Early outcomes for young adults transitioning from out-of-home-care in the USA. *Social Work, 11,* 209–219.

Courtney, M.; Dworsky, A.; Brown, A.; Cary, C.; Love, K.; & Vorhies, V. (2011). *Midwest evaluation of adult functioning of former foster youth outcomes at age 26.* Chicago: University of Chicago, Chapin Hall Center for Children.

Courtney, M.; Dworsky, A.; Cusick, G.; Havlicek, J.; Perez, A.; & Keller, T. (2009). *Midwest evaluation of adult functioning of former foster youth outcomes at age 21.* Chicago: University of Chicago, Chapin Hall Center for Children.

Courtney, M.; Dworsky, A.; Lee, J.; & Rapp, M. (2010). *Midwest evaluation of adult functioning of former foster youth outcomes at ages 23 & 24.* Chicago: University of Chicago, Chapin Hall Center for Children.

Courtney, M.; Dworsky, A.; & Peters, C. (2009). *California's Fostering Connections to Success Act and the costs and benefits of extending foster care to age 21.* Seattle: Partners for Our Children.

Courtney, M.; Dworsky, A.; & Pollack, H. (2007). *When should the state cease parenting? Evidence from the Mid-West Study.* Chicago: University of Chicago, Chapin Hall Center for Children.

Courtney, M. & Heuring, D.H. (2005). The transition to adulthood for youth "aging out" of the foster care system. In D. Wayne Osgood, E. Michael Foster, C. Flanagan, & G.R. Ruth (Eds.), *On your own without a net: The transition to adulthood for vulnerable populations.* Chicago: University of Chicago Press.

Courtney, M.; Hook, J.; & Lee, J. (2010). *Distinct subgroups of former foster youth during young adulthood: Implications for policy and practice.* Chicago: University of Chicago, Chapin Hall Center for Children.

Courtney, M. & Lyons, S. (2009). Mentorship relationships and adult outcomes for foster youth transition to adulthoods. *Presented at the13th Annual Meeting of the Society for Social Work Research,* New Orleans, LA.

Courtney, M. & Okpych, N. (2015, July). *Memo from CalYOUTH: Early findings on extended foster care and legal permanency.* Chicago: University of Chicago, Chapin Hall Center for Children.

Courtney, M.; Okpych, N.; Charles, P.; Dominique, M.; Stevenson, B.; Park, K.; Kindle, B.; Harty, J.; & Feng, H. (2016). *Findings from the California Transitions to Adulthood Study (CalYOUTH): Conditions at age 19.* Chicago: University of Chicago, Chapin Hall Center for Children.

Courtney, M.; Terao, S.; & Bost, N. (2004). *Mid-West evaluation of adult functioning of former foster youth: Conditions of youth preparing to leave care.* Chicago: University of Chicago, Chapin Hall Center for Children.

Courtney, M.; Zinn, A.; Koralek, R.; Bess, R.; Stagner, M.; Pergamit, M.; & Johnson, H. (2011a). *Evaluation of independent living employment service programs*, Kern County California.

Courtney, M.; Zinn, A.; Koralek, R.; Bess, R.; Stagner, M.; Pergamit, M.; & Johnson, H. (2011b). *Evaluation of the Massachusetts adolescent outreach programs for youth in intensive foster care*: Final Report. Multi-Site Evaluation of Foster programs. OPRE Report.

Courtney, M.E.; Piliavin, I.; Grogan-Kaylor, A.; & Nesmith, A. (2001). Foster youth transitions to adulthood: A longitudinal view of youth leaving care. *Child Welfare, 80* (6), 685–718.

Courtney, M.E.; Skyles, A.; Miranda, G.; Zinn, A.; Howard, E.; & Goerge, R.M. (2005). *Youth who run away from substitute care*. Chicago: University of Chicago, Chapin Hall Center for Children.

Courtney, M.E.; Zinn, A.; Zielewski, E.; Bess, R.; Malm, K.; Stagner, M.S.; Stagner, M.; & Pergamit, M. (2008). *Evaluation of the Life Skills Training Program Los Angeles County, California: Final report*. Washington, DC: U.S. Department of Health and Human Services.

Crosson-Towers, C. (2007). *Exploring child welfare: A practice perspective* (4th edition). Boston, MA: Pearson Education.

Crowley, S. (2003). The affordable housing crisis: Residential mobility of poor families and school mobility for poor children. *Journal of Negro Education, 72* (1), 22–38.

Culhane, D.; Metraux, S.; & Hadley, T. (2002). Public service reductions associated with placement of homeless persons with severe mental illness in supportive housing. *Housing Policy Debate, 13* (1), 107–163.

Curry, S. & Abrams, L. (2015). Housing and directions for future inquiry. *Child and Adolescent Social Work, 32* (2), 143–153. Reilly.

Cusick, G.R. & Courtney, M. (2007). *Offending during late adolescence: How do youth aging out of foster care compare with peers?* Chicago: University of Chicago, Chapin Hall Center for Children.

Cusick, G.R.; Havlicek, J.; & Courtney, M. (2012). Risk for arrest: The role of social bonds in protecting foster youth making the transition to adulthood. *American Journal of Orthopsychiatry, 82* (1), 19–31.

Cyphers, G. (2001). *Report from the Child Welfare Workforce Survey: State and county data and findings, 2001*. American Public Human Services Association. http://www.aphsa.org/policy/doc/cwwsurvey.pdf.

Daining, C. & DePanfilis, D. (2007). Resilience of youth in transition from out-of-home care to adulthood. *Children and Youth Service Review, 29*, 1158–1178.

Dane, A. & Schneider, B. (1998). Program integrity in primary and early secondary prevention: Are implementation effects out of control? *Clinical Psychological Review, 18*, 23–45.

Davidson, H. (2008). ABA policy update: ABA calls for reform in child welfare/delinquency "crossover" cases. *ABA Child Law Practice, 27* (2), 4.

Davis, M.; Banks, S.; Fisher, W.; & Grudzinskas, A. (2004). Longitudinal patterns of offending during the transition to adulthood in youth from the mental health system. *Journal of Behavioral Health Services Research, 31* (4), 351–366.

Davis, M.; Koroloff, N.; & Ellison, M.L. (2012). Between adolescence and adulthood: Rehabilitation research to improve services for youth and young adults. *Psychiatric Rehabilitation Journal, 35* (3), 167–170.

Davis, R.J. (2006). *College access, financial aid, and college success for undergraduates from foster care.* Washington, DC: National Association of Student Financial Aid Administrators.

Day, A.; Dworsky, A.; Fogarty, K.; & Damashek, A. (2011). An examination of post-secondary retention and graduation among foster care youth enrolled in a four-year university. *Children and Youth Service Review, 33,* 2335–2341.

Day, A.; Riebschleger, J.; Dworsky, A.; Damashek, A.; & Fogarty, K. (2012). Maximizing educational opportunities for youth aging out of foster care by engaging youth topics in partnership for social change. *Children and Youth Service Review, 34,* 1007–1014.

Dean, A. & Lin, N. (1977). The stress buffering role of social support. *Journal of Nervous and Mental Disease, 165* (6), 403–416.

Debski, L.; Spadafore, C.; Jacob, S.; Poole, D.; & Hixson, M. (2007). Suicide intervention training: Roles and knowledge of school psychologists. *Psychologists in the School, 44* (2), 157–170.

Delgado, M. (2013, December). *California's fostering connections: Ensuring that the AB 12 bridge leads to success for transition foster youth.* San Diego: Children's Advocacy Institute, University of San Diego School of Law.

DeMarco, A. & Cosner-Berzin, S. (2008). The influence of family economic status on home-leaving patterns during emerging adulthood. *Family in Society, 89* (2), 208–218.

DePaul, J. & Domenech, L. (2000). Childhood history of abuse and abuse potential in adolescent mothers: A longitudinal study. *Child Abuse and Neglect, 24,* 701–713.

DeWoody, M.; Ceja, K.; & Sylvester, M. (1993). *Independent Living Services for youth in out-of-home care.* Washington, DC: CWLA.

DiGiuseppe, D.L. & Christakis, D.A. (2003). Continuity of care for children in foster care. *Pediatrics, 111,* 208–213.

Dion, R.; Dworsky, A.; Huff, J.; & Kleinman, R. (2014, May). *Housing for youth aging out-of-foster care.* Washington, DC: Department of Housing and Urban Development.

Dogan-Ates, A. & Carrion-Basham, C.Y. (2007). Teenage pregnancy among Latinas: Examining risk and protective factors. *Hispanic Journal of Behavioral Sciences, 29* (4), 554–569.

Domonoske, C. (2016, April 4). Denying housing over criminal records may be discrimination, feds says. *The two way: breaking news from NPR.*

www.npr.org/sections/thetwo-way/2016/04/04/472878724/denying
-housing-over-criminal-record-may-be-discrimination-feds-say

Drapeau, S.; Saint-Jacques, M.C.; Lepine, R.; Begin, G.; & Bernard, M. (2007). Processes that contribute to resilience among foster youth. *Journal of Adolescence, 30* (6), 977–999.

DuBois, D.L.; Holloway, B.E.; Valentine, J.C.; & Cooper, H. (2002). Effectiveness of mentoring programs for youth: A meta-analytic review. *American Journal of Community Psychology, 10,* 157–197.

DuBois, D.L.; & Silverthorn, N. (2005). Natural mentoring relationships and adolescent health. *American Journal of Public Health, 95* (3), 518–524.

Duke-Lucio, J.; Peck, L.; & Segal, E. (2010). The latent and sequential costs of being poor: an exploration of housing. *Poverty and Public Policy, 2* (1), 185–194. http://psocommons.org/ppp/vol12/iss1/art11.

Dumaret, A.C.; Coppel-Batsch, M.; & Couraud, S. (1997). Adult outcomes of children reared for long-time periods in foster families. *Child Abuse and Neglect, 21* (10), 911–927.

Dunst, C. & Trivette, C. (1988). Toward experimental evaluation of the family, infant, and preschool program. In H.B. Weiss & F.H. Jacobs (Eds.), *Evaluating family programs* (pp. 315–346). New York: Aldine DeGruyter.

Durkheim, E. (1951). *Suicide.* New York: Free Press.

Dworsky, A. (2005). The economic self-sufficiency of Wisconsin former foster youth. *Children and Youth Service Review, 27,* 1085–1118.

Dworsky, A. (2010). *Assessing the impact of extending care beyond age 18 on homelessness.* Chicago: University of Chicago, Chapin Hall Center for Children.

Dworsky, A. (2015). Child welfare services involvement among children of young parents in foster care. *Child Abuse and Neglect, 45,* 68–79.

Dworsky, A. & Courtney, M. (2009a). Homelessness and the transition from care to adulthood. *Child Welfare, 88* (4), 23–56.

Dworsky, A. & Courtney, M. (2009b). Addressing the mental health needs of foster youth during the transition to adulthood: How big is the problem and what can the states do? *Journal of Adolescent Health, 44,* 1–2.

Dworsky, A. & Courtney, M. (2010a). *Assessing the findings of the impact of extending care beyond age 18 on homelessness: Emerging findings from the Midwest study.* Chicago: University of Chicago, Chapin Hall Center for Children. Retrieved from http://www.chapinhall.org/research/brief/assessing-impact
-extending-care-beyond-age-18-homelessness-emergingfindings-midwest.

Dworsky, A. & Courtney, M. (2010b). The risk of pregnancy among transitioning foster youth: Implications for extending state care beyond age 18. *Children and Youth Service Review, 32* (10), 135.

Dworsky, A. & Havlicek, J. (2009). *Experiences of foster youth in employment training and job placement program.* Chicago: University of Chicago, Chapin Hall Center for Children.

Dworsky, A. & Perez, A. (2010). Helping former foster youth graduate from college through campus support programs. *Children and Youth Service Review, 32,* 255–263.

Dworsky, A.; White, C.; O'Brien, K.; Pecora, P.; Courtney, M.; & Kessler, R. (2010). Racial and ethnic differences in outcomes of former foster youth. *Children and Youth Service Review, 32* (6), 902–912.

Eckenrode, J.; Rowe, E.; Laird, M.; & Brathwaite, J. (1995). Mobility as a mediator of the effects of child maltreatment on academic performance. *Child Development, 66,* 1130–1142.

Elder, G. (1980). Adolescence in an historical perspective. In J. Adelson (Ed.), *Handbook of adolescent psychology* (pp. 3–46). New York: Wiley.

Elder, G. (1995). The life course paradigm: Social change and individual development. In P. Moen, G. Elder, & K. Luscher, *Examining lives in context,* pp. 101–140. Washington, DC: American Psychological Society.

Elder, G. (1998). The life course development and human development. In R. Lerner & W. Dannon (Eds.), *Handbook of child psychology* (Vol. 1, pp. 939–992). New York: Wiley.

Elliott, D. & Ageton, S. (1980). Reconciling race and class differences in self-reported and official estimates of delinquency. *American Sociological Review, 45,* 95–110.

Elliott, D.S.; Huizinga, D.; & Ageton, S.S. (1985). *Explaining delinquency and drug use.* Beverly Hills, CA: Sage.

Enam, D. & Golden, D. (2014, April). *Affordable Care Act and youth aging out of foster care: New opportunities for action.* State Policy Advocacy Reform Center.

Ensign, J. & Santelli, J. (1997). Shelter based homeless youth: Health and access to care. *Archives of Pediatric Adolescent Medicine, 151* (8), 817–823.

Entwisle, D.; Alexander, K.L.; & Steffel-Olson, L. (2000). Early work histories of urban youth. *American Sociological Review, 65* (2), 279–297.

Erickson, E.H. (1968). *Identity and the youth crisis.* New York: Norton.

Ewart, S. (2012, February). What it's worth: Field of training and economic status in 2009. *Current Populations Reports,* 1–16.

Fain, P. (2014, November 18). Recession and completion. *Insider Education.* https://www.insidehighered.com/news/2014/11/18/enrollment-numbers-grew-during-recession-graduation-rates-slipped.

Fallesen, P. (2013). Time spent well: The duration of foster care and early adult labor market, educational, and health outcomes. *Journal of Adolescence, 36,* 1003–1011.

Family Connections Grant. (2012). http://www.federalgrants.com/Family-Connection-Grants-Combination-Family-finding-Family-Group-Decision-making-Projects-36111.html.

Feeding America. (2016). *Understand food insecurity.* Chicago: Feeding America. https://hungerandhealth.feedingamerica.org/understand-food-insecurity/.

Feldman, J. & Middleman, A. B. (2003). *Homeless adolescents: Common clinical concerns,* https://www.ncbi.nlm.nih.gov/pubmed/12748916.

Fernandes, A.L. (2006). *Child welfare: The Chafee Foster Care Independence Program. CRS Report to Congress.* Washington, DC: Congressional Research Service, Library of Congress.

Fernandes, A.L. (2008, May 21). *Youth transitioning from foster care: Background federal programs and issues for Congress.* Washington, DC: Congressional Research Service, Library of Congress.

Festinger, T. (1983). *No one ever asked us: A postscript to foster care.* New York: Columbia University Press.

Flanagan, C. & Levine, P. (2010). Civic engagement and the transition to adulthood. *Future of Childhood, 20* (1), 159–179.

Fowler, P.; Toro, P.; & Miles, B. (2009). Pathways to and from homelessness and associated outcomes among adolescents leaving the foster care system. *American Journal of Public Health, 99* (8), 1452–1458.

Fowler, P.; Toro, P.; & Miles, B. (2011). Emerging adulthood and leaving foster care: Settings associated with mental health. *American Journal of Community Psychology, 47,* 335–348.

Fowler, P.J.; Marcal, K.E.; Zhang, J.; Day, O.; & Landsverk, J. (2017). Homelessness and aging out of foster care: A national comparison of child welfare involved adolescents. *Children and Youth Service Review, 77,* 27–33.

Francisco, M.A.; Hicks, K.; Powell, J.; Styles, K.; Tabor, J.L.; & Hulton, L.J. (2008). The effect of child sexual abuse on adolescent pregnancy. *Journal of Specialists in Pediatric Nursing, 13* (1), 237248.

Freidman, M. (2015). Just as many Americans have criminal justice convictions as college degrees. *Brennan Center for Justice at New York University.* https://www.brennancenter.org/blog/just-facts-many-americans-have -criminal-records-college-diplomas.

Frerer, K.; Sosenko, L.D.; & Henke, R.R. (2013). *At greater risk: California foster youth and the path from high school to college.* San Francisco: Stuart Foundation.

Freundlich, M.; Avery, R. (2006). Transitioning from congregate care: Preparations and outcomes. *Journal of Child and Family Studies, 15,* 507–518.

Freundlich, M. & Avery, R.; & Padgett, D. (2007). Preparation of youth in care for independent living. *Child and Family Social Work, 12,* 64–72.

Frey, L.; Cushing, G.; Freundlich, M.; & Brenner, E. (2008). Achieving permanency for youth in foster care: Assessing and strengthening emotional security. *Child and Family Social Work, 13,* 218–226.

Friend, B. (2009). California Permanency Project. An overview. In T. LaLiberte & E. Snyder (Eds.), *Permanency of aging out—Adolescents in the child welfare system* (p. 24). Saint Paul: Center for Advanced Studies in Child Welfare, University of Minnesota, School of Social Work.

Fry, R. (2013, August 1). A rising share of young adults live in their parent's home. *Social and demographic trends. Pew Research Center.* http://www .pewsocialtrends.org/2013/08/01/a-rising-share-of-young-adults-live-in -their-parents-home/.

Furstenberg, F. (2010). On a new schedule: Transitions to adulthood and family change. *Future of Children, 20* (1), 67–87.

Furstenberg, F.; Kennedy, S.; McLoyd, V.C.; Rumbault, R.G.; & Setterstein, R.A. (2004). Growing up is harder to do. *Contexts, 3* (3), 33–41.

Fussell, E. & Furstenberg, F. (2004). The transition to adulthood during the twentieth century: Race, nativity, and gender. In F. Furstenberg, R. Rumbault, and R.A. Setterstein (Eds.), *On the frontiers of adulthood: Theory, research, and public policy*, pp. 3–25. Chicago: University of Chicago Press.

Galambos, N.; Kolaric, G.; Sears, H,; & Maggs, J. (1999). Adolescents and subjective age: An indicator of perceived maturity. *Journal of Research on Adolescence, 9*, 309–337.

Gardner, D. (2008). *Youth aging out of foster care: Identifying strategies and best practices*. National Association of Counties.

Geenen, S. & Powers, L. (2007). "Tomorrow is another problem." *Children and Youth Service Review, 29*, 1085–1101.

Geenen, S.; Powers, L.; Phillips, L.; Nelson, M.; & McKenna, J. (2015). Better futures: A randomized field test of a model for supporting young people in foster care with mental health challenges to participate in higher education. *Journal of Behavioral Health Services and Research, 42* (2), 150–17.

Geeraert, L.; Noorgate, W.; Grietens, H.; & Onghena, O. (2004). The effects of early prevention programs for families with young children at risk for physical child abuse and neglect: A meta-analysis. *Child Maltreatment, 9* (3), 277–291.

Georgiades, S. (2005). A multi-outcome evaluation of an independent living program. *Child and Adolescent Social Work, 22* (5–6), 417–439.

Gerber, J. & Dicker, S. (2005). Children adrift: Addressing the educational needs of New York's foster children. *Albany Law Review, 69* (1), 74–94.

Giele, J.Z. & Elder, G. (1998). *Methods of life course research*. London: Sage.

Goerge, R.; Bilaver, L.; Joo Lee, B.; Needell, B.; Brookhart, A.; & Jackman, W. (2002). *Employment outcomes for youth aging out of foster care*. Chicago: University of Chicago, Chapin Hall Center for Children.

Goerge, R.; Harden, A.; & Lee, B.J. (2008). Consequences of teen childbearing for child abuse, neglect, and foster parent. In *Kids having kids: Economic costs and social consequences of teen pregnancy*, 257–288. Washington, DC: Urban Institute Press.

Goldberg, G.S. (2012). Economic inequality and the economic crisis: A challenge for social workers. *Social Work, 57* (3), 211–224.

Golden, O. (2016). *Top five threats to child welfare from the ACA repeal and proposals to alter Medicaid*. Washington, DC: Center for Law and Social Policy.

Goldrick-Rab, S. & Broton, K. (2015). Hungry and homeless in college. *New York Times, 165*, (57,070), A33.

Goldscheider, F. & Goldscheider, C. (1999). *The changing transition to adulthood: Leaving and returning home*. Thousand Oaks, CA. Sage.

Goodkind, S.; Schelbe, L.; & Shook, J. (2011). Why youth leave care: Understanding of adulthood and transition successes and challenges among youth aging out of child welfare. *Children and Youth Service Review, 33*, 1039–1048.

Gotbaum, B. (2005). *Children raising children: City fails to adequately assist pregnant and parenting youth in foster care.* New York: Public Advocate for the City of New York.

Green, J. & Ringwalt, C. (1998). Pregnancy among three national samples of runaway and homeless youth. *Journal of Adolescent Health, 23* (6), 370–377.

Greeson, J.; Usher, L.; & Grinstein-Weiss, M. (2010). One adult who is crazy about you: Can natural mentoring relationships increase assets among young adults with and without foster care experience? *Children and Youth Service Review, 32,* 565–577.

Grossman, J.H. & Rhodes, J.E. (2002). The test of time: Predictors and effects of duration in youth mentoring programs. *American Journal of Community Psychology, 30,* 199–219.

Haight, W.; Finet, D.; Bamba, S.; & Helton, J. (2009). The beliefs of resilient African-American adolescent mothers transitioning from foster care to independent living. *Children and Youth Service Review, 31,* 53–62.

Harding, J.T. & Luft, J.L. (1995). Outcome evaluation of the PAL (Preparation for Adult Living). In E.V. Mech & J.R. Rycraft (Eds.), *Preparing foster youth for adult living. Proceedings of an invitational research conference* (pp. 144–146). Washington, DC: CWLA.

Harknett, K.S. & Harknett, C.S. (2011). Who lacks support and why? An examination of mothers' personal safety nets. *Journal of Marriage and Family, 73,* 861–875.

Harman, J.S.; Childs, G.E.; & Kelleher, K.J. (2000). Mental health problems of children in foster care. *Archives of Pediatric Adolescent Medicine, 154,* 1114–1117.

Harris, K.; Halpern, C.; Whitsel, E.; Hussey, J.; Tabor, J.; Entzel, P.; & Udry, J.R. (2009). *The national longitudinal study of adolescent health: research design.* http://www.cpc.unc.edu/edu/projects/addhealth/design.

Harris, M.; Jackson, L.; O'Brien, K.; & Pecora, P. (2009). Disproportionality in education and employment outcomes of adult foster care alumni. *Children and Youth Service Review, 31,* 1150–1159.

Harris, M.; Jackson, L.; O'Brien, K.; & Pecora, P. (2010). Ethnic group comparisons in mental health outcomes of adult alumni of foster care. *Children and Youth Service Review, 32,* 171–177.

Harvey, A.R. & Hill, R.B. (2004). Africentric youth and family rite of passage program: Promoting resilience among at-risk African-American youth. *Social Work, 49* (1), 65–74.

Hass, M.; Allen, Q.; & Amoah, M. (2014). Turning points of resilience for academically successful foster youth, *Children and Youth Service Review, 44,* 387–392.

Hass, M. & Graydon, K. (2009). Sources of resiliency among successful foster youth. *Children and Youth Service Review, 31,* 457–463.

Haussmann, L.R.; Schofield, J.W.; & Woods, R.L. (2007). Sense of belonging as a predictor of intentions to persist among African-American and White first year college students. *Research in Higher Education, 48* (7), 803–839.

Havalchak, A.; Roller, C.; O'Brien, K.; Pecora, P.; & Sepulveda, M. (2009). Foster care experiences and educational outcomes of young adults formerly placed in foster care. *School Social Work Journal, 34* (1), 1–27.

Havalchak, A.; White, C.R.; & O'Brien, K. (2008, March). *Casey Young Adult Survey.* Seattle: Casey Family Programs.

Havlicek, J.; Garcia, A.; & Smith, D. (2013). Mental health and substance use disorders among foster children transitioning to adulthood: Past research and future directions. *Children and Youth Services Review, 35* (1), 194–201.

Havlicek, J.; McMillen, J.C.; Fedoravicius, N.; McNelly, D.; & Robinson, D. (2012). Conceptualizing the step-down for foster youth approaching adulthood: perceptions of service providers, caseworkers, and foster parents. *Children and Youth Service Review, 34* (12), 1085–1118.

Hernandez, L. & Naccarato, T. (2010). Scholarships and support to foster care alumni: A study of 12 programs across the US. *Children and Youth Service Review, 32,* 758–766.

Herrenkohl, T.I.; Huang, B.; Tajima, E.A.; & Whitney, S.D. (2003). Examining the links between child abuse and youth violence: An analysis of mediating mechanisms. *Journal of Interpersonal Violence, 18* (10), 1189–1208.

Herrera, C.; Grossman, J.B.; Kauh, T.J.; Feldman, A.F.; McMaken, J.; & Jucovy, L.Z. (2007). *Making a difference in schools: The Big Brothers; Big Sisters school-based mentoring impact study.* Philadelphia: Public/Private Ventures.

Herrera, C.; Sipe, C.L.; & McClanahan, W.S. (2000). *Mentoring school age children: Relationship development in community based programs.* Philadelphia: Public/Private Ventures.

Hertz, D.; Lee, P.; Lutz, L.; Stewart, M.; Tuel, J.; & Wigg, J. (2012). *Addressing the needs of multi-system youth: Strengthening the connection between the child welfare and juvenile justice system.* Washington, DC: Georgetown University's Center for Juvenile Justice Reform and the Robert F. Kennedy Children's Action Corps. //cjjr.georgetown.edu/index.html.

Hill, K. (2009). Individuals with Disabilities Act of 2004 and the John Chaffee Foster Care Independence Act of 1999: What are the policy implications for youth with disabilities transitioning from foster care. *Child Welfare, 88* (2), 5–23.

Hines, A.M.; Merdinger, J.; & Wyatt, P. (2005). Former foster youth attending college: Resilience and transition to young adulthood. *American Journal of Orthopsychiatry, 75,* 381–394.

Hirschi, T. (1969). *Causes of delinquency.* Berkeley: University of California Press.

Hirschi, T. & Gottfredson, M. (1983). Age and explanation for crime. *American Journal of Sociology, 5,* 552–584.

Holzer, H.; Raphael, S.; & Stoll, M. (2003). *Employment barriers facing ex-offenders.* Washington, DC: Urban Institute.

Hook, J. & Courtney, M. (2011). Employment outcomes of former foster youth as young adults. *Children and Youth Service Review, 33,* 1855–1865.

Horney, J.; Osgood, D.W.; & Marshall, I.H. (1995). Criminal careers in the short term: Intra-individual variability in crime and its relation to local life circumstances. *American Sociological Review, 60,* 655–673.

Horrocks, C. (2002). Using life course theory to explore the developmental pathways of young people leaving care. *Journal of Youth Studies, 5* (3), 325–336.

Houshyar, S. (2014, October). *Medicaid to age 26 for former foster youth.* The State Policy Reform Center. http://childwelfaresparc.org/wp-content/uploads/2014/10/Medicaid-to-26-for-Former-Foster-Youth7.pdf.

Houtrow, A. & Okamura, M. (2011). Pediatric mental health and associated burdens on families. *Vulnerable Child Youth Studies, 6* (3), 222–233.

Huang, C.H. & Lee, I. (2008). The first 3 years of parenting: Evidence from the Fragile Families and Child Well-Being Study. *Children and Youth Services Review, 28,* 1447–1457.

Huebner, R.A.; Werner, M.; Hartwig, S.; White, S.; & Shewa, D. (2008). Engaging fathers: Needs and satisfaction in child protective services. *Administration in Social Work, 32* (2), 87–103.

Iglehart, A. & Becerra, R. (2002). Hispanic and African-American youth: Life after foster care emancipation. *Journal of Ethnic Cultural Diversity in Social Work, 11* (1–2), 79–107.

Iglehart, A.P. (1994). Adolescents in foster care: Predicting readiness for independent living. *Children and Youth Service Review, 16* (3/4), 159–169.

Irving, S.K. & Loveless, T.A. (2015, May). Dynamics of economic well-being: Participation in government programs: 2009–2012. In S.K. Irving & T.A. Loveless (Eds.), *Household economic studies,* pp. 70–141, U.S. Census Bureau.

Jackson Foster, L.; Beadnell, B.; & Pecora, P. (2015). Intergenerational pathways leading to foster care placement foster care alumni's children. *Child and Family Social Work, 20,* 72–82.

Jacobson, J.M.; Sander, R.; Svoboda, D.; & Elkinson, A. (2011). *Defining the role and contributions of social workers in the advancement of economic stability and capability of individuals, family and community.* Madison: Center for Financial Security, University of Wisconsin.

Jaffee, S.R. (2002). Pathways to adversity in young adulthood among early child bearers. *Journal of Family Psychology, 16* (1), 38–49.

Jaffee, S.R.; Caspi, A.; Moffitt, T.E.; Taylor, A.; & Dickson, N. (2001). Predictors of early fatherhood and whether those fathers live with their children: Prospective findings and policy reconsiderations. *Journal of Child Psychology and Psychiatry, 42* (6), 803–815.

James, S. (2004). Why do foster placements disrupt? An investigation of placement change in foster care. *Social Service Review, 78* (4), 601–628.

James, S.; Landsverk, J.; & Slyman, D. (2004). Placement movement in and out-of-home-care. *Children and Youth Services Review, 26,* 185–206.

Jee, S.H.; Barth, R.; Szilagyi, M.A.; Szilagyi, P.G.; & Davis, M.M. (2006). Factors associated with chronic conditions among children in foster care, *Journal of Health Care for the Poor and Underserved, 17,* 328–341.

Jim Casey Opportunities Initiatives (2011). *The adolescent brain and its implications for young people transitioning from foster care.* St. Louis: Casey Opportunities Initiatives.

Johnson, W.E. (2001). Paternal involvement among unwed fathers. *Children and Youth Service Review, 23,* 513–536.

Johnston, L.D.; O'Malley, P.M.; Bachman, J.G.; & Schulenberg, J.E. (2012). *Monitoring the future national results in adolescent drug abuse: Overview of key findings, 2011.* Ann Arbor: Institute for Social Research, University of Michigan.

Jones, J.; Mosher, W.; & Daniels, K. (2012). Current contraceptive use in the United States, 2006–2010, and changes, patterns, and use from 1995–2005. *National Health Statistics Report, 60* (18), 1–18. http://www.cdc.gov/nchs/data/nhsr/nhsr060.pdf.

Jones, L. (2004). The prevalence and characteristics of substance abusers in a child protective services sample. *Journal of Social Work in Addictions, 4* (2), 33–51.

Jones, L. (2008). Adaptation to early adulthood by a sample of youth discharged from residential placement. *Child and Youth Care Forum, 37,* 241–263.

Jones, L. (2014a). Former foster youth's perspectives on independent living preparation six months after discharge. *Child Welfare, 93* (1), 99–126.

Jones, L. (2014b). The family and social networks of recently discharged foster youth. *Journal of Family Social Work, 17* (1), 81–96.

Jones, L. (2015). "Was taking me out of the home necessary?" Perspectives of foster youth on the necessity for removal. *Families in Society, 96* (2), 108–115.

Jones, L. & Landsverk, J. (2006). Residential education: Examining a new approach for improving outcomes for foster youth. *Children and Youth Services Review, 28,* 1152–1168.

Jonson-Reid, M. & Barth, R. (2000). From placement to prison: The path to adolescent incarceration from child welfare supervised foster or group care. *Children and Youth Service Review, 22,* 493–516.

Katz, C. & Courtney, M. (2015). Evaluating the self-expressed unmet needs of emancipated foster youth over time. *Children and Youth Service Review, 57* (1), 9–18.

Kaufman, J.; Yang, B.; Douglas-Palumberi, H.; Houshyar, S.; Lipshitz, D.; & Krystal, J.H. (2004). Social support and serotonin transporter gene moderate depression in maltreated children. *Proceedings of the National Academy of Sciences, 101* (49), 17316–17321.

Keller, T.; Cusick, G.R.; & Courtney, M. (2007). Approaching the transition to adulthood: Distinctive profiles of adolescents aging out of the child welfare system. *Social Services Review, 81* (3), 453–484.

Keller, T.; Salazar, A.M.; & Courtney, M. (2010). Prevalence and timing of diagnosable mental health, alcohol, and substance use problems among older adolescents in the child welfare system. *Children and Youth Service Review, 32* (4), 626–634.

Kendall-Tackett, K. (2003). *Treating the lifetime effects of childhood victimization.* Kingston, NJ: Civic Research Institute.

Kendig, S.; Mattingly, M.; & Bianchi, S. (2014). Childhood poverty and the transition to adulthood. *Family Relations, 63,* 271–286.

Kenniston, K. (1971). *Youth and dissent: The rise of a new opposition.* New York: Harcourt Press.

Keogh, D.; Weed, K.; & Noria, C.W. (2007). The fate of adolescent mothers. In G. Borkowski, J.R. Harris, T.L. Whitman, S.S. Carothers, & K. Weed, (Eds.), *Risk and resilience: Adolescent mothers and their children grow up.* Mahwah, NJ: Lawrence Erlbaum.

Kerbow, D. (1996). Patterns of student mobility and local school reform. *Journal of Education for Students Placed at Risk, 1* (2), 147–170.

Kerman, B.; Barth, R.; & Wildfire, J. (2004). Extending transitional services to former foster children. *Child Welfare, 88* (3), 239–262.

Kerman, B.; Wildfire, J.; & Barth, R. (2002). Outcomes for young adults who experienced foster care. *Children and Youth Service Review, 24* (5), 319–344.

Kerr, D.C.; Leve, L.D.; & Chamberlain, P. (2009). Pregnancy rates among juvenile justice girls in two randomized trials of Multidimensional Treatment Foster Care. *Journal of Consulting and Clinical Psychology, 77* (3), 588–593.

Kertscher, T. (2013, August 11). On average, a college degree takes six years, U.S. Sen. Ron Johnson says. *Milwaukee Journal Sentinel.*

Ketteringham, E. (2017). Do poor parents have to be perfect parents? *New York Times,* August 22, A19.

Kilpatrick, D.G.; Ruggiero, K.J.; Acierno, R.; Saunders, B.E.; Resnick, H.S.; & Best, C.L. (2003). Violence and risk of PTSD, major depression, substance abuse/dependency, and comorbidity. *Journal of Consulting & Clinical Psychology, 71,* 692–700.

Kimberlin, S. & Lemley, A. (2012). *Exit outcomes for former foster youth participating in California's THP Plus transitional supportive housing programs.* San Francisco, California: John Burton Foundation.

King, B.; Putnam-Hornstein, E.; Cederbaum, J.A.; & Needell, B. (2014). A cross sectional examination of birth rates among adolescent girls in foster care. *Children and Youth Service Review, 36,* 179–186.

Kipke, M.D.; Simon, T.R.; Montgomery, S.B.; Unger, J.B.; & Iversen, E.F. (1997). Homeless youth and exposure to and involvement with violence while living on the streets. *Journal of Adolescent Health, 20* (5), 360–367.

Kirk, C.; Lewis, R.; Nilsen, C.; & Colvin, D. (2013). Foster care and college: The educational aspirations and expectations of youth in the foster care system. *Youth and Society, 45,* 307–323.

Klein, J.D.; Woods, A.H.; Wilson, K.M.; Prospero, M.; Greene, J.; & Greenwalt, C. (2000). Homeless and runaway youth access to care. *Journal of Adolescent Health, 27* (5), 331–339.

Kohlenberg, E.; Norlund, D.; Lowin, A.; & Treicher, B. (2012). *Alcohol and substance abuse among adolescents in foster care in Washington State: Results from*

1998–1999. Adolescent Foster Care Survey. Rockville, MD: Center for Substance Abuse.

Kortenkamp, K. & Ehrle, J. (2002). *The well-being of children involved in the child welfare system: A national overview.* Washington, DC: Urban Institute.

Kost, K. (2016). *Teen pregnancy in the US.* Washington, DC: Guttmacher Institute. www.guttmacher.org/united-states/teens/teen-pregnancy?gclid=CITzz _HYrc8CFU-Sfgodnk8JHQ.

Kozol, J. (1991). *Savage inequalities.* New York: Harper Perennial.

Kroner, M. & Mares, A. (2011). Living arrangements and level of care among clients discharged from a scatter-based independent living program. *Children and Youth Service Review, 33,* 405–415.

Kruszka, B.; Lindell, D.; Killion, C.; & Criss, S. (2016). "Its like pay or don't have it, and now I'm doing without:" The voice of transitional uninsured former foster youth. *Public Policy and Nursing Practice, 20* (10), 1–11.

Kulka, R.A.; Fairbank, J.A.; Jordan, K.; & Weiss, D. (1990). *Trauma and the Vietnam War generation: Report of findings from the National Vietnam Veterans Readjustment Study.* New York: Brunner Mazel.

Kushel, M.; Gupta, R.; Gee, L.; & Haas, J. (2006). Housing instability and food insecurity as barriers to health care among low-income Americans. *Journal of General Internal Medicine, 21* (1), 71–77.

Kushel, M.; Yen, I.; Gee, L.; & Courtney, M. (2007). Homelessness and health care access after emancipation: Results from the Mid-West Evaluation of Adult Functioning of Former Foster Youth. *Archives of Pediatric Adolescent Medicine, 161* (10), 986–993.

Landsverk, J.; Burns, B.; Stambaugh, L.; & Reutz, J. (2006). *Mental health care for children and adolescents in foster care: Review of research literature.* Seattle: Casey Family Programs.

Larimer, M.E.; Kilmer, J.R.; & Lee, C. (2005). College students drug prevention: A review of individually-oriented prevention strategies. *Journal of Drug Issues. 35* (2), 431–455.

Lawler, M.J.; Sayfan, L.; Goodman, G.; Narr, R.; & Cordon, I. (2014). Comprehensive residential education: A promising model to emerging adults in foster care. *Children and Youth Services Review,* (38), 10–19.

Leathers, S. & Testa, M. (2006). Foster youth emancipating from care: Caseworkers report on needs and services. *Child Welfare, 85* (3), 463–498.

Lee, B. & Barth, R. (2009). Residential education: An emerging resource for improving educational outcomes for foster care. *Children and Youth Service Review, 31* (5), 389–412.

Lee, J.S.; Courtney, M.; & Hook, J. L. (2012). Formal bonds during the transition to adulthood: Extended foster care support and criminal/legal involvement. *Journal of Public Child Welfare, 6* (3), 255–279.

Lee, J.S.; Courtney, M.; & Tajima, E. (2014). Extended foster care support during the transition to adulthood: Effect on the risk of arrest. *Children and Youth Services Review,* (42), 34-42.

Lee, T.; Festinger, T.; Jaccard, J.; & Munson, M. (2017). Mental health subgroups among vulnerable emerging adults and their functioning. *Journal for Society for Social Work, 8* (2).

Lemley, A. & Sepe, M. (2014). *THP-Plus foster care.* San Francisco: John Burton Foundation.

Lemon, K.; Hines, A.; & Merdinger, J. (2005). From foster care to young adulthood: The role of independent living programs in supporting successful transitions. *Children and Youth Service Review, 27,* 251–270.

Lenz-Rashid, S. (2006). Employment experiences of homeless young adults: Are they different for youth with a history of foster care? *Children and Youth Service Review, 28,* 235–259.

Leslie, L.; Rahghavan, Zhang, J.; & Aarons, G. (2010). Rates of psychotropic medication use over time among youth in child welfare/child protective studies. *Journal of the American Academy of Child and Adolescent Psychiatry, 20,* 135–143.

Leventhal, T. & Newman, S. (2010). Housing and child development. *Children and Youth Services Review, 32,* 1165–1174.

Levine, J. A.; Emery, C.R.; & Pollack. H. (2007). The well-being of children born to teen mothers. *Journal of Marriage and Family, 69* (February), 105–122.

Libby, A.M.; Kelleher, K.J.; & Leslie, L.K. (2007). Child welfare systems policies and practices affecting Medicaid health insurance for children: A national study. *Journal of Social Service Research, 33,* 39–49.

Lichtblau, E. (2017, January 16). Trump may reverse Obama policy of freeing inmates. *New York Times,* p. A12.

Lightfoot, E.; Hill, K.; & Laberte, T. (2011). Prevalence of children with disabilities in the child welfare system and out of home placement: An examination of administrative records. *Children and Youth Services Review, 33* (11), 2069–2075.

Lindsey, E. & Ahmed, F. (1999). The North Carolina Independent Living Program: A comparison of outcomes. *Children and Youth Services Review, 21* (5), 389–412.

Lopez, M.H. & Gonzales-Barrera, A. (2014, March 6). Women's college enrollment gains leave males behind. *Fact Tank, News in Numbers.* Pew Research Center. Retrieved November 2, 2015. http://www.pewresearch.org/fact-tank/2014/03/06/womens-college-enrollment-gains-leave-men-behind/.

Love, L.T.; McIntosh, J.; Rosst, M.; & Terzakian, K. (2005). *Fostering hope: Preventing teen pregnancy among youth in foster care.* Washington, DC: National Campaign to Prevent Teen Pregnancy.

Lowell, D.; Carter, A.; Godoy, L.; Paulicin, B.; & Briggs-Gowan, M. (2011). A randomized controlled trial of Child FIRST: A comprehensive home-based intervention translating research into early childhood practice. *Child Development, 82* (1), 193–208.

Macomber, J.; Kuehn, D.; McDaniel, M.; Vericker, T.; Pergamit, M.; Cuccaro, S.; Needell, B.; Duncan, D.; Kum, H.; K. Stewart, J.; Kwon-Lee, C.; & Barth, R.

(2008). *Coming of age: Employment outcomes for youth who age out of foster care through their middle twenties.* Presented at the 11ᵗʰ National Child Welfare Data and Technology Conference.

Mailman School of Public Health. (2016, October 19). Youth who age out of foster care leave behind critical health care coverage. *Policy Brief.* New York: Columbia University. www.mailman.columbia.edu/public-health-now /news/young-people-who-age-out-foster-care-may-leave-behind-critical -health-coverage.

Mallon, G.P. (1998). After care, then where? Outcomes of an independent living program. *Child Welfare, 77* (1), 61–79.

Maluccio, A.; Kreiger, R.; & Pine, B.A. (Eds.). (1990). *Preparing adolescents for life after foster care: The central role of foster parents.* Washington, DC: CWLA.

Mares, A. (2010). An assessment of independent living needs among emancipating foster youth. *Child and Adolescent Social Work, 27,* 79–96.

Mares, A. & Kroner, M. (2011). Lighthouse Independent Living Program: Predictors of client outcomes at discharge. *Children and Youth Services Review, 33,* 1749–1758.

Marshall, J.M. & Haight, W. (2014). Understanding racial disproportionality affecting African-American youth who cross over from child welfare to the juvenile justice system: Communication, power, race, and social class. *Children and Youth Services, 42,* 82–90.

Martinez, G.M. & Abma, J.C. (2015). *Sexual activity, contraceptive use, and child bearing of teenagers aged 15–19 in the United States.* NCHS Data Brief, No. 209.

Mason, M.; Castrianno, L.; Kessler, C.; Holmstrand, L.; Huefner, J.; Payne, V.; Pecora, P.; Schmaltz, S.; & Stenslie, S. (2003). A comparison of foster care outcomes across four child welfare agencies. *Journal of Family Social Work, 7* (2), 55–72.

Massinga, R. & Pecora, P. (2004). Providing better opportunities for older children in the child welfare system. *The Future of Children, 14,* 151–173.

Masten, A.S. (2006). Promoting resilience in development: A general framework for systems of care. In R.J. Flynn, P.M. Dudding, & J. Barber (Eds.). *Promoting resilience in child welfare* (pp. 3). Ottawa, ON: University of Ottawa Press.

Mathews, T.J. & MacDorman, F. (2013, January 24). Infant mortality statistics from the 2009 Period Linked Birth/Infant Death Data Set. *National Vital Statistics Reports, 61* (8), 1–13.

Mattison, D.; Jayaratne, J.; & Croxton (2002). Client or former client? Implications of ex-client definition on social work practice. *Social Work, 47* (1), 55–64.

McCarron, G.P. & Inkelas, K.K. (2006). The gap between educational aspirations and attainment for first-generation college students and the role of parental involvement. *Journal of College Development, 47,* 534–549.

McCoy, H.; McMillen, J.C.; & Spitznagel, E. (2008). Older youth leaving the foster care system: Who, what, when, where, and why? *Children and Youth Service Review, 30,* 735–745.

McDonald, T.P.; Allen, R.I.; Westerfelt, A.; & Piliavin, I. (1993). *Assessing the long term effects of foster care: A research synthesis.* Madison, WI: Institute for Research on Poverty.

McGinty, J. (2015, August). How many Americans have a police record? Far more than you think. *Wall Street Journal.* http://www.wsj.com/articles /how-many-americans-have-a-police-record-probably-more-than-you -think-1438939802.

McMahon, R. & Fields, S. (2015). Criminal conduct subgroups of "aging out" foster youth. *Children and Youth Service Review, 48,* 14–19.

McMillen, C.; Auslander, W.; Elze, D.; White, T.; & Thompson, R. (2003). Educational experiences and aspirations of older youth in care. *Child Welfare, 82* (4), 475–495.

McMillen, J. & Tucker, J. (1999). The status of older adolescents at exit from out-of-home care. *Child Welfare, 78* (3), 339–351.

McMillen, J.C. & Raghavan, R. (2009). Pediatric to adult mental health service use of young people leaving the foster youth care system. *Journal of Adolescent Health, 44,* 7–13.

McMillen, J.C.; Rideout, G.; Fisher, R.; & Tucker, J. (1997). Independent living services: The views of former foster. *Families in Society, 78* (5), 471–479.

McMillen, J.C.; Zima, B.T.; Scott, L.D.; Auslander, W.F.; Munson, M.R.; & Ollie, M.T. (2005). Prevalence of psychiatric disorders among older youth in the foster care system. *Journal of the American Academy of Child and Adolescent Psychiatry, 44* (1), 88–95.

McMillen, J.C.; Zima, B.T.; Scott, L.D.; Ollie, M.T.; & Munson, M.R. (2004). The mental health service use of older youth in foster care. *Psychiatric Services, 55,* 811–817.

McNaughton, C. (2008). *Transitions through homelessness: Lives on the edge.* New York: Palgrave MacMillan.

Mech, E.V. (2002). *Uncertain futures: Foster youth in transition.* Washington, DC: CWLA.

Mech, E.V. (2003). Transition systems for youth. In E.V. Mech (Ed.). *Uncertain futures in foster youth in the transition to adulthood* (pp. 1–22). Washington, DC: CWLA.

Mech, E.V. & Fung, C.C. (1999). Placement restrictiveness and educational achievement among emancipated foster youth. *Research on Social Work Practice, 9* (2), 213–228.

Mech, E.V.; Ludy-Dobson, C.; & Hulsemans, F.S. (1994). Life skills knowledge: A survey of foster adolescents in three placements. *Children and Youth Services Review, 16* (3–4), 181–201.

Mech, E.V.; Pryde, J.A.; & Rycraft, J.R. (1995). Mentors for adolescents in foster care. *Child and Adolescent Social Work Journal, 12,* 317–328.

Merdinger, J.; Hines, A.; Lemon, K.; Osterling, K.; & Wyatt, P. (2005). Pathways to college for former foster youth: Understanding factors that contribute to educational success. *Child Welfare, 84* (6), 867–896.

Merikangas, K.R.; He, J.; Burnstein, M.; Swanson, S.A.; Avenevoli, S.; & Cui, L. (2010). Lifetime prevalence of mental health disorders in US adolescents: Results from the National Comorbidity Study Replication-Adolescent Supplement. *Journal of the American Academy of Child and Adolescent Psychiatry, 49* (10), 980–989.

Merton, R.K. (1968). The Matthew Effect in science. *Science, 159,* 56–63.

Miller, W.R. & Brown, S.A. (1997). Why psychologists should treat alcohol and drug problems. *American Psychologist, 52* (12), 1269–1279.

Montgomery, P.; Donkoh, C.; & Underhill, K. (2006). Independent living programs for young people leaving the care system. *Children and Youth Services Review, 28,* 1435–1448.

Moore, K.; Manlove, J.; Glei, D.A.; Morrison, D.R. (1998). Non-marital school age motherhood: Family, individual, and school characteristics. *Journal of Adolescent Research, 13* (4), 433–447.

Mouw, T. (2004). The effect of timing and choice on the future of young adulthood. *Policy Brief, 8,* 1–3.

MSNBC. (2012, April 27). Romney tells students to "borrow money from your parents." http://www.msnbc.com/the-ed-show/romney-tells-students -borrow-money.

Munson, M.R.; Lee, B.R.; Miller, D.; Cole, A.; & Nedelcu, C. (2013). Emerging adulthood among former system youth: The ideal versus real. *Children and Youth Services Review, 35* (6), 923–929.

Munson, M.R. & McMillen, J. (2009). Natural mentoring and psychosocial outcomes among older youth transitioning from foster care. *Children and Youth Service Review, 31,* 104–111.

Munson, M.R.; Scott, L.D.; Smalling, S.E.; Kim, H.; & Floersch, J.E. (2011). Former system youth with mental health needs: Routes to adult mental health care insight, emotions, and mistrust. *Children and Youth Service Review, 33,* 2261–2266.

Munson, M.R.; Smalling, S.E.; Spencer, R.; Scott, L.D.; & Tracy, E.M. (2010). A steady presence in the midst of change: Non-kin natural mentors in the lives of youth exiting foster care. *Children and Youth Service Review, 34* (4), 527–535.

Murthi, M. & Espelage, D.L. (2005). Childhood sexual abuse. Social support, and psychological outcomes: A loss framework. *Child Abuse and Neglect, 29,* 1215–1231.

Naccarato, T.; Brophy, M.; & Courtney, M. (2010). Employment outcomes of foster youth: The results from the Midwest Evaluation of the adult functioning of foster youth. *Children and Youth Service Review, 32,* 551–559.

Naccarato, T. & DeLorenzo, E. (2008). Transitional youth services: Practice implications from a systematic review. *Child Adolescent and Social Work Journal, 25,* 287–308.

Nair, P.; Black, M.M.; Schuler, M.; Keane, V.; Snow, L.; & Rigney, B.A. (1997). Risk factors for disruption in primary caregiving among infants of substance abusing women. *Child Abuse and Neglect, 21* (11), 1039–1051.

Napolitano, L. & Courtney, M. (2014). *Residential settings of young adults in extended foster care: A preliminary investigation*. Chicago: University of Chicago, Chapin Hall Center for Children.

Narendorf, S. & McMillen, J.C. (2010). Substance use and substance use disorders as youth transition to adulthood. *Children and Youth Service Review, 32*, 113–119.

National Center for Education Statistics. (2015). *State non-fiscal survey of public elementary/secondary education*. Washington, DC: U.S. Department of Education.

National Foster Care Awareness Project. (2000a). *Answers to foster care independence questions. 1, (2)*, Seattle: Casey Foundation. https://cbexpress.acf .hhs.gov/index.cfm?event=website.viewArticles&issueid=4&articleid=51.

National Foster Care Awareness Project. (2000b). *Frequently asked questions II: About the Foster Care Independence Act of 1999 and the John H. Chafee Foster Care Independence Program*. Seattle: Casey Foundation.

National Survey of Child and Adolescent Well-Being. (2005). *CPS Sample Component, Wave 1: Data Analysis Report*. Washington, DC: Children's Service Bureau.

National Youth in Transition Database. (2012, September). *Highlights from the state reports to the National Youth in Transition Database, federal fiscal year 2011*. Washington, DC: Administration for Children and Youth.

National Youth in Transition Database. (2013, August). *Highlights from the state reports to the NYTB, federal fiscal year 2012*. Washington, DC: USDHHS.

National Youth in Transition Database. (2014a, July). *Highlights from the state reports to the National Youth in Transition Database, federal fiscal year 2013*. Washington, DC: Administration for Children and Youth.

National Youth in Transition Database. (2014b, September). *Comparing outcomes reported by young people at ages 17 and 19 in the NYTD Cohort 1*. Washington, DC: Administration for Children and Youth.

Needell, B.; Cuccaro-Alamin, S.; Brookhart, A.; Jackman, W.; & Shlonsky, A. (2002). *Youth emancipating from foster care in California: Findings using linked administrative data*. Center for Social Services: University of California Berkeley.

Newton, R.R.; Litrownick, A.J.; & Landsverk, J.A. (2000). Children and youth in foster care: Disentangling the relationships between problem behaviors and number of placements. *Child Abuse and Neglect, 24* (10), 1363–1373.

Nixon, R. & Jones, M.G. (2000). *Improving transitions to adulthood for youth served in the foster care system: A report on strengths and needs of existing aftercare services*. Washington, DC: CWLA.

Nolan, T. (2006). Outcomes for transitional living programs serving LGBTQ youth in New York City. *Child Welfare, 85* (2), 385–406.

Nollan, K.A.; Wolf, M.; Ansell, D.; Burns, L.; Barr, L; Copeland, W.; et al. (2000). Ready or not: Assessing youths' preparedness for independent living. *Child Welfare, 79* (2), 159–176.

O'Brien, K.; Pecora, P.; Echohawk, L.A.; Evans-Campbell, T.; Palamteer-Holder, N.; & White, C.R. (2010). Educational and employment achievements of American Indian/Alaskan Native alumni of foster care. *Families in Society, 91* (2), 149–157.

Okpych, N. (2012). Policy framework supporting youth aging out of foster care through college. *Children and Youth Service Review, 34,* 1390–1396.

Okpych, N. (2015). Receipt of independent living services among older youth in foster care: An analysis of national data from the U.S. *Children and Youth Service Review, 51,* 74–86.

Okpych, N. & Courtney, M. (2014). Does education pay for youth formerly in foster care? Comparisons of employment outcomes with a national sample. *Children and Youth Service Review, 43,* 18–28.

Osborn, C.; Manning, W.; & Smock, P. (2007). Married and cohabitating parents' relationship stability: A focus on race and ethnicity. *Journal of Marriage and the Family, 69,* 1345–1367.

Osgood, D.W.; Foster, M.; & Courtney, M. (2010). Vulnerable populations and the transition to adulthood. *Future of Children, 20* (1), 209–229.

Oshima, S.C.; Narendorf, J.C.; & McMillan, J.C. (2013). Pregnancy risk among older youth transitioning out of foster care. *Children and Youth Service Review, 35,* 1760–1765.

Osterling-Lemon, K. & Hines, A. (2006). Mentoring adolescent foster youth: Promoting resilience during development transitions. *Child and Family Social Work, 11,* 242–253.

O'Sullivan, J. & Lussier-Duynstee, P. (2006). Adolescent homelessness, nursing, and public health policy. *Public Policy Nursing Practice, 7* (1), 73–77.

Packard, T.; Delgado, M.; Fellmeth, R.; & McReady, K. (2008). A cost-benefit analysis of transitional services for emancipating foster youth. *Children and Youth Service Review, 30,* 1267–1278.

Packard, T.; Jones, L.; Gross, B.; Hohman, M.; & Fong, T. (2001). Using focus groups to design an inter-agency training for child welfare workers. *Professional development in social work: Journal of International Social Work Continuing Education, 3* (3), 18–26.

Pager, M. (2003). The mark of a criminal record. *American Journal of Sociology, 108* (5), 937–976.

Park, J.M.; Fertig, A.; & Metraux, S. (2014). Factors contributing to the receipt of housing assistance by low-income families with children in twenty American cities. *Social Service Review, 88* (1), 166–193.

Park, J.M.; Metraux, S.; & Culhane, D. (2005). Childhood out of home placement and the dynamics of public shelter utilization among homeless adults. *Children and Youth Service Review, 27* (5), 533–546.

Park, M.; Mulye, P.; Adams, S.; Brindis, C.; & Irwin, C. (2006). The health status of young adults in the United States. *Journal of Adolescent Health, 39* (3), 305–317.

Parrish, T.; Dubois, J.; Delano, C.; Dixon, D.; Webster, D.; & Berrick, J.D. (2001). *Education of foster group home children: Whose responsibility is it? Study of* the educational placement of children residing in group homes. Palo Alto, CA: American Institutes for Research.

Patel, S. & Roherty, M.A. (2007). *Medicaid access for youth aging out of foster care.* Washington, DC: American Public Human Services Association.

Pecora, P. (2007). Providing better opportunities for older children in the child welfare system. *Archives of Pediatric Adolescent Medicine, 161* (10), 1006–1008.

Pecora, P. (2010, Spring). Why should child welfare focus on promoting placement stability? *CW360*, University of Minnesota: Center for Advanced Studies in Child Welfare. https://cascw.umn.edu/wp-content/uploads/2013/12 /CW360_2010.pdf.

Pecora, P. (2012). Maximizing educational achieving of youth in foster care and alumni: Factors associated with success. *Children and Youth Service Review, 34,* 1121–1128.

Pecora, P.; Kessler, L.; Williams, J.; O'Brien, K.; Downs, A.; English, D.; & Holmes, K. (2005). *Improving family foster care: Findings from the Northwest Foster Care Alumni Study.* Seattle: Casey Family Programs.

Pecora, P.; Kessler, R.C.; O'Brien, K.; White, C.R.; Williams, J.; Hiripi, E.; English, D.; White, J.; & Herrick, M.A. (2006). Educational and employment outcomes of adults formerly placed in foster care: Results from the Northwest Foster Care Alumni Study. *Children and Youth Service Review, 28,* 1469–1481.

Pecora, P.; Kessler, W.; Downs, A.C.; O'Brien, K.; Hiripi, E.; & Morello, S. (2003). *Early results from the Casey National Alumni Study.* Seattle: Casey Family Foundation.

Pecora, P.; White, C.W.; Jackson, L.; & Wiggins, T. (2009). Mental health of current and former residents of foster care: A review of recent studies in the USA. *Child and Family Social Work, 14,* 132–146.

Pecora, P.; Williams, J.; Kessler, R.; Downs, C.A.; O'Brien, K.; & Hiripi, E. (2003). *Assessing the effects of foster care: Early results from the Casey National Alumni Study.* Retrieved November 20, 2004 from http://fostercarealumni.casey .org/index2.asp.

Pecora, P.; Williams, J.; Kessler, R.; Hiripi, E.; O'Brien, K.; Emerson, J.; Herrick, M.; & Torres, D. (2006). Assessing the educational achievements of adults who were formerly placed in family foster care. *Child and Adolescent Social Work, 11,* 220–231.

Perez, B. & Romo, H. (2011). "Couch surfing" of Latino foster care alumni: Reliance on peers as social capital. *Children and Youth Service Review, 34,* 239–248.

Pergamit, M. & Johnson, H. (2009). Extending foster care to age 21: *Implications and estimates of youth aging out of foster care in Los Angeles: Final report to the Stuart Foundation.* Washington, DC: Urban Institute.

Pergamit, M.; McDaniel, M.; & Hawkins, A. (2012, June 18). *Housing assistance for youth who have aged out of care: The role of the Chaffee Program.* Report for the Urban Institute to United States Department of Health and Human Services.

Perna, L.W. (2005). The benefits of higher education: Sex, racial/ethnic, and socioeconomic group differences. *Review of Higher Education, 29* (1), 23–52.

Perry, B.L. (2006). Understanding social network disruption: The case of youth in foster care. *Social Problems, 53* (3), 371–391.

Peters, C.M.; Dworsky, A.; Courtney, M.; & Pollack, H. (2009). *The benefits of costs of extending foster care to age 21.* Chicago: University of Chicago, Chapin Hall Center for Children.

Peters, C.M.; Sherraden, M.; & Kuchinski, A.M. (2016). From foster care to adulthood: The role of income. *Journal of Public Child Welfare, 10* (1), 39–58.

Pike, G.; Kuh, G.; & Massa-McKinley, R. (2009). First year students' employment, engagement, and academic achievement: Untangling the relationship between work and grades. *NASPA Journal, 45* (4), 560–582.

Piliavin, I.; Bradley, R.E.; Wright, R.; Mare, D.; & Westerfelt, A.H. (1996). Exits from and returns to homelessness. *Social Service Review, 70* (1), 33–57.

Pilowsky, D.J. & Wu, L.T. (2006). Psychiatric symptoms and substance abuse disorders in a nationally representative sample of foster adolescents involved with foster care. *Journal of Adolescent Health, 38,* 351–358.

Pine, B.A.; Kreiger, R.; & Maluccio, A. (1990). Preparing adolescents to leave foster family care: Guidelines for policy and program. In A. Maluccio, R. Krieger, & B.A. Pine (Eds.). *Preparing adolescents for life after foster care* (pp. 77–89). Washington, DC: CWLA.

Porter, K. (2002). *The value of a college degree.* Washington, DC: Clearinghouse on Higher Education.

Pottick, K.J.; Bilder, S.; Stoep, A.V.; Warner, L.A.; & Alvarez, M.F. (2008). US patterns of mental health service utilization for transition-age youth and young adults. *Journal of Behavioral Health Services, 35* (4), 373–379.

Powers, L.; Geenen, S.; Powers, J.; Pommier-Satya, S.; Turner, A.; Dalton, L.; Drummond, D.; & Swank, P. (2012). My life: Effects of a randomized study of self-determination enhancement on the transition outcomes of youth in foster care and special education. *Children and Youth Service Review, 34* (11), 2179–2187.

Powers, P. & Stotland, J.F. (2002). *Lost in the shuffle revisited.* Philadelphia: Law Center. Retrieved March 8, 2006 from http://www.elc-pa.org/pubs /downloads/english/dis-lost-in-the-shuffle-revisited-12–02.pdf.

Prince, D.; Vidal, S.; & Connell, C. (2016, January 14). *Effect of independent living supports and subsequent housing after youth exit foster care.* Washington, DC: Presented at the Society for Social Work Research.

Propp, J.; Ortega, D.; & NewHeart, F. (2003). Independence or interdependent: Rethinking the transition from "ward of the court." *Families in Society, 84* (2), 259–266.

Pryce, J. & Samuels, G. (2010). Renewal and risk: The dual risk: The dual experience of young motherhood and aging out of the child welfare system. *Journal of Adolescent Research, 25* (2), 205–230.

Pullman, M.D. (2010). Predictor of criminal charges for youth in public mental health during the transition to adulthood. *Journal of Child and Family Studies, 19*, 483–491.

Putnam-Hornstein, E.; Cederbaum, J.; King, B.; & Needell, B. (2013). *California's most vulnerable parents: When maltreated children have children.* Agoura Hills, CA: Conrad Hilton Foundation.

Raghavan, R. & McMillen, J.C. (2008). Use of multiple psychotropic medications among adolescents aging out of foster care. *Research on Social Work Practice, 14* (4), 240–248.

Raghavan, R.; Shi, P.; Aarons, G.; Roesch, S.; & McMillen, J.C. (2009). Health insurance discontinuities among adolescents leaving foster care. *Journal of Adolescent Health, 44* (1), 41–47.

Raghavan, R; Zima, B.T.; Anderson, R.M.; Leibowitz, A.A.; Schuster, M.A.; & Landsverk, J. (2005). Psychotropic medication use in a national probability sample of children in the child welfare system. *Journal of Child and Adolescent Psychopharmacology, 15* (1): 97–106.

Ramirez, E. (2015). *Literature review: Psychotropic medication and children and use in foster care.* Berkeley, California: CALSWEC.

RAND. (2001). *RAND health research highlights: Mental health care for youth 2001.* Santa Monica, California: RAND Corporation.

Raphael, S. (2007). Early incarceration spells out the transition into adulthood. In S. Danziger & C.E. Rouse (Eds.), *The price of independence: The economics of early adulthood* (pp. 278–305). New York: Russell Sage Foundation.

Rashid, S. (2004). Evaluating a transitional living program for homeless, former foster youth. *Research on Social Work Practice, 14* (4), 240–248.

Reilly, T. (2003). Transition from care: Status and outcomes of youth who age out of foster care. *Child Welfare, 82* (6), 727–746.

Requarth, T. (2017). A court calls on science. *New York Times*, April 18, 1,3.

Rhode, P.; Lewinsohn, P.M.; & Seeley, J.R. (1996). Psychiatric comorbidity with problem alcohol use in high school students. *Journal of the American Academy of Child Adolescent Psychiatric, 35* (1), 101–109.

Rhodes, J.E. & DuBois, D.L. (2006). Understanding and facilitating the youth mentoring movement. *Social Policy Support, 20* (3), 3–19.

Rice, D.L. & McFadden, F.J. (1988). A forum for foster children. *Child Welfare, 67*, 231–247.

Riggs, P.D. & Davies, R.D. (2002). A clinical approach to integrating treatment for adolescent depression and substance abuse. *Journal of the American Academy of Child and Adolescent Psychiatry, 41* (10), 1253–1255.

Rios, S. & Rocco, T. (2014). From foster care to college: Barriers and supports on the road to post-secondary education. *Emerging Adulthood, 2* (3), 227–237.

Robert, S. & House, J.H. (1996). SES differential in health by age and alternative indicators of SES. *Journal of Aging and Health, 8*, 359–388.

Rodriguez, M. & Avery, B. (2016, December). *Ban the box: U.S. cities, counties, and states adopt fair hiring policies.* New York: National Employment Law Project.

Rohe, W.M. & Stegman, M.A. (1994). The effects of homeownership on self-esteem, perceived control and life satisfaction of low-income people. *Urban Affairs Quarterly, 30*, 152–172.

Roman, N.P. & Wolfe, P.B. (1997). The relationship between foster care and homelessness. *Public Welfare, 55* (1), 4–9.

Rosenbaum, P.R. & Rubin, D.B. (1983). The central role of propensity score in observational studies for causal effect. *Biometrika, 70* (1), 41–55.

Ross, C.E. & Jang, S.J. (2000). Neighborhood disorder, fear, and mistrust: The buffering ties with neighbors. *American Journal of Community Psychology, 28* (4), 401–420.

Rostosky, S.S.; Regenerus, M.D.; & Comer-Wright, M.L. (2003). Coital debut: The role of religiosity and sex attitudes in the ADD Health Survey. *Journal of Sex Research, 40* (4), 358–367.

Rubin, D.M.; Alessandrini, E.A.; Feudtner, C.; Lovalio, R.; & Hadley, T. (2004). Placement changes and emergency department visits in the first year of foster care. *Pediatrics, 114*, 354–360.

Rubin, D.M.; Halfon, N.; Raghavan, R.; & Rosenbaum, S. (2005). *Protecting children in foster care: Why proposed Medicaid cuts harm our nation's most vulnerable children.* Seattle: Casey Family Programs.

Rubin, D.M.; O'Reilly, A.; Luan, X.; & Localio, A. (2007). The impact of placement stability on behavioral well-being for children in foster care. *Pediatrics, 119* (2), 336–344.

Rumbaut, R.; Komai, G.; & Morgan, C. (2007). *Demographic profiles of young adults in five cities.* Philadelphia: Network on Transitions to Adulthood.

Rumberger, R.W.; Larsen, K.A.; Ream, R.K.; & Palardi, G.J. (1999). *The educational consequences of mobility: California students and schools (Policy Analysis for California Education).* University of California, Berkeley.

Runtz, M.G. & Schallow, J.R. (1997). Social support and coping strategies as mediators of adult adjustment following childhood maltreatment. *Child Abuse and Neglect, 21*, 211–226.

Ryan, J.; Hernandez, P.; & Herz, D. (2007). Developmental trajectories of offending youth leaving foster care. *Social Work Research, 31* (2), 83–93.

Ryan, J.; Marshall, J.; Herz, D.; & Hernandez, D. (2008). Juvenile delinquency in child welfare: Investigating the role of group home effects. *Children and Youth Services Review, 30* (9), 1088–1099.

Ryan, J.; Perron, B.; & Huang, H. (2016). Child welfare and the transition to adulthood: Investigating placement status and subsequent arrest. *Journal of Adolescence, 45*, 172–182.

Ryan, J. & Testa, M. (2005). Child maltreatment and juvenile delinquency: Investigating the role of placement instability. *Children and Youth Services Review, 27*, 227–249.

Ryan, P.; McFadden, E.J.; Rice, D.; & Warren, B.L. (1988). The role of foster parents in helping young people develop emancipation skills. *Child Welfare, 79* (2), 563–572.

Ryan, R.M.; Kalil, A.; & Ziol-Guest, K.M. (2008). Longitudinal patterns of non-resident fathers' involvement: The role of resources and relations. *Journal of Marriage and the Family, 70*, 962–977.

Ryan, T. & Thompson, S. (2013). Perspectives on housing among emerging homeless adults. *Evaluation and Program Planning, 36* (1), 107–1144.

Sakai, C.; Mackie, T.I.; Shetgriri, R.; Franzen, S.; Partap, A.; Flores, G.; & Leslie, L.K. (2014). Mental health beliefs and barriers to accessing mental health services in youth aging out of foster care. *Academy of Pediatrics, 14* (6), 565–573.

Salazar, A. (2012). Supporting college success in foster care alumni: Salient factors related to postsecondary retention. *Child Welfare, 91* (5), 139–167.

Salazar, A. (2013). The value of a college degree for foster care alumni: Comparisons with general population samples. *Social Work, 58* (1), 139–150.

Salazar, A.; Keller, T.; & Courtney, M. (2013). Understanding social support's role in the relationship between maltreatment and depression in youth with foster care experience. *Child Maltreatment, 6* (2), 1–12.

SAMHSA. (2005). *Substance use and need for treatment of youth who had been out of foster care.* Washington, DC: Office of Applied Sciences, National Survey on Drug Use and Health. 2002–2003, the NSDUH.

SAMHSA. (2011). *Results from the National Survey on Drug Use and Health.* Washington, DC: U.S.D.H.H.S, Substance Abuse and Mental Health Administration.

SAMHSA. (2013). *Results from the National Survey on Drug Use and Health.* Washington, DC: U.S.D.H.H.S, Substance Abuse and Mental Health Administration.

Sampson, R.J. & Laub, J.H. (1990). Crime and deviance over the life course: The salience of adult social bonds. *American Sociological Review, 55* (5), 609–627.

Sampson, R.J. & Laub, J.H. (1992). *Crime in the making: Pathways and turning points throughout life.* Cambridge, MA: Harvard University Press.

Sampson, R.J.; Laub, J.H.; & Wimer, C. (2006). Does marriage reduce crime? A counterfactual approach to within-individual causal effects. *Criminology, 44*, 465–506.

Sampson, R.J.; Morenoff, J.; & Gannon-Rowley, T. (2002). Assessing neighborhood effects: Social processes and new directions in research. *Annual Review of Sociology, 28*, 443–478.

Samuels, G.M. (2009). Ambiguous loss of home: The experience of familial (im)permanence among youth with foster care backgrounds. *Children and Youth Service Review, 31*, 1229–1239.

Samuels, G.M. & Pryce, J. (2008). "What doesn't kill you makes you stronger:" Survivalist self-reliance as resilience and risk among adults aging out of foster care. *Children and Youth Service Review, 30*, 1198–1210.

Sawhill, I.W.; Winship, S.; & Grannis, K.S. (2012, September). *Pathways to the middle class: Balancing personal and public responsibilities.* Washington, DC: Brookings Institute.

Scannapieco, M. (2011). *Final report: Texas Foster Teen Conference.* University of Texas at Arlington.

Scannapieco, M.; Connell-Carrick, K.; & Painter, K. (2007). In their own words: Challenges facing youth aging out of foster care. *Child and Adolescent Social Work Journal, 24,* 425–435.

Scannapieco, M.; Schagrin, J.; & Scannapieco, T. (1995). Independent living programs? Do they make a difference? *Child and Adolescent Social Work Journal, 12* (5), 381–389.

Scannapieco, M.; Smith, M.; & Blakeney-Strong, A. (2016). Transition from foster care to independent living: Ecological predictors with outcomes. *Child and Adolescent Social Work Journal, 33,* 293–302.

Schelbe, L.A. (2011). Policy analysis of Fostering Connections to Success and Increasing Adoptions Act of 2008. *Journal of Human Behavior in the Social Environment, 21* (5), 555–576.

Schmitz, M. (2005). Effects of childhood foster care and adoption on adult childbearing. *Children and Youth Service Review, 27,* 85–98.

Schoeni, R. & Ross, K. (2005). Material assistance from families during the transition to adulthood. In R. Settersten, F. Furstenberg, & R. Rumbault (Eds.), *On the frontier of adulthood: Theory, research, and public policy.* Chicago: University of Chicago Press, pp. 3–25.

Schulenberg, J.E.; Sameroff, A.J.; & Cicchetti, D. (2004). The transition to adulthood as a critical juncture in the course of psychopathology and mental health. *Development and Psychopathology, 16* (4), 799–806.

Schwartz, R. (2009). Commentary. In M. Courtney, *The difficult transition to adulthood for foster youth in the US: Implications for the state as corporate parent.* Washington, DC: Research on Child Development, p. 13.

Scopelliti, D. (2014). *Housing: Before, during, and after the Great Recession.* Washington, DC: Bureau of Labor Statistics.

Shah, M.F.; Albrecht, C.; & Felver, B. (2013). *The housing status and well being of foster youth aging out in Washington State.* Washington State Department of Social and Health Services Research and Data Analysis Report 11.195.

Shanahan, M.J. (2000). Pathways to adulthood in changing societies: Variabilities and mechanisms in life course perspective. *Annual Review of Sociology, 26,* 667–692.

Shared Youth Initiative. (2008). https://www.childwelfare.gov/pubPDFs/louisville2.pdf.

Shaw, T.V.; Barth, R.P.; Svoboda, D.V.; & Shaikh, N. (2010). *Fostering safe choices: Final report.* School of Social Work, Ruth H. Young Center for Families and Children, Baltimore: University of Maryland, Baltimore.

Sheehy, A.; Oldham, E.; & Zhangi, M.; Ansel, D.; Correia, P.; & Copeland, R. (2001). *Promising practices: Supporting the transition of youth served by the foster care system.* Baltimore: Annie E. Casey Foundation.

Shin, S. (2006). Need for and actual use of mental health services by adolescents in the child welfare system. *Children and Youth Services Review, 27,* 1071–1083.

Shiner, M.; Young, T.; Newburn, T.; & Groben, S. (2004). *Mentoring disaffected young people: An evaluation of mentoring plus.* York, England: Joseph Rowntree Foundation.

Shirk, C. (2008). *Medicaid and Mental Health Services.* Background paper 66. Washington, DC: National Health Policy Forum. http://www.nhpf.org /library/background-papers/Bp66_MedicaidMentalHealth_10–23–08 .pdf.

Shook, J.; Goodkind, S.; Herring, D.; Pohlig, R.; Kolivoski, K.; & Kim, K. (2013). How different are their experiences and outcomes? Comparing aged-out and other system involved. *Children and Youth Service Review, 35,* 11–18.

Shook, J.; Goodkind, S.; Pohlig, R.; Schelbe, L.; Herring, D.; & Kim, K. (2011). Patterns of mental health, substance abuse, and justice system involvement among youth aging out of child welfare. *American Journal of Orthopsychiatry, 81* (3), 420–427.

Shpiegel, S. & Cascardi, M. (2015). Adolescent parents in the first wave of the National Youth in Transition Database. *Journal of Public Child Welfare, 9* (3), 277–298.

Silver, D. (2014, September 8). Who makes minimum wage? Pew Research Center FACTTANK. Retrieved from http://www.pewresearch.org/fact-tank/2014 /09/08/who-makes-minimum-wage/.

Silver, J.; DiLorenzo, P.; Zukoski, M.; Ross, P.; Amster, B.; & Schlegel, D. (1999). Starting young: Improving the health and developmental outcomes of infants and toddlers in the child welfare system. *Child Welfare, 78* (1), 148–165.

Simms, M.D.; Dubowitz, H.; & Szilagyi, M.A. (2000). Health care needs of children in the foster care system. *Pediatrics, 106,* 909–918.

Singer, A. (2004). *Assessing outcomes of youth transitioning from foster care.* Salt Lake City: Utah Department of Human Services.

Singer, E. & Berzin, S.C. (2015). Early adult identification among youth with foster care experience: Implications for emerging adulthood. *Journal of Public Child Welfare, 9,* 65–87.

Skidmore, M. (2010). Health in America. Poverty and public policy and everywhere else: A review essay. *Poverty and Public Policy, 2* (1), 185–194.

Smithgall, C.; Gladden, R.M.; Howard, E.; Goerge, R.; & Courtney, M. (2004). *Educational experiences of children in out-of-home care.* Chicago: University of Chicago, Chapin Hall Center for Children.

Smithgall, C.; Gladden, R.M.; Yang, D.H.; & Goerge, R. (2005). *Behavior problems and educational disruptions among children in out-of-home care in Chicago* (Working Paper). Chicago: University of Chicago, Chapin Hall Center for Children.

Spencer, R. (2006). Understanding the mentoring process between adolescents and adults. *Youth and Society, 37,* 287–315.

Spencer, R.; Collins, M.E.; Ward, R.; & Smashnaya, S. (2010). Mentoring for young people leaving foster care: Promise and potential pitfalls. *Social Work, 13* (3), 226–233.

Stahmer, A.; Leslie, L.K.; Hurlburt, M.; Barth, R.; Webb, M.; & Landsverk, J. (2005). Development and behavioral needs and service use for children in child welfare. *Pediatrics, 116*, 891–900.

Steinberg, L. (1990). Autonomy, conflict, and harmony in family relationships. In S. Feldman & G. Elliot (Eds.), *At the threshold: The developing adolescent*, pp. 255–276. Cambridge, MA: Harvard University Press.

Steinberg, L. (2005). Cognitive and affective development in adolescence. *Trends in Cognitive Sciences, 9* (2), 69–74.

Steinberg, L. (2007). Risk taking in adolescence: New perspectives in brain and behavioral science. *Current Directions in Psychological Science, 16* (2), 55–59.

Stoddard, S. (2014). *Disability Statistics Annual Report*. Durham: University of New Hampshire, Institute on Disability.

Stone, S. (2006). Child maltreatment, out-of-home placement, and academic vulnerability: A fifteen-year review of the evidence and future directions. *Children and Youth Services Review, 29*, 139–161.

Stone, S.; D'Andrade, A.; & Austin, M. (2007). Educational services for children in foster care: Common and contrasting perspectives of child welfare and education stakeholders. *Journal of Public Child Welfare, 1*, 53–70.

Stoner, M. (1999). Life after foster care: services and policies for former foster youth. *Journal of Sociology and Social Welfare, 25* (4), 159–172.

Stott, T. (2012). Placement instability and risky behaviors of youth aging out of foster care. *Child and Adolescent Social Work, 29*, 61–83.

Stott, T. (2013). Transitioning youth: policies and outcomes. *Children and Youth Service Review, 35*, 218–227.

Stott, T. & Gustavsson, N. (2010). Balancing permanency and stability for youth in foster care. *Children and Youth Service Review, 32*, 619–625.

Suede, M. (2014). What percentage of the US adult population has a felony conviction? *The Libertarian News*, https://www.libertariannews.org/2014/06/05/what-percentage-of-us-adult-population-has-a-felony-conviction.

Sullivan, M.; Jones, L.; & Mathiesen, S. (2010). School change, academic progress, and behavior problems in a sample of foster youth. *Children and Youth Services Review, 32*, 164–170.

Sun, A.; Shillington, A.; Hohman, M.; & Jones, L. (2001). Caregiver AOD use: Case substantiation, and AOD treatment: Studies based on two Southwestern Counties. *Child Welfare, 80* (2), 151–178.

Sweet, M. Appelbaum, M. (2004). Is home visiting an effective strategy? A meta-analytic review of home visiting programs for families with young children. *Child Development, 75* (5), 1435–1456.

Tach, L.; Mincy, R.; & Edlin, K. (2010). Parenting as a "package deal:" Relationships, fertility, and non-resident father involvement among unmarried parents. *Demography, 47*, 181–204.

Telzer, E.H. & Fuligni, A.J. (2009). Daily family assistance and the psychological well-being of adolescents from Latin American, Asian, and European backgrounds. *Developmental Psychology, 45,* 1177–1189.

Testa, M. (1992). Racial and ethnic variation in the early life course of adolescent welfare mothers. In M. Rosenheim & M. Testa (Eds.), *Early parenting and coming of age in the 1990's.* New Brunswick, NJ: Rutgers University Press.

Thompson, R.G. & Auslander, W. (2007). Risk factors for alcohol and marijuana among adolescents in foster care. *Journal of Substance Abuse Treatment, 32,* 61–69.

Thompson, S.J.; Bender, K.A.; Lewis, C.M.; & Watkins, R. (2008). Runaway and pregnant: Risk factors associated with pregnancy in a national sample of runaway/homeless female adolescents. *Journal of Adolescent Health, 43* (2), 125–132.

Tierney, W.G.; Bailey, T.; Constantine, J.; Finkelstein, N.; & Hurd, N. (2009). *Helping students navigate the path to college: What high schools can do.* Washington, DC: U.S. Department of Education.

Traube, D.S.; James, S.; Zhang, J.; & Landsverk, J. (2012). A national study of risk and protective factors for substance abuse among youth in the child welfare system. *Addictive Behavior,* http://dx.doi.org/10.1016/j.addben.2012.01.2015.

Tyler, K.T. & Melander, L. (2010). Foster care placement, poor parenting and negative outcomes among homeless young adults. *Journal of Child and Families Studies, 19,* 787–794.

Uggen, C. & Wakefield, S. (2005). Young adults reentering the community from the Criminal Justice System: The challenges of becoming an adult. In D.W. Osgood (Ed.), *On your own without a net: The transition to adulthood for vulnerable populations.* Chicago: University of Chicago Press.

Uggen, C. & Wakefield, S. (2008). What have we learned from longitudinal studies of crime? In A.M. Lieberman (Ed.), *The long view of crime: A research synthesis,* pp. 192–219. New York: Springer.

Unrau, Y.A.; Font, S.; & Rawls, G. (2012). Readiness for college engagement among youth who have aged out of foster care. *Children and Youth Service Review, 34,* 76–83.

Unrau, Y.A.; Seita, J.R.; & Putney, K.S. (2008). Former foster youth remember multiple placement moves: A journey of loss and hope. *Children and Youth Service Review, 30* (11), 1256–1266.

U.S. Bureau of Labor Statistics. (2003). *The national longitudinal surveys handbook, 2003.* Washington, DC: U.S. Department of Labor.

U.S. Bureau of Labor Statistics. (2015). *Median weekly earnings by educational attainment in 2014.* http://www.bls.gov/opub/ted/2015/median-weekly-earnings-by-education-gender-race-and-ethnicity-in-2014.htm.

U.S. Census Bureau. (2009). *Income, poverty and health insurance coverage in the United States.* www.census.gov/www/cpstables/032010/health/h01_001.htm

U.S. Census Bureau. (2016). *Percentage of U.S. children ages 0–17 by race and Hispanic origin 1980–2015, and projected 2016–2050.* Washington, DC.

U.S. Department of Health and Human Services. (2003). *Positive youth development*. Washington, DC: Administration for Children and Families and Children's Bureau.

U.S. Department of Health and Human Services. (2004). *Adoption and foster care analysis and reporting system*. Washington, DC: Administration for Children and Families and Children's Bureau.

U.S. Department of Health and Human Services. (2005). *A report to Congress on adoption and other permanency outcomes for children in foster care: Focus on older children*. Washington, DC: Administration for Children and Families and Children's Bureau.

U.S. Department of Health and Human Services. (2008a). *Multi-site evaluation of foster youth programs: Evaluation of the Early Start to Emancipation Preparation—Tutoring Program, Los Angeles California—final report*. Washington, DC: Administration for Children and Families.

U.S. Department of Health and Human Services. (2008b). *Evaluation of the life skills training program, Los Angeles County, California*. Multi-Site Evaluation of Foster Programs. Prepared for Office of Planning and Research Evaluation. Washington, DC: Administration for Children and Families.

U.S. Department of Health and Human Services. (2008c, February 8). *General funding from the federal child and family services review*. Washington, DC: Administration for Children and Families.

U.S. Department of Health and Human Services. (2012). *Child welfare outcomes, 2007–2010, report to Congress*. http:www.acf.hhs.gov/programs/cb/resources/cwo-07–10.

U.S. Department of Health and Human Services. (2014a). *Adoption and foster care analysis and reporting system*. Washington, DC: Administration for Children and Families and Children's Bureau.

U.S. Department of Health and Human Services. (2014b, November). *Serving youth who run away from care*. Administration for Children and Families and Children's Bureau. http://www.acf.hhs.gov/sites/default/files/fysb/info_memo_rhy_foster_care_20141104.pdf.

U.S. Department of Health and Human Services. (2015a). *The AFCARS report: Preliminary FY 2014 estimates as of July 2015 (22)*. http://www.acf.hhs.gov/sites/default/files/cb/afcarsreport22.pdf.

U.S. Department of Health and Human Services. (2015b). *Transitional program fact sheet*. Washington, DC: Administration for Children and Families, Family and Youth Services Bureau. https://www.acf.hhs.gov/fysb/resource/tlp-fact-sheet (CH 1–3).

U.S. Department of Health and Human Services. (2015c, April). *Foster statistics for 2013*. Washington, DC: Administration for Children and Families and Children's Bureau.

U.S. Department of Health and Human Services. (2016, March). *Foster care statistics 2014*. Washington, DC: Administration for Children and Families and Children's Bureau.

U.S. Department of Labor. (2000). *Employment status of the civilian non-institutional population by sex, age, race, and Hispanic origin: 2000 annual average.* Washington, DC: Bureau of Labor Statistics.

U.S. Government Accountability Office. (1994). *Foster care: Parental drug abuse has an alarming impact on young children.* Washington, DC: United States Government Accounting Office.

U.S. Government Accountability Office. (1999). *Foster care: Effectiveness of independent living programs not known.* Report no. GAO/HEHS-00–13. Washington, DC: U.S. General Accounting Office.

U.S. Government Accountability Office. (2004). *Foster youth: HHS actions could improve coordination of services and monitoring of the states' independent living programs.* Report no. GAO-05–25. Washington, DC: U.S. General Accounting Office.

U.S. Government Accountability Office. (2007). *Child welfare: Actions would help states prepare youth in foster care system for independent living.* Retrieved from http://www.gao.gov/new.items/d071097t.pdf.

Valentine, E.J.; Skemer, M.; & Courtney, M. (2015). *Becoming adults: One-year impact findings from the youth villages transitional living evaluation.* Oakland, CA: MDRC.

Valentino, K.; Nuttall, A.; Cmoas, M.; Borkowski, J.; & Akai, C. (2012). Intergenerational continuity of child abuse among adolescent mothers: Authoritarian parenting, community violence, and race. *Child Maltreatment, 17* (2), 172–181.

Vandivere, S.; Chalk, R.; & Moore, K.A. (2003). Children in foster homes: How are they faring? *Research Brief, Publication #2003–23.* Washington, DC: Child Trends.

Van Leeuwen, J.M.; Hopfner, C.; Hooks, S.; White, R.; Petersen, J.; & Pirkopf, J. (2004). A snapshot of substance abuse among homeless youth in Denver, Colorado. *Journal of Community Health, 29* (3), 217–229.

Van Zandt, S. & Rohe, W.M. (2006). Do first time homeowners improve their neighborhood quality, *Journal of Urban Affairs, 28* (5), 491–510.

Vaughan, M.; Ollie, M.; McMillen, J.C.; Scott, L.; & Munson, M. (2007). Substance abuse among older youth in foster care. *Addictive Behavior, 32* (9), 1929–1935.

Vaughan, M.; Shook, J.; & McMillen, J.C. (2008). Aging out of foster care and legal involvement: Towards a typology of risk. *Social Service Review, 82* (3), 419–446.

Vespa, J.; Lewis, J.; & Kreider, R. (2013, August). *American family living arrangements.* Washington, DC: U.S. Department of Commerce, Bureau of the Census.

Villegas, S.; Rosenthal, J.; O'Brien, K.; & Pecora, P. (2014). Educational outcomes for youth formerly in foster care: The role of ethnicity. *Children and Youth Service Review, 36,* 42–52.

Vinnerjung, B.; Hjern, A.; & Lindbald, F. (2006). Suicide attempts and severe psychiatric morbidity among former child welfare clients—a national cohort study. *Journal of Child Psychology and Psychiatry, 47* (7), 723–733.

Vranceanu, A.; Hobfoll, S.; & Johnson, R.J. (2007). Child multi-type maltreatment and associated depression and PTSD symptoms: The role of social support and stress. *Child Abuse and Neglect, 31* (11), 71–84.

Wagner, M.; Iida, E.; & Spiker, D. (2001). *The multisite evaluation of the Parents as Teachers home visiting program: Three-year findings from one community.* Menlo Park, CA: SRI International.

Wahler, R.G. (1994). Child conduct problems: Disorders in conduct or social continuity. *Journal of Child and Family Studies, 3,* 143–156.

Waldinger, G. & Furman, W. (1994). Two models of preparing foster youth for emancipation. *Children and Youth Services Review, 16* (3–4), 201–212.

Wall, A.E. & Kohl, P.L. (2007). Substance use in maltreated youth: Findings from the National Survey of Child Adolescent Well-Being. *Child Maltreatment, 12* (1), 20–30.

White, C.; O'Brien, K.; Pecora, P.; & Buher, A. (2015). Mental health and educational outcomes for youth transitioning from foster care in Michigan. *Families and Society, 96* (1), 17–24.

White, C.R.; O'Brien, K.; White, J.; Pecora, P.; & Phillips, C.M. (2008). Alcohol and drug use among alumni of foster care: Decreasing dependency through the improvement of the foster care experience. *Journal of Behavioral Health Services and Research, 35* (4), 419–434.

Widom, C. & Maxfield, M. (2001, February). *An update on the "cycle of violence."* Washington, DC: National Institute of Justice.

Widom, C.B. (1996). Childhood sexual abuse and its criminal consequences. *Society, 33* (4), 47.

Wiegmann, W.; Putnam-Hornstein, E.; Barrat, V.; Magruder, J.; & Needell, B. (2016). *The invisible achievement gap: How foster care experiences of California public school students are associated with their educational outcomes.* San Francisco: Center for the Future of Teaching and Learning.

Wildeman, C. & Emanuel, N. (2014). Cumulative risks of foster care placement by age 18 for U.S. children, 2000–2011. *PLOS/ One,* http://dx.dol .org/10.1371/journal.pone.0092785.

Williams, C. (2005). The independent living program: Today's challenge. In K.A. Nolan & A.C. Downs (Eds.), *Preparing for long-term success* (pp. 1–14). Seattle: Casey Family Programs.

Wilson, B.D.M.; Cooper, K.; Kastanis, A.; & Nezhad, S. (2014). *Sexual & gender minority youth in Los Angeles foster care.* Los Angeles: Williams Institute.

Wiltz, T. (2015, March 3). Racial and ethnic disparities persist in teenage pregnancy rates. Stateline. http://www.pewtrusts.org/en/research-and-analysis/blogs /stateline/2015/3/03/racial-and-ethnic-disparities-persist-in-teen-pregnancy-rates.

Wolanin, T. (2005). *Higher education opportunities for foster youth: A policy primer for policy makers.* Available at http://www.ihep.org/Pubs?PDF/foster youth.pdf.

Won, J. (2008). *The relationships between social ties, social support, and material hardship among youth aging out of foster care.* (Unpublished Doctoral Dissertation), University of Chicago.

Wulczyn, F. (2004). Family reunification. *Future of Children, 14* (1), 95–113.

Wulczyn, F. & Brunner Hislop, K. (2001). *Growth in the adoption population. Issue papers on foster care and adoption #2: Growth in the adoption population.* Washington, DC: Administration of Children and Families and Children's Bureau.

Wulczyn, F.; Kogan, J.; & Harden, B.J. (2003). Placement stability and movement trajectories. *Social Service Review, 77* (2), 212–236.

Wylie, L. (2014). Closing the crossover gap: Amending fostering connections to provide independent living services for foster youth who crossover to the justice system. *Family Court Review, 52* (2), 298–315.

Yadama, G.N. & Sherraden, M. (1996). Effects of assets on attitudes and behaviors: Advance test of social policy proposal. *Social Work Research, 54,* 353–363.

Yates, T. & Grey, I. (2012). Adapting to aging out: Profiles of risk and resilience among emancipated foster youth. *Development and Psychopathology, 24,* 475–492.

Youth Advocacy Center. (2001). *The impact of foster care on teens and a new philosophy for preparing teens for participating in citizenship.* New York: Youth Advocacy Center.

Yu, E.; Day, P.; & Williams, M. (2002). *Improving educational outcomes for youth in care: A national collaboration.* Washington, DC: Child Welfare League of America Press.

Yu, M.; Lombe, M.; & Nebbit, V. (2010). Food Stamps program participation, informal supports, household food security and child food security: A comparison of African-American and Caucasian households in poverty. *Children and Youth Services Review, 32,* 767–773.

Zeeshan, A. (2015, June 10). *Minimum wage to rent an apartment in any state.* Policy.mic. http://mic.com/articles/120428/1-map-shows-how-many-hours -you-need-to-work-minimum-wage-to-rent-an-apartment-in-any-state# .a3xIRsSu0.

Zetlin, A.; Weinberg, L.; & Luderer, J.W. (2004). Problems and solutions to improving education services for children in foster care. *Preventing School Failure, 48* (2), 31–36.

Zima, B.T.; Bussing, R.; Freeman, S.; Yang, X.; Belin, T.R.; & Forness, S.R. (2000). Behavior problems, academic skill delay and school failure among school-aged children in foster care: Their relationship to placement characteristics. *Journal of Child and Family Studies, 9* (1), 87–103.

Zimmerman, R.B. (1982). *Foster care in retrospect. Studies in social welfare.* New Orleans: Tulane University Press.

Zito, J.M.; Safer, D.J.; Sai, D.; Gardner, J.F.; Thomas, D.; Coombes, P.; Dubowski, M.; & Mendez-Lewis, M. (2008). Psychotropic medication patterns among youth in foster care. *Pediatrics, 121,* 157–163.

Zlotnick, C.; Tam, T.; & Soman, L. (2012). Life course outcomes on mental and physical health: The impact of foster care on adulthood. *Research and Practice, 102* (3), 534–540.

Index

About the Author

Loring Paul Jones is a professor in the School of Social Work at San Diego State University, where he teaches courses in social policy, child welfare, research, and child and family policy. For the past 15 years, his research has examined the experiences of former foster youth after discharge. He has published more than 65 scholarly articles and presented his work to more than 50 national and international audiences. Dr. Jones spent five years following a group of foster children both as they were preparing to leave and after they left care, observing their adaptation to independence.